North Korea, Intern: and the Dual Crises

MW00862057

The Democratic People's Republic of Korea (DPRK) has a reputation as one of the worst human rights situations in the world. This book utilizes a unique international law perspective to examine the actions and inactions of North Korea with regard to international security and human rights.

Adopting political, military, historical, and legal perspectives, the book explores how the two issues of nuclear weapons and the human rights abuses in North Korea are interconnected, and why the international community should apply the same international law framework to find a solution for both. Drawing on eyewitness accounts, such as refugee and defector testimony, Morse Tan offers a real-life story of North Korea that covers the pertinent law, and constructive approaches of its regime. Tan examines the specific objectives and actions of the North Korean government, and measures these according to international legal obligations such as applicable treaty law, *jus cogens* norms, and customary international law.

The book concludes by offering solutions for dealing with international security surrounding the Korean Peninsula, and forwards a proposal for the creation of a tribunal to prosecute those at the top of the regime for international crimes and human rights abuses.

As a project exploring the extremes of international law violation, this book will be of great interest and use to readers interested in the history, and political and legal implications of the strategies employed by the North Korean government.

Morse Tan is Associate Professor of Law at Northern Illinois University, USA.

"Professor Tan's research is impressive, given the dearth, if not inaccessibility, of even basic information from such a hermetically closed system ... Professor Tan's analysis in Section 2 of applicable international law, especially human rights treaties, is accurate and comprehensive ... Professor Tan's book offer[s] a wealth of information and analysis of the world's sovereign outlier ... with a straight-forward exposition and analysis ... His command of the governing international law is clear, as is his ability to marshal cogent facts and political insights ... Along with his other writings and public appearances, [the book] clearly establishes his credentials as a well-informed critic of an opaque and puzzling country whose deliberate isolation greatly inhibits useful research of the sort he has admirably undertaken. As a legal scholar, Professor Tan is truly a pioneer."

James A.R. Nafziger, Thomas B. Stoel Professor of Law, Director of International Programs, Wilammette University College of Law

"Prof. Tan has written a thoroughly documented treatment of the North Korean situation in all of its many dimensions. This is the most comprehensive schol-arly book on the subject now and Prof. Tan undoubtedly will gain considerable exposure and prominence ... in both the legal and political science academies and in diplomatic and media circles once the book is published ... It reminds me of a scholar at the University of Oklahoma who has great expertise on Syria and projected OU into the headlines during the first year of the Syrian civil war as he was interviewed regularly by major media. That will happen to Prof. Tan as well because the North Korean story will only grow in the years ahead ... I have to honestly conclude that Prof. Tan covered all of the bases. In fact, I kept anticipating my criticism of his text by wondering whether he would include one point or another, and then within pages he did so. That was extremely pleasing to see him accomplish time and again throughout the text ... I looked through the relevant endnotes as well and found them quite impressive ... This is a very readable book and it will lead to numerous high-profile opportunities for Prof. Tan, including Congressional testimony and interaction with the United Nations. I strongly endorse the value of its scholarship, its sourcing, and its role in building the foundation..."

David Scheffer, Mayer Brown/Robert A. Helman Professor, Director of the Center for International Human Rights, Northwestern University School of Law, and the 1st War Crimes Ambassador in U.S. history

North Korea, International Law and the Dual Crises

Narrative and Constructive Engagement

Morse Tan

Routledge
Taylor & Francis Group

LONDON AND NEW YORK

First published 2015
by Routledge
2 Park Square, Milton Park, Abingdon, Oxon, OX14 4RN

and by Routledge
711 Third Avenue, New York, NY 10017

First issued in paperback 2018

Routledge is an imprint of the Taylor & Francis Group, an informa business

British Library Cataloguing in Publication Data
A catalogue record for this book is available from the British Library

Library of Congress Cataloging-in-Publication Data
Tan, Morse, author.
North Korea, international law, and the dual crises : rightlessness
in a nuclear state / Morse Tan.
pages cm
Includes bibliographical references and index.
ISBN 978-0-415-83062-1 (hardback) -- ISBN 978-0-203-38162-5 (ebk)
1. Human rights--Korea (North) 2. International crimes--Korea (North)
3. International criminal courts--Korea (North) 4. Political prisoners--
Abuse of--Korea (North) 5. Defectors--Korea (North) 6. Nuclear weapons--
Korea (North) 7. Security, International. 8. Korea (North)--Politics and
government. I. Title.
KPC2460.T36 2015
342.519308'5--dc23
2014039401

ISBN 13: 978-1-138-61450-5 (pbk)
ISBN 13: 978-0-415-83062-1 (hbk)

Typeset in Baskerville MT Pro by
Servis Filmsetting Ltd, Stockport, Cheshire

For the longsuffering people of North Korea: may they live in justice, peace, security, and freedom to flourish!

Contents

Preface

David Scheffer

On 22 December 2014 the United Nations Security Council met for the first time for a briefing about the human rights debacle that has plagued the people of North Korea for decades. The fifteen member states of the Council were driven to this moment because of the United Nations Human Rights Council's *Report of the Commission of Inquiry on Human Rights in the Democratic People's Republic of Korea*, a set of findings so devastating in their content that the Commission of Inquiry recommended the Security Council refer the human rights situation in North Korea to the International Criminal Court. Not surprisingly, China and Russia sought to prevent the Security Council meeting from being convened, but this time they lost that procedural bid. Ivan Šimonović, the U.N. Assistant Secretary-General for Human Rights, aptly noted during the briefing, "Rarely has such an extensive charge-sheet of international crimes been brought to this Council's attention."

One can only barely forgive the Security Council for its evasion of the issue for so long as it grappled with the nuclear arms threat posed by North Korea since the early 1990s. U.S. Permanent Representative to the United Nations Samantha Power finally seemed to cast aside that trade-off as a "false choice" during her remarks at the Security Council briefing. Perhaps the turning point on North Korea's human rights record occurred that day; there is no longer any plausible means of denying the reality of what horrors exist in that country.

Long before the Commission of Inquiry commenced its investigative work in 2013, scholars and non-governmental organizations had been researching, publishing, and sounding the alarm on the abhorrent human rights conditions in North Korea. They were joined by the voices of refugees who have had the courage to speak out through interviews and their own publications. Twice in the last decade I joined the analysts seeking to bring to the world's attention the atrocity crimes that were enveloping North Korea. Each time I recall the wall of silence these efforts confronted from major governments and from the United Nations. During the years (1993–1997) when I was senior counsel to the U.S. Permanent Representative to the United Nations, Dr. Madeleine Albright, and while I was the U.S. Ambassador at Large for War Crimes Issues (1997–2001), the nuclear arms threat growing inside North Korea and the persistent waves of starvation there prevented any serious effort on the human rights agenda in Washington or at the United Nations in New York from gaining traction with bureaucrats, politicians, diplomats, and even to a large extent the media.

Professor Morse Tan now steps forward with this book, which provides a compelling and fulsome account of what has transpired in North Korea since the Korean War on several interconnected fronts: political repression, nuclear defiance, human rights violations across the spectrum of human endeavor, and the commission of crimes against humanity against significant numbers of its people. He also examines the diplomatic history of China's unique role in facilitating, but also failing to influence at times, North Korea's foreign policy.

Tan's ten years of research, including interviews and research into both known and previously undiscovered sources of information, has resulted in a meticulously documented account that shocks the conscience and educates the international community of the realities that can no longer be cast into the "deep fog" Tan describes. He has achieved his goal magnificently, which is "a readable and accessible book that introduces readers to the astonishing realities of North Korea, the relevant law, and some constructive approaches." But this book also will propel further into the public realm the situation that is now before the Security Council as a continuing agenda item and shame any government that ignores or undermines the hard facts set forth on the following pages.

Tan paints a dark and foreboding landscape of North Korea. His recordings of refugee accounts about the sheer horror endured daily are the opening snapshots of reality in modern-day North Korea. The most obvious candidate in the world for implementation of the responsibility to protect principle is North Korea, a political and legal mandate that Tan explores. While the Security Council has approved non-military measures sanctioning the North Korean leadership, any suggestion of military intervention under the responsibility to protect principle almost certainly would be blocked by at least China and Russia in the Council.

Tan examines the judicial options that should be considered by the international community in the years ahead. There will be a day of reckoning for North Korea's leaders, Tan infers, and there must be credible judicial forums in which to investigate and prosecute them. One would hope that some day national courts in a reunified Korea or in a North Korea liberated from brutally repressive governance and from criminal assaults against its own citizens will be enforcing justice against the North Korean political and military leaders responsible for such egregious conduct.

Joined with national justice may be the prospect some day of an international effort, particularly at the International Criminal Court. The latter probably will depend on a Security Council referral, as recommended by the Commission of Inquiry, or through creation of a hybrid tribunal that has a narrowly drawn jurisdiction over atrocity crimes committed on North Korean territory beginning on a particular date in the past. Tan, who prefers the hybrid tribunal, examines these and other options from a comparative perspective with judicial initiatives elsewhere in the world.

The International Criminal Court will have sitting on the bench from 2015 through 2024 Judge Chang-ho Chung, a citizen of South Korea. (He was preceded from 2003 to 2015 by the South Korean jurist, Judge Sang-Hyun Song, who also served as the president of the Court from 2009 to 2015.) Chang-ho Chung served from 2011 to 2015 as an international judge on the Pre-Trial Chamber of the Extraordinary Chambers in the Courts of Cambodia (ECCC), before which the atrocity crimes of the Pol Pot regime in Cambodia from 1975 to 1979 are being investigated and prosecuted. I have long viewed Judge Chung's service at the ECCC as, in part, preparation to confront the judicial challenge presented by North Korean atrocity crimes. If the North Korean human rights situation falls within the jurisdiction of the International Criminal Court by Security Council referral or otherwise, then Judge Chung may play a critical role in adjudicating the cases emerging from such an opportunity. If, in the alternative, a hybrid tribunal is created, then he may also serve a critical role on that tribunal following his International Criminal Court tenure.

One could imagine a hybrid tribunal arising from an explicit grant of extraterritorial jurisdiction under South Korean law for the atrocity crimes that have been committed in North Korea. This could be done on the grounds that under the Constitution of the Republic of Korea, there exists a basis for determining that residents of North Korea in fact are nationals of the Republic of Korea. Indeed, the enabling legislation of the hybrid tribunal could so classify the people of North Korea as nationals of the Republic of Korea for this particular purpose. The commission of atrocity crimes against such nationals would trigger the jurisdiction of South Korean courts in a manner similar to how counterterrorism laws of many nations today invoke extraterritorial jurisdiction to prosecute terrorist acts against a country's nationals located anywhere in the world. There could be negotiated a treaty between the United Nations and South Korea whereby that extraterritorial jurisdiction is embodied within the treaty.

Under such a treaty, foreign judges and a foreign prosecutor could be joined with perhaps a majority of South Korean judges and a South Korean co-prosecutor. The atrocity crimes would be drawn from those already embedded in South Korean law by virtue of that country's membership in the International Criminal Court. The grant of extraterritorial jurisdiction, in the context of extending the reach of the tribunal over atrocity crimes committed on North Korean territory, would be explicitly established under both the enabling legislation of the tribunal in South Korea and within the treaty with the United Nations. The hybrid tribunal, no less than the International Criminal Court, may find it exceptionally difficult, if not impossible in the short term, to gain custody of any North Korean political or military leader charged with atrocity crimes. But that is a reality that should not defeat the pursuit of justice on the Korean peninsula any more than it should in Africa or the Americas or Europe or elsewhere in Asia.

International criminal justice is a long game and that reality may prove no less real for North Koreans as it has for other victims globally. But the hand of justice ultimately must rest firmly over the defiant masters of atrocity crimes and human rights abuses in North Korea, whose people are entitled to the simple joy of living healthy, safe, and prosperous lives. Morse Tan admirably explains why in this book.

David Scheffer
Chicago, January 2015

Foreword

by Jasper Becker

It is shameful that so little has been done to free the people of North Korea from the dictatorship of the Kim family. The North Koreans have lived for over a century in one or another kind of brutal rule. Japan annexed Korea in the early part of the nineteenth century and immediately set out to destroy the Korean identity and enslave the Koreans as colonial subjects of a Japanese empire. After Japan's unconditional surrender, Stalin seized half the country and installed a puppet leader, Kim Il Sung, a member of the Chinese Communist Party, who barely spoke Korean. With the support of Stalin and Mao Zedong, Kim Il Sung invaded the South. He conducted a savage war which devastated the country and caused immense suffering. Three or four million Koreans died and millions of others became refugees. The invasion became an international conflict which ended in stalemate after a combined military death toll estimated at 1.2 million.

Kim Il Sung stayed in power and installed a state faithful to the ideas of Lenin and Stalin. He died in 1994 after witnessing the disintegration of the Soviet Union in 1990. His son, Kim Jong-Il, took over as the country endured a devastating famine. Yet he remained in power too and rejected any substantial change. When he died in 2011, his son Kim Jong-Eun was installed as his successor and soon launched an internal purge, which saw the swift arrest and summary execution of his uncle, Jang Song Thaek, his former tutor to groom him for the Supreme Ruler position and second in the ruling hierarchy.

North Korea, or to give its official name, the Democratic People's Republic of Korea (DPRK), now remains as the last country left on earth which can be truly called Stalinist. That means no commerce, massive military spending, Gulags, wastefully poor investment, perennial food shortages, a pampered elite and a division of the population according to their political loyalty. It stands as the only hereditary Communist state. The populace must worship its ruling family as deities. The state has remained committed to one overriding goal – the unification of the Korean peninsula under the rule of the Kim family by military force. The 'military first' policies means that the country's resources have been concentrated on maintaining the largest military threat possible, which now includes long range missiles and nuclear weapons. As there are no legal markets, no real money, and no trade, economic statistics from the State become as rare as hen's teeth:

Pyongyang has not released any data for decades. We do not even know precisely how many people live there. We can surmise that at least a third of the economy is devoted to defence, that some four million have perished in the North Korean labor camps, and that three million died in the 1990s famine. The total number of deaths that can be laid at the door of the Kim family is now in the region of 15 million, a staggering figure given that North Korea's population may not be much more than 20 million.

Western thinking about North Korea has changed over the years. Some used to regard it sympathetically, as a socialist developing nation standing up to American imperialism. Prominent American historians have attempted to excuse its record as the tortured response of a scarred victim fighting back and have argued for more understanding for its paranoia.

The nature of the North Korean question has also changed over time. In the 1970s, it became notorious as a sponsor of international terrorism after a series of violent attacks, such as the 1987 destruction in mid-air of Korean Air flight 858 after North Korean agents planted a bomb.

Then in the 1980s, a belief sprang up that North Korea was willing to undertake reforms and should be encouraged to do so. This line of thinking led the Clinton administration in the early 1990s to engage North Korea by promising to build nuclear light water reactors for it. It also led the South Korean government to pursue a fruitless Sunshine policy of engagement, which included secretly transferring huge sums of cash to Pyongyang in the conviction that a sudden unification would be a costly mistake.

During President George W. Bush's first term, Washington tried a much tougher line by naming North Korea as a part of an axis of evil building nuclear weapons. Bush invaded one member, Iraq, and spoke out against the other members, Iran and North Korea. North Korea was the only member which was able to shrug off this tougher stance and continued with its program, culminating in several nuclear tests. It demands to be treated as a *de facto* nuclear power.

As it did so, North Korea's main ally, China, claimed that it was sponsoring diplomatic solutions to the North Korean crisis, such as by hosting the Six Party Talks. It claimed it was restraining North Korea, fostering economic reforms, and finding a solution. As a result, international pressure on North Korea has been weak despite some economic sanctions. Few now believe China has the will to change anything in North Korea.

In the media, North Korea is often treated as a joke rather than a real threat or a pressing human rights issue. The *Economist*, for instance, ran a jokey cover in 2000 showing Kim Jong Il with the caption 'Greetings Earthlings'. Hollywood ignored the famine and the death camps in favour of comedies like *Team America: World Police* (2004) or *The Interview* (2014). In response to the latter, North Korea hacked the computer system of Sony Pictures Entertainment and made threats to intimidate the distributors, who initially delayed and then pulled the film's release in theatres. After a storm of protest, Sony reversed its decision by making the film available online, through which they have raked in massive revenues through an extensive viewership.

As hopes of change from within have dimmed, and efforts to engage North Korea in negotiations have been abandoned, the United Nations has taken a new tack. In November 2014, the United Nations General Assembly passed a ground-breaking resolution that calls on North Korea's leaders to be prosecuted at the International Criminal Court. The resolution was the strongest ever taken against the country and follows the presentation of 400 pages of investigation by the UN Human Rights Council's Commission of Inquiry. It described that the gravity and nature of abuses is "without parallel in the contemporary world."

Although China is expected to continue protecting its client state to ensure its survival, the willingness of so many UN member states to challenge both Beijing and Pyongyang on its human rights record opens a fresh and potentially significant front. For the first time, North Korea's leaders are not being treated with respect because they are no longer seen as the vehicle that will bring change but as the chief obstacle to positive change. The possibility that members of the Kim dynasty could be put on trial like Slobodan Milošević of Yugoslavia and Liberia's Charles Taylor creates a new situation.

Finally, the notion firmly held by diplomats for many years that the Kim family's crimes should be forgotten as the price for ensuring peaceful change has been dropped. This means that for the first time, the law can become a profoundly important tool.

For these reasons, it is immensely helpful that Professor Tan has written a book that will help arm and inform all those dealing with North Korea. By doing so, he powerfully augments the legal scholarship on North Korea, which is scarce relative to its importance. As Professor Tan makes clear, the DPRK government acts in violation of both its domestic laws and the numerous international treaties to which it is a signatory and a party to as member of the United Nations. He also details the ways in which China, as the chief ally of North Korea, is also acting in violation of such treaties as the Convention Relating to the Status of Refugees.

The first section of the book describes how North Korea has broken laws relating to human rights before moving on to breaches of laws relating to nuclear non-proliferation and the Geneva Convention. He presents the history of the DPRK, its history of provocations and attacks against other states, and the theory behind its strategy of brinkmanship. He then delves into North Korea's persistent violations of the human rights of its own citizens, such as the system of penal colonies and arbitrary executions, the treatment of returning refugees and religious believers. He specifically explains how routinely the DPRK government breaches both its own domestic laws and many international laws, such as the International Covenant on Civil and Political Rights or the Convention on the Rights of the Child.

In the third section Professor Tan examines the many issues to be considered when deciding on the best way of dealing with North Korea under international law. Among the interesting questions it discusses is that of prosecuting the North Korean leadership under the terms of the Genocide Convention.

"North Korea stands next in line among the precedents set in the Nuremberg Trials and Tokyo Trials after World War II, the ad hoc tribunals for Rwanda and the former Yugoslavia, the hybrid tribunals concerning places such as Cambodia, Sierra Leone, East Timor, Bosnia and Herzegovina, and Kosovo, and the establishment of the International Criminal Court through the Rome Treaty," he writes.

"The magnitude, severity, and frequency of human rights violations in North Korea calls for the redress that such courts have sought to bring. Sufficient ratification of the Rome Treaty by enough countries established the International Criminal Court, the first permanent international criminal court based on a treaty, and the start of analyzing possible redress options for the Korean peninsula," he says.

He also considers whether it is practical to start organizing a prosecution now or to wait until the regime falls, which he believes is inevitable. If the North Korean regime was suddenly swept from power, then it is almost inevitable that a sudden unification would follow. That would mean that the North Korean leaders could be tried by South Korean courts or an international tribunal.

So Professor Tan discusses the merits of creating a hybrid tribunal, which brings together local judges and international jurists so that violations of both international and domestic law could be dealt with in a fair way that does not smack of victor's justice. Although dealing with any rogue regime is by definition profoundly difficult in any situation, it is not an abstract or theoretical issue. One day even China may weary of defending North Korea or its own people may tire of living in an economic failure. Its leaders and officials will then have to face justice, and it is imperative that we are prepared.

Jasper Becker

January 2015

Becker authored *Rogue Regime: The Looming Threat of North Korea* (Oxford University Press)

Acknowledgments

I am grateful that as well-regarded a publisher as Routledge has given me this opportunity to publish my first book.

My wife Sarah and four children (Hope, Enoch, Isaiah, and Moses) have sacrificed considerable time with her husband and their dad to make this book possible. My parents-in-law and parents freed up critical portions of time for me to work on and finish this volume.

I want to thank all the authors who have contributed, directly and indirectly, to this book.

My current and former research assistants helped make this book a reality. Among them, attorney Kevin Zickterman deserves the most applause. Kevin, as my right-hand man, did far more than anyone else in aiding me with this whole project—starting from the book proposal, extending to the endnotes, and much in between. In sequential order starting from the one who contributed most, I acknowledge the work of Weston Sedgwick, Sonya Chung, Jeremy McCabe, Michael Nealis, Dino Delic, Amanda Beveroth, Sarah Walsh, Matt Palucki, Christian Hall, and Ryan Leibforth. As appropriate, I recognize their work also in the first footnotes of chapters.

My thanks to Dean Jennifer Rosato Perea, Provost Dr. Lisa Freeman, Associate Vice President for Research Dr. David Stone, and Northern Illinois University for the support that encouraged this book to materialize. Grants from the law school and the university both supported the making of this book.

Allow me to add the customary statement of my authorial responsibility for any errors that made their way into this book. As I told my assistants, the buck stops with me as the one with overall responsibility for the entire project. Any faults and flaws that may remain fall upon my figurative shoulders. Much of whatever positive aspects may exist in the book usually involved people other than myself, whether other authors, the publisher, or my assistants.

Most of all, I want to acknowledge and honor the One who received much worship in Pyongyang before the Kim cult entered the scene. Before anyone on the horizontal plane of mortal relationships, I want to consecrate this work to the Rock of Ages, faithful and steadfast without fail, the greatest Lover of the people of North Korea and the world.

Introduction

Personal background

This book could not be written in North Korea by a North Korean without the cruelest consequences falling on that person's head. Here in the United States, as an American law professor, I can do so with drastically minimal risk by comparison. Yet I realize that I have this opportunity because of decisions by my forbears, not initially by me.

If my parents' families fled North rather than South during the Korean War, I could have found myself living in North Korea. Instead, I was born in Seoul, South Korea. Fulfilling a dream since my dad's youth, my parents flew over the Pacific to the United States before I reached two years of age.

Another reason that it would not be hard to imagine an alternate destiny of living in North Korea instead is because my paternal great-grandfather served as Governor of Pyongyang Province within a unified Korea. Governor Yoo's son, my dad's late father, died when my dad was very young. My grandmother remarried with grandfather Tan, the father of my aunts and uncles on my paternal side.

My mother's side has the most common Korean last name: Kim (like "Smith" in the United States). This particular branch of Kims (Gwang-Sahn Kim) historically served as scholars in the King's court.

I came to know this slice of family history as a college student, which is when I became more aware of the suffering of the North Korean people during the famine of the mid-1990s. This knowledge moved me deeply, provoking me to write a personal statement regarding wanting to make a difference for the people of North Korea in my application to Northwestern University School of Law, my law school *alma mater*.

After serving as a founding professor of the first American JD program in Asian history, I embarked on researching and writing about North Korea as a Visiting Scholar and then a Senior Research Fellow at the University of Texas Law School, delving deeply into its extensive library collections and making ample use of inter-library loan. This book comes after over a decade of such research and writing: it attempts to continue fulfilling the words of my personal statement applying to Northwestern.

The dual crises

In what some consider the worst totalitarian regime in history, resides a state of rightlessness (a neologism needed to describe North Korea) along with one of the most serious security threats in the world: the Democratic People's Republic of Korea (DPRK). Sadly, in that official appellation, only "of Korea" rings true: it is neither democratic, for the people, nor a republic. The security and human rights crises merge to present perhaps the worst combined crisis in the world.

Most treatments of North Korea that touch on the dual human rights and security crises only treat one to the neglect of the other. Recent exceptions exist, such as David Hawk's *Pursuing Peace While Advancing Rights: The Untried Approach to North Korea*[1] and Lord David Alton and Rob Chidley's *Building Bridges: Is There Hope for North Korea*.[2] Like these books, this book proposes that addressing both crises increases the prospect of resolving either one—contrary to the bulk of the diplomatic history, which tended to focus on security issues while avoiding the human rights ones.

The approach of this book

While books regarding North Korea come from many angles, very few delve deeply into legal analysis as this book does. One monograph surveys North Korea vis-à-vis the United Nations, but it is an exception. When I began writing law review articles on North Korea, the law review literature formed a tiny trickle. Now, a growing stream of law review notes and articles has emerged, which with many books and other sources feed into this book, ideally in a way that a general audience can consume with more ease than the scholarly literature itself.

Not many books on North Korea give much attention to possible solutions;[3] this book dares to devote an entire, interdisciplinary section to it after much wrestling and reflection. It seeks to do so with humble hope, meek boldness, and unpretentious wisdom. I do not claim to have fully hit the mark, only that I have tried to do so.

I have tried to approach the book as a scholar, following the evidence where it leads, weighing and sifting through it as best as I can. As such, I did not approach it to try to vindicate partisan political agendas, whether here in the United States, Korea, Japan, China, or elsewhere. Rather, I tried to use truth, justice, and wisdom as my lodestars, not unlike what the late William Stuntz of Harvard Law School recommends for scholarship. Accuracy is the aim more than accumulating accolades. I do not claim to have achieved perfection in these regards—only that these have been my good-faith goals.

While the book does not shy away from analyzing the human rights violations of North Korea in vivid and straightforward terms, it does not engage in name-calling or demonizing.[4] The facts themselves speak starkly—without any embellishment or exaggeration needed. Description obviates demonizing; accurate analysis makes name-calling superfluous.

Longing for peaceful reunification

Let me make clear in this introduction that I long for a peaceful reunification of North and South Korea. I am deeply concerned about the ongoing ravages of war. Personally, about half of my blood relatives, not to mention others that I have known, reside in South Korea. I have no ulterior motivation for ongoing conflict.

However, I try not to avoid the difficult realities on the peninsula. A just peace does not reign in North Korea. I try to face the unfathomable horrors of North Korea with a keen desire for constructively addressing them. The people of North Korea and those threatened by North Korea deserve no less.

The culmination of a decade

This book represents the culmination of about a decade of research regarding North Korea. Prior to this book, I have published a series of law review articles on North Korea, as it turns out, more than any other scholar. I have consulted other leading scholars, activists, and specialists in the field. I have read and learned from a mountain of sources, some of which are reflected in the endnotes. I chose endnotes rather than footnotes to not encumber the text for those who have little interest in the references. I included references in these endnotes to credit sources and satisfy scholars as well as others who want to know the sources and dig deeper.

Frankly, I wish I was wrong in my assessment of the DPRK. It would be convenient to be in denial that it has had one of the worst, if not the worst human rights crisis in the world in terms of the depth and breadth of gross, systematic violations. I would like to think the U.S. Department of Defense was incorrect in considering the DPRK as the worst security threat in the world. However, to hide my head in a hole like an ostrich and deny these difficult-to-face realities would be cowardly and dishonest. I attempt to resist these temptations, albeit with imperfect results.

Defying denial, neglect, and ungrounded over-optimism

At a talk given at the University of Texas, I suggested that the analysis of Hwang Jang-Yop, the highest level defector from North Korea, would be helpful to understand North Korea.[5] I did so not only because he had the highest inside view of North Korea as the architect of their political philosophy, the president of the DPRK's most prestigious university, personal tutor to Kim Jong-Il, general secretariat of the party and the former head of its legislature; I suggested his work because it crystallized the massive amount of research I have been conducting.[6] Hwang, who died on October 11, 2010, lamented his involvement in a criminal regime and wanted to dedicate the remainder of his life to help solve the Korean crisis. He had agonized about leaving his wife but finally left to prevent the impending doom in the Korean Peninsula. Because he knew too much, the North Korean government declared him Public Enemy Number One. He lived out his days in South Korea under the constant protection of bodyguards and an electronic security system. Yet one of the members of the panel derisively spoke of Hwang's analysis as *passé*, outdated and currently inaccurate.

One might be inclined to agree with this assessment if North Korea has fundamentally shifted its objectives, goals, and political philosophy. However, North Korea has proven remarkably persistent in its primary goals, objectives, and political philosophy. The burden of proof should fall much heavier upon those who would claim *perestroika*- and *glasnost*-type reform, or even China-like economic reform. One strains to find convincing evidence of sweeping reform of this nature up to the present. If anything, conditions under Kim Jong-Un have taken a turn for the worse, with tighter borders (that tell border guards to shoot refugees), the execution of his uncle (who as regent seemed to want to take North Korea toward China-like reforms), the most extreme rhetoric (threatening aggressively to attack Washington, D.C. with nuclear weapons), and the expulsion of South Korean workers from the Kaesong industrial complex.

Yet many media sources and observers made inaccurately rosy prognostications about how North Korea would turn in a fundamentally brighter direction under the third Kim dictator. For support, they tried to claim that the fact that he studied for a short amount of time in Switzerland shows that he would swing North Korea in a better direction. While he became a Chicago Bulls fan during that time, inviting Dennis Rodman to visit has hardly led to sweeping reform.

Primary goals and the recurring pattern

Instead, the bulk of evidence supports Hwang's assertion that North Korea has maintained three primary goals, which I have explained to my classes and to news sources like the Channel 4 News and United Press International: (1) Remove the U.S. commitment to South Korea, which is why they persistently ask for a peace treaty to do so. The U.S. commitment to South Korea is the largest deterrent to North Korean aggression. (2) Foster positive sentiment toward North Korea in South Korea. North Korea has succeeded remarkably in this goal, especially among the younger generations, who have no firsthand memory of the Korean War; the Korean War generation has been increasingly aging and passing on. (3) Finally and ultimately, reunify Korea by force. It does not take a shrewd observer to see that North Korea has built up the fourth largest military in the world, north of the most militarized border on the planet, the 38th parallel. They themselves have articulated a "Military First" policy. The DPRK has not produced stockpiles of chemical, biological and nuclear weapons in order to win a worldwide popularity contest. Understanding these three linchpin goals enables one to make sense of what North Korea has done to a great extent.

Couple these goals with the common pattern of saber-rattling brinkmanship, and one attains an even better framework for understanding North Korea. The DPRK has repeatedly employed the pattern of: (1) precipitate a crisis; (2) bring to the table whom they want; (3) negotiate benefits; (4) swallow these benefits; (5) break the agreement and precipitate another crisis, thus repeating the cycle. They come to agreements not with the intention to abide by them, but for their own tactical gains.

So, contrary to the popular view that the rulers of North Korea have been simply irrational, North Korea's actions and tactics have often been tightly woven quite rationally around their primary goals and methods. Rather than the assessment that these rulers are simply stupid, they have been cunning and calculating—as well as Machiavellian—in pursuing their ends.

I agree with the commonly heard remarks that these rulers are "crazy" if one means morally crazy. I disagree with that assessment if one means irrational. I partially agree and partially disagree if one means disconnected from reality.

Evidence that can stand

In order to research North Korea, one cannot reliably depend upon DPRK government sources to gain an accurate picture. Kim Il-Sung declared that the country must put its enemies in a deep fog; the DPRK accomplishes it through continuous mendacity. Indeed, it is exceptional when the DPRK government tells the truth because they only do so when it fits their purposes.

Thus, one must rely on other sources. Primary sources, especially refugee and defector testimony and insights provide a particularly rich vein for research. Credible secondary sources, including those who researched based on primary sources, provide additional corroboration.

The cumulative weight of testimony from eyewitnesses as well as experts would be sufficient to stand in a properly functioning court of law. Indeed, this book makes the case that the chief perpetrators of this criminal regime should be prosecuted for crimes against humanity, among other charges. More than enough evidence exists for such convictions.

The breakfast test and exploitation

Admittedly, the cruel and harsh realities that the North Korean people face do not go well with breakfast and the morning paper. In other words, most of the media had shied away from reporting on the terrible suffering of the North Korean people because it is not pleasant to dwell on. Thankfully, there has been a shift in a better direction, especially by certain media sources such as the Washington Post and the Wall Street Journal. The New York Times has also moved in a better direction along these lines.

However, the media has also been exploited by North Korea. For example, CNN breathlessly covered North Korea blowing up an easily replaceable cooling tower from their nuclear facility. It was nothing but a public relations stunt by North Korea, as they rapidly replaced the tower after giving CNN exclusive coverage of the charade.

Also, the media placed undue significance on positive events, such as the performance of the New York Philharmonic in Pyongyang. While I am favorable toward such cultural exchanges and would like to see them only increase and flourish, they have not, as of yet, resulted in a basic shift in stance by the North Korean government. I do not mean to deprecate such efforts at all; indeed, I applaud them. However, the overly optimistic pronouncements that have emanated in connection with such things ought to be tempered by a sober-minded regard for the ongoing realities that the North Korean people suffer.

In South Korea, much of the media, certain members of academia, and some members of the government have willfully ignored or downplayed many of North Korea's provocations and malfeasances. Reasons given along these lines have included: (1) not provoking North Korea; (2) they are fellow Koreans; (3) their deeds are not much worse than those of other countries. In my view, such media sources have failed the South Korean population by cooperating with North Korea's purpose of perpetuating positive sentiment toward North Korea that have a superficial basis at best. At times, by omission and commission, they have helped lull segments of the Korean populace to sleep regarding the realities in North Korea.

By contrast, these same sources drive a wedge between South Korea and the United States, the chief deterrent of North Korean aggression and the major ally throughout the history of the country. They try to magnify anything negative pertaining to the United States, especially the government and military thereof. This approach again plays into North Korea's hands, toward the objective of removing the American deterrent.

Given all the North Korean spies that have been caught in South Korea, it is reasonable to surmise that more of the thousands of operatives from North Korea have yet to be caught. Some spies caught in the past had burrowed into strategic positions, such as the chair of the sociology department at Seoul National University, widely considered the most prestigious university overall in South Korea. Media, government as well as academic positions would be prize areas for North Korean spies to penetrate, in order to turn the country from within.

This book's goal

My goal is to provide a readable and accessible book that introduces readers to the astonishing realities of North Korea, the relevant law, and some constructive approaches. While a great deal of research undergirds the book, it tries not to indulge too much in hyper-technical scholarly approaches that try harder to impress than to inform, or overwhelmingly dense prose that tends to mask rather than reveal its meaning. On the other hand, I do aim to weave some eloquence into the text. Put another way, the book tries to take a different approach than North Korea itself: it does not try to put the reader in a dense fog.

At the same time, the endnotes (in legally American academic Blue Book format) provide sources for further exploration, whether for the scholar or the general reader. Ideally, even scholars will find satisfactory the level of research supporting the book. The author is quite cognizant that endnotes depart from the footnote convention of American law reviews, the primary scholarly outlet for legal scholarship, including for this author up to this point. I do so to improve the flow of the main text.

I try to connect the reader with the real-life story of North Korea, the pertinent law, and constructive approaches, whether legal or not. This final, main section, while fraught with perils, also holds the most promise.

In other words, Section One tells the story of North Korea thematically. Section Two analyzes the legal implications. Finally, Section Three ventures to provide potential solutions. Appendices provide supplemental information of various kinds to motivate and enable positive responses.

Notes

1 David Hawk, *Pursuing Peace While Advancing Rights: The Untried Approach to North Korea*, U.S.-KOREA INST. AT SAIS (2010), www.uskoreainstitute.org/wp-content/uploads/2010/05/HawkPeaceHR_0514101.pdf.
2 DAVID ALTON & ROB CHIDLEY, BUILDING BRIDGES: IS THERE HOPE FOR NORTH KOREA (2013).
3 For example, JASPER BECKER, ROGUE REGIME: KIM JONG IL AND THE THE LOOMING THREAT OF NORTH KOREA (2005), as wonderfully as it weaves narratives, explicitly states that it will not attempt to propose solutions.
4 NORTH KOREA: TOWARD A BETTER UNDERSTANDING (Sonia Ryang ed., 2009) accuses some politicians and authors of demonizing and name-calling.
5 I am honored that one of my former students translated for Hwang Jang-Yop when he spoke to Congress and other U.S. audiences.
6 The book JOHN H. CHA WITH K.J. SOHN, EXIT EMPEROR KIM JONG-IL: NOTES FROM HIS FORMER MENTOR (2012) bases its insights on Hwang Jang-Yop's insights and direct mentoring. It also summarizes the story of Hwang's defection, among other things.

Section One

The story of a criminal regime

1 War, incursions, and provocations*

But more than the litany of crimes committed against South Koreans or the kidnapping of Japanese citizens or the axe-murder of UN guards in the Demilitarized Zone, more than the macabre nature of the North Korean regime which allows its citizens to starve to death by the hundreds of thousands while pouring in one-third of its GDP into the military, more than the habitual violations of international agreements and the predictable pattern of blackmail and willful deceit that has always underlain North Korean diplomacy, there is a basic irrefutable fact that shows that North Korea always has been and remains to this day a grave threat to South Korea's national security and to peace in the region. It is North Korea's explicitly stated national goal as enshrined in the preamble of its Korean Workers' Party Rules and in its Constitution and repeated over and over again by the various channels of state propaganda machinery: "Liberate the South and bring about the complete victory of socialism on the fatherland."[1]

The Korean War

After finding itself no longer under the ignominy of the Japanese colonial period (which lasted from 1905 to the end of World War II),[2] Korea was experiencing a new kind of problem. The Soviet Union, after a period of relative inaction, decided to actively pursue military efforts at the end of World War II in order to strengthen its hand during post-war settlements.[3] The Soviets poured south into Manchuria.[4] The resulting U.S.–Soviet agreement, disregarding the will of the Korean people, split this small peninsula into the U.S.-aligned South Korea and the Soviet-aligned North Korea, with the Soviets agreeing to push no further south than the 38th parallel.[5]

Border skirmishes ensued over the next few years until, on the early morning of June 25, 1950, after Joseph Stalin gave the green light, North Korean forces embarked on a full-scale war by launching out over the 38th parallel.[6] Premier Kim Il-Sung had eight full divisions (135,000 troops) at his disposal; many of these soldiers fought previously in World War II. By contrast, South Korea counted only 95,000 generally less-seasoned soldiers.[7] The North Korean divisions drove deep into South Korea, overmatching the smaller South Korean forces, who were pushed down to the Pusan Perimeter, a relatively small swath of land at the southernmost tip of the peninsula.[8] The North Korean troops made full use of their advantages of surprise and initiative.[9]

As the North steamrolled the South, the United States called upon the U.N. Security Council to take action against North Korean aggression.[10] The Security Council, with the approbation of forty-four out of forty-nine U.N. member states, called upon its members to send military and other assistance: sixteen states sent soldiers and twenty-five total countries provided materials and other assistance.[11] General Douglas MacArthur stepped forward as the U.N. commander of the combined forces. The Soviet Union, as a permanent member of the U.N. Security Council, could have vetoed this first UNSC Resolution denouncing aggressive war, but instead boycotted the meetings, which did not constitute a veto.

MacArthur led a key counter-initiative known as the Inchon Landing, a tricky military maneuver due to the tides.[12] By the middle of September 1950, MacArthur's forces not only plowed back to the 38th parallel, but they also continued on north.[13] As the U.N. forces proceeded closer to the North Korean-Chinese border, Chinese soldiers poured into North Korea, driving the U.N. forces back. After two more pushes, one northward by the U.N. troops and one southward by the Chinese, the battle lines hardened for two more years back where they started—the 38th parallel.[14]

After three years of bloodshed and two years of negotiations, the "longest, most violated military armistice in modern history," the Korean Armistice Agreement, took shape near the village of Panmunjom.[15] It was signed on July 27, 1953.[16] July 27 marked a momentous date in Korean history. The signing of the Korean Armistice on that date not only marked an official cessation of hostilities on the Korean Peninsula, but it also represented the end of the first test of U.N. military forces and a joint military response of U.N. member states.[17] Found within this historic cease-fire agreement lies a promise that a permanent peace treaty would soon be signed between the U.N. forces and the Korean People's Army and China.[18] That promise was broken, as negotiations for a political conference between the parties to resolve this and other matters on the peninsula fell apart by mid-1954.[19] Since that time, Korea has teetered on the brink of resuming all-out war, with a communist north and a democratic south, separated only by the ironically named Demilitarized Zone (DMZ), a mere 2.5 miles wide, part of the most militarized border in the world.

The Armistice Agreement, intended as a temporary measure by its own terms, was supposed to be replaced by a peace treaty through a conference convening within three months after the agreement.[20] While a treaty emerging from the conference was supposed to settle the remaining issues, such as withdrawal of foreign forces from Korea and a new peace for the Land of the Morning Calm, this anticipated peace treaty did not come about as planned. Due to this failure, the two Koreas instead signed the Agreement of Reconciliation, Non-Aggression and Exchanges and Cooperation between North and South toward the end of 1991, and the Joint Declaration by South and North Korea of the Denuclearization of the Korean Peninsula in 1992.[21]

A short history of provocations

Notwithstanding the Armistice, the U.S. Congressional Research Service had documented some 124 provocations by North Korea against the United States, South Korea, and/or Japan from June 1950 to March 2003.[22] They ranged from multiple assassination attempts on South Korean presidents,[23] to the infiltration of thousands of armed agents involved in kidnapping and terrorism,[24] and from the mid-air bombing of a South Korean Boeing 707 passenger plane in 1987,[25] to the capture of the *U.S.S. Pueblo*, a surveillance ship.[26] More recent Congressional and other sources put these numbers even higher. For example, one Korean journal found that from 1953 to 1996, North Korea initiated a total of 361 armed attacks, 539 armed incursions, and 687 exchanges of gunfire, aggregating a total of 1,587 incidents.[27] From 1997 to 2003, infiltrations and abductions by North Korean agents, infantry and naval military skirmishes, and gunfire exchange remained commonplace. For example, North Korean ships provoked a nine-day naval confrontation with South Korea in the Yellow Sea over disagreement about the Northern Limit Line in June 1999.[28] Over the last decade, the DPRK has continued its provocations by launching a series of short-range and medium-range missiles into the Sea of Japan (East Sea according to Korea) and conducting several nuclear tests.[29]

Air and naval encounters over the years have proven especially deadly. In April 1969, North Korean MiG jet fighters destroyed a U.S. EC-121 reconnaissance plane over the Sea of Japan, taking thirty-one lives. This unarmed plane was flying about ninety miles off the North Korean coast.[30] As recently as March 2003, four North Korean fighters intercepted an American Air Force reconnaissance plane in international airspace above the Sea of Japan.[31] "The North Korean Navy has captured and detained numerous South Korean merchant ships that have entered North Korea's territorial sea."[32] The list goes on.

One particular incident illustrates North Korea's brutal treatment of those individuals that it actually does capture. On January 23, 1968, North Korea attacked and seized the intelligence ship, the *U.S.S. Pueblo*, in international waters, killing one crewman and detaining eighty-two others. The DPRK incarcerated the crew until mid-December of that year when it returned them to South Korea. However, the ship stayed behind as a trophy museum piece for the regime.[33] Within that time period, North Korea quartered several to a room and the POWs were "threatened with death, interrogated, and some were severely beaten," eliciting supposed "confessions" as to their "criminal aggressive acts." Their treatment was documented through interviews shortly after their return by the Naval Health Research Center in California:

> Their treatment by the North Koreans varied; in general the living quarters, sanitation facilities and medical care were unsatisfactory by western standards. Food was deficient in both quality and quantity. Physical maltreatment was concentrated in two specific periods—the first three weeks (i.e. until all had "confessed") and a "purge" two weeks prior to release in an effort

to obtain names of those crew members who had attempted to communicate their lack of sincerity to the western world. (Propaganda photographs often showed smiling faces in association with obscene gestures.) Physical abuse consisted of fist assaults or kicks in the head or groin. Several crew members who were forced to squat with an inch square stick behind their knees reported losing consciousness and, as a result of the beatings, one man had a fractured jaw. Through lectures, field trips, and written material, the North Koreans attempted to convince crew members of the injustices of their "imperialist" government.[34]

Because of such treatment, researchers discovered that the men were initially depressed and anxious upon return and weeks later were angry and increasingly hostile toward others.

Particularly over the last few years, tension has increased dramatically. On March 26, 2010, as a recent independent investigation revealed, North Korea sank the South Korean navy corvette *Cheonan*, killing forty-six South Korean sailors. Later on in 2010, on November 23, "North Korea fired over 170 artillery rounds toward Yeonpyeong Island in the Yellow Sea, killing two South Korean Marines and two civilians, injuring many more and damaging multiple structures." In 2012, the DPRK attempted to launch two satellites, one successfully, which many observers considered to be equivalent to ballistic missile tests and in violation of the Leap Day Agreement it had just signed with the U.S.[35]

The year 2013 saw the apogee of such tension. The latest nuclear test of February 2013, conducted less than a month after the U.N. Security Council condemned North Korea's satellite launches,[36] provoked another strongly-worded resolution by the Council to impose immediate, greater economic sanctions.[37] This brazen provocation accentuates the North's continued and systematic "fist-shaking" at the international community, the East Asian region, and the United States.[38]

North Korea's defiance has not only included provocations and skirmishes with South Korea and the U.S., but North Korea has aggressively exported ballistic missile technology during the course of several decades.[39] North Korea has sold this technology to countries such as Libya,[40] Pakistan, Syria, Egypt, Iran, and the United Arab Emirates,[41] grossing hundreds of millions of dollars per year, its largest source of hard currency.[42] North Korea's financial stake in the development and sale of missile technology and other military sales drive its economy.[43]

In October 2002, North Korea threatened to resume long-range missile tests and a higher level of weapons proliferation to other countries. This activity falls in line with the intermediate range ballistic missiles supplied to Pakistan in the 1990s.[44] In the late 1990s, North Korea furnished Pakistan with twelve to twenty-five complete No-Dong medium-range missiles.[45] Ominously, North Korea gained nuclear centrifuge technology from Pakistan, which it has used for producing nuclear weapons.[46]

Such proliferation in efforts have continued through the years. For example, a North Korean vessel transported Scud missiles to Yemen in December 2002.[47]

A spokesman for the Nigerian government indicated that a North Korean delegation showed the Nigerian government a catalogue of weapons—but that Nigeria
had not made a definite commitment to purchase them yet.[48]

It does not stop there. North Korea joined the Biological Weapons Convention,
an international treaty that, for the most part, does not even permit possession of biological weapons.[49] However, it appears that North Korea has developed biological weapons such as anthrax, yellow fever, and the plague.[50] Unlike
the Biological Weapons Convention, however, North Korea did not sign the
Chemical Weapons Convention. Consistent with its refusal to sign, North Korea
has a formidable assemblage of such weapons.[51] North Korean military doctrine
asserts the use of chemical weapons as standard weaponry, which makes the use of
chemical weapons, in a fashion akin to conventional weapons, a deadly concern.[52]
The decision not to sign the Chemical Weapons Convention involved conflict
within the regime and illustrates the dominance of military considerations in the
country.[53]

North Korea's goals

On March 7, 2013, the U.N. Security Council unanimously passed additional
economic sanctions against North Korea through a strongly-worded resolution.
This resolution, recalling the 2006 and 2009 resolutions that implemented similar
sanctions on the DPRK, responded to yet another nuclear test performed by
North Korea on February 12, 2013 mentioned previously.[54] Resolution 2094
bears greater significance for two reasons: (1) the Republic of China, North
Korea's closest ally, partially drafted it;[55] and, more importantly, (2) North Korea
threatened again to "withdraw" or otherwise not abide by the armistice agreement. Four days later, on March 11, 2013, the North Korean state newspaper
claimed that the nation did just that.[56]

Why would a country like North Korea promulgate such a withdrawal? Why
would a state like North Korea, a state that has repeatedly and egregiously violated every international agreement it has made,[57] engage in such defiance? North
Korea repeatedly engages in brinkmanship, already having attempted withdrawal
from the Treaty on the Non-Proliferation of Nuclear Weapons (NPT).[58] North
Korea also knows that the Korean War has not reached its conclusion and that the
armistice stands as a roadblock to resumption of full-scale war on the peninsula—
a war that could yield more than a million casualties—but more on this later.[59]

The denunciation of the armistice continues an intentional pattern of precipitating crises and engaging in provocations. The DPRK expelled mandated
neutral armistice observers and closed their facilities to increase diplomatic pressure many years ago.[60] In addition to North Korea's proliferation of media dance
and defiance, it has systematically perpetuated a series of hostilities against several
other nations to achieve particular goals, as briefly highlighted earlier.[61]

Hwang Jang-Yop has provided the highest inside view to explain North Korea's
systematic goals and motivations. He indicated that North Korea had been
fervently seeking to foment favorable political conditions within South Korea for

decades.[62] From the government, there historically have been elements that have been favorable toward North Korea and its system—which is strange, given the disaster that is North Korea, and the relative paradise by comparison that South Korea has become.

Additionally, according to the Seoul bureau chief of *Time Magazine*, much of the South Korean media has evinced a strange reluctance to report North Korean abuse and aggression, whether to Japan or to South Korea itself, but it is quick to trumpet stories that magnify any real or perceived transgression of a soldier or anyone else from the United States. There has emerged a naiveté combined with wishful thinking about the intentions of North Korea, and a willful disbelief of the bellicose intentions of North Korea on the part of a good number of South Korean youth, who never experienced the Korean War. The *Time Magazine* bureau chief said that the South Korean media tends to downplay or even ignore a lot of North Korean acts of aggression, whether sending submarines down to South Korea where spies emerge and infiltrate, or naval skirmishes between North and South Korea near the borderline, or North Korea's wrongful actions against Japan, such as the kidnapping of innocent Japanese civilians conscripted into teaching North Korean officials Japanese.[63] These stories receive little to no press, whereas when anything seems even remotely like a U.S. soldier doing wrong, the headlines magnify disproportionately. Such reporting tends to drive a wedge between South Korea and the United States. North Korea actively has sought to take advantage of, and deepen, any rifts or disagreements between these allies, as well as with other involved countries (such as Japan, Russia, and China).[64]

In addition, South Korean media and other sources, such as books, have tended to demonize the U.S. while indicating attractive points of North Korea. These sources have helped to inculcate in the younger generations a sizable degree of anti-Americanism as well as pro-North Korean sentiments. North Korea regularly seeks to implant anti-American and pro-North Korean propaganda in South Korea, and it seems that it has done so successfully to a large extent. As an example, North Korea likes to say that it has to liberate South Korea from U.S. imperialism and domination, and thus damages the pride of South Korea by, in essence, speaking of South Korea as if it were a colony under the thumb of the United States.[65]

Several years ago a professor at Seoul National University (considered the leading university in South Korea), who had taught sociology at the university for more than thirty years, was discovered to be a North Korean spy after two fellow spies were linked to him. These spies confessed that this professor emeritus had been a North Korean spy all along.[66] North Korea has thus been able to infiltrate influential centers of South Korean culture, and the culture, sadly enough, seems to be swallowing more of the North Korean propaganda and other reinforcing messages. Ironically enough, such devious communication exists in South Korea because as a developing democracy, it allows incomparably more freedom of speech than North Korea.

There are also appeals to Korean nationalism, such that the common bond of Korean ethnicity is touted as being more important than other pieces of common ground, such as the extensive common ground that the United States and South Korea share, both in terms of their inner relationship, but also politically, economically, religiously, and socially. North Korea is an entirely different sort of society economically, politically, religiously, and socially; there exists much more common ground, and much more of a relationship, between South Korea and the United States than between South Korea and North Korea.[67] The South Korean media, a significant portion of university students, and now many government officials in South Korea who are sympathetic with the North Korean regime, see the United States as a big bully against North Korea and an exploiter of South Korea.[68] These South Koreans say they see North Korea as one of them, "our people," as fellow ethnic Koreans. For many, especially in the generations in South Korea who did not experience the Korean War, affinities with the U.S. politically, socially, economically, and legally can be overshadowed by the common ethnic blood shared between North and South Korea.

The strong nationalism of Koreans as Koreans (not North and South Koreans) feeds this misguided identity politics and a strong sense of ethnic identity that has not only survived many invasions, many attacks, and many attempts to dominate or even colonize it, but has grown stronger in resistance to outside attacks. So a distinct susceptibility exists to this sort of propaganda and rhetoric. There are many in Korea, especially among the younger generations and the media, who want the United States out. Indeed, that attitude plays into the hands of North Korean propaganda, which says South Korea is not free and must be liberated by North Korea from under the imperialist fist of the U.S.[69] This attitude lends indirect support to North Korea's goal of consolidating its power over the entire peninsula. If not for the deterrent of the American military forces in South Korea, the country likely would already have been overrun by North Korea, leaving a unified Korea under Kim Jong-Un.

One jail of a country

The North Korean regime puts the entire society in a straitjacket. It has at least ten known concentration camps, where it enslaves, tortures and murders dissidents and others under its disfavor.[70] The regime has starved many of its own people to death; the bulk of the country suffers greatly from malnutrition and starvation. North Koreans do not have the ability to socialize freely. They have no freedom of association, no freedom of press, no freedom of expression, no freedom of speech, and no freedom of religion. The rights, freedoms, and privileges that Americans, and even South Koreans, can at times take for granted, get trampled in North Korea. With no freedom of movement either, a North Korean citizen cannot travel freely within or out of the country.[71] It is an iron cage of a society with the canary inside wasting away—and certainly not singing.

This is all possible because politics flow from the top—presently North Korean dictator Kim Jong-Un ruling in a totalitarian way, just like his father. Early intelligence wrongfully assessed Kim Jong-Il as unintelligent. Later intelligence corrected this earlier assessment, and concluded instead that Kim possessed a high-powered intellect. Estimates of his I.Q. had placed it at around 150.[72] Kim Jong-Un may have similar intellectual capabilities but too little is known of him to be sure at this early point in his reign.[73]

Kim Il-Sung groomed his son Kim Jong-Il to take the reins of power from him starting in the early 1970s.[74] As Korean Workers' Party Secretary, Kim Jong-Il ran the organization, including its propaganda function. In 1980, the Sixth Party Congress named him the official successor. In 1991, Kim Jong-Il ascended to the position of Supreme Commander of the People's Army, and in 1993, he rose to Chairman of the National Defense Committee. Throughout this time, propaganda deifying Kim Jong-Il drummed its way into the day-to-day life of North Korea.[75]

The succession of Kim Jong-Un took place over a much shorter span of time, but his rule so far emphasizes continuity over discontinuity with the rule of the elder Kims. In some ways though, North Korea has fared worse under the current Kim, the least experienced of the three prior to assuming the place of Supreme Ruler.[76]

However, according to defectors from North Korea itself, the North Korean populace, in spite of the regime's propaganda, is aware of Kim Jong-Il and his son's immoral behavior, the failure of their economic policies, and the politicized nature of their inner circle. The deterioration of the country on many fronts would tend to diminish the glorified image of this totalitarian dictator.[77] However, this awareness has not led to the crumbling of the regime yet, but to a continued crushing of the North Korean people.

Failed diplomacy

Kim Jong-Un's recent behavior on the international scene has corroborated Hwang Jang-Yop's insights on North Korea's goals. North Korea, while proliferating weapons, continues to creep ever closer to its ultimate goal: reunifying the Korean Peninsula by force. Its continued hostilities have not only kept the region on the brink of full-scale war, but it also has twisted the arms of the international community to wrest concessions from other nations.[78] It has also sought to intimidate the international community and to buy time to perfect nuclear capabilities, especially inter-continental ballistic missile capability along with the technology to shrink a nuclear device onto a missile warhead. North Korea, by continuing its systematic military hostilities and provocations, has continued the Korean conflict, ensuring that the state of war persists.

North Korea thinks that by continuing its crisis politics, it can leverage for more carrots. Peering into the background of what has been traditionally called the Agreed Framework presents a good example of how North Korea uses the continuing conflict to conjure benefits for its regime. The 1994 Agreed Framework resulted from intensive negotiations during the Clinton administration.[79] U.S. policy toward North Korea, dubbed "limited engagement by necessity," emerged out of heated discussion and debate, both within the Clinton administration and also within the Republican-led Congress. During this debate, policymakers considered a range of options, including preemptive strikes against the known nuclear facilities, proposed sanctions, and a negotiated agreement with North Korea. What was seen as nothing more than a focused preemptive attack solely on the nuclear facilities carried with it, even according to the military leaders at the time, too much risk of a full-blown war.[80] The Clinton administration had actually started pursuing the sanctions option when a visit to Pyongyang by former president Jimmy Carter renewed negotiation efforts.[81]

Jimmy Carter went on a peacemaking mission to Pyongyang in June, 1994. Upon Carter's return, he pronounced the end of the crisis, with Kim Il-Sung agreeing to freeze North Korea's nuclear program under International Atomic Energy Agency (IAEA) inspections, and willing to come back to the bargaining table with the current U.S. administration at the time.[82] This trip served as a catalyst for the negotiations that led to the Geneva Protocol, also known as the Agreed Framework.

The planned initial meeting between the DPRK and the United States in Geneva found itself suspended due to the demise of Kim Il-Sung, the self-styled "Great Leader" who had ruled North Korea from its inception until July 9, 1994. After a one-month delay, the negotiation resumed. A joint statement emerged on August 12, which announced the core of the agreement. U.S. Ambassador Gallucci and North Korea's First Vice Foreign Minister concluded the agreement on October 17, and signed it on October 21. The four-page agreement included eventually transitioning the DPRK from graphite-moderated nuclear reactors to light water reactors. This staged agreement, scheduled to take place over a decade, called for substantial commitments from the U.S. and South Korea to replace lost generating capacity through shipments of heavy oil. The agreement met resistance from some quarters as a "sellout and an act of appeasement." Others hailed it as a major achievement for peace on the peninsula.[83]

If you read the paragraph above carefully, you will notice the carrot, heavy oil, and the stick, IAEA inspections. How well did the Agreed Framework work? As events unfolded afterwards, it became obvious that North Korea had materially breached the Agreed Framework. In 1998, U.S. intelligence discovered a large underground facility that could support nuclear weapon development.[84] In a 2002 meeting with Ambassador Kelly, a North Korean official disclosed North Korea's possession of nuclear weaponry, a statement later denied by Pyongyang.[85]

Given the material breach, in November 2002 (eight years later, mind you) the Korean Peninsula Energy Development Organization (KEDO) suspended shipment of heavy oil and scrapped the light water reactor (LWR) project.[86] North Korea claimed the U.S. breached the agreement and stated that it must develop and produce nuclear weapons as a deterrent against potential American aggression, which it claimed to genuinely fear. North Korea then withdrew from the ongoing Six-Party Talks—formerly involving itself, South Korea, the U.S., Japan, China, and Russia.[87] The result over eight years: free heavy oil shipments and more time for North Korea to build nuclear weapons.

Conclusion

As mentioned previously, international negotiations with North Korea have followed a predictable, cyclical nature: North Korea precipitates a crisis to gain attention and gets who it wants to the negotiating table, makes promises to obtain concessions, and then reneges on any commitments it made. This discernible pattern has emerged time and again. This cycle flies in the face of the customary international legal principle of *pacta sunt servanda* ("promises must be kept"), which embodies the notion that agreements and stipulations between parties of an agreement must be honored.[88] North Korea normally has violated this principle, such as its material breach of the Agreed Framework. In another example, China, maintaining that North Korea reciprocates to friendly gestures, convinced the George W. Bush administration to return frozen funds to Pyongyang in 2007, and to remove Kim's insidious government from the U.S. State Department's list of state sponsors of terrorism the following year as a way to stimulate positive discussions during the Six-Party Talks.[89] Shortly after it pocketed both concessions, North Korea withdrew from the Six-Party Talks in 2009 and proceeded to defiantly carry out a series of nuclear weapons tests. As we will discuss further, North Korea has yet to return to these talks or to reciprocate positively—standard behavior for this criminal regime.

North Korea attempts to justify its behavior by claiming a blanket sovereignty that supposedly immunizes it against its violations of its own domestic as well as applicable international law. Claims of sovereignty should not seek to eliminate the rule of law or *pacta sunt servanda*. North Korea has contempt for the rule of law and proportional consequences should follow.

Notes

*   I am grateful for Kevin Zickterman's assistance in organizing this chapter.

1   *See* Sung-Yoon Lee, *Global Pressure Point: Nuclear Diplomacy vis-à-vis the DPRK: A Dead-End Street*, 27 FLETCHER F. WORLD AFF. 151, 156–57 (2003).

2   *See* MAX HASTINGS, THE KOREAN WAR 25–26 (1987); HENRY CHUNG, KOREA AND THE UNITED STATES THROUGH WAR AND PEACE 43–85 (2000); Michael Hickey, *The Korean War: An Overview*, BBC ONLINE, www.bbc.co.uk/history/worldwars/coldwar/korea_hickey_01.shtml (last visited Aug. 11, 2014).

3   ROBERT J. MYERS, KOREA IN THE CROSS CURRENTS 78–79 (2001); Chung, *supra* note 2, at 97–108.

4   Chung, *supra* note 2, at 103–05; Myers, *supra* note 3, at 78.

5   Chung, *supra* note 2, at 109–24; Myers, *supra* note 3, at 78–79; M.P. SRIVASTAVA, THE KOREAN CONFLICT: SEARCH FOR UNIFICATION 23–33 (1982).

6   Chung, *supra* note 2, at 155; BRUCE CUMINGS, KOREA'S PLACE IN THE SUN: A MODERN HISTORY 260 (1997).

7   UNITED STATES ARMY, OFFICE OF THE CHIEF MILITARY HISTORY, AMERICAN MILITARY HISTORY 545 (1973).

8   Chung, *supra* note 2, at 169.

9   *But see* Cumings, *supra* note 6, at 261–63. South Korean intelligence expected an attack on the Ongjin peninsula, which was repulsed—the surprise may have been that the attack continued and was more widespread than the Ongjin peninsula.

10 Chung, *supra* note 2, at 158–59; Srivastava, *supra* note 5, at 37–45.

11 Hickey, *supra* note 2; Chung, *supra* note 2, at 160–62; CHI YOUNG PAK, KOREA AND THE UNITED NATIONS 78 (2000).

12 Chung, *supra* note 2, at 165–66, 170–77.

13 Cumings, *supra* note 6, at 275–78.

14 *See id.* at 284–86, 289; Hickey, *supra* note 2.

15 *See* Scott R. Morris, *America's Most Recent Prisoner of War: The Warrant Officer Bobby Hall Incident*, THE ARMY LAW., Sept. 1996, at 3, 45; Morse Tan, *The North Korean Nuclear Crisis: Past Failures and Present Solutions*, 50 ST. LOUIS U. L.J. 517, 521 (2006) (explaining that military strategists claim that a full-scale North Korean invasion could produce over one million casualties).

16 Chung, *supra* note 2, at 90, 296–98, 300–02. Note that South Korea had no desire to sign an armistice and had to be persuaded to sign by President Eisenhower, largely through repeated assurances that the United States was committed to unifying Korea.

17 *See* Morris, *supra* note 15, at 3–4; Samuel Pollack, *The Korean Armistice: Collective Security in Suspense*, THE ARMY LAW., Mar. 1984, at 43.

18 Agreement Between the Commander-In-Chief, United Nations Command, on the One Hand, and the Supreme Commander of the Korean People's Army and the Commander of the Chinese People's Volunteers, on the Other Hand, Concerning a Military Armistice in Korea, art. IV, *opened for signature* July 27, 1953, 4 U.S.T. 234 (entered into force July 27, 1953) [hereinafter Korean Armistice].

19 David M. Morriss, *From War to Peace: A Study of Cease-Fire Agreement and the Evolving Role of the United Nations*, 36 VA. J. INT'L L. 801, 885 (1996).

20 Korean Armistice, *supra* note 18, at art. IV; Chung, *supra* note 2, at 300.

21 *See* Agreement on Reconciliation, Non-Aggression and Exchanges and Cooperation Between the South and the North (entered into force Feb. 19, 1992), *available at* www.state.gov/t/ac/rls/or/2004/31012.htm; Joint Declaration of the Denuclearization of the Korean Peninsula, N. Korea-S. Korea, Jan. 20, 1992, 33 I.L.M. 569, *available at* www.state.gov/t/ac/rls/or/2004/31011.htm.

22 Dick K. Nanto, *Report for Congress*, Congressional Research Service, North Korea: Chronology of Provocations, 1950–2003 (2003), *available at* www.fas.org/man/crs/RL30004.pdf; *see generally* THE INST. FOR EAST ASIAN STUDIES, FOREIGN POLICY FOR PEACE AND UNIFICATION (1975) (tracking the South Korean-Japanese relationship during the early 1970s); Korean Unification: Problems and Prospects (C.I. Eugene Kim ed., 1973).

23 Nanto, *supra* note 22, at 6, 8–9. One assassination plot succeeded in killing the wife of President Park Chung-hee only two days before the capture of the *U.S.S. Pueblo; see also* ROBERT S. LITWAK, ROGUE STATES AND U.S. FOREIGN POLICY: CONTAINMENT AFTER THE COLD WAR 202 (2000).

24 "From 1954 to 1992, North Korea is reported to have infiltrated a total of 3,693 armed agents into South Korea," Nanto, *supra* note 22, at Summary; *see also* Richard P. Cronin, *The North Korean Nuclear Threat and the U.S.-Japan Security Alliance: Perceived Interests, Approaches, and Prospects*, 29 FLETCHER F. WORLD AFF. 51, 52 (2005), for more on the kidnapping of Japanese nationals by North Korea.

25 Nanto, *supra* note 22, at 10. The plane was traveling from Baghdad to Seoul. Twenty crew members and ninety-five passengers died. This egregious act sought to discourage participation in the Seoul Olympics.

26 *Id.* at 4. The North Koreans held the crew of eighty-three prisoners for eleven months; *see also* Litwak, *supra* note 23, at 202.

27 James M. H. Lee, *The Korean Armistice and North-South Dialogue*, THE KOREA SOCIETY Q., Summer 2001, at 9, 11.

28 Nanto, *supra* note 22, at 14–26.

29 *E.g., id.* at 17, 25, 26 (August 8, 1998 saw the test fire of "a new 3-stage Taepodong-1 missile in an arc over Japan," February 4, 2003, saw the firing of "a short-range,

anti-ship missile into the Sea of Japan, " and March 2003, saw the firing of "a Silkworm ground-to-ship nonballistic missile into the Sea of Japan"); Emma Chanlett-Avery, Mark E. Manyin & Hannah Fischer, Cong. Research Serv., RL33389, North Korea: A Chronology of Events in 2005, 15 (2006) (May 1, 2005: "The BBC reports that North Korea has test-fired a short-range missile into the Sea of Japan. The missile was believed to have traveled about 100 kilometers, or 60 miles, into the sea between the two countries"); Hannah Fischer, CONG. RESEARCH SERV., RL30004, *North Korean Provocative Actions*, 1950–2007 32 (2007) ("03/10/06—North Korea test-fires two short-range missiles from a coastal site on the Sea of Japan. According to a South Korea government official, the missiles probably dropped into the sea about 100 km away … 07/04/06—Defying broad international pressure, North Korea test-fires six missiles into the Sea of Japan, including a long-range Taepodong-2 with the theoretical capacity to reach the continental U.S. However, the Taepodong-2 failed 40 seconds into its flight … 07/05/06—North Korea launches a seventh missile, despite broad international condemnation of the earlier launches.")

30 Nanto, *supra* note 22, at 5; *see also* Litwak, *supra* note 23, at 202.

31 Nanto, *supra* note 22, at 25.

32 Stephen Kong, Comment, *The Right of Innocent Passage: A Case Study on Two Koreas*, 11 MINN. J. GLOBAL TRADE 373, 375–76 (2002).

33 Richard Mobley, *Pueblo: A Retrospective*, NAVAL WAR C. REV. Spring 2001, at 98, *available at* www.usnwc.edu/getattachment/08740ee7-e8a4-497e-83c8-6a12bb3e3827/Pueblo--A-Retrospective---Mobley, -Richard.aspx; Nanto, *supra* note 22, at 4.

34 Raymond C. Spaulding, *Some Experiences Reported by the Crew of the USS Pueblo and American Prisoners of War from Vietnam*, NAVAL HEALTH RESEARCH CTR., www.history.navy.mil/library/special/pueblo.htm (last visited Mar. 28, 2013)

35 Emma Chanlett-Avery & Ian E. Rinehart, CONG. RESEARCH SERV., R41259, *North Korea: U.S. Relations, Nuclear Diplomacy, and Internal Situation* 8–9 (2013).

36 S.C. Res 2087, U.N. Doc. S/RES/2087 (Jan. 22, 2013); Press Release, Security Council, Security Council Condemns Use of Ballistic Missile Technology in Launch by Democratic People's Republic of Korea, in Resolution 2087 (2013), U.N. Press Release SC/10891 (Jan. 22, 2013).

37 S.C. Res. 2094, U.N. Doc. S/RES/2094 (Mar. 7, 2013); Edith, M. Lederer & Hyung-Jin Kim, *UN Approves New Sanctions against North Korea*, CHI. DAILY LAW BULL. (Mar. 7, 2013), www.hosted2.ap.org/ILDLB/8ef5320729ce4298abefc1903704c7d5/Article_2013-03-07-UN-North%20Korea/id-8a27f53d080146fc8257fa8aadecb074?utm_source=subscriber&utm_medium=CDLBemail&utm_content=APhed_UN%20approves%20new%20sanctions%20against%20North%20Korea&utm_campaign=headlines.

38 *See, e.g.*, Tan, *supra* note 15, at 522–23.

39 *See* Joseph S. Bermudez, Jr., *A History of Ballistic Missile Development in the DPRK*, MONTEREY INST. OF INT'L STUDIES, CTR. FOR NONPROLIFERATION STUDIES, 18–19 (1999), www.cns.miis.edu/pubs/opapers/op2/op2.pdf.

40 Libya in 2004 relinquished tons of uranium likely supplied to it by North Korea. *See* William J. Broad & David E. Sanger, *After Ending Arms Program, Libya Receives a Surprise*, N.Y. TIMES, May 22, 2004, at A6.

41 Bermudez, *supra* note 39, at 1. According to the U.S. Weapons Inspector David Kay, in an interesting twist of events, Kim Jong-Il defrauded Saddam Hussein out of $10 million in a deal that Kim failed to fulfill. The contract included ballistic missile technology and other verboten missile equipment before the Second Gulf War. Bob Drogin, *Botched Iraqi Arms Deal Is Detailed*, L.A. TIMES, Oct. 4, 2003, at A1.

42 *See* Andrew Ward, *Trade Ties Grow Between the Two Koreas*, FIN. TIMES (LONDON), Dec. 10, 2003, at 2; *see also* Douglas Frantz, *N. Korea's Nuclear Success Is Doubted*, L.A. TIMES, Dec. 9, 2003, at A1.

43 *See, e.g.*, Bertil Lintner, *North Korea's Missile Trade Helps Fund its Nuclear Program*, YALE GLOBAL ONLINE (May 5, 2003), www.yaleglobal.yale.edu/display.article?id=1546.

44 *See* Larry A. Niksch, CRS Issue Brief for Congress, *North Korea's Nuclear Weapons Program* 1–2 (2003), *available at* www.fas.org/spp/starwars/crs/IB91141.pdf.

45 Bermudez, *supra* note 39, at 24.

46 *See Nuclear Duplicity from Pakistan*, N.Y. TIMES, Dec. 2, 2002, at A20.

47 Lintner, *supra* note 43.

48 Editorial, *Missiles for Sale: North Korea Spreading Weapons Technology to Largest African Nation*, COLUMBUS DISPATCH (OHIO), Jan. 30, 2004, at 10A.

49 *See* Convention on the Prohibition of the Development, Production and Stockpiling of Bacteriological (Biological) and Toxin Weapons and on Their Destruction, Apr. 10, 1972, 26 U.S.T. 585 [hereinafter Biological Warfare Convention]. North Korea joined on March 13, 1987.

50 *North Korea Special Weapons Guide: Biological Weapons Program*, FED'N OF AM. SCIENTISTS, www.fas.org/nuke/guide/dprk/bw/ (last visited Aug. 11, 2014).

51 *See* Convention on Chemical Weapons: Hearing on Treaty Doc. 103–21 Before the S. Comm. on Foreign Relations, 104th Cong. 2 (1996) (statement of Sen. Jesse Helms, Chairman, S. Comm. on Foreign Relations). North Korea is purported to possess the technology to produce nerve, blister, choking, and blood agents in large quantities. It already has copious stockpiles of sarin and mustard gas, as well as blood agents, choking gases, VX, and riot control agents in unknown amounts. In all, U.S. intelligence reports—as a low figure—some 180–250 tons of chemical weapons. High estimates place the figure at between 2,500 to 5,000 tons. Director of Central Intelligence, U.S. Central Intelligence Agency, Unclassified Report to Congress on the Acquisition of Technology Relating to Weapons of Mass Destruction and Advanced Conventional Munitions, Jan. 1 through June 30, 2001; *North Korea Special Weapons Guide: Chemical Weapons Program*, FED'N OF AM. SCIENTISTS, www.fas.org/nuke/guide/dprk/cw/ (last visited Aug. 11, 2014); U.S. DEP'T OF DEFENSE, PROLIFERATION: THREAT AND RESPONSE (1997).

52 *See generally Attack Across the DMZ Special Report*, JANE'S INTELLIGENCE REV., Apr. 1, 1994, at 22.

53 This confrontation took place between the Ministry of Foreign Affairs (MFA) and the Ministry of the People's Armed Forces (MPAF). SUNG CHULL KIM ET AL., NORTH KOREA IN CRISIS: AN ASSESSMENT OF REGIME SUSTAINABILITY 58 (1997). The MFA briefed Kim Jong-Il on the tactical value of signing the Chemical Weapons Convention. However, rather than take the MFA's advice, the Deputy Minister of the MFA had to complete a full year "revolutionization course" before he could resume his post. The reason for this punishment was the violation of reporting rules.

54 Edith, M. Lederer & Hyung-Jin Kim, *UN Approves New Sanctions against North Korea*, CHI. DAILY LAW BULL. (Mar. 7, 2013), www.hosted2.ap.org/ILDLB/8ef5320729ce 4298abefc1903704c7d5/Article_2013-03-07-UN-North%20Korea/id-8a27f53d080 146fc8257fa8aadecb074?utm_source=subscriber&utm_medium=CDLBemail&utm_ content=APhed_UN%20approves%20new%20sanctions%20against%20North%20 Korea&utm_campaign=headlines; S.C. Res. 2094, U.N. Doc.S/RES/2094.

55 Lederer & Kim, *supra* note 37.

56 Hyung-Jin Kim & Foster Klug, *North Korea Says it Cancels 1953 Armistice*, CHI. DAILY LAW BULL. (Mar. 11, 2013), www.hosted2.ap.org/ILDLB/8ef5320729ce4298abefc1 903704c7d5/Article_2013-03-11-Koreas-Tension/id-ef180ced68b746fb8766b921b8 1eef4b?utm_source=subscriber&utm_medium=CDLBemail&utm_content=APhed_ North%20Korea%20says%20it%20cancels%201953%20armistice&utm_ campaign=headlines.

57 *See, e.g.*, Morse Tan, *Finding a Forum for North Korea*, 65 SMU LAW REVIEW, *passim* (2012).

58 *See, e.g.*, Frederic L. Kirgis, *North Korea's Withdrawal from the Nuclear Nonproliferation Treaty*,

AM.SOC'Y OF INT'L LAW (2003), www.asil.org/insigh96.cfm (explaining North Korea's alleged withdrawal from the NPT on January 10, 2003); S.C. Res. 1874, U.N. Doc. S/RES/1874 (June 12, 2009) (one of the many Security Council resolutions demanding "that the DPRK immediately retract its announcement of withdrawal from the NPT").

59 Morris, *supra* note 15, at 885 ("The Korean Armistice has prevented renewed large-scale hostilities for over forty years ... Despite the breakdown of some of its major provisions, the Armistice has been durable enough to withstand failures and violations and to prevent the eruption of another full-scale war on the Korean peninsula."); Tan, *supra* note 15, at 525–26 (explaining that military strategists claim that a full-scale North Korean invasion could produce over one million casualties).

60 Morris, *supra* note 15, at 33.

61 Tan, *supra* note 15, at 522–23.

62 Hyung-Jin Kim & Foster Klug, *North Korea says it cancels 1953 armistice*, CHI. DAILY LAW BULL., Mar. 11, 2013

63 Donald Macintyre, *Time Magazine* Seoul Bureau Chief, Speech delivered at Handong International Law School (July 11, 2003).

64 *See* Yoon-Ho Alex Lee, *Criminal Jurisdiction Under the U.S.-Korea Status of Forces Agreement: Problems to Proposals*, 13 J. TRANSNAT'L L. & POL'Y 213, 215–16 (2003) (providing the example of large demonstrations that followed the trial of two U.S. soldiers who were acquitted by U.S. tribunals, as opposed to South Korean tribunals, of negligent homicide for running over two South Korean girls in 2002); Lee, *supra* note 1, at 156–58.

65 Lee, *supra* note 1, at 156–59.

66 Nicholas D. Kristof, *Seoul Said to Foil Spy Ring for North that Included Top Scholar*, N.Y. TIMES, Nov. 21, 1997, at A7.

67 Cecilia Y. Oh, Comment, *The Effect of Reunification of North and South Korea on Treaty Status*, 16 EMORY INT'L L. REV. 311, 312–15 (2002) (explaining that since the Armistice, the political and economic interests of the two nations have diverged considerably).

68 *See* Lee, *supra* note 1, at 155–59.

69 *Id.* at 156–58.

70 *See* Robert Windrem, *Death, Terror in N. Korea Gulag*, NBCNEWS.COM (Jan. 15, 2003), www.msnbc.msn.com/id/3071466.

71 *Starved of Rights: Human Rights and the Food Crisis in the Democratic People's Republic of Korea (North Korea)*, AMNESTY INT'L, www.amnesty.org/fr/library/asset/ASA24/003/2004/en/f5daaf5b-d645-11dd-ab95-a13b602c0642/asa240032004en.pdf (last visited Aug. 11, 2014).

72 *See* Peter Carlson, *Sins of the Son: Kim Jong Il's North Korea Is in Ruins, But Why Should that Spoil His Fun?* WASH. POST, May 11, 2003, at D1.

73 Chanlett-Avery & Rinehart, *supra* note 35, at 4 (stating that the "'Great Successor' Kim Jong-un, is unpredictable and opaque." So little is known about the new leader that the uncertainty surrounding policymaking in Pyongyang may be more murky than it was under Kim Jong-il.)

74 Kim et al., *supra* note 53, at 35; SANG-WOO RHEE, SECURITY AND UNIFICATION OF KOREA 7 (1983).

75 Kim et al., *supra* note 53, at 35–36.

76 Chanlett-Avery & Rinehart, *supra* note 35, at 1, 13–14 (discussing how the missile and satellite launches were likely done to bolster legitimacy across North Korea and show the regime's continued defiance in the international arena). Kim Jong-Un has reportedly (and unfortunately) continued the nation's *Songun*, or "Military First" policy despite his openness with western culture.

77 Kim et al., *supra* note 53, at 36, 38.

78 *See, e.g.*, Tan, *supra* note 15, at 527, 533–34.

79 Agreed Framework to Negotiate Resolution of the Nuclear Issue on the Korean Peninsula, U.S.-N. Korea, Oct. 21, 1994, 34 I.L.M. 603; Litwak, *supra* note 23, at 198.

80 Litwak, *supra* note 23, at 198–99. 214–16.

81 *Id.* at 214–16; William M. Drennan, *Nuclear Weapons and North Korea: Who's Coercing Whom?* in THE UNITED STATES AND COERCIVE DIPLOMACY 157, 158–59 (Robert J. Art & Patrick M. Cronin eds., 2003).

82 Litwak, *supra* note 23, at 216; Drennan, *supra* note 81, at 177; B. K. GILLS, KOREA VERSUS KOREA: A CASE OF CONTESTED LEGITIMACY 243 (Michale Liefer ed., 1996).

83 Litwak, *supra* note 23, at 218–220. Of course, the Clinton administration was under the misapprehension that the North Korean regime was not going to last long. *Id.* at 227. They felt that "the Agreed Framework is almost certainly a sufficient period of time for [the North Korean] regime to have collapsed."

84 *Id.* at 222, 225; *see also No Nukes Warning from Clinton to N. Korea*, CNN.COM (Nov. 21, 1998), www.cnn.com/WORLD/asiapcf/9811/21/korea.01/index.html.

85 *See Timeline: N. Korea Nuclear Dispute*, CNN.com (Sept. 28, 2005), www.cnn.com/2005/WORLD/asiapcf/02/10/nkorea.timeline/ [hereinafter *Timeline*]; Paul Kerr, *North Korea Chronology*, ARMS CONTROL TODAY, June 2003, *available at* www.armscontrol.org/act/2003_06/nkoreachron_june03.asp. In 2005, North Korea publicly announced that it had already developed nuclear weapons.

86 Kerr, *supra* note 85.

87 *See, e.g.*, Daniel A. Pinkston et al., CTR. FOR NONPROLIFERATION STUDIES, MONTEREY INST. OF INT'L STUDIES, *Special Report on the North Korean Nuclear Weapons Statement* (2005), *available at* www.cns.miis.edu/stories/050211.htm; *Timeline*, *supra* note 85.

88 *See* The Free Legal Dictionary, www.legal-dictionary.thefreedictionary.com/Pacta+Sunt+Servanda.

89 The Six-Party Talks sought an end to North Korea's nuclear program through negotiations involving China, the United States, North and South Korea, Japan, and Russia.

2 Multiple menaces, including cyber-nuclear*

A brief history of proliferation

On March 12, 1993, North Korea first informed the world that it would be the first nation in history to withdraw (or attempt to withdraw) from the NPT supposedly through the treaty's Article X provisions.[1] The DPRK claimed that recent, routine South Korean military exercises and a lack of objectivity of IAEA inspections threatened its state sovereignty and supreme national interests. It proceeded to attempt this withdrawal just a day before the three-month required notice under Article X. Then, after reactivating its nuclear facilities in December 2002, on January 10, 2003, North Korea again announced that it would officially withdraw from the NPT the following day. It claimed that the aggregate notice of the two withdrawal statements fulfilled the three-month required notice.[2]

Since these purported withdrawals, North Korea has acted as though the NPT never existed at all. After several years and rounds of the Six-Party Talks and after the United States discovered North Korea's extensive money laundering in late 2005, the DPRK threatened to completely withdraw from the Six-Party Talks.[3] Tensions grew until July 4, 2006, when the attempted launching of a long-range missile triggered a Security Council resolution condemning the test-firing.[4] Three months later, on October 9, 2006, North Korea announced that it had success-fully conducted its first underground nuclear test.[5] This led to a strongly-worded Security Council resolution condemning the test, urging North Korea to abandon the program and return to the NPT, and imposing widespread military and economic sanctions on the nation.[6] It did not.

Less than three years later and after years of further negotiations and nuclear tension, North Korea conducted a second nuclear test on April 5, 2009.[7] Another strong Security Council resolution was passed shortly thereafter condemning the test, extending sanctions, and allowing for the inspection of all cargo to and from the DPRK.[8] However, such sanctions did not induce North Korea to return to the NPT. As if the DPRK did not understand the gravity of its offenses, in 2012, after years of test firing short and medium-range missiles mentioned ear-lier, it attempted to launch two satellites, bringing forth more Security Council condemnation.[9] Most recently, North Korea conducted another nuclear test on February 12, 2013, sparking international criticism, including from China, the

DPRK's closest ally, and more specifically targeted language by the Security Council.[10]

The threat from the North

Military planners project that in the event of a North Korean full-scale invasion, the first several months of conflict could see some 300,000 to half a million casualties in the South Korean and U.S. militaries, as well as additional "hundreds of thousands of" civilian casualties.[11] According to Doug Bandow of the Cato Institute, total casualties for such a war could exceed *one million*.[12] Oplan 5027, the U.S. military's plan for the region, anticipates massive attacks on Seoul with artillery and rockets, possibly turning Seoul into a "sea of fire" through launching up to half a million shells per hour.[13] A pre-emptive strike on North Korea could result in a counter-attack by North Korea that would inflict huge levels of casualties and damage before the South Korean and U.S. military could do much to block such attacks or pre-emptively defang the North Korean military by military force.[14] While analysts typically project an eventual South Korean/American victory, this victory would likely come at a great price.[15]

There exists a more devious possibility that North Korea has hinted at by firing missiles over Japan, kidnapping Japanese citizens, and other hostile actions: North Korea may have the ability to attack U.S. bases in Japan to launch the first attack. In this scenario, North Korea would probably seek to fray or split the alliance between the U.S. and South Korea, and possibly move toward uniting the two Koreas.[16] Given the rising anti-U.S. sentiment, especially among the younger generations of South Koreans, the friendly overtures of South Korea (both governmental and private) to North Korea, the prevalent pro-North Korean and anti-American media bias, North Korean infiltrations in South Korea, and the strong desire of the Korean populace to unite, such a scheme takes on increased credibility.

Regardless of whether or not North Korea attacks U.S. military bases in Japan, it can still attack, or threaten to attack, Japanese targets. In one conceivable scenario, North Korea can blitzkrieg the South, and then threaten to destroy major Japanese cities if the United States sends reinforcements. North Korea seeks to weaken America's will to defend South Korea, foment favorable political conditions in South Korea, and then wage war to distract its own populace from its extensive woes. After all, official North Korean policy maintains the objective of re-unifying Korea by force; it considers a violent Communist revolution of the South as its manifest destiny.[17]

North Korea possesses devastating capabilities. In conventional weapons alone, it is one of the leading countries in the world in total number of military units.[18] In fact, "[f]our to five percent of North Korea's 24 million people serve on active duty, and a further 25–30 percent are assigned to a reserve or paramilitary unit and subject to wartime mobilization."[19] While some of these units do not employ the most state-of-the-art technology, the sheer overwhelming numbers nonetheless make North Korea a menacing foe indeed. North Korea has many artillery, mortars, rockets, and missiles pointed and ready to turn the city of Seoul into rubble.[20] North Korea boasts the ability to field approximately five to seven million troops; it already has over 1,100,000 soldiers in its standing forces, thousands of special operation forces, 8,500 field artillery pieces, 1,300 aircraft, over 800 ships and naval craft, 170-millimeter guns and 5,100 220-millimeter multiple-launch rocket launchers, 70 submarines, 6,200 tanks and armored vehicles, surface-to-air missiles and anti-aircraft artillery, cave and underground bases, air defense weapons, mobile missile launchers, and other potential causes of military mayhem.[21]

North Korea presently has the missile delivery technology to strike South Korea and Japan, and, if it so foolishly desired, to strike various parts of China as well.[22] Missile launches over Japan have demonstrated so. The U.S. Department of Defense has also found that in addition to North Korea's "mobile theater ballistic missiles (TBM)" that can reach places around the Pacific, "North Korea continues to develop the TD-2, which could reach parts of the United States if configured as an intercontinental ballistic missile (ICBM) capable of carrying a nuclear pay-load."[23] The huge population densities of both South Korea and Japan would make such weapons, especially nuclear weapons, particularly destructive as they would take more lives per square mile. A nuclear warhead launched to the west coast of the United States, such as Los Angeles or Silicon Valley, would prove devastating as well.

Additionally, and more alarmingly, another Korean war could draw in China again.[24] After all, during the Korean War, the Chinese forces turned back the U.N. forces as they approached the Yalu River near the Chinese border. China would want to maintain North Korea as a buffer between it and South Korea, both geographically and ideologically.[25]

We must also keep in mind that the U.S. nuclear presence in Korea has steadily dwindled to none. In 1967, the United States had 2,600 nuclear weapons in Korea and Okinawa.[26] The number of nuclear weapons in Korea decreased to 151 by 1985,[27] and in 1991, the United States removed all of its nuclear weapons from Korea.[28] However, because the United States has long-range delivery systems that can strike anywhere in the world from anywhere in the world, the presence of nuclear weapons in Korea—or even Asia—does not matter except perhaps symbolically.[29]

The U.S. Army has recently placed approximately 20,000–40,000 troops in South Korea.[30] These troops have ample equipment, such as Apache helicopters and Patriot missile batteries.[31] The largest forward-deployed fleet of the Navy, the Seventh Fleet, rests not far from the shores of North Korea. Around 140 aircraft, 80 ships,[32] and some 40,000 Navy and Marine personnel constitute the Seventh Fleet.[33] Air Force deployment in the Pacific numbers 45,000 military and civilian personnel—with about 340 fighter and attack aircraft under its control.[34] The Seventh Air Force perches in Korea with the Fifth in Japan.[35] These forces in the Pacific, some in and around Korea and Japan, can respond briskly to an outbreak of hostilities. At the same time, the ability to quickly deploy additional military resources enables rapid reinforcement of the present numbers.

With mandatory military service for male citizens, South Korea can also mobilize approximately 4,500,000 well-equipped soldiers with newer armaments than their North Korean counterparts, such as more than 3,000 tanks and 1,500 strike aircraft.[36] Approximately 5,300 mortars and two surface-to-surface battalions add to the South Korean military resources.[37]

The robust South Korean economy, once the second poorest at the end of the Korean War, now stands among the dozen or so largest economies in the world, with a GDP of U.S. $1.14 trillion.[38] It would have large capabilities to sustain a war effort, if those capabilities would not already find themselves devastated by a North Korean attack. However, after another war with North Korea, the South Korean economy might end up flattened even more than after the first Korean War[39] because there exists more to destroy—whether infrastructure, industry, edifices, or people. Additionally, South Korea, for many reasons—including economic, political, historical, and humanitarian—has strong incentives to avoid the outbreak of another war on the Korean Peninsula.[40] In one form or another, war does not present itself as an attractive option.

While the might of the U.S. military with the help of South Korea would likely eventually win or at least maintain or return to the status quo in a fight against North Korea alone, it would probably do so at great cost. The cost of human lives and property on the Korean Peninsula could dwarf the casualties suffered during the first Korean War.

Instead, the North Korean situation requires a delicate balance. At one extreme, the risk of war, which would prove disastrous for the entire peninsula; and at the other extreme, the risk of blackmail and exploitation, in which North Korea would receive benefits that it would divert for its own devious ends. Exploring both ends of the continuum in order to find the parameters for the best solutions, the last section of this book makes an attempt to do so.

The cyber threat

Even without the potentially impending conventional or nuclear armament usage from North Korea, which would likely prove catastrophic, the DPRK poses another rather problematic technological threat. Cyber warfare, a modern technology-based arms race akin to the nuclear arms race of the Cold War, presents more adversaries on the battleground and unique conflict-engagement dynamics. Technology creates a relatively low barrier to entry and the cost associated with waging war in the virtual world, enticing sovereign states like the United States, China, Syria, Iran, and North Korea, as well as terrorist cells such as Al-Qaeda, to develop and continue to invest heavily in furthering their offensive and defensive cyber capabilities. As U.S. Representative Mike Rogers, chairman of the House Select Committee on Intelligence said, "We need to assume that hostile nation states—even non-state actors like al Qaeda—have offensive cyber-capabilities, and we need to be in a position to render their capabilities moot."[41]

Additionally, geographic distance and other barriers, such as mountains, oceans, and physical borders no longer provide a strategic buffer; in the virtual world, enemies can orchestrate war activities inside enemy lines from thousands of miles away. Furthermore, because North Korea cordons off its Internet system, it can defend it more easily in contrast to places like the United States and South Korea, where the Internet remains more openly accessible and laws, often tilted in favor of individual freedom and privacy, restrict government monitoring. Thus, North Korea operates in favorable conditions, allowing it to focus primarily on offensive cyber capabilities.[42]

North Korea appears to prepare for escalation of a cyber war. The DPRK recently doubled the size of its cyber war unit to over 6,000 elite cyber warriors, making it a formidable, sophisticated cyber-foe capable of carrying out advanced technological attacks using its own hacking codes.[43] In a closed-door meeting with the intelligence committee of South Korea's National Assembly, the NIS quoted North Korean leader Kim Jong-Un as saying, "cyber warfare is just as strategically important to Pyongyang as missiles and nuclear weapons," and went on to describe seven North Korean hacking organizations—as well as a network of spies operating in China and Japan.

In addition, experts' analysis of the number of attacks on South Korea over the last five years reveals a pattern that looks more like a coordinated war than the work of random hackers. As Jarno Limnéll, director of cybersecurity at Stonesoft Corp., a McAfee cybersecurity company, summarized: "cyber-capabilities [are] something [North Korea] has taken very seriously … and what they are saying quite publicly is they have several thousand men and women working on a daily basis on cyber. They want to give a very clear impression that they are a strong player in this field."[44]

Computers have crept into nearly every facet of our modern lives, including military strategy and combat. As C. Matthew Curtin, founder of the computer security consulting firm Interhack, pointed out, "If someone was trying to shut down our power grid when there is a huge polar vortex blowing through the country, that would have a serious impact on us."[45] This example highlights how cyber attacks can not only cripple an enemy during a time of war, but also facilitate global blackmail or extortion schemes. As such, North Korea's cyber-military strategy has a core focus of conducting cyber attacks on national infrastructure—including gas, electricity, transportation, and nuclear power. In pursuit of this goal, North Korean hackers have used malware deployments and virus-carrying emails to carry out cyber attacks on South Korean military institutions, commercial banks, government agencies, TV broadcasters, and media websites. A few examples include:

- Carrying out a wave of "distributed denial of service (DDoS)" attacks in 2009 that struck both U.S. government and South Korean websites. A virus, allegedly launched from Pyongyang, sent waves of Internet traffic to a number of websites in the two countries through a series of "zombie" computers. The action took down the U.S. Treasury and Federal Trade Commission websites for several days and crippled a number of government sites and media outlets in South Korea, which cost an estimated £29 million ($48 million) to fully recover.[46]

- Another DDoS attack in March 2011 on South Korean banks left 30 million people without ATM access for days. At the time, Dmitri Alperovitch, vice president of threat research for McAfee Labs, said the attacks had the mark of a North Korean "cyberwar drill" and theorized that Pyongyang had built an army of zombie computers, or "botnets," to unleash malicious software. He guessed that the 2009 attack had been a similar operation. This led to over £470 million ($780 million) in economic damages.[47]
- It appears that North Korea launched the March 2013 attack that wreaked havoc on major South Korean banks, media, and government agencies. The attack crippled systems for days, having wiped the critical master boot records of 48,000 computers and servers associated with South Korean banks and media outlets, using *their own networks* to carry out the destructive activity. Post-forensic analysis revealed the perpetrators tried to mask their identity by transmitting the "cyberweapon" through a series of over 1,000 different IP addresses across multiple continents, and South Korean officials estimated the economic cost at $800 million.[48]

North Korea appears to launch cyber attacks from overseas bases in cooperation with countries such as China.[49] In addition, somewhere in the gray area between cyber and conventional warfare lay chilling reports of North Korea aiding the development of other state's nuclear programs, and actively participating in the underground market for nuclear military technology such as centrifuge construction.[50] In one instance, *Popular Science* magazine recently confirmed that Mossad, the Israeli intelligence agency, secretly accessed a Syrian government official's laptop in 2006 while on a trip to London. While analyzing the contents of the hard drive, it found a photo of two men meeting in the middle of the desert: Chon Chibu, a leader of North Korea's nuclear program, and Ibrahim Othman, director of the Syrian Atomic Energy Commission. When viewed in light of other documents on the machine, Mossad concluded that North Korea was helping Syria build a facility in al Kibar to process plutonium![51]

Before leaving that hotel in London, Mossad planted a Trojan-horse into the Syrian official's machine, and set Israeli government *Operation Orchard* in motion. *Operation Orchard* reached its climax just after midnight on September 6, 2007 when seven heavily armed Israeli F-151 fighter jets flew hundreds of miles into Syrian airspace and leveled the Kibar complex. The Syrian air-defense system never detected the planes or fired a single shot since the Israeli military had used the Trojan-horse to introduce dummy radar images and disable the system while the planes carried out their sortie. This account sheds light on the fine line between cyber and conventional war; "if planting the Trojan-horse was an act of cyberespionage, *Operation Orchard* was its armed cousin."[52]

The potential for cyber attacks to precipitate an armed conflict is real and on the rise. Besides the North and South Korean cyber attack accusations flying back and forth, China has accused the U.S. of cyber snooping, while the U.S. has retorted with accusations against China of spying as well as carrying out offensive cyber attacks against public and private networks in the U.S. For instance, Israel and the U.S. exposed the globe to the Stuxnet virus in 2010. While Stuxnet successfully crippled Iran's nuclear program, it also inflicted collateral damage. In the short term, public and private enterprises inadvertently infected with the virus had to spend time cleaning up their networks, and in the long run *everyone* had to erect barriers to defend against a new genus of computer virus exemplified by Stuxnet. Cyberwar constitutes a new genus of warfare spawned by the application of technology to otherwise traditional military methodologies.[53]

Rep. Mike Rogers, chairman of the House Select Committee on Intelligence, has proposed that continually investing in securing domestic networks addresses the threat of cyber attacks by forcing other countries to ramp up their spending to try to penetrate a layered defensive front. In his words, it then "becomes like the [Cold War-era] Soviet Union, where they will eventually have nothing left to spend."[54] Despite its dismal economy, North Korea has amassed the fourth largest military on the planet through its dogmatic commitment to furthering its military ambitions, even while leaving its people to suffer, starve, and die. North Korea's ability to focus primarily upon offensive cyber capabilities may provoke the world to seriously consider coordinated, aggressive offensive cyber attacks upon North Korea with the intention of wholly destroying or capturing its technological infrastructure. By taking this more assertive course of action, the international community will disrupt North Korea's cyber military program, force it to divert resources toward defensive capabilities, and render its cyber threat moot by attacking from the inside out. The world should also follow Rogers' advice and continue to strengthen its defensive posture as well as staying circumspect of North Korea should it sit at the negotiating table. "We should never underestimate Pyongyang's willingness to engage in dangerous and provocative behavior to extract more aid and concessions from the international community."[55] This quote, alluding to North Korea's notorious pattern of precipitating a crisis, obtaining concessions, and reneging on its promises, applies as well to its cyber attack capabilities.

Conclusion

Many decades ago, nuclear physicists Otto Hahn and Fritz Strassmann changed the course of history through the small but stupendous act of splitting a uranium atom.[56] The devastating power of an atomic bomb itself came about through the efforts of American nuclear scientists through the Manhattan Project.[57] At the intersection of irony and destruction, Americans ponder in the latter half of the 2010–2020 decade how to keep such power over destruction away from one of the most devious nations in world history. Atomic weapons in the hands of a nation with a stated goal to reunite the Korean Peninsula by force, a nation that has violated all of its major international agreements, a nation with missile systems capable of reaching South Korea, Japan, and possibly even the United States, may prove the international community's gravest concern since the Nazis crossed the Rhine.[58]

For the past sixty years, North Korea has lied, broken its word, and pushed tensions to the brink of nuclear war, and negotiations with this country have routinely been unproductive, if not outright failures. With nuclear weapons in the equation, though, the need for effective solutions has never been greater. At the same time, one scholar has called nuclear diplomacy with North Korea "a dead-end street."[59] The entire situation worsens with North Korea's ongoing refusal to return to multi-nation talks that include South Korea, the United States, and Japan, plus North Korea's own traditional allies China and Russia.[60] As with its repeated violations and defiance in the realm of international human rights, North Korea's continued provocations, hostilities and acts of military aggression should trigger consequences—as its actions have violated some of the longest standing international law in human history.

Notes

* I appreciate the aid of Kevin Zickterman and Michael Nealis, especially on the cyber warfare portion.

1 *A Timeline of North Korea's Nuclear Development*, THE PROGRAM IN ARMS CONTROL, DISARMAMENT, AND INT'L SEC., UNIV. OF ILL. AT URBANA-CHAMPAIGN, www.acdis. illinois.edu/resources/arms-control-quick-facts/timeline-of-north-koreas-nuclear-development.html (last visited Mar. 13, 2013) [hereinafter *A Timeline of North Korea's Nuclear Development*].

2 George Bunn & Roland Timerbaev, *The Right to Withdraw from the Nuclear Non-Proliferation Treaty (NPT): The Views of Two NPT Negotiators*, YADERNY KONTROL (NUCLEAR CONTROL) DIG., Winter/Spring 2005, at 20, 20–21.

3 *See A Timeline of North Korea's Nuclear Development*, *supra* note 1.

4 *See* S.C. Res. 1695, U.N. Doc. S/RES/1695 (July 15, 2006) ("Condemns the multiple launches by the DPRK of ballistic missiles on 5 July 2006 local time").

5 Hannah Fischer, CONG. RESEARCH SERV., RL30004, *North Korean Provocative Actions*, 1950–2007, 32–33 (2007).

6 S.C. Res. 1718, U.N. Doc. S/RES/1718 (Oct. 14, 2006) (*"Condemns* the nuclear test proclaimed by the DPRK on 9 October 2006 in flagrant disregard of its relevant resolutions, in particular resolution 1695 (2006), as well as of the statement of its President of 6 October 2006 (S/PRST/2006/41), including that such a test would bring universal condemnation of the international community and would represent a clear threat to international peace and security").

7 *A Timeline of North Korea's Nuclear Development*, *supra* note 1.

8 *See generally* S.C. Res. 1874, U.N. Doc. S/RES/1874 (June 12, 2009).

9 Emma Chanlett-Avery & Ian E. Rinehart, CONG. RESEARCH SERV., R41259, *North Korea: U.S. Relations, Nuclear Diplomacy, and Internal Situation* 7 (2013); S.C. Res 2087, U.N. Doc. S/RES/2087 (Jan. 22, 2013) (*"Condemns* the DPRK's launch of 12 December 2012, which used ballistic missile technology and was in violation of resolutions 1718 (2006) and 1874 (2009).").

10 Edith M. Lederer & Hyung-Jin Kim, *UN Approves New Sanctions against North Korea*, CHI. DAILY LAW BULL. (Mar. 7, 2013), www.hosted2.ap.org/ILDLB/8ef5320729ce 4298abefc1903704c7d5/Article_2013-03-07-UN-North%20Korea/id-8a27f53d080 146fc8257fa8aadecb074?utm_source=subscriber&utm_medium=CDLBemail&utm_ content=APhed_UN%20approves%20new%20sanctions%20against%20North%20 Korea&utm_campaign=headlines; S.C. Res. 2094, U.N. Doc. S/RES/2094 (Mar. 7, 2013) (*"Condemns* in the strongest terms the nuclear test conducted by the DPRK on 12 February 2013 (local time) in violation and flagrant disregard of the Council's relevant resolutions").

11 R. Jeffrey Smith, *North Korea Deal Urged by State Dept.*, WASH. POST, Nov. 15, 1993, at A15; William M. Drennan, *Nuclear Weapons and North Korea: Who's Coercing Whom?*, in THE UNITED STATES AND COERCIVE DIPLOMACY 191 (Robert J. Art & Patrick M. Cronin eds., 2003); Phillip C. Saunders, *Military Options for Dealing with North Korea's Nuclear Program*, CTR. FOR NONPROLIFERATION STUDIES (Jan. 27, 2003), www.cns.miis.edu/north_korea/dprkmil.htm.

12 Doug Bandow, *N. Korea Is No Place to Apply Iraq "Lessons,"* L.A. TIMES, Apr. 22, 2003, at B13.

13 Paul Richter, *Two-War Strategy Faces Test*, L.A. TIMES, Feb. 13, 2003, at A1.

14 Saunders, *supra* note 11 ("The biggest military concern in striking North Korean nuclear facilities is the threat of North Korean counter-attacks."). North Korea's military assets are numerous. To make it even more difficult, these arms often have mobile capabilities or find shelter in caves or underground. Although a number of nuclear sites are known, some of the sites are heavily reinforced and armored, and other sites, such as nuclear reactors and reprocessing plants (especially for uranium), could be functional in small, underground facilities; *see also* North Korean Missile Proliferation: Hearing Before the Subcomm. on Int'l Security, Proliferation, and Fed. Services of the S. Comm. on Governmental Affairs, 105th Cong. 6–7 (1997) (statement of Choi Ju-Hwal, Former Official, Ministry of the People's Army, stating that "since the North uses mostly mobile rocket launchers, not fixed ones, it is assumed that the North does not have fixed rocket launchers").

15 *See generally Attack Across the DMZ Special Report*, JANE'S INTELLIGENCE REV., Apr. 1, 1994; *see also* Linda D. Kozaryn, *Despite Progress, North Korea Poses Major Threat*, AM. FORCES INFO. SERVICE NEWS ARTICLES (Apr. 3, 2001), www.defense.gov/news/newsarticle.aspx?id=45044; Eleanor Hall, "North Korea a Greater Threat than Iraq: Analyst", *The World Today*, ABC (radio broadcast, Australia, Feb. 13, 2003), *available at* www.abc.net.au/worldtoday/stories/s783676.htm.

16 *See* Hall, *supra* note 15.

17 *See* Sung-Yoon Lee, *Global Pressure Point: Nuclear Diplomacy vis-à-vis the DPRK: A Dead-End Street*, 27 FLETCHER F. WORLD AFF. 154–58 (2003) (describing the North's power with respect to the South, Japan, and the United States).

18 *See generally* Kathleen T. Rhem, *North Korean Military "Very Credible Conventional Force,"* AM. FORCES INFO. SERVICE NEWS ARTICLES (Nov. 18, 2003), www.defense.gov/news/newsarticle.aspx?id=27769.

19 Anthony H. Cordesman & Ashley Hess, *The Evolving Military Balance in the Korean Peninsula and Northeast Asia* 109 (2013).

20 Seoul, one of the most populous cities in the world, contains nearly one-fifth and its metropolis includes nearly half of the total population of the Republic of Korea. *See* Wikipedia, Seoul, www.en.wikipedia.org/wiki/seoul (last visited July 1, 2014). It sits not more than 30 miles away from the DMZ. Denis Warner, *A Village Thrives Near the DMZ*, INT'L HERALD TRIB., Apr. 11, 1996, at 9.

21 *Annual Report to Congress: Military and Security Developments Involving the Democratic People's Republic of Korea*, OFFICE OF THE SEC'Y OF DEFENSE 8–15, 18–20 (2012), www.defense.gov/pubs/report_to_congress_on_military_and_security_developments_involving_the_dprk.pdf.

22 *See generally* Daniel A. Pinkston et al., CTR. FOR NONPROLIFERATION STUDIES, MONTEREY INST. OF INT'L STUDIES, *Special Report on the North Korean Nuclear Weapons Statement* (2005), *available at* www.cns.miis.edu/stories/050211.htm; *Timeline: N. Korea Nuclear Dispute*, CNN.COM (Sept. 28, 2005), www.cnn.com/2005/WORLD/asiapcf/02/10/nkorea.timeline/.

23 *Annual Report to Congress: Military and Security Developments Involving the Democratic People's Republic of Korea*, *supra* note 20.

24 *But see* CHARLES M. PERRY & TOSHI YOSHIHARA, THE U.S.-JAPAN ALLIANCE 78 (2003) (China told Pyongyang in the mid-1990s that China will not participate in any future Korean conflict).

25 JAMES E. HOARE & SUSAN PARES, CONFLICT IN KOREA: AN ENCYCLOPEDIA 145 (1999).

26 Robert S. Norris et al., *Where They Were*, 55 BULL. ATOMIC SCIENTISTS 26, 26–35 (1999); *see also A History of U.S. Nuclear Weapons in South Korea*, THE NUCLEAR INFORMATION PROJECT (Sept. 28, 2005), www.nukestrat.com/korea/koreahistory.htm.

27 Robert S. Norris & William M. Arkin, *Nuclear Notebook: U.S. Nuclear Weapons Locations*, 1995, 51 BULL. ATOMIC SCIENTISTS 74, 74–75 (1995).

28 *See* Benjamin Friedman, *Fact Sheet: North Korea's Nuclear Weapons Program*, Jan. 23, 2003. South Korea was the last forward nuclear base for the United States in the Pacific. *See* Norris et al., *supra* note 25.

29 *See* CHARLES J. MOXLEY, JR., NUCLEAR WEAPONS AND INTERNATIONAL LAW IN THE POST COLD WAR WORLD 501–14 (2000).

30 Friedman, *supra* note 27.

31 *U.S. Forces Order of Battle*, GLOBALSECURITY.ORG, www.globalsecurity.org/military/ops/korea-orbat.htm (last visited Aug. 11, 2014).

32 *About the 7th U.S. Fleet*, U.S. NAVY, www.c7f.navy.mil/about.htm (last visited Aug. 11, 2014). The ships typically include three to five Aegis guided-missile cruisers, five to ten destroyers and frigates, and one to two aircraft carriers.

33 *Id.* Many of these ships use Japan and Guam as their bases.

34 *United States Air Force Factsheet: Pacific Air Forces*, U.S. AIR FORCE, www.pacaf.af.mil/library/factsheets/factsheet.asp?id=3597 (last visited Aug. 11, 2014).

35 *The United States Security Strategy for the East Asia-Pacific Region*, U.S. EMBASSY IN THAILAND, www.dod.gov/pubs/easr98/easr98.pdf (last visited Aug. 11, 2014). The Seventh Air Force includes the Fifty-first and Eighth Fighter Wings, with a combined 117 planes and 8,300 air force personnel. See *7th Air Force*, PACIFIC AIR FORCES, www.pacaf.af.mil/library/factsheets/factsheet.asp?id=3602 (Dec. 2006).

36 Kozaryn, *supra* note 15.

37 *Orders of Battle and Major Equipment South Korea and North Korea*, GLOBALSECURITY.ORG, www.globalsecurity.org/military/world/rok/orbat-comp.htm (last visited Aug. 11, 2014).

38 *Travel and Tourism Trade Mission to Taiwan, Japan and Korea*, FEDERAL REGISTER, www.federalregister.gov/articles/2013/06/07/2013-13489/travel-and-tourism-trade-mission-to-taiwan-japan-and-korea#h-6 (last visited July 2, 2014).

39 Bruce Howard, Professor of Economics, Wheaton College, Economics Lecture (1996) (asserting that war in a country devastates a country's economy more than anything else).

40 *See, e.g.*, Saunders, *supra* note 11 (speculating on the negative consequences to South Korea, both physical and political, should war break out).

41 Kelley Beaucar Vlahos, *Special Report: The Cyberwar Threat from North Korea*, FOXNEWS.COM (Feb. 14, 2014), www.foxnews.com/tech/2014/02/14/cyberwar-experts-question-north-korea-cyber-capabilities/.

42 Daniel Schearf, *North Korea's 'World Class' Cyber Attacks Coming from China*, VOICE OF AMERICA (Nov. 21, 2013), www.voanews.com/content/north-koreas-world-class-cyber-attacks-coming-from-china/1795349.html.

43 *Id.*

44 Kelley Beaucar Vlahos, *supra* note 40.

45 *Id.*

46 Alex Hern, *North Korean 'Cyberwarfare; Said to Have Cost South Korea £500m*, GUARDIAN (Oct. 16, 2013) www.theguardian.com/world/2013/oct/16/north-korean-cyber-warfare-south-korea.

47   *Id.*

48   *Id.; see also Cyber Attack Hits South Korea Websites,* BBC NEWS (June 25, 2013), www.bbc.
      com/news/world-asia-23042334.

49   Jeyup S. Kwaak, *North Korea Ramps Up Cybersecurity,* KOREA REALTIME (Jun. 3, 2014),
      www.blogs.wsj.com/korearealtime/2014/06/03/north-korea-ramps-up-
      cybersecurity/?mg=blogs-wsj&url=http%253A%252F%252Fblogs.wsj.com%252Fkor
      earealtime%252F2014%252F06%252F03%252Fnorth-korea-ramps-up-cybersecurity.

50   *Khan "Gave N Korea Centrifuges,"* BBC NEWS (Aug. 24, 2005), www.news.bbc.co.uk/2/
      hi/south_asia/4180286.stm.

51   Peter W. Singer, *The War of Zeros and Ones,* POPULAR SCIENCE, Sept. 2014, *available at*
      www.popsci.com/article/technology/war-zeros-and-ones.

52   *Id.* at 42.

53   *Id.* "[M]ore than 90 percent of conflict casualties over the past two decades have been
      civilians. It would not be surprising to see the same dynamic in cyberwar." *Id.* at 46.

54   Kelley Beaucar Vlahos, *supra* note 40

55   Kelley Beaucar Vlahos, *supra* note 40.

56   HARALAMBOS ATHANASOPULOS, NUCLEAR DISARMAMENT IN INTERNATIONAL LAW 1
      (2000).

57   *Id.;* Geoffrey P. Hammond, *Nuclear Energy into the Twenty-first Century,* 54 APPLIED ENERGY
      327, 328 (1996).

58   *See, e.g.,* Pinkston et al., *supra* note 21.

59   *See* Lee, *supra* note 17, at 152, 155–57.

60   *See, e.g., North Korea's Threat,* WASH. POST, Feb. 12, 2005, at A18.

3   Hell's doorstep[*]

In the midst of the important discussion of geopolitical security concerns regarding nuclear weapons and cyberwarfare, the stifled cry of the North Korean people, whose rights have been grossly and systematically trampled upon, pleads for redress. The egregious conditions and unthinkable treatment of the North Korean people by their own government clamours for worldwide attention. The dictatorships of Kim Jong-Un and his father and grandfather who reigned before him have defied treaties entered into throughout the international community and have made decisions that focus purely on the gain of the government to the extreme detriment of its citizens. Media attention regarding these violations has improved over the years. For instance, the U.S. news sources appropriately informed us about the plight of American journalists in North Korea (who have since returned); yet not much attention focuses upon the astonishing absence of a free press, free speech, and free-association rights inside North Korea. Media outlets readily cover North Korea's missile launches, but do not provide as much coverage for the concentration camps that can stun even the calloused conscience. The story of North Korean counterfeiting U.S. currency makes for a fine news headline, yet the wrenching narratives of refugees sent back to North Korea to face cruel torture, unrelenting labor on less than subsistence rations, and possible execution receive less recognition.

The story of Robert Park briefly increased international awareness of human rights violations in North Korea. Park, a courageous man who sought to increase worldwide attention to the human rights atrocities in North Korea, knowingly put himself at risk by walking into North Korea with requests for Kim Jong-Il and other top leadership to desist from their human rights abuses and step down from power. After enduring severe abuse in prison, he was released in February 2010 after spending forty-three days in DPRK custody.[1] North Korean officials had beaten Mr. Park within an inch of his life.

Hundreds of thousands of citizens have found themselves enslaved in one of the many concentration camps. The on-going vile activities taking place within the North Korean camps almost defy description. While North Korea denies the existence of any concentration camps, modern global satellite imagery, such as Google Earth, provides imagery to the world.[2] Furthermore, common themes emerge from the numerous accounts by refugees who have escaped from North

Korea after captivity inside a North Korean concentration camp.[3] North Korea imprisons its citizens for shockingly small reasons, and even sometimes for no reason other than guilt by association; domestic North Korean law provides, as stated by Kim Il-Sung, "Factionalists or enemies of class, whoever they are, their seed must be eliminated through three generations," which allows any prisoner's children or grandchildren to be sent to a camp at any time during their lives.[4] The DPRK propaganda goes to great lengths to try to dehumanize the human beings inside the concentration camps.

This chapter steps into the relative dearth (given the situation's gravity) of popular and legal academic treatment to analyze this egregious state of rightlessness (an intentional neologism). Experts in the human rights field have averred that the human rights situation in North Korea is the worst in the world, or even the worst in human history.[5] Meanwhile, the North Korean government denies any human rights abuses, insisting "that, there is no human rigths [sic] problem in North Korea."[6] This book challenges this outright denial by providing an analysis of various human rights abuses persisting north of the most heavily armed border in the world.

North Korea epitomizes and seems to justify the "realist" view of international relations, descriptively speaking, in terms of how it actually operates. As such, North Korea acts as if neither international law, nor the international treaties it has already ratified, apply to it. *Pacta sunt servanda* does not constitute North Korea's *modus operandi*. Furthermore, North Korea does not accept accountability to any other country or international organization; rather, it clings only to its own oppressive "sovereignty."

Along these lines: "North Koreans claim that, 'Human rights is [sic] unthinkable apart form [sic] national independence, and what imperialists call rights is their power to do whatever they please; thus, the biggest enemies of human rights are the imperialists who intervene in other states internal affairs under the pretense of protecting human rights.'"[7] The claim that human rights is unthinkable is accurate when put in another context: the current state of rightlessness for many North Koreans causes a bleak sense that under the present government, human rights do seem unthinkable because the government has deprived them of their most basic human rights. The accusation against "imperialists" of "doing whatever they please" actually provides an apt description of the Kims who have historically done whatever they so please. Unfortunately, what the Kims have done against their own people include massive and egregious violations of human rights.

Contrary to the constant denial of the North Korean government, this chapter seeks to help start the criminal case against this state of rightlessness, the egregious case of North Korea. It lays the foundation for subsequent chapters regarding judicial redress of these gross and systematic violations of human rights. Before any need for judicial redress raises itself for consideration, the case that cries out for such a forum must receive delineation: this chapter proposes to expound on the major violations of human rights in North Korea together with the context that makes such violations possible. Entire volumes document human rights abuses in the North.

The prison system

Adverse as conditions in the DPRK remain for most of its population, it degrades into a Kafkaesque nightmare for those whom the regime deems its enemy. While international law and even DPRK law require respect for basic human rights and due process in various forms for prisoners, North Korea disregards these standards. The DPRK government directs the most disturbing methods of abuse at those accused of political crimes. From the time of arrest, political prisoners hear that they are no longer human.[8] This move to dehumanize has long served as the pretext and precursor for the perpetration of gross injustices. The government officials frequently foist this fib upon its prisoners, which rationalizes the horrors inflicted upon them.

Life inside the North Korean concentration camps amounts to a miserable, inhumane existence, with reports estimating around a half million "prisoners" have previously perished while in them.[9] As many as 40 percent of prisoners die as the natural result of daily 12–18 hour-long hard labor shifts in combination with intense malnutrition and starvation; many of them literally starve and work to death.[10] Woefully, severe torture and abuse constitute typical concentration camp conditions in the DPRK.

The wanton disregard for human beings displayed in the camps includes such atrocious, grotesque, acts like "doctors" forcibly removing the unborn fetus from the wombs of pregnant women without anesthesia, and then making the mothers watch the henchmen mercilessly torture and kill the defenseless baby in front of their eyes. They must watch as they toss the tiny, lifeless body into a bloody box overflowing with the remains of similar victims, whose brief existence on this earth featured severe suffering in malignant hands. In an infanticidal variation, "doctors" snatch live newborn babies immediately upon delivery, and then subsequently torture and slaughter the child while their grieving mothers watch on in horror. Sometimes, the grieving mothers, having suffered severe psychological torture and been deprived of any contact with their babies, face subsequent torture, rape, or murder themselves.

Horrific accounts of human experimentation upon prisoners using chemical and biological weapons exist. In one instance, Kwon Hyok, a former prison Head of Security at Camp 22, provided a first-hand account of having watched a family of four, the parents, son and a daughter, live out their final moments inside a chamber filled with suffocating gas. As the room filled with gas, the parents frantically tried to save their children using mouth-to-mouth resuscitation up to their last breath, and all four died gasping for air.[11]

These sorts of firsthand accounts prompted the U.N. to take further action. In February 2014, a United Nations Human Rights Council commission released a report of detailed findings, including countless human rights violations related to crime and punishment in the DPRK.[12] These findings, documented by many sources, corroborate the ongoing violations transpiring in the DPRK.

In North Korea, the Ministry of People's Security (MPS) operates police stations and detention interrogation centers, while the State Security Department (SSD) operates interrogation centers that detain those accused of political crimes.[13]

Non-political crimes garner a maximum two-month detention period—typically respected for standard crimes.[14] However, officials often subject those accused of political crimes to extensive interrogation by the SSD and transfer them to the MPS for further interrogation.[15]

> After his forced repatriation from China, Mr Kim Song-ju was first brought to the SSD interrogation centre in Musan (North Hamgyong Province), where he was kept in an underground prison that appeared to him like a *"cave"*. Such underground cells are a common feature of SSD interrogation centres.
>
> Subsequently, Mr Kim was transferred for further interrogation to the MPS interrogation detention centre in Musan. Mr Kim explained that he had to crawl on his hands and knees into the cell he shared with 40 other prisoners, because the entrance door was only about 80 cm high. The guards told him that *"when you get to this prison you are not human, you are just like animals, and as soon as you get to this prison, you have to crawl just like animals."*[16]

Torture typically accompanies interrogations for either the SSD or MPS.[17] They essentially beat confessions out of suspects. The government purposely employs more sophisticated and terribly "efficient" methods of torture for this purpose.[18] MPS officials receive training on torture methods to induce the maximum amount of pain by confining detainees in painful physical positions.[19] For example, they employ the "pigeon torture" position, which involves handcuffing and suspending prisoners, rendering them unable to sit or stand, sometimes for days at a time.[20] A former prisoner testified that he would have preferred death over the pigeon torture, the worst torture he endured.[21]

Unspeakable horror

The North Korean government consistently argues that torture and human rights violations have disappeared as a result of relevant law revisions and the thorough education of law enforcement officers.[22] However, the Office of the United Nations High Commissioner for Human Rights has officially acknowledged the widespread human rights violations that regularly occur in North Korea, well before the U.N. Commission did the same in 2014. In fact, the very notion of individual rights are considered subversive to the goals of the state and the party. "The regime uses extreme repression and a pervasive surveillance network to intimidate and instill fear in the population. It maintains control through terror, threat of severe punishment, and the manipulation of privileges, including the privilege of food allotments."[23]

Torture and cruel punishment of political prisoners occurs with routine banality daily in North Korean concentration camps.[24] Consider this report of a North Korean political prisoner:

> One day in early March 1997, I was taken into a torture chamber that I had never been in before. I saw a big kettle on a small table and a low wooden table

with straps, about 20 centimeters high. By surprise, one of the two interrogators tripped me with his leg. They strapped me on to the table and forced the kettle spout into my mouth. The spout was made so that it forced my throat wide open and I could not control the water running into my body. Close to suffocation, I had to breathe through my nose. My mouth was full of water and it overflowed from my nose. As I began to faint from the pain and suffocation, I could not see anything but felt sort of afloat in the air. I had been through all kinds of torture, such as whippings, beatings with rubber bands or hard sticks, or hand twisting with wooden sticks between my ten fingers, but this was worse. I do not remember how long it lasted but when I woke up I felt two interrogators jumping on a board which was laid on my swollen stomach to force water back out of my body. I suddenly vomited and kept vomiting with terrible pain. I had no idea how much water ran into my body but I felt like the cells in my body were full of water and water was running out of my body through my mouth, nose, anus and vagina. I faintly heard somebody saying, "Why doesn't this bitch wake up. Did she die?" I could not get up so I was dragged to my cell that day. From that day on, I suffered from high fever and often fainted. My whole body was so swollen that I could not open my eyes. I could only urinate a few drops of milk-like liquid with blood and felt a severe pain in my bladder. I was able to get up and walk again in about two weeks' time. I cannot explain how I could have survived such an ordeal. I would have died if that had happened to me in my ordinary life. I must have developed a mysterious super power to sustain myself under an emergency situation.[25]

This account provides an emblematic example of the horrific practices of the regime. The following gives another instance of the egregious practices of torture:

In 1987, a school principal in Chongjin city found two female teachers murdered the previous night in the night duty chamber of the school. He immediately reported the murders to the police. When the police made little progress in the investigation, they arrested him for murder. He was subject to all kinds of severe torture for two years and forced into confessing the murder. When I saw him in the police jail, both his ears were gone with only ear holes in their place. I have no idea how it happened but his fingers were cut short and clustered together. He was badly crippled, one leg shorter than the other, and unable to walk. His mouth was slanted and he could not control his lips, which made it very difficult to understand what he said. He was a tall and handsome person before he was arrested but became as short as a ten year-old boy in the two years in the police jail.[26]

One common form of torture involves tying a prisoner against iron bars, spreading his hands and legs apart, and beating him repeatedly all over his body with a rubber or cow-skin whip. Just the pain from hanging by his body weight makes the ordeal unbearable. The beatings cause the prisoner's skin to tear and gush blood to the point where his skin does not even feel human anymore. When the torturers release the prisoner from the iron bar, his whole body is so swollen that he cannot bend his back or knees. As a result, the prisoner must evacuate and urinate while standing.[27] As a result of extended torture, North Korean citizens look incredibly stunted. People aged nineteen or twenty look no older than twelve.[28]

Here is another stark example of such cruelty by the SSD and MPS toward someone suspected of a political crime:

> Mr Jeong Kwang-il was detained in an underground interrogation facility operated by the SSD in Hoeryoung (North Hamgyong Province). He was held there on suspicion of being a spy of the Republic of Korea because Mr Jeong had engaged in trading with ROK citizens. During the 10 months he spent in detention, Mr Jeong was given so little food that his weight dropped from 75 kilograms to 36 kilograms.
>
> In order to make him confess, Mr Jeong was beaten with clubs, while hanging upside down. Like numerous other witnesses interviewed by the Commission, Mr Jeong was also subjected to the so-called "pigeon torture". *"[Y]our hands are handcuffed behind your back. And then they hang you so you would not be able to stand or sit"* Mr Jeong described. On repeated occasion, Mr Jeong had to spend a full three days at a time in the pigeon torture stress position, enduring excruciating pain.[29]

Unconsciousness poses no defense for inmates. Multiple means and methods of torture inflict so much gratuitous suffering:

> In February 2011, the witness was repatriated from China. After enduring 12 days of beatings and interrogations by the SSD, she was handed over to the MPS. During two months of detention in an MPS interrogation detention Center, she and other inmates were beaten with various objects, in particular during interrogations. People who fainted during an interrogation session were accused of faking their unconsciousness and made to start again. Although she paid bribes in exchange for more lenient treatment, the witness was still subjected to beatings with wheelbarrow handles, gun barrels and pieces of wood. Detainees had to engage in forced labour during the day. Two men were beaten to death because they had not reached their work targets. A woman starved to death. While in their cells, inmates had to sit still the entire time in a cross legged position with their hands on their knees. If they moved, they would be forced to do head-stands and squats or they were beaten. Some guards took advantage of the coercive setting to rape female inmates, who were taken to a nearby field for "questioning".

In addition to starvation and interrogation, guards coerce inmates at detention centers to perform difficult labor, even before conviction of any crime.[30] Additionally, the detention centers fail basic standards for preventing or treating disease, leaving detainees to waste away or starve with little or no medical attention.[31] Detainees face one form of misery or another almost constantly, such as interrogation, physically grueling work, or maintaining a fixed bodily position.[32] Any deviation from instruction, even looking around or speaking, results in further draconian punishment.[33]

The U.N. Human Rights Council Commission Report[34] detailed the following startling account, offering a glimpse into the DPRK's torture chambers:

> A former SSD official described how a special torture chamber existed at the SSD interrogation detention facility in the province where the witness was deployed. The torture chamber was equipped with a water tank, in which suspects could be immersed until the suspect would fear drowning. The room also had wall shackles that were specially arranged to hang people upside down. Various other torture instruments were also provided, including long needles that would be driven underneath the suspect's fingernails and a pot with a water/hot chili pepper concoction that would be poured into the victim's nose. As a result of such severe torture, suspects would often admit to crimes they did not commit.[35]

Similar conditions also exist in MPS detention centers, especially concerning suspects accused of political "crimes".[36] Former detainees describe the pigeon torture position, beatings, and physical stress positions used to obtain false confessions under severe duress.[37] Former detainees testified that they sustained numerous permanent injuries, including broken legs, spinal fractures, and kidney damage.[38]

For those sentenced to a highly secretive political prison camp, their already dreadful ordeal of undergoing arbitrary arrest, unlawful detention and torture, starvation, as well as a preordained "legal" sentence decided without any due process becomes even more horrific.[39] The sentence of a political prison detainee tolls most ominously in this benighted land. The government fails to inform families whether their accused family members are alive or dead, but everyone knows that a family member who disappears in the night generally remains "disappeared".[40] Witness testimony corroborates public awareness and fear of political prison camps, but the government cloaks details in secrecy, leaving the North Korean public to imagine their worst nightmares. Such punishments intimidate people from questioning the government.[41]

Operation devastation

The DPRK government does not acknowledge the existence of political prisons.[42] In a calculated move to deny and disguise the existence of unlawful conditions surrounding prison camps, the government of the DPRK distorts reality with inaccurate labels. The government explains away the physical existence of these camps, notwithstanding their visibility through satellite imagery. It disguises the prison camps as farming communities or military compounds, and calls them by such false appellations. Even in classified government documents, officials call the prison camps "controlled areas." They refer to inmates as "moved people," and call the SSD Bureau in charge of prison camps the "Farming Bureau."[43]

Beyond the "lies of disguise," political prison camp orders seek to ensure their existence remains secret at all costs. The government tucks away political prisons in remote mountain regions, and it threatens and forbids anyone from disclosing information about these camps. Testimony has revealed elaborate plans and infrastructure in place, should direct discovery occur, to execute all prisoners in a short amount of time and to destroy all evidence that the prison ever existed. Multiple witnesses corroborate the orders in place to "wipe out" inmates and "eliminate any evidence" of prison existence in the case of war.[44] According to former prison guards, the officials conduct drills to prepare for this possibility.[45]

The DPRK government has gone to such lengths to hide these prisons in part because the ongoing atrocities destroy adverse witnesses and evidence of past and ongoing crimes. The continuous and systematic operation of prison camps has been gradually eliminating those suspected of opposing the government.[46] When I brought my students to an event about North Korean concentration camps, officials at the Illinois Holocaust Museum called these camps a "Holocaust in slow motion." The North Korean government designed the camps in the 1950s with the purpose of purging anyone (along with three generations of that person's family) who did not fall in line with the Supreme Leader.[47] Through a multi-faceted system of deliberate starvation, forced labor, execution, torture, and sexual violence,[48] the prison camps have functioned to silence anyone who poses any perceived threat to the government, including those deemed guilty by association.[49]

Political prison camps intended to "permanently remove from society those groups, families and individuals that may politically, ideologically or economically challenge the current political system and leadership of the DPRK." Not only do the political prison camps eradicate any opposition to the DPRK, but the prison camps also terrorize the populace through fear. In testimony to the Commission, Ms. Jeong Jin-hwo explained:

> [E]very North Korean knows [about the camps]. We have a perception that once you are in, there is no way out. It's a cruel, cruel place, and you would guess, you are sometimes beaten by the police and so from that you can imagine how harsh the treatment would be inside.[50]

As Ms. Jeong Jin-hwo's testimony illustrates, the political prison camps, well known throughout the DPRK, strongly discourage any political opposition to the Supreme Ruler and the fellow criminals in cahoots with him.[51] According to the Commission, "political prison camp inmates are considered to have lost their rights as DPRK citizens."[52]

Prison official-arranged marriages, used as a reward for exceptional prisoners, runs against the general prohibition against having children. Couples created by these arranged marriages do not live together; rather, they may stay overnight together a couple of times a year. Any children born of an arranged marriage become prisoners of the camp at birth. The camp authorities separate them from their mothers at school age. The environment of the political prison camps and the separation of family members, reinforces "no concept of family" for the members of these families. Mr. Shin Dong-Hyuk testified about his family stating, "We were all inmates and there was nothing that I could do to them … And, they had nothing they can do as parents, so I guess I did not feel any attachment or feeling for my parents."[53] Ordinary family life remains out of the question for those in these concentration camps.

Despite the prohibition against rape in the political prisons, rape commonly occurs as guards and privileged prisoners take advantage of female prisoners' vulnerability. In some instances, the guards rape women using physical force. At other times, women receive pressure to trade sexual relations in order to receive special treatment, such as favorable work conditions or food. If the rape of a female prisoner becomes known to prison authorities, the perpetrator receives no punishment, while the victim often experiences harsh labor or execution. Mr. Ahn Myong-chol testified that "[o]n one occasion, the commander of his unit raped a woman, who became pregnant and gave birth to a baby. The mother and her child were taken to the detention and punishment block, where the baby was thrown in the feeding bowl for the dogs." The Commission also described the horrible ordeal one woman endured when sent to a political prison camp while pregnant:

> The witness was sent to Political Prison Camp whilst pregnant. Toward the end of her pregnancy, she was kicked by a guard triggering premature labour. When the child was born, guards beat her until they could pull away the crying baby from her. She lost consciousness because of the ordeal. When she woke up she found her baby dead. The body was gathered with other corpses in a storeroom until enough corpses had accumulated to merit throwing them into a single grave site. Still in pain and bleeding, the witness was forced to work the next day and beaten because she could not keep up with her work quota.[54]

This political prisoner's experience illustrates the negative impact the DPRK's policy of forced abortions has on the mothers' well-being. Additionally, the policy of forced abortions demonstrates the DPRK's disregard of the lives of both the mother and child, further emphasizing that the DPRK regards political prisoners as "enemies of the state," and thus must stay under complete state control.[55] The perpetrators of rape, forced abortions, and sexual violence do so with impunity.

Pregnant women entering the concentration camps face particularly unfortunate conditions due to the unfathomably heartless treatment of newborns. For instance, concentration camp guards, nurses, and inmates murder all newborns and unborn babies with any non-Korean lineage, most commonly Chinese. The following summarizes the refugee testimony of a sixty-four-year-old grandmother:

The first baby was born to a twenty-eight-year-old woman named Lim, who had been happily married to a Chinese man. The baby boy was born healthy and unusually large, owing to the mother's ability to eat well during pregnancy in China. Former Detainee #24 assisted in holding the baby's head during delivery and then cut the umbilical cord. But when she started to hold the baby and wrap him in a blanket, a guard grabbed the newborn by one leg and threw it in a large, plastic-lined box. A doctor explained that since North Korea was short on food, the country should not have to feed the children of foreign fathers. When the box was full of babies, Former Detainee #24 later learned, it was taken outside and buried.

She next helped deliver a baby to a woman named Kim, who also gave birth to a healthy full-term boy. As Former Detainee #24 caressed the baby, it tried to suckle her finger. The guard again came over and yelled at her to put the baby in the box. As she stood up, the guard slapped her, chipping her tooth. The third baby she delivered was premature—the size of an ear of corn—and the fourth baby was even smaller. She gently laid those babies in the box. The next day she delivered three more very premature babies and also put them in the box. The babies in the box gave her nightmares.[56]

Most of the prisoners do not make it out alive.[57] According to a former prison guard, the officials drilled into them that inmates, as enemies of the state, should not be thought of as humans, that prisoners are meant to die from hard labor, and that they erase any record of the prisoners' existence.[58] These concentration camps starve the prisoners and work them to death as slaves in order to produce a maximum number of goods with minimal labor costs.[59] The prisoners slave away at factories, farms, and mines. Inmates work in excess of twelve hours most days to meet quotas, regardless of their physical condition or environmental factors.[60] When a starving, diseased, and exhausted worker cannot meet the quota, the guards make no adjustment and show no mercy.[61] Even dangerous jobs, including building a hydropower dam, often employed the labor of teenagers.[62] Accidents would fill the water with corpses, but the government did not care.[63]

Regardless of the overall food situation in the DPRK, the policy of starvation through sub-subsistence rations persists.[64] Starvation and inadequate food rations have created a situation so dire, one witness testified that she ran to work with broken bones to avoid tardiness, which would result in reduced rations.[65] Those who survive supplement their diet with things like mice, snakes, insects and grass at the risk of severe punishment.[66]

The camp officials and guards exact severe, extrajudicial punishment upon those who disobey.[67] Incentives reward prison guards for cruelty and harshness; their training and propaganda supports treating the prisoners in a subhuman and inhumane fashion.[68] Select prisoners gain oversight of their fellow prisoners.[69] These informants have authorization to use discretionary violence and do so with the hopes of ensuring their own survival. They also instruct other prisoners to report any perceived wrongdoing lest they incur punishment themselves. Snitching on fellow prisoners and tipping off the authorities gain rewards. One former inmate informant, aged 13 at the time, testified reporting a conversation he overheard between his own mother and brother in which they discussed plans to escape the camp. After denouncing his mother, the witness had to witness the public execution of his mother, brother, and others involved in the alleged plan. The informant gained a full serving of cooked dried rice, a rare reward indeed for betraying his own family members.[70]

In addition to starvation, intimidation, and actual violent punishment, political prisoners have grossly inadequate clothing, substandard shelter from harsh elements, little hygiene and medical treatment, if any.[71] The system seeks to eliminate any trace of a challenge to the reigning Supreme Leader's authority, which has resulted in the extermination of hundreds of thousands of people over the years.[72]

Despite acknowledgment and regulation by DPRK law, inmates of ordinary prisons experience many of the same conditions as political prisoners.[73] While regulations provide for bedrooms, bathrooms, lighting, water, clothing, medical treatment, libraries, eight-hour work days, and family visits,[74] most inmates suffer in a different reality.[75] Aside from the model prison DPRK has shown to the world,[76] prisons generally overflow with too many prisoners, and prisoners do not have access to showers or hygiene materials.[77] Rather than the purported goal of reforming prisoners, ordinary prisons seek to subdue and exert absolute control over inmates and re-establish absolute allegiance and obedience to the government and its leaders.[78] In their starved conditions, many prisoners survive only because family members have brought them food.[79] One inmate witnessed another inmate receiving a meal from outside the prison. Not used to consuming a full meal, he thereafter vomited. The on-looking inmate collected the vomit and saved it to eat later.[80]

Due to starvation, long work hours, and manual labor performed elsewhere by machines rather than humans, prisoners often suffer injuries through accidents or severe punishment.[81] In this environment with no regard for prisoner safety, the physically incapable inmates cannot meet the demands of the job, and therefore find themselves in further peril of severe punishment.[82]

Egregious executions

The recent U.N. Commission of Inquiry, as well as numerous eye witnesses, has also confirmed the widespread use of public and private executions.[83] The SSD, not a neutral decision maker by any means, carries out a large number of these executions in detention centers and determines if, how and when to execute a prisoner. The officials often force other prisoners to watch these executions.[84] Stunningly to ordinary sensibilities, these executions on often ludicrous grounds systematically fulfill *state policy*.[85]

North Korea outright rejects the charge of public executions as absolute fabrications of hostile elements.[86] Nonetheless, direct, firsthand testimonies exist of public executions after summary sentencing. Some political prisoners know neither the nature of their crime nor the scope of their sentence.

The U.N. review subcommittee urged North Korea to revise the criminal code provisions relating to capital punishment in a way that would comply with the relevant articles of international covenants; however, North Korea refuses to do so.[87] Amnesty International has received reports of public executions carried out at places where large crowds gather. The officials announce these executions in advance to encourage attendance by those in schools, enterprises, and farms. Additionally, the executions of some prisoners take place in front of their own families. Hanging and firing squad constitute common methods.[88] So many of these executions occur for political, trivial, or manifestly unjust reasons, and take place without the benefit of legal protections that would safeguard the innocent.

The North Korean government, in practice, fails to uphold human rights in general; the concentration camps form the nadir of this state of rightlessness.[89] Arbitrary arrests, executions and forced disappearances not only punish individuals, but also warn others to continue towing the state line.[90]

Modern slavery

As a leader that keeps his people in line through a Machiavellian utilization of fear, Kim Jong-Un has seized a stranglehold on his raw power through these concentration camps. Political prisoners make up the vast majority of inmates suffering from what the U.N. defines as "arbitrary detention."[91] The concentration camps serve the purpose of thoroughly purging anyone standing against the Kim regime, as well as providing a means of free labor to power the regime.[92] The plight of Hun-sik Kim, the principal of Pyongyang Light Engineering College, serves as an example. She received a sentence of five years imprisonment for simply suggesting to the City Education Board that her students' labor responsibility diminish so that they could spend more time studying.[93]

As already mentioned, many inmates die before the completion of their sentence due to the horrendous living and working conditions inside the prison camps. The crowded and cramped prison chamber might count as torture in and of itself. "Some eighty to ninety prisoners sleep in a flea-infested chamber about six meters long by five meters wide (about 19 feet by 16 feet)."[94] Thus, the prisoners sleep with the stinking feet of other prisoners right under their nose. The prisoners naturally emit a stench due to permission to shower only twice a year.[95] Additionally, prisoners receive only enough food to leave them perpetually teetering on the verge of starvation, even while working long hours. Their hunger drives them to eat anything remotely edible, such as plants, grass, bark, rats, snakes, or food provided for the labor-camp farm animals, if they can get away with it.[96] Much of this scavenging happens in the work fields if prisoners can (again) "get away with it."

Not only do the living arrangements inside these camps earn about negative seven stars on a scale of one to five, but working conditions frequently kill inmates. The prisoners work around 12–18 hours every day without wages. Leather whips line the prison walls, used to beat inmates on a daily basis with little or no reason.

The guards restrict prisoners from talking, laughing, or taking a rest, and they must literally keep their heads down at all times. They must monotonously repeat the same motions throughout their workday. As a result, more than half of the women suffer from lumps on their heads or shoulders, they develop hunched backs, or they become crippled.[97]

Death by beating, starvation, and outright execution commonly occur in these concentration camps. Consider this report on Kyohwa-so Number 1, located in South Pyongan Province:

> The whole group would be punished for the infraction of one of its members, a common infraction being the failure to meet individual—or group—production quotas. The most common and immediate punishment was reduced food rations. Frequently the threat of reduced food rations drove the women prisoners to work through constant pain. In winter, hands and fingers numb from cold were prone to accidents from the sewing needles and scissors. Mindful of their production quotas, prisoners continued at their workstations, doubly fearful that their dripping blood would soil the garments they were sewing. Repeated infractions led to transfer to the prison's shoe factory. Even more severe punishment included prolonged solitary confinement in a cell too small to allow for a person to fully stand up or lie down inside, leading to loss of circulation and severe pain.[98]

Conclusion

Massive and varied crimes against humanity take place in North Korea on a regular basis, most especially in its prison camps. Human extermination, torture, crimes by association, and collective retribution abound. Without exception, crime-by-association applies to all political crimes. The concluding observations from the UNHRC's 2004 report and the most recent report demanded North Korea guarantee that all unfair treatments, tortures, and other inhuman treatments be swiftly reported to and investigated by an independent organization.[99] Nonetheless, North Korea fails to protect its citizens from the most severe human rights abuses to this day.

A final example puts an exclamation mark upon these barbarous practices and demonstrates how these camps are used as tools of the regime to keep *all* in line, even the elite. In December 2013, the DPRK executed Jang Song-thaek, the uncle by marriage to the Supreme Leader Kim Jong-Un and the head of the Administration Department of the Central Committee of the Workers' Party of Korea. Kim Jong-Un ordered his execution three days after his arrest and immediately after a special military court pronounced judgment. He had no opportunity to appeal his preordained judgment before execution. As the Commission so succinctly stated, "[i]f such violations [of international law] could affect one of the highest officials in the land, it is not difficult to appreciate the standards of law and justice that are afforded to ordinary citizens."[100] In other words, if the

Supreme Leader's uncle did not have a chance at any sort of dignified treatment in his arrest and trial, an ordinary citizen sent to one of these nightmarish camps has even less.

Kim Jong-Un currently stewards at least one of the most oppressive regimes in the world, if not the most. In spite of North Korea's every attempt to hide this repulsive reality, human rights violations remain numerous and well documented. In North Korea, due to guilt by association, children die of starvation in concentration camps because their grandfather or grandmother was deemed anti-Party. "People are executed in public because they ask the question: Why is the Great Leader not giving us rations?"[101] May the day come when Hell's doorstep closes forever in the DPRK.

Notes

* Thanks to Sarah Walsh and Kevin Zickterman for their assistance with this chapter.

1 Adam Gabbot, *U.S. Human Rights Campaigner Freed by North Korea Returns Home*, GUARDIAN (Feb. 7, 2010), www.guardian.co.uk/world/2010/feb/07/robert-park-north-korea-home.

2 *North Korea's Largest Concentration Camps on Google Earth*, ONE FREE KOREA, www.free-korea.us/camps/ (last visited Aug. 1, 2014).

3 *See generally* DAVID HAWK, THE HIDDEN GULAG: EXPOSING NORTH KOREA'S VAST SYSTEM OF LAWLESS IMPRISONMENT (2d ed. 2012), *available at* www.davidrhawk.com/HRNK_HiddenGulag2_Web_5-18.pdf.

4 *Id.* at 29.

5 *See generally* David Scheffer & Grace Kang, Editorial, *North Korea's Criminal Regime*, N.Y. TIMES, (July 7, 2006), www.nytimes.com/2006/07/06/opinion/06iht-edkang.2131969.html; Stephanie Ho, *VOA NEWS, Freedom House Calls for Action on North Korean Human Rights Violations*, US FED NEWS, June 6, 2007. North Korea is also included in the report by Freedom House titled *The Worst of the Worst 2010: The World's Most Repressive Societies*, *available at* www.freedomhouse.org/uploads/special_report/88.pdf.

6 Sung-Chul Choi, *Human Rights in North Korea in the Light of International Covenants*, in INTERNATIONAL COMMUNITY AND HUMAN RIGHTS IN NORTH KOREA 53, 56 (Sung-Chul Choi ed., 1996) (quoting a statement by Nam-Joon Paek in 1993 at the World Conference on Human Rights in Vienna).

7 *Id.* at 55 (quoting Kim Jong-Il, *Socialism is a Science*, RODONG SHINMOON [THE LABOR NEWSPAPER], Nov. 4, 1994).

8 U.N. Human Rights Council, Rep. of the Comm'n of Inquiry on Human Rights in the DPRK, Feb. 7, 2014, ¶704, U.N. Doc. A/HRC/25/63 (2014) [hereinafter *H.R.C. Rep.*].

9 *Holocaust Now: Looking Down into Hell at Camp 22*, ONE FREE KOREA, www.freekorea.us/camps/22-2/ (last visited Aug. 1, 2014).

10 *Torture, Starvation Rife in North Korea Political Prisons*, CNN (May 4, 2011), www.edition.cnn.com/2011/WORLD/asiapcf/05/04/north.korea.amnesty/.

11 Jamie Frater, *Top 10 Evil Human Experiments*, LISTVERSE (Mar. 14, 2008), www.listverse.com/2008/03/14/top-10-evil-human-experiments/.

12 *See generally H.R.C. Rep.*, *supra* note 8.

13 *Id.* ¶700.

14 *Id.* ¶701.

15 *Id.* ¶703.

16 *Id.* ¶704.

17 *Id.* ¶840.

18 *Id.* ¶707.

19 *Id.*

20 *Id.* ¶717.

21 *Id.*

22 Lee Keum-Soon et. al., *White Paper on Human Rights in North Korea*, Korea Inst. for Nat'l Unification, 96 (2004) [hereinafter KINU 2004].

23 North Korea: Humanitarian and Human Rights Concerns: Hearing Before the Subcomm. on East Asia and the Pacific of the H. Comm. on Int'l Relations, 107th Cong. 62, 4 (2002), *available at* www.internationalrelations.house. gov/archives/107/79392.pdf [hereinafter NKHR].

24 *See generally* David Hawk, *The Hidden Gulag: Exposing North Korea's Prison Camps*, U.S. Comm. For Human Rights in N. Korea (2003), *available at* www.hrnk.org/HiddenGulag.pdf.

25 NKHR, *supra* note 23, at 65.

26 *Id.* at 66.

27 *Id.*

28 *Id.* at 10.

29 H.R.C. Rep., *supra* note 8, ¶715

30 *Id.* ¶712.

31 *Id.* ¶715.

32 *Id.* ¶713.

33 *Id.*

34 *See generally* H.R.C. Rep., *supra* note 8.

35 *Id.* ¶707

36 *Id.* ¶717.

37 *Id.* ¶717.

38 *Id.* ¶717.

39 *Id.* ¶729.

40 *Id.* ¶730.

41 *Id.*

42 *Id.* ¶731.

43 *Id.*

44 *Id.* ¶732.

45 *Id.*; International Group of Human Rights Volunteers, Brutality Beyond Belief: Eye-Witness Accounts from North Korean Prison Camps 35 (2004) [hereinafter Brutality Beyond Belief].

46 H.R.C. Rep., *supra* note 8, ¶746.

47 *Id.* ¶¶743–48.

48 *Id.* ¶842.

49 *Id.* ¶738.

50 *Id.* ¶730 (alterations in original) (quoting witness).

51 *Id.* ¶¶729–31.

52 *Id.* ¶754.

53 *Id.* ¶¶763–64.

54 *Id.* ¶¶764–66.

55 *Id.* at 227–33.

56 *Id.* at 61–62.

57 *Id.* ¶755.

58 *Id.* ¶767.

59 *Id.*

60 *Id.* ¶775.

61 *Id.* ¶777; BRUTALITY BEYOND BELIEF, *supra* note 52, at 37, 39.

62 H.R.C. Rep., *supra* note 8, ¶779.

63 *See e.g.*, BRUTALITY BEYOND BELIEF, *supra* note 52, at 71–77 (giving numerous examples of such atrocities). "On one occasion, 150 corpses were rolled up in straw mats and buried under the fruit trees. The families were never informed and identification is no longer possible, once buried." The individuals had died from the sheer amount of labor they were subjected to. *Id.* at 71.

64 H.R.C. Rep., *supra* note 8, ¶770.

65 *Id.*

66 *Id.* ¶772; *see also* BRUTALITY BEYOND BELIEF, *supra* note 52, at 73 (explaining the purposeful lack of food circulated throughout the prisons and the horrific health problems that result).

67 H.R.C. Rep., *supra* note 8, ¶758.

68 *Id.* ¶761.

69 *Id.* ¶762.

70 *Id.*

71 *Id.* ¶773.

72 *Id.* ¶781.

73 *Id.* ¶822.

74 *Id.* ¶786.

75 *Id.* ¶787.

76 *Id.* ¶786.

77 *Id.* ¶800.

78 *Id.* ¶801.

79 *Id.* ¶805.

80 *Id.*

81 *Id.* ¶802.

82 *Id.* ¶802.

83 *Id.* ¶823.

84 *Id.* ¶834.

85 *Id.* ¶845; *see also* BRUTALITY BEYOND BELIEF, *supra* note 52, at 176–77 (giving an example of workers who slipped off a path that were shot to death on site for falling while working).

86 KINU 2004, *supra* note 22, at 91, 112.

87 *Id.* at 91.

88 The Hidden Gulag: Putting Human Rights on the North Korea Policy Agenda: Hearing Before the Subcomm. on East Asian and Pacific Affairs, Comm. On Foreign Relations, 108th Cong. 42 (2003), (statement of David Hawk, Human Rights Investigator, U.S. Comm. for Human Rights in North Korea), *available at* www.ftp.resource.org/gpo.gov/hearings/108s/92834.pdf.

89 H.R.C. Rep., *supra* note 8, ¶838.

90 *Id.* ¶839.

91 Hawk, *supra* note 24, at 26.

92 North Korea: Human Rights, Refugees, and Humanitarian Challenges: Joint Hearing Before the Subcomm. on Asia and the Pacific and the Subcomm. on Int'l Terrorism, Nonproliferation and Human Rights of the H. Comm. on Int'l Relations, 108th Cong. 102 (2004), *available at* www.internationalrelations.house.gov/archives/108/93390.pdf [hereinafter North].

93 North Korea: Humanitarian and Human Rights Concerns: Hearing Before the Subcomm. on East Asia and the Pacific of the H. Comm. on Int'l Relations, 107th Cong. 62 (2002), *available at* www.internationalrelations.house.gov/archives/107/79392.pdf.

94 *Id.* at 60.

95 NKHR, *supra* note 23, at 69.
96 Hawk, *supra* note 24, at 25.
97 NKHR, *supra* note 23, at 69.
98 Hawk, *supra* note 24, at 44–45.
99 KINU 2004, *supra* note 22, at 9, 96–97.
100 *See* H.R.C. Rep., *supra* note 8, ¶832.
101 North, *supra* note 109, at 100.

4 The perils and hardships of refugees*

Under the oppression of the feared demagogue, Kim Jong-Un, thousands of North Koreans flee their home country every year in search of a better life. The combination of extreme hunger, fear, and potential economic opportunity motivates refugees to risk their families' lives by making the dangerous trek to China, or to abandon their families and make the journey alone.[1] This unfortunate situation allows human traffickers the opportunity to exploit refugees, of whom nearly 75 percent are women. In fact, 70–90 percent of women who venture into China fall prey to sex traffickers.[2]

At the height of the famines in the 1990s, crossing the border into China provided the desperate solution for some to escape the starvation and persecution. For several years, this solution worked, as the Chinese and North Korean governments turned a blind eye to these "defectors," many of whom returned to North Korea after obtaining food, money, or other goods for their families.[3] After the early 2000s, however, China had a change of heart and viewed these defectors as a threat to the region's already weakened regional job market and political well-being.[4]

China began rounding up around 2,000 of these defectors to send back to North Korea every month.[5] Initially, as the DPRK's criminal code has always sanctioned those for illegally leaving the country, mild (at least by North Korean standards) punishments followed,[6] and, up until recently, centered on the motivation of the defectors.[7] Even more recently, however, defectors have found themselves receiving much harsher punishment, in some cases formal execution or even shooting on sight.[8] This "crime" of leaving the country, or "treason against the fatherland," more frequently gets several years of hard labor in a concentration camp and/or various forms of torture.[9] The Chinese government understands the return of such persons could mean more than just a slap on the wrist for them, yet Chinese officials forcibly repatriate these North Korean citizens anyway and show reluctance only when under the international spotlight.[10]

Forcibly repatriating North Koreans seeking refuge in China contravenes China's obligations under the 1951 Convention Related to the Status of Refugees and its 1967 Protocol. Well over 150,000 North Korean refugees currently live in China. In December 2003, the Commission to Help North Korean Refugees (CNKR) reported that Chinese security forces captured over 850 North Korean refugees, holding them in five separate Chinese detention centers in the Yanbian region. Well-informed sources reported that the Chinese authorities repatriated the refugees from the five camps to North Korea at a rate of roughly 100 per week or more. Each week, the officials repatriate 50 to 100 additional refugees from Dandong, China to Sinuiju, North Korea.[11]

Upon return

Upon arrival in North Korea, North Korean officials subject refugees to intense interrogations that may last for several days or even weeks. Torture often accompanies the interrogation process, along with sexual humiliation and exploitation of female detainees, as well as the horribly common practice of infanticide.[12] Reports indicate that the interrogators ask very similar questions such as: Why did you leave? Were you trying to get to South Korea? Did you talk to any South Koreans? Did you talk to any Christians? Did you listen to South Korean television or radio? Did you attend a Christian church? If at any time the interrogators become convinced that the detainee has either been influenced by South Koreans or a community of faith, that individual will face either execution or banishment to one of the North Korean concentration camps.[13] Shorter-term work camp and torture sentences have emerged as the least cruel options.

North Korean defectors understand, therefore, that getting caught before, at, or over the Chinese border can prove just as lethal as starving back home. North Koreans walk for days through dangerous terrain to avoid the numerous armed guards and barbed wire on the border to reach passable rivers to cross.[14] Numerous human rights organizations have facilitated these defectors' escapes and an "underground railroad" of sorts has formed.[15] South Korean, Chinese, and other foreign brokers "escort" these individuals to freedom in countries like South Korea, the United States, or Japan.[16] Human traffickers gather up thousands of these border crossers, an overwhelming number female, and sell them into slavery or forced marriages to Chinese men,[17] while China rewards those that turn in these defectors by returning them to North Korea.[18]

In its report, the U.N. Commission noted that the DPRK "routinely subject[s] person[s] who speak out about the human rights situation in the DPRK to summary executions, enforced disappearances and other acts of violence." Approximately 30,000 North Koreans have left the DPRK, yet many of these witnesses do not speak out, fearing for the safety of their families.[19] As a result, many of the witnesses who speak out believe that their families have either escaped from North Korea or that they have already died.[20] Still others who fear for their families risk providing testimony, often requesting that their identities remain confidential in an effort to protect their families.[21]

However, satellite images and information from the press and non-governmental organizations (NGOs) provide evidence outside that of testimonials from North Korean witnesses and victims.[22] The U.N. Commission of Inquiry on Human Rights in the DPRK (the Commission) further "obtained clandestinely recorded videos and photographs showing relevant sites, documents and correspondence" that evidenced human rights abuses in the DPRK. These additional sources serve to confirm the existence of political prison camps and corroborate the testimonies from escaped North Korean prisoners and refugees.[23] Additionally, as the number of people who have escaped North Korea has increased, their accounts have provided cumulative evidence.[24] In the face of the DPRK's denial that human rights abuses occur in North Korea, the testimony of numerous courageous North Koreans raises awareness of the shocking abuses and provides the grounds for future accountability of DPRK authorities.

The vulnerability of refugee women

Refugee women make up "two-thirds of North Korean refugees hiding in China".[25] Many of the following testimonials emanate from these women, who have fortunately escaped repatriation.

The high number of North Korean women refugees exists for at least several reasons. The state's assumption of the responsibility of child rearing reconfigured the traditional family unit into a means of strengthening Kim's totalitarian grip on the country and its people.[26] Kim Il-Sung's depiction as the father figure of the state and all North Koreans as his children also contributed to the dismantling of traditional family units.[27] Jung and Dalton note that "by 1960, 65% of children under five were sent to child care centers, and by 1970, the vast majority of children were in state-provided child care."[28] In reality, the state's assumption of child care served to strengthen the state's control over its citizens by providing an opportunity for years of indoctrination of young children. The government taking away children from their mothers eliminated a major reason for them to stay.

The role of domestic violence, pervasive throughout North Korean society also factors into the mix.[29] A witness testified before the Commission that "[d]omestic violence is quite common. There is no law on this: family issues stay within the family. Even if a woman complains, the police will not interfere in family business." Violence against women extends beyond the houses to public instances. DPRK officials do not fear reprisal as rape is not "really considered a crime."[30] One witness told the story of a girl, recalling, "Lee was caught on a train without a ticket but could not pay the penalty. She was taken to the railroad inspector's home and sexually assaulted."[31] Another witness testified to the Commission about sexual violence in the military, explaining:

> There were a lot of cases of sexual abuse and rape committed often by senior officers. Normal soldiers would also engage in rape, exacerbated by the fact that these young men were denied the right to have sexual relations while serving in the army. The rapes were typically covered up, although male comrades would talk about them and some even bragged. It was common knowledge that rapes were taking place.[32]

Sexual violence meets with impunity, so women remain reluctant to even report such abuse.[33] Factors such as these contribute to the fact that women leave the

DPRK at a higher rate than men, making them more vulnerable to repatriation and/or human trafficking.[34]

Trafficking of women

After women have escaped North Korea, as refugees they fall prey to human trafficking and forced marriages with Chinese men. In addition to the reasons given already, the famine in the 1990s also drove many women to seek outside resources to survive.[35] Women also have historically had more opportunities to leave in comparison to men because women have more freedom of movement and are under less surveillance than men. Human traffickers also contribute to North Korean women's mobility into China as "brokers are more willing to assist the travel of a woman with the intention of selling her to a Chinese household, or into prostitution once in China, with or without the woman's knowledge and/or consent."[36] One witness described to the Commission how brokers lure women to China:

> In 2003, a broker who came regularly to the market convinced me I could work in China and earn a lot of money growing ginseng. Brokers came on a daily basis to the market to get women out of the DPRK. I know a lot of women who left this way. I went with the broker on the impression I would be going to a farm, but once in China I realized I was being trafficked, and sold by the broker. I was with 8 other women, when we got to … [a] location in China 4 or 5 men were waiting for us in a car. I later learned I was sold for 8,000 North Korean won.[37]

Another woman described her experience once she was sold to her Chinese "husband," informing the Commission:

> I was sold off to a man with disabilities. Despite having a disability, he beat me often. He did not speak Korean and I did not speak Chinese, we communicated in body language. I was locked inside the house for 6 months and did not know where I was. After 6 months, I was finally able to convince him I would not run away, that I would work, then I was able to leave the house. I was expected to sleep in his bed, and have sex from the first day. I begged every time not to have sex, but was beaten when I tried to resist. He used to hit me with anything until I was bruised and bleeding. I tried not to get pregnant by avoiding sex during my fertile periods by saying I was sick. I do not know if he wanted children because I could not communicate with him. I lived with the man for 3 years, in the same area the other eight women I was trafficked with lived.[38]

The above survivor's experience illustrates the confinement as well as mental and physical abuse trafficked North Korean women endure.[39] North Korean trafficked women also face more isolation due to language and cultural barriers in addition to their often rural locations. The isolation experienced by trafficked North Korean women makes escape and building support systems impossible and reinforces Chinese "husbands" control over their refugee wives.[40] In addition, trafficked North Korean women have no rights in China, leaving them without the protection of the law, without necessary health services, particularly for pregnancy, and nowhere to report crimes, such as domestic violence. One North Korean witness details the state of North Korean refugee women in China:

> Even if you die in China, you have nowhere to be buried. You have no rights there. Because you are unregistered, even if your "husband" beats you to death, there is nothing that can be done. If this happens, your friends will take the body and bury it for you. This happened to one of my friends.[41]

North Korean trafficked women have no rights in China because the Chinese government does not recognize the marriages between North Korean refugee women and Chinese men. As a result, North Korean refugee women cannot obtain the proper documentation necessary to find employment in China.[42] This leaves trafficked women little opportunity to escape from their forced marriages.

Perhaps surprisingly to some, a sizable portion of the marriages turn out well, as happy unions. Others turn out middling, but much better than life in North Korea. Not all the marriages play out as tragedies, although some do, as this section explains.

The National Human Rights Commission of Korea estimated that between 20,000 and 30,000 children, born to North Korean refugee women, currently live in China.[43] Despite entitlement to Chinese citizenship, children born as a result of the marriages between refugee North Korean women and Chinese men are often "effectively rendered stateless" because in order to be a Chinese citizen, a child must be registered, which puts their North Korean mothers in danger of repatriation.[44] Because they lack proper registration, these children face the constant threat of deportation to North Korea based on their maternity, cannot receive education and health care, and are often separated from their mothers.[45] Further, Chinese "husbands" sometimes use the children's welfare and status as "stateless" citizens as blackmail over their trafficked mothers.[46] Ms. Park, a North Korean woman able to reunite with her son, explains this difficult situation faced by many trafficked North Korean women and their Chinese/North Korean children:

> Children born to DPRK mother do not have ID, so they cannot go to schools. When their mothers are arrested and sent back to the DPRK, they become literally homeless. When mother go to the [ROK] and try to take their children, some men use the children to blackmail their mothers for money. [They say] 'if you send this much, I will send the child,' but they never do. Women can't go there themselves for fear of being arrested and repatriated.[47]

Repatriated women

Women constitute the majority of repatriated persons and experience punishments of sexual violence, humiliating acts, and forced abortions, which impose the most mental and physical pain against the repatriated individuals.[48] DPRK authorities impose forced continual naked squats and groping, and speak to prisoners in a derogatory manner. Witnesses recalled guards asking prisoners questions such as: "Do you like the taste of Chinese men?" and "Do you enjoy sleeping with that Chinese man?" The DPRK authorities employ invasive body searches under the pretense of searching for evidence. The authorities confiscate and steal money. One female witness recounted an extremely humiliating experience:

> She and others were taken to a detention facility where women were placed in a room separate to the men and had all their clothes and belongings removed and taken away. They were made to lie down on their backs with their legs spread and an invasive thorough body search was conducted by the guards who were looking for cash, letters and phone numbers. A female guard wearing rubber gloves conducted a search of their body cavities. The witness saw that other guards were looking and laughing at them through the open windows of the facility while this search was conducted. The witness heard that a man who was caught concealing a credit card was taken to a separate room and severely beaten up. After one month, the witness was transferred to another detention facility where she was subjected to another round of thorough body searches. In her group, there were an elderly woman and a woman at a very advanced stage of her pregnancy. Both were not spared from physical and verbal abuse. They were made to squat and stand up 100 times. When the old woman was too weak to carry this out, female guards kicked her until she fell, bringing down with her the pregnant detainee who was standing next to her. The pregnant detainee was in pain from the fall but the guards simply started cursing her and shouted that she was carrying a Chinese baby in her womb. The guards eventually took her to the medical facility of the detention centre. When the pregnant detainee returned three days later, she was no longer carrying a child and she informed the rest of the detainees that she had a miscarriage.[49]

The DPRK also utilizes forced abortions against women as an intentional form of punishment for leaving the DPRK. These abortions suggest a genocidal intention to maintain ethnic homogeneity. Officials inflict abortions upon repatriated women by using physical force to inflict trauma on the fetus, forcing the woman to engage in heavy physical activity and denying women proper food and nutrition, invasively inserting chemicals, physically removing the fetus through the use of invasive procedures, and administering drugs that either induce labor or kill the baby in utero. In Korean culture, a newborn baby counts as a one year old, providing some cultural context to this matter. Ms. Jee Heon A testified about her forced abortion before the Commission:

I was found to be pregnant, three months pregnant at that time. I was so surprised that I was pregnant. And I remember in 1999 ... they said that they were going to make me get an abortion, and what they meant by abortion was instead of giving me a shot, they make me lie on a table, and get a surgery right away. There was a lot of bleeding ... I could not stand straight.[50]

At other times, women carry their babies to full term and they witness the infanticide of their newborn infant. Ms. Jee Heon A also testified before the Commission about witnessing a mother forced to kill her own child immediately after giving birth:

[T]here was this pregnant woman who was about 9 months pregnant. She worked all day. The babies who were born were usually dead, but in this case the baby was born alive. The baby was crying as it was born; we were so curious, this was the first time we saw a baby being born. So we were watching this baby and we were so happy. But suddenly we heard the footsteps. The security agent came in and this agent of the Bowibu said that ... usually when a baby is born we would wash it in a bowl of water, but this agent told us to put the baby in the water upside down. So the mother was begging. "I was told that I would not be able to have the baby, but I actually got lucky and got pregnant so let me keep the baby, please forgive me", but this agent kept beating this woman, the mother who just gave birth. And the baby, since it was just born, it was just crying. And the mother, with her shaking hands she picked up the baby and she put the baby face down in the water. The baby stopped crying and we saw this water bubble coming out of the mouth of the baby. And there was an old lady who helped with the labour, she picked up the baby from the bowl of water and left the room quietly. So those kinds of things repeatedly happened. That was in the detention centre in the city of Chongjin of Hamgyong Province.[51]

Ms. Jee Heon A's experiences demonstrate not only the DPRK's complete disregard for human life, but also the North Korean government's pervasive employment of genocidal acts in the labor camps.

Escaping

As we saw in earlier chapters, not only has North Korea created one big prison for its citizens, it also has perfected a heartless propaganda machine that mocks what the world would consider free speech and press. Because of these two factors, much of the information that North Koreans have about the outside world and freedom comes by word of mouth.[52] Typically the only escape routes available to them take them to China. South Korea and the United States shimmer like promised lands of sorts.

Bribing officials, paying brokers, and/or utilizing friends and family most commonly contribute to escape efforts. This usually happens through the northeastern part of the country near the border with China as explained earlier. Defectors typically travel to northeast China, are escorted to Southeast Asian countries, and missionaries take the defectors the rest of the way to Seoul. A major alternative to this common route is to pay for a forged passport to fly directly to Seoul from China, but this requires three times the cash, a price few North Koreans can afford while hiding and making menial wages in one of the poorer areas of China.[53] Many refugees trek across the comparatively unguarded Mongolian border from China, braving the difficult terrain. Those with boats have increasingly attempted to escape by sea.

Many refugees find themselves swept up by labor traffickers, exploited through menial jobs and stuck in a cycle of poverty, and the majority of these refugees remain in China for many years. Many of them merely survive in China for so long because of the support of the Korean–Chinese community, as well as local missionaries that risk their lives to support escapees.[54] However, even though many defectors remain in China, almost none of them have plans to return home. More than 97 percent express no intention to return to the North even though more than 90 percent generally still have family there. Few return of their own volition, and even those repeatedly repatriated often attempt to cross the border again.[55] The fact that escapees risk imprisonment, torture, and death repeatedly demonstrates the desperate plight of the North Korean people.

Challenges in the promised land

No matter how they get there or where exactly "there" is, be it China, South Korea, or the Unites States, survivors of this treacherous journey do not necessarily manage well in the receiving culture. The majority of escapees have experienced torture, rape, experimentation, imprisonment, and watching their relatives die and fall apart before them, leading to "an indelible imprint of horror and helplessness on the body and the mind." Their world feels unsafe, devoid of love, with their sense of trust all but destroyed.[56] The trauma runs deep:

> Trauma can manifest itself in a number of specific behavioral responses. One is a permanent heightening of the natural response of fear and anxiety to a dangerous situation. This happens when victims' views of the world and a sense of safety have changed. Memories of the trauma may provoke fear or anxiety. Other common responses to trauma include increased and/or continuous arousal, manifested in feeling jumpy, being easily startled, having trouble concentrating or sleeping, and impatience and irritability. Such reactions—themselves unusual—may further distress trauma victims as well, particularly if loved ones bear the brunt of this behavior. Sometimes people feel angry because of sustained anxiety.[57]

Refugees also experience grief and depression, including hopelessness, and in extreme cases have suicidal or even homicidal thoughts or behavior. The majority of the refugees stay anxious about possible arrest and return to North Korea, living in a strange place, and worrying about their family in North Korea. Sadly, these psychological and social problems do not end when they reach South Korea or their destination, "with rates of PTSD ranging from 30 percent to 48 percent."[58]

Unfortunately, when refugees actually reach their destination, or their "promised land," their high expectations of freedom do not necessarily find full satisfaction. Many of these refugees neither make a decent living nor sustain a healthy lifestyle. Many find themselves unhappy in this promised land.[59] The refugee unemployment rates dwarf the national average in South Korea:

> The typical defector of the early 2000s is a former manual worker or farmer, and is seldom successful in the South. Indeed, most of these defectors live in poverty. According to a 2003 survey of 780 defectors, only 19 percent of them had regular full-time jobs while 42 percent described themselves as "unemployed." In a 2004 survey, the number of "unemployed" defectors was 38 percent. These are very large figures for a country where the unemployment rate fluctuates around 2 to 4 percent … Moreover these and other studies suggest that those who were employed tended to find work in parttime [sic] and casual jobs.[60]

While refugees receive settlement money and monthly scholarships, these do not necessarily last for long. Cultural differences also make it challenging. Defectors typically go through assimilation classes specifically designed for them to learn South Korean culture and important life skills; the novelty of a culture based on capitalism and income jars them.[61] Unless that person is considered a relatively important refugee, refugee incomes generally move toward the low side. Connections to the elite in South Korea or the upper class are rare. Most refugees claim that they do not have jobs that match their skills, do not have the ability to do their work, or suffer discrimination at work.[62]

Add these issues to a myriad of other concerns, and the lives of refugees become all the more difficult and isolated. Many North Koreans (45% by some surveys) claimed that at first they could not understand the South Korean language at all, twice the amount of those that claimed that they understood the language and dialect clearly. Similarly, younger refugees in South Korea also do not tend to understand lessons and remain behind in school, which may mean a menial job further down the road for them and their families.[63] While far better than life in a North Korean concentration camp, life in South Korea also presents challenges.

A diminished welcome

South Korea has cut the benefits it offers to defectors for resettlement. It did this in 2005 to cut down on what is called "chain defection," a process by which defectors use their settlement and other benefit money to help family members navigate to South Korea. This process continues with the next relative making it to South Korea and receiving their benefits and continues until all of the family has made it out of the North. South Korea has quietly made it harder for Northern defectors to settle in the nation (except for important refugees of course) to keep up its image. In essence, "[t]he South Korean government is closing the door in front of aspiring defectors, but trying to do it quietly since an explicit rejection of 'brothers and sisters' from the desperate North remains a political impossibility."[64] South Korea should pass the proposed North Korean Human Rights Act (see Appendix 1).

Although the United States invites refugees through its North Korean Human Rights Act of 2004, few (between 100 and 200) have come to the United States. The process can take as long as two years, and most refugees give up. Most of the refugees find waiting for up to two years under conditions like house arrest in an embassy or consulate more than they can bear.

Notes

* Kevin Zickterman again helped with this chapter, as did Amanda Beveroth.

1 Rhoda Margesson, Emma Chanlett-Avery & Andorra Bruno, CONG. RESEARCH SERV., RL34189, *North Korean Refugees in China and Human Rights Issues: International Response and U.S. Policy Options* (2007) *available at* www.fas.org/sgp/crs/row/RL34189. pdf.

2 North Korea: Human Rights, Refugees, and Humanitarian Challenges: Joint Hearing Before the Subcomm. on Asia and the Pacific and the Subcomm. on Int'l Terrorism, Nonproliferation and Human Rights of the H. Comm. on Int'l Relations, 108th Cong. 76 (2004), *available at* www.internationalrelations. house.gov/archives/108/93390.pdf [hereinafter North].

3 *See* Elisa Gahng, Note, *North Koran Border-Crossers in Yanbian: The Protection Gap Between the Economic Migrants and Refugee Regimes,* 24 GEO. IMMIGR. L.J. 361, 363–65 (2010). Up to 66 percent of these border-crossers were returning to North Korea after obtaining food and money from China.

4 Benjamin Neaderland, *Quandary on the Yalu: International Law, Politics, and China's North Korean Refugee Crisis,* 40 STAN. J. INT'L L. 143, 172–73 (2004).

5 Alison Carrinski, Note, *The Other North Korean Dilemma: Evaluating U.S. Law Toward North Korean Refugees,* 31 SUFFOLK TRANSN'L L. REV. 647, 652 (2008). These numbers are estimates from 2002 and could be higher today. *Id.* at n. 24.

6 Gahng, *supra* note 3, at 366.

7 Kyu Chang Lee, *Protection of North Korean Defectors in China and the Convention Against Torture,* 6 REGENT J. INT'L L. 139, 151 (2008).

8 *See, e.g., id.* at 156; Richard Shears & Daily Mail Reporter, *New Leader But Still No Mercy: Three North Korean Defectors Shot Trying to Cross Frozen River to Reach the Chinese Border,* MAIL ONLINE (Jan. 3, 2012), www.dailymail.co.uk/news/article-2081581/New-leader-mercy-Three-North-Korean-defectors-shot-trying-cross-frozen-river-reach-Chinese-border.html.

9 Lee, *supra* note 7, at 155.

10 *See, e.g.,* Neaderland, *supra* note 4, at 150–55 (giving numerous examples of the Chinese allowing North Koreans to proceed to South Korea after finding their way into foreign embassies throughout China).

11 *Id.* at 2, 76.

12 David Hawk, *The Hidden Gulag: Exposing North Korea's Prison Camps,* U.S. COMM. FOR HUMAN RIGHTS IN N. KOREA 59, 63 (2003), *available at* www.hrnk.org/HiddenGulag. pdf.

13 *Id.* at 8.

14 *See Perilous Journeys: The Plight of North Koreans in China and Beyond,* INT'L CRISIS GRP., 8–9 (Oct. 26, 2006), www.crisisgroup.org/--/ media/Files/asia/north-east-asia/north-korea/

erilous_journeys___the_plight_of_north_koreans_in_china_and_beyond [hereinafter *Perilous Journeys*].

15 *See, e.g.*, Carrinski, *supra* note 5, at 664–65; *Perilous Journeys*, *supra* note 14, at 19–20.

16 Carrinski, *supra* note 5, at 664–65; *Perilous Journeys*, *supra* note 14, at 15–16 (providing the prices for certain trafficking and escort services for defectors).

17 *See* Albery Suh, Note, *First Steps Are Better than None: Distinguishing the Practical from the Rhetorical in the North Korean Human Rights Act of 2004*, 37 RUTGERS L.J. 585 (2006) (stating that 70–90 percent of these women fall into human traffickers' hands).

18 *E.g.*, Carrinski, *supra* note 5, at 652; *Perilous Journeys*, *supra* note 14, at 15–16 (quoting rewards as high as $630 and fines as high as $3,600).

19 U.N. Human Rights Council, Rep. of the Comm'n of Inquiry on Human Rights in the DPRK, Feb. 7, 2014, 14–15, U.N. Doc. A/HRC/25/63 (2014) [hereinafter *H.R.C. Rep.*].

20 *See* David Hawk, *The Hidden Gulag: The Lives and Voices of "Those Who are Sent to the Mountains:" Exposing North Korea's Prison Camps*, COMMITTEE FOR HUMAN RIGHTS IN N. KOREA, 15 (2d ed. 2012), *available at* www.hrnk.org/uploads/pdfs/HRNK_HiddenGulag2_Web_5-18.pdf.

21 *See id.*; H.R.C. Rep., *supra* note 19, at 15.

22 *See* Hawk, *supra* note 12, at 17.

23 H.R.C. Rep., *supra* note 19, at 60–61.

24 *See* Hawk, *supra* note 20, at 12.

25 Jane Kim, *Trafficked: Domestic Violence, Exploitation in Marriage, and the Foreign-Bride Industry*, 51 VA. J. INT'L L. 443, 457 (2011).

26 Kyungia Jung & Bronwen Dalton, *Rhetoric Versus Reality for the Women of North Korea: Mothers of the Revolution*, 46 ASIAN SURVEY 741, 750 (2006).

27 H.R.C. Rep., *supra* note 19, at 86.

28 Jung & Dalton, *supra* note 26, at 743.

29 Jung & Dalton, *supra* note 26, at 750.

30 H.R.C. Rep., *supra* note 19, at 90.

31 Jung & Dalton, *supra* note 26, at 756.

32 H.R.C. Rep., *supra* note 19, at 90.

33 Jung & Dalton, *supra* note 26, at 756.

34 H.R.C. Rep., *supra* note 19, at 90.

35 *See* Jane Kim, *Trafficked: Domestic Violence, Exploitation in Marriage, and the Foreign-Bride Industry*, 51 VA. J. INT'L L. 443, 457 (2011); *H.R.C. Rep.*, *supra* note 19, at 133.

36 H.R.C. Rep., *supra* note 19, at 133–4.

37 H.R.C. Rep., *supra* note 19, at 133–4.

38 *Id.* at 137.

39 *Id.* at 139.

40 Kim, *supra* note 34, at 463.

41 H.R.C. Rep. *supra* note 19, at 134.

42 *See* Kim, *supra* note 34, at 464.

43 Cho Jung-hyun et al., *White Paper on Human Rights in North Korea*, KOREA INST. FOR NAT'L UNIFICATION 44 (2013) [hereinafter KINU 2013].

44 H.R.C. Rep., *supra* note 19, at 139–40.

45 *Id.* at 141; Kim, *supra* note 34, at 465.

46 Kim, *supra* note 34, at 464–65.

47 H.R.C. Rep., *supra* note 19, at 141.

48 *See* Hawk, *supra* note 20, at 166.

49 H.R.C. Rep., *supra* note 19, at 119–20.

50 *Id.* at 124–25.

51 *Id.* at 126.

52 *The North Korean Refugee Crisis: Human Rights and International Response* (Stephan Haggard & Marcus Noland eds.), U.S. COMM. FOR HUMAN RIGHTS IN N. KOREA 20 (2006), www. hrnk.org/uploads/pdfs/The_North_Korean_Refugee_Crisis.pdf [hereinafter *Refugee Crisis*].

53 *Id.* at 20, 59.

54 *Id.* at 20–21.

55 *Id.* at 22.

56 *Id.* at 24.

57 *Refugee Crisis, supra* note 50, at 24.

58 *Id.* at 24–25.

59 *Id.* at 62–63.

60 *Id.* at 63.

61 *Id.* at 60–61.

62 *Refugee Crisis, supra* note 50, at 63 ("The five most common complaints were, in order: 'the job does not suit my aptitude' (46 percent of all those who responded to the question), 'my future [at this work] is uncertain' (40 percent), 'I have no ability to do this work' (37 percent), 'problems with discrimination of defectors' (27 percent), and 'income is not sufficient' (21 percent).")

63 *Id.* at 64.

64 *Id.* at 58–59, 67.

5 Jerusalem of the East no more*

Although guaranteed by North Korea's constitution, the DPRK sharply curtails religious freedom in practice. Refugees and defectors held on the basis of their religious beliefs generally receive worse treatment than other inmates. North Korea sends many Christians to labor camps due to their religious beliefs.[1] A North Korean concentration camp prisoner explains:

> I have seen many scenes of Christians being punished because they would not change their belief. They would not say, okay, I will not believe in Christ anymore, and that is what the prison guards wanted to hear. I have seen eight women who were dragged out and being punished because they did not say they would not believe in Christ anymore. These women were burned.[2]

Refugees who convert to Christianity during their fugitive life in China face a particularly grim fate when repatriated to North Korea. For instance, a family of four refugees practiced their religion without interference for over a year while under the protection of an undercover missionary in China until May 2002, when Chinese police discovered and detained them. The family attempted to retain some of their religious reading by hiding it in their clothing; however, the North Korean State Security Agency investigators searched and seized it. Countless repatriated refugees have testified that the interrogators ask as their very first question whether the refugees had any contact with Christians while in China or if they believe in Jesus Christ. Although many newly converted refugees hesitate, this family stood firm and forthright in its profession of faith. Following a bold declaration of faith in Jesus Christ, the authorities led the family to so-called "Hepatitis Street", a small courtyard adjacent to the liver ward of a hospital in Namyang City. As the authorities forcibly assembled their neighbors, gunshots rang out and all four family members fell to the ground with mortal wounds to the head. "The message to the stunned cluster of neighbors was unmistakably clear: anyone who attempts to exercise a religious belief other than the worship of the Dear Leader [at the time, Kim Jong-Il] will meet the same fate."[3] With that brutality in mind, further historical background can help as context.

Protestant Christianity's entry into Korea

Protestant Christianity was first introduced in Korea by Robert J. Thomas, who arrived in 1865. On September 2, 1866, Mr. Thomas was beheaded on the banks of the Daedong River after a conflict with the Korean government.[4] Though the Korea that Thomas encountered still largely lived up to its hermit kingdom moniker, by the 1890s, northwestern Korea opened up to missionary work and many Presbyterian and Methodist missionaries founded "stations", where they worked to spread Christianity through education and medical work.[5]

The number of conversions among Koreans gradually grew and eventually led to the Wonsan Revival Movement in 1904. During this revival, over 10,000 Koreans in Pyongyang alone converted to Christianity, and in the next couple of years, over 20,000 people turned to Jesus, once again dramatically increasing the numbers of Christians in Korea.[6] Soon after this first revival came another in 1907, known as the Great Revival Movement, "one of the most discussed growth experiences in the history of Korean Protestantism."[7] Yoon Tahk-Sohn, Doctor of Theology at the Presbyterian College and Theological Seminary in South Korea, describes the causes of the 1907 revival:

> The immediate cause is the bliss of the Holy Spirit at the Bible and prayer congregation at Jangdaehyeon Church in Pyongyang in 1907. The Bible and prayer congregation didn't only begin in January 6 and focus on studying the Bible but in the evening, the congregation focused more on the evangelical movement. Two nights of January 14 and 15 were the critical moment. Normally, about 900 people from the countryside gathered to study the Bible in the morning, but in the evening, up to about 15,000 people from the city congregated.[8]

The ripples of these revivals extended broadly. Church leaders started a campaign for "a million new souls" in that year, and the religious experiences of the revival gave the Korean church a distinct character. As Paek Nak-Chun wrote, "The Revival left its mark in the mode of worship that still defines the Korean church: an emphasis on fervent prayer, often before dawn or at retreats in the mountains, confessional prayer, prayer for healing and wholeness, and prayer for deliverance."[9]

Benefits of Christianity to the Korean Peninsula

In addition to the spiritual transformation, Korea reaped many benefits from the Christian missionaries' presence. Churches sprang up alongside clinics and schools, and the Christian worldview introduced new ways of thinking that positively influenced society.

A turning point in this history took place through Dr. Horace N. Allen, first appointed by the Presbyterian Church as missionary to Korea in 1884 and the first American missionary to Korea. Providence would grant him access to royalty when on December 4, 1884, assassins attacked Korea's Prince Min Young Ik and severely wounded him. Dr. Allen was at the scene and attended to the Prince until he had fully recovered. Gaining the trust and favor of the royal court during this time, Dr. Allen became the King's personal physician. From that position of influence, Dr. Allen established the first Western medical hospital in 1885. Later on, Dr. Allen played a part in founding the Severance Medical Hospital and University, which would later become Yonsei University, a renowned university in Seoul today. In the same manner, Mary F. Scranton and her son Dr. W.B. Scranton came to Korea in 1885 and established Ehwa Girls School and Ehwa University, a prestigious women's college in Korea.[10] These seminal events transpired even while Korea still officially outlawed Christianity.

Early Protestant missionaries continued to establish schools offering Korean language education in modern subjects such as math and science. These mission schools also offered educational opportunities for girls. As such, the missionaries held the reputation for initiating the educational system that still exists among the Korean people.[11] The missionaries' spheres of influence in society grew, and soon children from all over Asia were sent to these mission schools. The Pyongyang Foreign School (PYFS) was one such school for missionary children from China, Korea, and Japan, including Ruth Bell Graham, the late wife of Billy Graham. Along with PYFS, more than 800 Christian schools across the nation taught an estimated 41,000 children.[12] Korean cities and towns began to acquire large Christian populations, especially among the growing middle class; Pyongyang, the current capital of North Korea, became known as one of the most thriving centers of Christianity in Asia—enough to garner the sobriquet "Jerusalem of the East". As many as one out of every five or six Koreans in Pyongyang embraced Jesus by the 1930s.[13] Korea historian Ki-Baek Lee said, "Protestantism was warmly welcomed not only as a religious creed but also for its political, social, educational, and cultural ideals and activities."[14]

Christianity's peculiar reputation in North Korea

The religious history of the Korean Peninsula illustrates the existence of various belief systems, of which Christianity especially thrived in the North Korean region. Though official creation of the DPRK under Kim Il-Sung in 1948 resulted in mass purging of religious activities, the regime could not completely stamp out the deeply embedded culture of belief within the North Korean people. Kim Il-Sung himself co-opted this culture by employing religious notions to establish control of the state. False religion, such as the cult of the Kims, makes an awful cloak.

Christianity stood among the largest of the religions in North Korea when that country formed, and has emerged as noteworthy in a number of ways. First, the Kim trilogy has persecuted Christianity more than any other belief system. After an encounter with North Korean border guards, one former North Korean refugee stated that the DPRK government fears that Christianity will topple its ruling philosophy.[15] These perceptions by the regime led to attempts to root out every sign of Christianity after the end of World War II:

Christian churches, literature, and symbols have been burned and destroyed. The persecution of Christians as documented by the UN Human Rights Commission is reminiscent of the days of Ancient Rome when Christians were brutally fed to lions or set on fire and burned alive.[16]

A former North Korean security agent testified to the special focus placed on Christianity above other religions:

> The target of the search is Protestantism. None of the North Korean defectors are asked, "Did you go to a Buddhist temple?" when repatriated. Protestantism is the only religion that is so persecuted because basically, it is related to the United States ... and is considered spying. Since Americans conveyed Christianity and since they are the ones who attempted to invade our country, those who are Christians are spies. Spies are executed. The level of punishment for Christians is different from that of fortune-tellers. Although [the authorities] regulate and interrogate fortune-tellers, they just ask, "How many times did you provide your service? What did you receive as payments?" and send them to a lockup for a few days.[17]

Also, unlike the other religions present in the DPRK, loyalty to Christianity does not comport with the absolute loyalty demanded by the state's Juche ideology. Juche teaching has effectively incorporated elements of Confucianism, while Shamanism, Buddhism, and Chondokyo do not appear as threatening to the regime due to their introspective traits that do not require active devotion to an outside deity the way Christianity does. Christianity and Juche, in part because Juche counterfeited aspects of Christianity, do not meld neatly together. These reasons may partially explain why the DPRK regime regards Christianity as a threat and responds with concentrated persecution.

Second, Christians in North Korea persist in practicing their faith despite the great risks involved. Though followers of other belief systems do engage in some religious activity, they do not engage to quite the same extent that Christians do. Another North Korean security agent stated in an interview:

> Buddhism is tolerated a little. Buddhists tend to keep their religion to themselves, but Christianity spreads fast unlike Buddhism. [Christians] don't pray alone, but try to get together in numbers and also they spread fast. Kim Jong Il is more afraid of his own people than the United States. The great god of North Korea is Kim Jong Il and if that changes to a real god, it can stir up people.[18]

Though there is a higher risk in participating in Christian religious practice due to government oppression, the underground churches, the smuggling of Bibles, and clandestine missionary activity continue to occur. Such activity catches the attention of those North Koreans who witness it firsthand, as well as the attention of foreign religious communities. Former North Korean political prisoner Kang

Chol-Hwan shared his confusion with the Christians he encountered: "I could not understand why they put themselves through this horrible experience at the camp when they could go home with just one denial of the existence of an invisible God."[19] These factors suggest that Christianity is the religion with the most potential as a belief system rigorous enough to be an alternative to Juche. Christianity does not permit syncretism with incompatible portions of Juche teachings. The dedicated devotion of its adherents also keeps them from recanting. The persistence of practice despite persecution has enabled the existence and growth of Christianity and has resulted in the continuation of the underground church in the DPRK despite massive persecution.

The underground church

Views vary on the existence of the underground church in North Korea. From the mid-1950s, most of the insights about the church come from defectors, and they do not always state identical things. Those who have witnessed or even participated in religious activities attest to its existence, but the majority cannot fathom how an underground church could have existed in the DPRK, with all its restrictions and outright persecution. However, these restrictions may be the very reason why the majority have not witnessed religious practice, as the survival of the underground church rests on its invisibility.

Despite the hidden nature of the church, a number of accounts support the existence of underground religious activity. In 2008, the United States Commission on International Religious Freedom (USCIRF) stated in its report:

> Though refugees cannot confirm the size or scope of clandestine religious activity, they can confirm its existence … Ironically, another indicator of the existence of clandestine Protestant religious activity came from the testimony of former security agents tasked with curtailing it. There is testimony of police operations to set up a "false underground church" to attract repatriated refugees who had converted in China and also to infiltrate religious groups in China.[20]

The underground church operates under severe constraint. Two former missionaries in North Korea describe its choked practices:

> Of necessity, the underground church was not formally organized or networked. Links between believers always proved to be deadly. Pastoral training and oversight was impossible. The majority of Christians worshipped in secret with only family members present. Those who had come to believe in Christ before the end of the Korean War—those who had had comprehensive discipleship training—were aging; the average age of Christians was over sixty. Only a few damaged Bible chapters and crosses remained.[21]

Another missionary said, "Since it is impossible to sing Christian songs out loud, these small household churches of at most five people can only quietly read the hymns when they worship."[22] The close monitoring of words and actions, as well as an enforced culture of reporting any suspicious behavior makes it extremely difficult to trust anyone regarding religious convictions. Parents cannot talk freely about religion to their own children, as public school teachers trick the young students into revealing their family's practices, resulting in the arrest of the parents and often the children as well. Normally, if Christian parents died before their children turned fifteen, the offspring might never know their family's faith.[23]

Despite all these limitations, a survey of actual conditions of religion in the North shows that since the early 2000s, clandestine religious activities have increased in the North, with projections for it to continue in the future.[24] The Database Center for North Korean Human Rights in South Korea also surveyed 2,047 North Korean defectors who arrived in South Korea since 2007, and among them, twenty respondents said they had participated secretly in religious activities. At the same time, 4.5 percent of respondents reported witnessing clandestine religious activities. Also, sixty, or 3.2 percent, of respondents saw a Bible while living in North Korea.[25] The majority, or 50.5 percent, of the defectors who arrived in South Korea before the end of 2008 counted themselves Protestants; Catholics made up 12.9 percent, 2.2 percent identified as Buddhists, and 34.4 percent said they had no religion.[26] The vast majority of religious defectors began participating in religious activities while in China. This phenomenon relates to the relative inaccessibility of the Gospel of Jesus on the North Korean side of the border along with the high intensity of missionary activity in the Chinese region bordering North Korea.

During the period of famine in the mid-1990s, known as the March of Tribulation, hundreds of thousands of North Koreans escaped to China and Russia. North Korean defectors who lived in China with the help of religious organizations had exposure to religion and engaged in religious activities, which led to many conversions to Christianity. "Along the China–North Korea border there are churches, Bible schools, mission schools, language schools, the refugee underground railroad, orphanages, safe houses, and whatever else the Christian can do to help the people in North Korea."[27] When these refugees returned home, either voluntarily or by deportation, unofficial religious activities increased in the North. These returning defectors made it possible for outside religious organizations to give support to religious activities in the North as extensions of the missionaries' efforts:

> Over the years, The Voice of the Martyrs, Cornerstone Ministries International, and other ministries have launched thousands of Scripture balloons into North Korea, smuggled in tons of Bibles, and financed radio broadcasts on behalf of the underground church … At the cost of only pennies apiece, balloons were printed with a Gospel tract … the balloons also include 49 pages of Scriptures explaining the good news of Jesus Christ. Random launches of these helium-filled balloons have caused the Korean People's Army to mobilize large numbers of troops near the North Korean border to try to gather all the balloons to prevent anyone from reading them.[28]

The secrecy of the underground church community makes it more difficult to gather information, but enough corroboration from defector accounts have given rise to the strong inference that it not only exists, but also grows.

Legal violations of religious liberties

North Korea remains culpable of gross religious persecution ever since the founding of the DPRK when Kim Il-Sung sought to suppress political rivals, and especially after the Korean War, when Kim turned to policies of eliminating all religious practice in North Korea.[29] The North Korean Dictionary on Philosophy and Religion considers it an imperialistic intrusion into society, defining religion in this way: "Religion historically was seized by the ruling class to deceive the masses and was used as a means to exploit and oppress, and it has recently been used by imperialists as an ideological tool to invade underdeveloped countries." Borrowing from Marx's description of religion, the Choson Central Annual in 1950 recorded Kim Il-Sung saying that religion is like opium because, "If they [the people] believe in religion, people will see their class consciousness paralyzed, and they will no longer be motivated to carry out revolution." The DPRK regime targeted religious belief, especially Christianity, as a hindrance and threat, distracting North Korean citizens from full devotion to the regime and to Kim Il-Sung. In a speech made at the Ministry of People's Security in 1962, Kim stated:

> [We] cannot carry such religiously active people along on our march toward a communist society. Therefore, we have tried and executed all religious leaders higher than deacon in the Protestant and Catholic churches. Among other religiously active people, those deemed malignant were all put to trial. Among ordinary religious believers, those who recanted were given jobs while those who did not were held in concentration camps.

Solidifying total control, the Kims' exclusive claim to the lives and rights of the people resulted in widespread oppression and suffering.

The North Korean leadership claims that it provides religious freedom and even has various churches and religious federations to show for it. These developments came about in the 1970s, when a changed international environment led to the DPRK's decision to allow the re-emergence of public religious practice:

> [I]t is this revival of highly circumscribed and tightly monitored and controlled religious practice, organized and supervised through a series of religious 'federations' for Buddhism, Chondokyo, and Catholic, Protestant, and, most recently, Orthodox Christianity, that is cited by DPRK authorities to indicate that North Korea respects religious freedom.[30]

For Buddhism, there is the Korean Buddhist Federation, mostly tolerated in Juche-dominated North Korea. Buddhist temples and texts are viewed more as cultural accomplishments and the Federation allows for interaction with

Buddhist communities across the world.[31] The Chondoist Association formed for Chondokyo boasts 15,000 members, 800 meeting halls, and even has a political party, the Cheong'u (Young Friends) Party, that fills several seats in the North Korean parliament [32] Similarly, the Korean Catholic Association supervises the Catholics. The Catholics still await a resident priest, and the government built the church for diplomacy with Catholic communities outside North Korea.[33]

In North Korea's Protestant Christianity, all Protestants supposedly belong to the Korean Christian Federation. The federation oversees two Protestant churches in Pyongyang, with a claimed membership of about 10,000 people.[34] As with Catholicism and Buddhism, this organization serves as a platform for engaging foreign Protestant communities. The DPRK built the accompanying religious buildings over a short period of time: Bongsu Protestant Church in 1988, located in the outskirts of Pyongyang; Changchung Catholic Church, also in 1988; and another smaller Chilgol Protestant Church in 1992, in the middle of an apartment complex in Pyongyang. Kim Il-Sung ordered the construction of Chilgol Church on the site of the church where his mother had worshipped.[35] Though services at the churches used to be sporadic, since 1995, international humanitarian aid workers living in Pyongyang report regular worship services every Sunday.[36] However, Party members control and conduct the sham "worship services".

These religious federations and church buildings certainly hint at positive progress toward religious freedom, but as of yet, the current religious activities that take place reflect "emanations of the North Korean party-state."[37] All church activity stays under consistent government monitoring, and the Korean Workers' Party controls both membership and attendance at the services. As of 2005, the congregations at these churches comprise old society pre-World War II Christians and their families, and new converts introduced to Christianity through contact with missionaries cannot attend. The DPRK government disallows religious activity apart from these churches, criminalizing all acts of the underground church. Likewise, the National United Front for the Unification of the Fatherland, monitored by the Korean Workers' Party controls the federations. The regime forbids any religious interaction between North Koreans and foreign religious adherents that takes place outside of the prescribed boundaries. A German church official who has visited Pyongyang notes that the head of the Korean Christian (Protestant) Federation, Rev. Kang Yong Sop, worked as a former ambassador to Romania and Malta as well as a former Chairman of the highest North Korean court, and says "Certainly [the North Korean Christian Federation] is not independent. It functions as one of the channels through which the North Korean Government operates diplomatically."[38]

Accordingly, many North Korean observers maintain the absence of religious freedom despite official statements and public displays of religious practice. Careful observation reveals a country where Christianity has stayed systematically oppressed. The government position that simplistically caricatures Christians as enemies of the state and counter-revolutionaries who deserve punishment has not changed. The murder of close to 700,000 Christians killed in prison camps between 1948 and 1987 amounts to genocide.[39] Open Doors, an international missionary group, released *World Watch List 2012*, an annual report on the oppression of Christians around the world. North Korea finished as the worst country for severely persecuting Christians for the eleventh straight year. The report added that the number of Christians arrested in North Korea increased yearly.[40] Likewise, a USCIRF report states that North Korea qualifies as the worst oppressor of religious freedom in the world, especially with respect to those of Christian beliefs.

Religious persecution in North Korea

The political prison camp system in North Korea magnifies religious persecution. The government regards people found engaged in Christianity as political criminals and sends them to these camps. Prisoners arrested for religious reasons endure worse treatment than other inmates, and among those repatriated from China, defectors who had been in contact with religious organizations suffer harsher penalties than others. One defector and former political prisoner, Kang Chol-Hwan, affirmed:

> Religious people are considered one of the targets for extermination spanning three generations. There were a few Christians where I was, at the Yodok Political Prison Camp in South Hamgyong Province. They suffered the indignity of being called "crazy people" and were subjected to harsher forced labor than the other political prisoners.[41]

North Korea regularly carries out special searches for Christians operating clandestinely in underground churches, and many Christians disappear, die under torture, or endure public execution. These searches even extend beyond North Korean borders, and into China as a former North Korean security officer testifies:

> As large numbers of North Koreans ... started to escape and information [about North Korea] started to leak, the NSA created the 8th Division to stop the leaks. I was recruited in this new division and went to China as an undercover North Korean defector. My boss gave me a mission [to find out if] political defectors received help from religious groups or Christian groups. The NSA still sends spies posing as Christians in order to uncover [missionaries] among the North Korean refugees.[42]

Public executions for religious offense still take place in North Korea. The U.S. State Department's Report on International Religious Freedom reported in 2009 that Son Jong-Nam was executed for contacting Christian groups in China and attempting missionary work in North Korea. Also, in June 2009, an article in Daily NK, South Korea's online newspaper reporting on North Korea, said that a woman by the name of Ri Hyon-Ok had been publicly executed for believing in and spreading Christianity. The DPRK regime actively investigates and cracks down on missionary activity because of its opposition to the DPRK's unjust, totalitarian rule:

The current regime is aware of the dangers that Christianity poses to their stronghold over the people and is willing to spare no expense to root it out and crush it completely. The government makes every effort to keep missionaries from having contact with North Koreans and vice versa.[43]

The following defector's testimony illustrates this crushing, in this case literally:

The steamroller started up. The ultimatum was offered again: Reject Jesus and live or refuse to deny Him and die. They remained silent. They had made their choice. It was clear that they would rather die than deny the wonderful name of Jesus Christ. The steamroller began to roll toward the pastor, the assistant pastors, and the elders and drove over their bodies. They were immediately crushed to death. Onlookers said that they could hear the sound of the skulls popping as the steamroller ran over their heads. Some of the Christians who knew the pastor fainted when they saw the crushed bodies.[44]

Most North Koreans find such steadfast commitment incomprehensible. Yet Christian believers continue to practice their religion at the risk of death, even to their deaths.

The stark disconnect between the state's official religious policies, and its continued religious persecution qualifies as sheer deceit. In 2000, the DPRK officially informed the U.N. Human Rights Committee that:

People have the legal freedom to select any religious belief, to build religious facilities or structures, to have or refuse to have religious ceremonies individually or collectively in an open or closed way, to organize religious bodies and have activities, to teach religion. ... In the DPRK, religion is completely independent of the state and all religions are equal. No religion is either interfered in or discriminated against and people are free to believe in any religion according to their own choice. Now there are such religious bodies in the DPRK as the Korean Christian Federation, the Korean Buddhist Federation, the Korean Association of Roman Catholics, and the Korean Central Guidance Committee of the Believers in Chondokyo, and the Korean Religionist Association.[45]

Clearly religion, particularly Christianity, has great significance for the North Korean government and society. The North Korean leadership includes threats for religious practice in its indoctrination in television programs such as *Choi Haksin's Family*. This dramatized North Korean show depicts a Christian pastor who received ordination during the Japanese occupation and rejects Communism. As a result of his refusal to recant, his mother gets killed, his wife goes insane, his daughter is raped, and his son fights for South Korea and becomes an American spy.[46] Such anti-religious propaganda regularly emanates from Pyongyang, and the country similarly implements anti-Christianity education programs specifically to denounce Christianity as evil.[47] As such, the regime not only persecutes Christianity, but vilifies it, while pretending to tolerate religions to the outside world. Christianity's championing of justice threatens this unjust regime such that: "the state of North Korea is deathly afraid of Christianity."[48] Pyongyang, no longer the "Jerusalem of the East", crushes Christians more than any other government in the world.

Defectors' testimonies of religious persecution[49]

In 1998, I, then a teenager, sought food by traveling to and from China. I lived there with the help of a Korean–Chinese church. At a deacon's request, I attempted to smuggle Bibles into the North. I was arrested, but was released because I was underage at the time of the investigation. But North Koreans, who attempted to receive the Bibles, were taken into custody at political prison camps. Nothing is known about them even now.

Between 1998 and 2000, a man and his wife held a Christian meeting with three or four neighbors in a county of North Hamgyong Province. All of them were arrested by the chief of the county State Security Agency. After their arrest only one returned alive, and it is unknown whether the rest are dead or alive.

In 2000, I was in custody at a regional State Security Agency detention cell. A so-called "Xian incident" occurred. It was a well-known incident in which 60 defectors were caught studying Christianity in Xian, China. Five leaders were executed publicly in a city of North Hamgyong Province as a public warning.

In 2001, a woman was taken into custody at a political prison camp for having talked with her neighbors, who had been to China, about religion. One of the neighbors was a government spy. She was forced to divorce her husband, and was detained at a political prison camp and died there.

Around 2001–2002, a younger brother of a woman, who lived in a city of North Hamgyong Province, returned from China. He brought a Bible to his sister's home. His sister tore it to pieces, regarding religion as a dangerous opiate. Her brother, however, took the pieces from her, promising to burn them himself. But he hid them in every corner of the house. One day, she found some pieces and asked her brother if he would continue to believe in Christianity. Without saying a word, he said a prayer. Later, he was taken into custody by security agents and died.

In 2002, North Korea sent agents to churches in China to arrest devout Christians based on information that defectors were attending churches in China. At such a church, a defector and her son led a devout Christian life. Because it was difficult to arrest them inside the church, agents reportedly called them out into another place, put them into a burlap sack, and took them to the North. The agents investigated them after putting them into a State Security Agency's detention cell, where only Christians were detained. But nobody knew what happened to them afterwards.

In 2003, I watched three men being taken to a place of public execution in a county of North Hamgyong Province. Among them was a man with whom I had studied the Bible together in China. He was gagged with rags before his execution. When told to say what he wanted to say before dying, he said, "O Lord, forgive these miserable people." And he was shot dead.

A 40-something woman, who lived in a city of North Pyongan Province, was caught keeping a Bible in her home. She was taken out of her home. An army officer arrived to live there. The woman was publicly shot to death at a threshing floor of a farm. I was told by superiors to go and see the public execution. I was curious why she was to be shot. Somebody told me she had kept a Bible at her home. Guards tied her head, her chest, and her legs to a post, and shot her dead. It happened in September 2005.

The wife of a tactical staff officer of Air Command in China's military, North Hamgyong Province was publicly executed for possessing a Bible around 2009.

The source heard from her mother that three family members, including a husband, wife and son who had lived in Sambong-gu, Onseong-gun, North Hamgyong Province, were caught conducting a family worship service and taken to a Political Concentration Camp in 2010.

Notes

* Sonya Chung provided tremendous assistance on this chapter.

1 The Hidden Gulag: Putting Human Rights on the North Korea Policy Agenda: Hearing Before the Subcomm. on East Asian and Pacific Affairs, Comm. On Foreign Relations, 108th Cong. 42 (2003) [hereinafter Gulag], (statement of David Hawk, Human Rights Investigator, U.S. Comm. for Human Rights in North Korea), *available at* www.ftp.resource.org/gpo.gov/hearings/108s/92834.pdf.

2 Examining the Plight of Refugees: The Case of North Korea: Hearing Before the Subcomm. on Immigration, Comm. on the Judiciary, 107th Cong. 28 (2002) (statement of Sun-ok Lee), *available at* www.access.gpo.gov/congress/senate/pdf/107hrg/86829.pdf.

3 North Korea: Human Rights, Refugees, and Humanitarian Challenges: Joint Hearing Before the Subcomm. on Asia and the Pacific and the Subcomm. on Int'l Terrorism, Nonproliferation and Human Rights of the H. Comm. on Int'l Relations, 108th Cong. 76–77 (2004), *available at* www.internationalrelations. house.gov/archives/108/93390.pdf [hereinafter North].

4 LUTHER MARTIN & EUGÈNE BACH, BACK TO THE JERUSALEM OF THE EAST: THE UNDERGROUND HOUSE CHURCH OF NORTH KOREA 25 (2010).

5 Kim Sun Joo, *The Northern Region of Korea: History, Identity & Culture*, SEATTLE: CTR. FOR KOREA STUDIES, U. OF WASH., 235 (2010).

6 Martin & Bach, *supra* note 4, at 26.

7 Kim, *supra* note 5, at 241.

8 Yoon Tahk-Sohn, *The Great Revival Movement in 1907 and the Korean Church Growth*, 18 SEONGYOWAH SHINHAK, 230 (2006).

9 *Id.* at 241.

10 Kim Young-sik, *A Brief History of the US-Korea Relations Prior to 1945*, ASSOCIATION FOR ASIAN RESEARCH (June 14, 2003), www.asianresearch.org/articles/1413.html.

11 Lee Jung-bae, *Protestantism*, in RELIGION IN KOREA, 97 (2003).

12 Martin & Bach, *supra* note 4, at 17.
13 *Id.* at 19.
14 Lee Ki-baik, A New History of Korea 335 (1967).
15 David Hawk, *"Thank you Father Kim Il Sung": Eyewitness Accounts of Severe Violations of Freedom of Thought, Conscience, and Religion in North Korea*, U.S. Comm'n on Int'l Religious Freedom (USCIRF) (2005), www.uscirf.gov/sites/default/files/resources/stories/pdf/nkwitnesses_wgraphics.pdf [hereinafter USCIRF].
16 Martin & Bach, *supra* note 4, at 6.
17 USCIRF, *supra* note 15, at 39.
18 *Id.* at 40.
19 Yeo-sang Yoon & Sun-young Han, *White Paper on Religious Freedom in North Korea*, Seoul: Database Ctr.for N. Korean Human Rights (2009), www.uscirf.gov/sites/default/files/resources/2009%20report%20on%20religious%20freedom%20in%20north%20korea_final.pdf.
20 USCIRF, *supra* note 15, at 21.
21 Eric Foley, These Are the Generations: The Story of How One North Korean Family Lived out the Great Commission for More than Fifty Years in the Most Christian-hostile Nation in Human History 10 (2012).
22 Martin & Bach, *supra* note 4, at 115.
23 *Id.* at 10.
24 Yoon & Han, *supra* note 19, at 41.
25 *Id.* at 79–82.
26 *Id.* at 86.
27 Martin & Bach, *supra* note 4, at 101.
28 Thomas J. Belke, *Juche*: A Christian Study of North Korea's State Religion. Bartlesville 152 (1999).
29 USCIRF, *supra* note 15.
30 *Id.*
31 3 Donald L. Baker, *North Korea, in* Worldmark Encyclopedia of Religious Practices (Thomas Riggs ed., 2006).
32 *Id.*
33 *Id.*
34 *Id.*
35 *Id.*
36 *Id.*
37 *Id.*
38 Lutz Drescher, *Threatening Gestures as Cries for Help? Questioning an Overly Fixed Image of North Korea*, Nautilus Inst., Policy Forum Online (Sept. 21, 2004), www.nautilus.org/fora/security/0434B_ReligionII.html.
39 Martin & Bach, *supra* note 4, at 63.
40 *Id.*
41 Yoon & Han, *supra* note 19.
42 USCIRF, *supra* note 15, at 22–37.
43 Martin & Bach, *supra* note 4, at 132.
44 *Id.* at 65.
45 *Democratic People's Republic of Korea, Second Periodic Report of the Democratic People's Republic of Korea on its implementation of the International Covenant on Civil and Political Rights*, 111–12, 114–15 (2000).
46 Martin & Bach, *supra* note 4, at 61.
47 USCIRF, *supra* note 15.
48 *Id.* at 130.
49 Kim Kook-shin et al., *White Paper on Human Rights in North Korea*, Seoul, Korea: Res. Inst. for Nat'l Unification (2011).

6 The China–North Korea connection*

Introduction

With its crimes against humanity, such as extermination, torture, starvation, and crimes of association, as well as collective retribution inside and outside its system of concentration camps, North Korea today presents one of the worst human rights situations in the world.[1] As North Korean isolation increases worldwide because of its actions, can the Kim regime continue to depend on the People's Republic of China for economic survival and political cover? This chapter looks to evaluate the past and present economic and political relationships between the People's Republic of China and North Korea and investigate any shifting policies that might provide insight to mitigating the dual human rights and security crises currently ongoing in North Korea.

China and North Korea: A contentious and multifaceted relationship

China is North Korea's closest ally, only significant trade partner, and largest provider of food, fuel, and industrial machinery. China, more than any other country, has the greatest potential to wield influence in North Korea's capital, Pyongyang.[2] Without China, North Korea as we know it today would possibly cease to exist and its people would die unless something else replaced China's role. China has supported North Korea since Chinese soldiers flooded onto the Korean Peninsula to fight for the DPRK in 1950. Since the division of the peninsula after the Korean War between the North and South along the 38th parallel, China has lent significant political and economic backing to North Korea's leaders—Kim Il-Sung, Kim Jong-Il and now Kim Jong-Un.[3] In order to understand why China would provide both economic and political cover to such a severely problematic regime, one must understand the history of the North Korean–Chinese relationship.

History of the relationship

Despite Korea's concerns about possible Chinese domination, since the seventh century, the various Korean kingdoms managed to largely retain their independence by not opposing China's imperial vision and accepting a special relationship with the Chinese dynasties. This cooperation allowed China to remain confident in Korea's loyalty on the border the two countries share, and gave Korea some assurance that China would not invade it. For both, a combination of convenience and necessity fueled relations. The pattern continued with only a few interruptions into the nineteenth century, even though China constantly fought off expansionist-minded European colonial powers. China continued to defend Korea's isolation from the rest of the world; however, its obvious objective to retain its buffer required keeping Korea out of the hands of foreigners. Ultimately, China failed. Amid the complex maneuvering between the Chinese, Japanese, Russians, Koreans, and others in the early twentieth century, Japan took control of the Korean Peninsula. Holding Korea effectively ensured that there was little chance that China or another power could use the territory to stage an invasion of Japan. Possession of Korea also helped the Japanese to seize more of Manchuria, reinforcing to China just how important Korea remained to China's national security interests.[4]

At the end of World War II, China focused on its internal civil war and had not yet prepared to re-establish a relationship with Korea. However, by 1949, the Chinese Communists had emerged victorious from its internal power struggle and the Soviet occupying forces in North Korea leftover from World War II had left the region. North Korea's new Communist government, formed after the peninsula's division by the Allied Powers in 1945, invaded South Korea in 1950 with the authorization and support of Moscow and Beijing.[5]

At the same time that Pyongyang prepared for its invasion into South Korea, China prepared a cross-strait invasion of Taiwan. China, however, placed its plans on hold. Only days after hostilities broke out between North and South Korea in June of 1950, the United States deployed ships to the Taiwan Strait to protect the government in Taipei. When the U.N. coalition halted the North's forces and pushed them back to the China–North Korea border months later, China had no choice but to shift its attention away from Taiwan and enter the Korean War to deal with the much more pressing threat along its border.[6] North Korea's actions, while they could have benefited China had they succeeded, instead undermined Beijing's re-capture of Taiwan and ultimately left China responsible for supporting a faltering state on a critical border after the Korean War ended. The Chinese intervention stopped the reunification of Korea under the South Korean government. The Chinese could settle for a divided Korea, so long as they could retain their buffer.[7]

Although the North Koreans took advantage of the emerging China–Soviet split after the Korean War in order to gain economic concessions from the competing Communist powers, the collapse of the Soviet Union and the end of the Cold War left the North Korean regime with dwindling economic resources. China largely filled the void left in the wake of the Soviet collapse. In response, Pyongyang decided it would build a strong domestic military, which it has sometimes successfully used to extract concessions out of the Americans, Japanese, South Koreans, and anyone else concerned about peace and stability. Pyongyang would also draw on China's continued fear of losing its strategic buffer to the East to draw out significant amounts of economic assistance.[8]

What motivates China to continue its support of North Korea?

North Korea shares an 870 mile-long (1400 km) border with China, and provides a buffer for China from South Korea, Japan, and by extension, the U.S. China and North Korea formally established the Yalu river as their border in the tenth century, and that has remained the border ever since.[9] This geographic position has made North Korea a center of the action in a region with divided alliances. North Korea geographically separates China from South Korea, a close ally of the U.S. and a democratic and capitalistic nation itself. It also lies between China and Japan, another close ally of the U.S. and a country embroiled in its own territorial disputes with China.[10]

China's first priority on the Korean Peninsula remains stability, both in the ruling regime—the Kim family—as well as the country as a whole. The known status quo appears preferable to China over the prospect of an economic or political collapse that would send refugees flooding into China and would create conditions that could trigger U.N., U.S., or South Korean intervention.[11] Additionally, China's support for Pyongyang maintains an ally on its northeastern border, and provides a buffer zone between China and South Korea, home to around 20,000–40,000 U.S. military personnel. China also gains economically from its association with North Korea. Chinese companies have made major investments aimed at developing mineral resources in North Korea's northern region.[12] North Korea actually contains more natural resources than South Korea. For China, stability and the avoidance of war have persisted as the top priorities. From this point of view, North Korea threatens stability because Pyongyang could trigger a war on its own. Hundreds of thousands of North Korean refugees flooding into China continue to be a major concern for Beijing.[13]

China also worries about the effects of a North Korean collapse on the strategic balance in East Asia. If North Korea collapsed and the two Koreas reunited, China might have a U.S.-aligned Korea on its border, including U.S. troops. If North Korea provokes a war, and it may, China, the United States, and South Korea would likely bear the brunt of any military confrontation on the Korean Peninsula.[14] Because the specter of North Korea's collapse could potentially destabilize the region, China may continue to shield Pyongyang to some extent. However, the two countries' increasingly divergent interests suggest that China's dissatisfaction with North Korea will only likely increase rather than diminish.[15]

Although largely effective in the past, North Korea's policy of making threats in order to extract concessions, as well as the threat to China of losing a buffer along its border, has yielded diminishing returns after the Geneva Protocol. While North Korea has waxed even more dependent upon China than before, Chinese dependence on North Korea has waned. Beijing has used the various North Korean crises to its own advantage, offering to mediate talks in return for political concessions from the United States or South Korea, by simultaneously asserting a special relationship with North Korea and denying responsibility for North Korean actions. For China's leaders, this once served as a very useful way of managing regional relations and countering U.S. challenges to Chinese policies, such as currency manipulation. Yet for China too, the policy has begun to lose efficacy, and Washington has increasingly called on China to either assert itself in dealing with Pyongyang or to step aside.[16]

For China, North Korea remains a strategic buffer, and Beijing would prefer a unification that results in a neutral Korea that leans toward red China. For North Korea, Beijing's desire for a buffer may ensure that China will defend the North against an attack, but it does not guarantee that Beijing would preserve the North Korean regime if it began attacking others. Beijing may prove just as satisfied with a North Korea that does not threaten nuclear attacks or violate the human rights of its people like the current government does. China has already suggested that in a collapse or a war scenario, it might seize Pyongyang and control the strategically important northern portion of the Korean Peninsula, effectively taking on responsibility for the management of that geographic area.[17] Accordingly, if North Korea's saber-rattling continues, this may illustrate to the world China's impotence in influencing its unstable neighbor, which could detract from China's own interests. China has already begun to spread this message via its academics and news media, both through domestic and international channels.[18]

China and North Korea's nuclear intimidation

Does China have concerns about Pyongyang's nuclear weapons? Yes, but this concern straggles behind China's main focus on preventing state failure. A coup or leadership struggle that expands into external conflict, or a popular rebellion that leads to a regime change, could send large numbers of refugees across the border into China. Additionally, if the North Korean government would collapse, South Korea would plausibly seek reunification. China may find such a situation unpalatable due to South Korea's close relationship with the U.S.[19]

Subsequently, China has stayed on the sidelines as a mute spectator in the multiple cases of North Korea–Pakistan nuclear centrifuge and related defense technology deals. However, recently China has expressed misgivings about the proliferation of nuclear and missile technologies by North Korea. In 2003, China hosted the Six-Party Talks, a forum comprised of China, the U.S., Japan, Russia, South Korea, and North Korea with the primary goal of complete, verifiable, irreversible dismantlement (CVID) of North Korea's nuclear program.[20] The Six-Party Talks started in 2003 after earlier bilateral negotiations between the U.S. and North Korea failed to stop the North's nuclear weapons program, and North Korea announced its withdrawal from the Non-Proliferation Treaty. The six nations signed an agreement in 2005 in which North Korea agreed to dismantle all its nuclear weapons facilities in return for economic aid and security guarantees. A follow-up agreement came in 2007. Despite these agreements, the talks foundered on differences over how to implement those agreements and by deep-seated mistrust between the U.S. and North Korea.[21] In an insubstantial and overblown move, CNN broadcast North Korea blowing up an easily replaceable cooling tower for a five-megawatt nuclear reactor at Yongbyon in 2008, whose spent fuel could be reprocessed into weapons grade plutonium. The U.S. State Department temporarily removed the DPRK from its list of state sponsors of terrorism in response.[22] Unfortunately and unsurprisingly, the talks collapsed the next year because of differences over the nuclear inspections. The U.S. maintained that a critical failure to the talks resulted from North Korea's refusal to admit running a clandestine uranium enrichment program for alternative nuclear fuel. In 2010, North Korea vindicated this concern when it unveiled a uranium enrichment plant.[23]

Prior to Pyongyang's 2013 nuclear test, Beijing attempted to persuade the North against proceeding, and even summoned the North Korean envoy and warned of serious repercussions if it proceeded with the test. North Korean Ambassador to China, Ji Jae-Ryong, responded to China that "the nuclear test is part of the North's sovereign right to self-defense and not a matter for Beijing to interfere with."[24] After the 2013 nuclear test by North Korea, China severely criticized Pyongyang and gave full support to the U.N. Security Council Resolutions 2087 and 2094, which has distressed North Korea's leaders and added additional economic pressures to the already financially strapped nation.[25] The most recent nuclear test rattled nerves more than previous episodes because of the youth and inexperience of North Korea's new leader, Kim Jong-Un. Kim Jong-Un and the North responded predictably to China's signing on to sanctions by threatening to disengage from any future denuclearization talks, a script Pyongyang has returned to time and time again. North Korea launched criticisms of China and Russia, both permanent members on the Security Council with veto power that could have stopped the U.N. Security Council Resolutions.[26] China not only did not exercise its veto power, but it even helped draft the resolution, marking what could turn out to be a major turning point.

China's economic relations with North Korea

For the DPRK, China remains its partner of first and last resort. To the extent that the DPRK does so at all, it turns to China for outside validation of its plans. China tries to soften and mitigate the reactions to North Korean provocations. Additionally, Beijing stands at the head of a short line of countries willing to side with, or at least accommodate, North Korea. Pyongyang turns most to the People's Republic of China when dealing with shortages of food, fuel, investment capital, and economic expertise.[27] China has served as North Korea's most important ally, biggest trading partner, and main source of food and fuel. China has helped sustain Kim Jong-Il's and now Kim Jong-Un's regime, and has historically opposed harsh international economic sanctions in attempting to avoid regime collapse and an uncontrolled influx of refugees across its eight-hundred-mile border with North Korea.[28]

However, after Pyongyang's third nuclear test in February 2013, it appears that China's patience with its ally has finally begun to wear thin. Immediately

following the nuclear test, the Chinese government took unprecedented measures to implement sanctions against North Korea. Among the most prominent
steps, the state-run bank of China halted business with North Korea's main
foreign exchange bank. Additionally, the central government instructed local
governments to implement U.N. Resolution 2094, which has led to more rigorous
inspections of North Korea-bound cargo.[29]

The Chinese–North Korean trade relationship: Increasing dependency

As the moribund economy of the DPRK finds itself even more isolated through
the U.N. sanctions, it depends more and more on the People's Republic of China
for survival and development. As North Korea's largest provider of food, fuel,
machinery, consumer goods, and direct investment, China has the most economic
leverage over Pyongyang.[30]

Recent trade data details the close relationship between the two countries. In
2012, China accounted for an estimated 67 percent of North Korea's exports and
61 percent of its imports, the majority in both directions. Additionally, experts
estimate China provides 80 percent of North Korea's consumer goods and 45
percent of its food.[31] North Korea has been incurring a $1.25 billion-dollar bilat-
eral trade deficit with China every year. Some experts view this trade deficit as an
indirect Chinese subsidy, given that North Korea cannot finance its trade deficit
through borrowing. North Korea's economic dependence on China continues to
grow, as indicated by the substantial trade imbalance between the two countries.[32]

However, Chinese trade data shows that during the first six months of 2013,
exports to North Korea fell for the first time in four years. The figures from China's
General Administration of Customs shows exports to North Korea shrank by
more than 13.6 percent from January to June. The last time exports from China
to North Korea fell was during the global financial crisis in 2009.[33] According to
Lu Chao, a Korean scholar at the Liaoning Academy of Social Sciences, Chinese
exports dropped due to China beginning to implement the U.N. Security Council
resolutions regarding North Korea.[34] By implementing measures that limit the
types of equipment and chemicals that could bolster North Korea's weapons
programs, China directly decreases production in North Korea's factories.[35] This
decrease in manufacturing production directly correlates to a decrease in con-
sumption of petroleum and crude oil in North Korea, leading to the 13.6 percent
drop in exports from China to North Korea in the first six months of 2013.[36] The
simultaneous direct investment from China in other non-military areas provides
North Korea with the opportunity to diversify and expand its economy—if the
ruling faction controlled by Kim Jong-Un ever decides to take advantage of
the opportunity. Up until now, the indications point otherwise; Kim Jong-Un
considers China-style economic reform as a threat to his power.

While 2013 exports from China to North Korea declined significantly during
the first six months of the year, possibly as a result of China punishing Pyongyang
for its reckless actions, 2014 trade data shows a year-over-year increase in overall

trade from 2012 to 2013. China's 2013 (recorded) trade with North Korea grew by over 10 percent from that recorded in 2012 to $6.5 billion, following modest but steady growth in 2012 over 2011. This steady growth in China–North Korea trade relations has continued to occur despite the rising political risks for China, as it remains aligned with Kim Jong-Un's internationally disruptive regime.[37] North Korea's trade with China fell 2.1 percent ($2.89 billion) in the first six months of 2014, according to data compiled by South Korea's government trade agency.[38] During the first six months of 2014, North Korea's exports to China declined 3.9 percent to $1.31 billion and imports slipped 0.6 percent to $1.58 billion, according to the data provided by the Beijing unit of the South's Korea Trade and Investment Promotion Agency (KOTRA).[39] The data showed no shipments of crude oil from China to North Korea from January to June. However, a diplomatic source with knowledge of the matter cautioned against reading too much into the official trade figures because China has provided crude oil to North Korea in the form of grant aid and this "aid" does not count as trade. "Despite the six-month absence of oil shipments, the scale of North Korea's decline in imports is minimal," the source said on condition of anonymity. Meanwhile, North Korea's exports of rare earth minerals to China jumped 153.7 percent one year during the January–June period, the data showed, without providing the precise value of the exports.[40]

China's direct investment in North Korea

For years, China has urged the ever-resistant Pyongyang to follow its development pattern of reform that has led to its own successful economic growth. Despite China's urging, the Kim regime has always remained hesitant to take any steps to reform the economy because it might lead to a loosening of its straightjacket-like grip on society.[41] However, the economic development strategy that has emerged in North Korea nevertheless appears to benefit both countries to some extent.

The first major step in this developing economic development strategy is the Rason Industrial Complex, launched officially in May 2011 and located near the two North Korean towns of Rajin and Sonbong. A Chinese plan with Chinese companies manages the investments and operations. The development plan calls for building or upgrading roads and port facilities, establishing international freight brokerage, export processing, and financial institutions, as well as investing in generating electricity, coal mining, oil refineries, manufacturing, and tourism. The Chinese operate the Rason Complex, and Chinese companies may hire North Korean workers.[42] One Chinese company, the Sangdi Guanqun Investment Company, has signed a memorandum of understanding with Pyongyang's Investment and Development Group in which the company agrees to construct a coal-fired power plant for the DPRK in exchange for the right to build an oil refinery. The refinery will represent a $2 billion investment and will refine crude oil imported from the Middle East and Russia in order to sell it to China and other countries.[43]

China plans to establish a free-trade zone on the Whwa and Huangjinbing Islands on the Yalu River, which separates the Chinese city of Dandong and the North Korean city of Sinuiju. China has reportedly negotiated a 100-year lease on the two islands and intends to invest $800 million there for industrial development through an industrial park on the islands similar to the Kaesong industrial complex on the border between North Korea and South Korea. Such a project would provide an enormous boost to the economy in China's poor northeastern region.[44] Given the size of the planned investments in the Rason and Sinuiju projects, China's direct investment in North Korea stands poised to increase dramatically.

Additionally, according to an Open Source Center report on PRC companies in North Korea, approximately 200 Chinese companies operate in the DPRK. However, China's Ministry of Commerce website only lists eighty-six companies currently operating in North Korea. Of those companies listed, the distribution breaks into thirty-five in mining, seventeen in industrial parts and materials, eleven in agriculture and timber, nine in transportation or trading, seven in apparel, four in other consumer goods, one in iron and steel, and one in automotive vehicles and parts.[45]

Chinese investors hesitant after 2013 nuclear test

North Korea's tactic of ratcheting up tensions so the international community will listen to its demands has backfired lately. Chinese businesses, which comprise the primary group of investors in ventures in North Korea, started the process of pulling out of the country. Chinese tourists have avoided the volatile state after the country's most recent nuclear test. Chinese authorities told travel agencies in Dandong to temporarily halt visits to North Korea in view of the tensions on the Korean Peninsula.[46]

Additionally, Chinese businesses for the most part have stopped any new investment into the North since Pyongyang's third nuclear test in February 2013. One seafood company in Dalian shelved plans in early March to build a factory in North Korea capable of processing 20,000 tons of seafood a year. The company had close ties with North Korea, and former premier Cho Yong-Rim even toured the company's facilities during his visit to China in 2010. "We decided to halt our investment plans for the time being due to the unstable conditions in North Korea," a staffer said.[47] Another Chinese company based in Zhejiang Province had invested 560 million Yuan (approximately $90.2 million) in a mine project in Hyesan, North Korea since 2007 but now considers withdrawing, according to Chinese media reports.[48] Construction of basic infrastructure such as roads and power lines in the Rajin-Sonbong special economic zone has also seen delay. Officials in the Chinese city of Hunchun last month announced that work would start soon on a transformer substation to power Chinese businesses there. A source in Yanbian indicated an indefinite postponement earlier this month. Rumblings exist that China has decided to postpone all investments into the zone for three years.[49] With North Korea regularly halting production at the inter-Korean Kaesong Industrial Complex and issuing war threats frequently, Chinese businesses and regional governments have taken a risk-minimization approach by pausing investments and taking a wait-and-see attitude.

Conclusion

In the past, China had taken a fundamentally risk-averse stance in its approach to North Korea. However, due to a number of the aforementioned shifts in priorities, China may seek to "shape" its neighbor gradually from various angles rather than employing drastic measures stemming from dramatic policy changes.[50] Whereas China previously maintained a one-dimensional policy with North Korea based on a "friendship sealed in blood," Beijing has shifted to a multi-dimensional policy focused on risk minimization instead of risk aversion.[51] This multi-dimensional approach utilizes diverse strategies to manage different types of risks surrounding the Korean Peninsula. A more in-depth discussion on the potential for China to direct a global effort to actively address the North Korean challenge appears in the third section of this book in Chapter 15.

Whether China's changing policy toward North Korea emerges as a long-term trend will depend on China continuing an increasingly vigorous approach with North Korea. Consistent and additional implementation of U.N. sanctions would signal a long-term trend. The cooperation between China and the U.S. based on the common interest to manage risk on the Korean Peninsula would also indicate movement toward a solution. Further tightening of Chinese export controls and sanctions at its borders of key material and technology related to North Korea's nuclear program could prod North Korea toward changing its course. To its credit, China has recently banned a long list of items usable for nuclear armament purposes.[52]

The answers to solving the North Korean challenge lie tightly intertwined with the willingness of China to put an end to its recurrent nuclear saber-rattling and the horrific human rights atrocities, primarily against its own people. China possesses singular advantages found in its own substantial economic contributions, as well as its prominent standing in the world, to turn the Kim regime toward a functioning economy, decent international relations, and movement toward upholding human rights. While North Korea has a long track record of engaging in joint initiatives with other nations for mutually beneficial economic development purposes, most such initiatives have, to a large extent, failed. However, recent evidence of continuing joint economic development initiatives between China and North Korea, regardless of hesitation from investors after the 2013 nuclear test, tips toward a promising direction, both economically as well as on a humanitarian angle.

The North Korea challenge, *sui generis* in ways, constitutes arguably one of the most complex and difficult international policy problems in the world. China's role as the North's main benefactor and protector places it in the preeminent position to bring about positive change. China, South Korea and the U.S. working in concert toward economic reform in North Korea, reducing human rights abuses, and stabilizing North Korea would multiply the impact.

Notes

* Weston Sedgwick co-authored this chapter. He is an expert in international trade and policy, a former economic advisor to Indiana Governor Mitch Daniels, and a Juris Doctor candidate at Northern Illinois University College of Law with a focus in international law.

1 *See generally* Morse H. Tan, *A State of Rightlessness: The Egregious Case of North Korea*, 80 Miss. L.J. 681 (2010) (illustrating multiple cases of North Korea's human rights abuses).

2 Dick Nanto, *Increasing Dependency: North Korea's Economic Relations with China*, Korea Econ. Inst. of Am., 77 (2011), www.keia.org/publication/increasing-dependency-north-korea's-economic-relations-china.

3 Jayshree Bajoria and Beina Xu, *The China-North Korea Relationship*, Coun. on Foreign Relations, 1–7, 1 (Feb. 21, 2013), www.cfr.org/china/china-north-korea-relationship/p11097.

4 David C. Kang, *An Historical Perspective on the China-North Korea Border*, Ctr. for Strategic and Int'l Studies, 1–4, 1 (Feb. 7, 2011), www.csis.org/files/publication/110207_Historical_Perspective_on_China-North%20Korea_Border.pdf.

5 *Id.*

6 Lin Cheng-Yi, *The Legacy of the Korean War: Impact on U.S. Taiwan Relations*, Journal of Ne. Asian Studies, Winter 1992, at 40.

7 David C. Kang, *An Historical Perspective on the China–North Korea Border*, Ctr. for Strategic and Int'l Studies, 1–4 (Feb. 7, 2011), www.csis.org/files/publication/110207_Historical_Perspective_on_China-North%20Korea_Border.pdf.

8 *Id.*

9 *Id.*

10 Austin Ramzy, *A Troubled Outlook for Japan–China Ties*, N.Y. Times, (July 25, 2014), www.sinosphere.blogs.nytimes.com/2014/07/25/a-troubled-outlook-for-china-japan-ties/?_php=true&_type=blogs&_r=0.

11 Nanto, *supra* note 2, at 77–83, 75.

12 *Id.* at 75, 79.

13 Jayshree Bajoria & Beina Xu, *The China-North Korea Relationship*, Coun. on Foreign Relations, 1–7 (Feb. 21, 2013), www.cfr.org/china/china-north-korea-relationship/p11097.

14 *Id.* at 4.

15 Jennifer Lind, *Will China Finally 'Bite' North Korea?* CNN.com (Mar. 14, 2013), www.cnn.com/2013/03/11/opinion/lind-north-korea/.

16 Rodger Baker, *China and North Korea: A Tangled Partnership*, Stratfor Global Intelligence (April 16, 2013), www.stratfor.com/weekly/china-and-north-korea-tangled-partnership#axzz3ACpizTG1.

17 *Id.*

18 *Id.*

19 Paul Carroll, *The Mouse that Keeps Roaring: The United States, China, and Solving the North Korean Challenge*, Yale J. of Int'l Affairs, Sept. 2012, at 57–67, *available at* www.yalejournal.org/2012/09/18/the-mouse-that-keeps-roaring-the-united-states-china-and-solving-the-north-korean-challenge/.

20 Ranjit Dhawan, *China and its Peripheries: Contentious Relations with North Korea*, Inst. of Peace and Conflict Studies (2014), www.ipcs.org/issue-brief/china/china-and-its-peripheries-contentious-relations-with-north-korea-231.html.

21 Choe Sang-Hun et al., *In Focus: North Korea's Nuclear Threats*, N.Y. Times, (Apr. 16, 2013), www.nytimes.com/interactive/2013/04/12/world/asia/north-korea-questions.html?_r=0.

22 *Id.*

23 *Id.*

24 Staff Report, *N. Korea-China Rift Deepens Over Nuclear Test*, THE CHOSUN ILBO (Feb. 7, 2013), www.english.chosun.com/site/data/html_dir/2013/02/07/2013020701150. html.

25 Dhawan, *supra* note 20.

26 *Id.*

27 Nanto, *supra* note 2, at 77–83.

28 *Id.*

29 Bonnie S. Glaser, *A New Type of Major Power Relations on North Korea*, CTR. FOR STRATEGIC & INT'L STUD., 1–4, 1 (Sept. 2013), www.csis.org/publication/thoughts-chairman-new-type-major-power-relations-north-korea.

30 Bajoria & Xu, *supra* note 13, at 1–7, 3.

31 Nanto, *supra* note 2, at 77.

32 Bajoria, *supra* note 13, at 3.

33 William Ide, *China Exports to North Korea Fall*, VOICE OF AMERICA (July 30, 2013), www.voanews.com/content/china-exports-to-north-korea-fall/1712903.html.

34 *Id.*

35 Jane Perlez, *China Bans Items for Export to North Korea, Fearing Their Use in Weapons*, N.Y. TIMES, (Sep. 24, 2013), www.nytimes.com/2013/09/25/ world/asia/china-bans-certain-north-korean-exports-for-fear-of-weapons-use.html?_r=0.

36 Ide, *supra* note 33.

37 Scott Snyder, *China–North Korea Trade in 2013: Business as Usual*, FORBES (Mar. 27, 2014), www.forbes.com/sites/scottasnyder/2014/03/27/44/.

38 Staff Report, *N. Korea's Trade with China Falls 2.1 pct in H1*, THE KOREA HERALD (Aug. 4, 2014), www.koreaherald.com/view.php?ud=20140804001040.

39 *Id.*

40 *Id.*

41 Nanto, *supra* note 2, at 77–83.

42 *Id.* at 80.

43 *Id.*

44 *Id.*

45 *Directory of PRC Enterprises in North Korea*, China–OSC Report in English (Apr. 19, 2011), available in Open Source Center, document no. FEA20110420016995 (Apr. 20, 2011).

46 *All Investment in N. Korea Grinds to a Halt*, THE CHOSUN ILBO (Apr. 11, 2013), www.english.chosun.com/site/data/html_dir/2013/04/11/2013041101379.html.

47 *Id.*

48 *DPRK Mining and Investment Woes*, N. KOREA ECON. Watch (Sept. 13, 2012), www.nkeconwatch.com/category/dprk-organizations/state-offices/musan-mine/.

49 *All Investment in N. Korea Grinds to a Halt*, *supra* note 46.

50 Jenny Jun, *Dealing with a Sore Lip: Parsing China's "Recalculation" of North Korea Policy*, 38 North Blog (Mar. 29, 2013), www.38north.org/2013/03/jjun032913/.

51 *Id.*

52 Perlez, *supra* note 35.

7   Iron fists in a fog*

Life inside North Korea

Like a virus tries to go undetected by its host while its cells multiply and it grows in strength, so too have the leaders of North Korea gone to painstaking lengths to maintain a "dense fog" over North Korea.[1] For instance, when taking foreign government diplomats on a tour of North Korea, Pyongyang features movie-set-like facades of buildings with electrical power turned on only during the parade passing through.[2] Excluding the present reader, an astounding number of people have stayed unaware or grossly misinformed about what actually takes place inside North Korea. When people gain knowledge about the dreadful realities inside North Korea, they often begin to care. Dr. Suzanne Scholte poignantly remarked:

> I am asked all the time: why are you involved in this issue, you are not even a Korean? The fact is this is not a Korean issue, this is an issue that should effect the conscience of the world—no one asks why do you care about the Holocaust, you are not Jewish? Why do you care about Darfur, you are not African? What is happening on the Korean Peninsula is the world's worst human rights tragedy; no people are more suffering, no people are more per-secuted and this is a tragedy that has continued for 65 years—longer than the Jewish holocaust, longer than the Soviet gulags, longer than China's cultural revolution, longer than the Rwanda genocide … I [have come] to know that what is happening in North Korea is breaking God's heart.[3]

Starvation as a weapon

Starving the population weakens the citizens, rendering them too feeble to revolt. When used as a weapon, starvation can turn family members against each other, even mother against son. Shin In Geun, the only person born into a North Korean "total control zone" who has managed to escape and live to talk about it, illustrates the tragic consequences of starvation as a weapon.

Shin's tale of life inside the concentration camp begins with his first memory from childhood at four years of age: he watched a firing squad execute another prisoner. Over the years, he would witness many more executions, including those of both his brother and mother. At the time of her execution, Shin did not cry, but rather felt anger toward his mother.

Shin Dong-Hyuk (as he later changed his name) did not have the chance to have the natural bond grow between his mother and him. Instead, he saw her as just another competitor for food. Shin remembers as a young boy, not yet old enough to attend school, that his mother would leave him alone in the house each morning as the camp authorities forced her to work in the fields. As soon as his mother left, Shin would eat his lunch rations, and, as a constantly hungry growing boy, he would often eat his mother's rations too. When his mother would return home for her midday rations and find no food to eat, she would use a hoe or a shovel to beat Shin mercilessly. Shin would later describe the violent nature of his mother's beatings as indistinguishable from the prison guards.[4] Only after his escape did Shin come to understand what words like *mother* and *love* connote at their best. In the concentration camp, these words did not exist or became contorted beyond ordinary recognition. Shin did not ever hear the word *love* uttered by anyone during his 23 years in the camp, not even by his own mother.

This systematic, intentional starvation and enslavement of the North Korean people, both in and outside the concentration camps, causes untold suffering. Shin says he never experienced a full stomach for the first 23 years of his life, and recalls hunger constantly gnawing at him. Eating the unprocessed grain out of animal feces just to survive, or other comparably desperate actions, occur all too often both inside and outside the camps.[5] The government diverts food aid to the government and military, preventing it from reaching those most in need of it. The Kim regime has generally prohibited people from growing their own food in a private garden. Such privation has driven the people to eat feces, sacrifice pets, or even turn to cannibalism within their own family to survive.[6]

This quote explains the stratified use of starvation as a weapon for the Kim regime:

> The famine, while itself largely a government creation, also created another means by which the government can persecute its opponents. Despite tremendous reliance on international food aid, the North Korean government fails to operate a transparent food distribution system and often denies NGOs access to the country's most vulnerable people—a situation that has led many NGOs to cease operations in North Korea. The government categorizes its population based on perceived loyalty and usefulness to the regime, and channels food aid—and many other entitlements—accordingly.[7]

This politicized caste system directly impacts the availability of necessities, including food, clothes and shelter.

North Korea has rejected humanitarian aid it may not control from the international community, despite the increased food shortages and economic hardships the country continues to face. Consider this account as an example: "As the number of defectors increased amid food shortages and economic hardship and as international concerns over the human rights situation in North Korea mounted, North Korea has seemed to worry more about the possibilities of the international community's humanitarian intervention to fulfill the duties of human rights protection."[8] As a result, in spite of the dire shortages, North Korea has resorted to acts such as ejecting humanitarian relief organizations, including the U.N. World Food Programme.

Aid organizations have learned to send food that the elite disdain to eat (like barley) and that perishes more quickly, so that it does not get stored as emergency war rations. These steps seek to diminish the diversion of humanitarian aid to the elite and military.

The cult of Kim Jong-Un

As we have already seen, the entire nation finds itself under the thoroughgoing sway of a single individual: Kim Jong-Un. North Korea has only had three rulers, Kim Il-Sung, his son Kim Jong-Il, and his grandson Kim Jong-Un.

The state religion of North Korea is the apotheosis, the deification of the only three individuals who have ruled North Korea: the deceased Kim Il-Sung, referred to as the Great Leader and his son Kim Jong-Il, called the Dear Leader, and now Kim Jong-Un, who has taken the title of "Dear Leader" from his deceased father. The government submerges its people under a deluge of propaganda and every manner of cultural influence to this effect, orienting the entire society around exaltation of the Kims.[9]

The press cannot engage in any criticism of the leadership or the instructions of the Supreme Ruler:

> [T]he North Korean press disregards the proper function of the press, such as providing critical commentary and providing objective information to citizens, but instead focuses on the propaganda of Kim Il-Sung based on the Juche ideology and upon indoctrinating the population. All radio dials are fixed to the DPRK official broadcasting service channels and sealed ... [I]f a seal is found broken, [the person is] ... treated as a political criminal. Nothing else may be worshipped other than Juche ideology and its founder, the Great Leader ... The worship of Kim Il-Sung and Kim Jong-Il is specifically stipulated in the Ten Great Principles of Unique Ideology.[10]

The people, starting from childhood, sing songs praising the Kims; a woman found herself in a concentration camp for singing a South Korean pop song instead.[11] The government inculcates in its people the belief that they must thank the Kims for any food that they might have, or any other positive feature, if any, in their lives. When a doctor (even a foreign doctor) performs surgeries to restore eyesight, the first thing that people do, in accordance with the massive conditioning and draconian pressures they have been subjected to along these lines, is to thank the Kims.[12] A whole web of legends is spun about the Kims that attribute superhuman abilities and incredible phenomena surrounding their births and their lives. However, notwithstanding the cascade of propaganda, the people still know about the immoral life of Kim Jong-Un and his father, which cannot remain completely concealed through the state-produced mélange of fabrications.

This false apotheosis does not leave room for human rights and freedoms: "Under the unitary ruling system and the deification efforts for the supreme leader, North Korea is predisposed to regard any expansion of individual rights and freedoms as a challenge and potential danger to the government and the leader."[13] Indeed, North Korea "forc[es] people even to sacrifice their lives to save portraits of Kim Il-Sung and Kim Jong-Il in accordance with the Ten Great Principles."[14] So, in the event of a fire at their residence, a family has a legal imperative to safeguard portraits of the Kims before anything else, even if it means risking their lives. The cult of the Kims thoroughly deprecates the rights and freedoms of the bulk of their people and reserves such freedom and rights for the corpulent despot who rules over an emaciated populace and an ever-increasing pile of corpses through cruelty and neglect.

Quite frankly, if Kim Jong-Un counts as a demigod, he descends from Hades, not Heaven.[15] The Kims have created one large prison within which to torment and brainwash the population. North Korean law coerces all citizens to worship Kim Jong-Un, as well as his father Kim Jong-Il and grandfather Kim Il-Sung: the state religion is the Cult of the Kim Dynasty. The government controls access to any and all information, even outside media portals. Only the ruling elite, for example, can legally access the Internet.[16] In addition to controlling access to information, Kim Jong-Un mercilessly uses starvation as a means to literally put a stranglehold on his people, creating a starkly divided class structure within North Korea. Kim Jong-Un and the ruling elite live in the lap of luxury and perverse extravagance, while the vast majority of citizens are reduced to living like hungry animals who fear for their lives, scrounge for food, and struggle to survive one more day under the iron fists.

A thoroughly totalitarian regime

This rulership accurately merits the use of the adjective "totalitarian" as merely a descriptive term. Kim Jong-Un skates effectively above the law within North Korea, and violates it with utter domestic impunity. In effect, the will and whim of the Dear Leader substitutes for the rule of law. The North Korean constitution says it guarantees a total of seventeen rights, but they in fact play only supporting roles for the six duties imposed on its citizens.[17] Article 75 newly added citizens' rights to free travel and residence. "The most important duty for all North Koreans in their daily lives is the duty of absolute loyalty and obedience to the supreme leader, or Suryong."[18] In other words, allegiance to Kim Jong-Un trumps everything else, including human rights.

Thus, even though the basic rights listed in North Korea's constitution may be similar to those of free democratic countries, the document's fundamental purpose is the strict regimentation of the people. The purported list of the people's basic rights may be interpreted to be solely for external/internal propaganda.[19]

The unimplemented rights claimed by the constitution form a thin patina over a ghastly and morally moribund state.

The society of North Korea stays under the control of one Supreme Leader rather than a more institutional means of governance. Consequently, to even maintain power, the totalitarian leadership in North Korea must exert considerable effort to force allegiance and loyalty to the leader.

Decades ago, the North Korean government supplied goods and services at minimal or no cost to the people, but in recent times, such supply functions have diminished drastically.[20] North Korean citizens cannot control the provision of their basic needs, including food, clothing, and shelter because the Dear Leader controls the supplies of all. Thus, even though North Korea's constitution declares the state shall provide food, clothing, and housing to all the working people, there exists a yawning chasm between the law and reality in North Korea today.[21]

The North Korean regime controls and distributes food to its citizens through a "Food Supply System", which essentially provides food to those higher in its caste system while eliminating those deemed enemies. Such a system encourages citizens toward at least external obedience, gratitude, and loyalty to their ruler. A citizen's clothing supply depends on his or her political status: thus, laborers receive free work clothes once or twice a year, and students and engineers receive discounted formal clothing less frequently. The government has further tightened its grasp on citizens by controlling housing. Every house in North Korea counts as "the haven of the state;" no recognition of any individual ownership exists and housing goes to "the people from the best up to the 5th degree."[22] The "5th degree" references the categorization of the populace into over fifty categories based on political loyalty.

Crimes by association and collective retribution

Citizens of North Korea face the fear of punishment for "guilt by association" to an extent unique in the world. If the regime considers the "crime" serious enough, a relative or associate of that person may also suffer,[23] which may extend through three generations.[24] Suicide also follows this extension of punishment because, in North Korea, suicide counts as treason because it "complains" about the regime and places that individual outside of its power. As such, those related to a person who commits suicide suffer at the hands of the government for their family member's act. Admitting that a person died of starvation is considered a political crime—so it is never stated as the cause of death by the deceased's family members out of fear of punishment.[25]

North Korea as a criminal syndicate

North Korea operates much like a modern organized criminal syndicate (e.g. the Mafia). While North Korea stands as a sovereign state, because it imprisons and/or enslaves its population, its per capita GDP in 2011 tallied a mere $506 to $1,800 with growth estimated between -0.1 and +0.8%. By comparison, per capita GDP in South Korea dwarfed its northern neighbor at $31,700 with a growth rate of 3.6% for the same time period.[26] North Korea directly participates in and/or facilitates carrying out global cyberattacks, espionage, fraud, blackmail, and money laundering; it supplies much of the world's illicit opium and methamphetamine drug trade; and, of course, it parlays the materials and/or technology related to illegal international military proliferation. Through it all, Kim Jong-Un has amassed a personal net worth in excess of $5 billion.[27]

Why there is no rule of law

The North Korean regime effectively consigns human rights to oblivion. "North Korea classifies its populace into the people and the enemy, and it argues that human rights mean the exercise of absolute dictatorship over the class enemies in order to build a socialist society."[28] Somehow, the regime rationalizes crushing of perceived "enemies" as upholding human rights. An absolute, totalitarian dictatorship that regularly oppresses its populace must be considered antithetical to the rule of law and recognition of human rights, not as supportive of human rights. "Under these circumstances, no one can insist on individual freedoms and rights (such as the freedom of speech, press, religion, association, and political participation) unless one is prepared to risk personal safety. It is reported that those who ask for individual rights and freedoms often disappear without a trace."[29] The deprivation of these human rights forms the antithesis of an embrace of human rights.

North Korea claims a "style" of human rights, referred to as "our style of human rights concept." Unfortunately, the policies of this "style" clash completely with respect for human rights in that it has strong political tendencies: every citizen's life gets strangled by political necessity. The Constitution of North Korea itself states its own subordination to the supreme dictator's will.[30]

The "socio-political organism" metaphor, at the core of North Korean political theory, makes individual human rights guarantees even more difficult. An individual may not act outside of the guidance of the Great Leader and the Party under the philosophy that establishes a one-leader (Workers') party, which combines with the masses to form a socio-political organism. The Supreme Ruler assumes the center of society as the "founder of life".[31] Anything even mildly contravening, non-conforming or seen as undermining this totalitarian state has no place in the "socio-political organism."

The absence of an effective, politically independent judiciary also renders these rights and freedoms unprotected. As previously stated, trials, if they take place at all, often mock the idea of due process, often leading to summary sentencing without any semblance of a full judicial process, much less anything approximating a just result on the merits. Ironically, the lack of justice and rule of law appears as just another way for the "all-powerful" Dear Leader to subjugate the proletariat and support the bourgeoisie.

Conclusion

When friends have asked about human rights in North Korea, sometimes I half-facetiously quip that the description should be one word long: "none." These blatant violations of international law at every corner of the DPRK call for redress. This criminal regime pummels its own people with iron fists while trying to hide these atrocities in a fog of lies. If a threat to justice anywhere is a threat to justice everywhere (with due credit to Martin Luther King, Jr.), this state of rightlessness, this egregious case of gross, systematic violations of human rights in North Korea, simply demands redress. That redress serves as the subject for this book's later chapters.

Notes

* My thanks to Michael Nealis for his help on this chapter.
1 Gordon G. Chang, *Finding Truth in the North Korean Fog*, Wall St. J. (Jan. 6, 2010), www. online.wsj.com/news/articles/SB10001424052748703436504574641082982104094 (last visited Aug. 1, 2014).
2 Alastair Bonnett, *North Korea's Creepy Fake Civilian Village Fools No One*, BOINGBOING.NET (Jul. 8, 2014) www.boingboing.net/2014/07/08/north-koreas-creepy-fake-civ.html.
3 North Korea Freedom Coalition, *Remarks by Dr. Suzanne Scholte at the North Korea Freedom Day Rally on April 28, 2011 in Seoul, South Korea*, www.nkfreedom.org/About-Us/Message-from-the-Chairman.aspx (last visited Aug 1, 2014).
4 BLAINE HARDEN, ESCAPE FROM CAMP 14: ONE MAN'S REMARKABLE ODYSSEY FROM NORTH KOREA TO FREEDOM IN THE WEST 16 (2013).
5 Stephanie Hegarty, *North Korea: Defectors Adjust to Life Abroad*, BBC (April 22, 2013), www.bbc.com/news/magazine-22209894.
6 Charlotte Meredith, *North Korean Reveals Cannibalism is Common after Escaping Starving State*, EXPRESS (April 17, 2013), www.express.co.uk/news/world/392610/North-Korean-reveals-cannibalism-is-common-after-escaping-starving-state.
7 *The North Korean Refugee Crisis: Human Rights and International Response* (Stephan Haggard & Marcus Noland eds.), U.S. COMM. FOR HUMAN RIGHTS IN N. KOREA 43 (2006), www. hrnk.org/uploads/pdfs/The_North_Korean_Refugee_Crisis.pdf [hereinafter *Refugee Crisis*].
8 Lee Keum-Soon, et al., *White Paper on Human Rights in North Korea*, KOREA INST. FOR NAT'L UNIFICATION 18 (2004) [hereinafter KINU 2004].
9 *See generally* Sung-Chul Choi, *Human Rights in North Korea in the Light of International Covenants*, in INTERNATIONAL COMMUNITY AND HUMAN RIGHTS IN NORTH KOREA 126–30 (Sung-Chul Choi ed., 1996).
10 *Id.* at 142–43, 161.
11 David Hawk, *The Hidden Gulag: Exposing North Korea's Prison Camps*, U.S. COMM. FOR HUMAN RIGHTS IN N. KOREA 46 (2003), *available at* www.hrnk.org/ HiddenGulag.pdf.
12 "Inside: Undercover in North Korea", Nat'l Geographic (television broadcast, Jan. 18, 2009), *available at* www.natgeotv.com/asia/listings/weekly/ngc/170410/3.
13 KINU 2004, *supra* note 8, at 16.
14 Choi, *supra* note 9, at 163.

15 In Greek mythology, Zeus was the god of the heavens and supreme ruling deity over the upper world. Hades, ruler of darkness, oversaw the lower world, where he would goad the souls of the damned to their eternal place of torment following "judgment."

16 *North Korea's Tightly Controlled Media*, BBC News (Dec. 19, 2011), www.bbc.com/news/world-asia-pacific-16255126.

17 KINU 2004, *supra* note 8, at 10.

18 *Id.* at 10.

19 Choi, *supra* note 9, at 97.

20 KINU 2004, *supra* note 8, at 6, 15–16, 113, 139.

21 *Id.* at 10.

22 Choi, *supra* note 9, at 103–04.

23 KINU 2004, *supra* note 8, at 11.

24 *See* Robert Windrem, *Death, Terror in N. Korea Gulag*, MSNBC (Jan. 15, 2003), www.msnbc.msn.com/id/3071466.

25 KINU 2004, *supra* note 8, at 11–12.

26 Susannah Cullinane, *How Does North Korea Make its Money?* CNN (April 10, 2013), www.edition.cnn.com/2013/04/09/business/north-korea-economy-explainer/.

27 *How Much Is Kim Jong-Un Worth?* CELEBRITY NETWORTH, www.celebritynetworth.com/richest-politicians/presidents/kim-jong-un-net-worth/ (last visited Aug. 1, 2014).

28 KINU 2004, *supra* note 8, at 8, 10

29 KINU 2004, *supra* note 8, at 8, 10.

30 Choi, *supra* note 9, at 98.

31 *Id.* at 94.

Section Two

Dissecting the crimes

Introduction

To call the legal case against North Korea strong understates the matter dramatically. Based primarily upon a foundation of the international treaties and agreements to which North Korea has voluntarily agreed, the DPRK's behavior has been grossly inconsistent with each one's terms and conditions in almost all cases. The following short list is a summary of the major treaties and agreements to which North Korea has subscribed and broken.

- The *International Covenant on Civil and Political Rights*[1] bars nations from willfully starving or testing chemical weapons on its own people, and prohibits slavery. Article 9 requires that citizens receive due process of law. The concentration camps and countless refugee accounts provide a mountain of evidence of the willful starvation, human experimentation, and enslavement. Additionally, North Korea's "3 from the seed" policy fundamentally violates due process of law as well as the customary international law principle of individual accountability because citizens are punished absent any "justified basis" for receiving the negative consequence(s); people find themselves imprisoned for no valid reason at all and North Korean judges merely act as the mouthpiece of the executioner to pronounce guilt and read the sentence.
- The *International Covenant on Economic, Social, and Cultural Rights*[2] calls for nations to continually progress with regard to furthering an individual citizen's right to find work, his or her right to health, to education, and to an adequate standard of living. While the ICESCR puts forth the continual progression requirement rather than setting a requirement of immediate compliance, the data generally show a downward, regressive trend in North Korea for each of the categories of rights under the ICESCR.
- The *Convention on the Rights of the Child*[3] basically requires nations to act in the best interests of children under the age of 18. North Korea's genocidal tendencies toward partly Chinese children makes it apparent that North Korea does not spend much time pondering the well-being of its children. The large number of homeless orphans wandering its streets also testify eloquently against the DPRK regarding this treaty.

- The ***Convention on the Elimination of All Forms of Discrimination Against Women***[4] presents another ironic example of North Korea pretextually ratifying a treaty in an attempt to appease and attract international goodwill.

- Most recently, in July 2014, North Korea became a ***provisional member*** of the ***Asia Pacific Group on Money Laundering (APG)***,[5] an international group that vows to combat money laundering and terror-related financing.[6] Justifiably, many question whether this counts as another political stunt by North Korea. Time will corroborate whether North Korea survives three years of close scrutiny by the APG, which will look for any sign of involvement in illicit financial activities.[7] In the unlikely event it proves its doubters wrong, North Korea may then move from an "observer" to a "full member country" of the APG.[8] As we have already seen, North Korea has on numerous occasions already supported terrorism financially and militarily.

- The ***Treaty on the Non-Proliferation of Nuclear Weapons (NPT)*** applies to the DPRK, at a minimum, for the time period in which it indubitably stayed a member. It remains in question whether North Korea complied with the procedural terms set forth by the NPT to effectuate its stated withdrawal in January 2003. As a practical matter, North Korea committed numerous violations of the NPT between December 1985 and January 2003. Minimally, its violations of the safeguard provisions during this time follow it into the present.

- The ***Biological Weapons Convention*** states, in Article 1, that every ratifying party will never, "in any circumstances … develop, produce, stockpile or otherwise acquire or retain: (1) Microbial or other biological agents, or toxins whatever their origin or method of production, of types and in quantities that have no justification for prophylactic, protective or other peaceful purposes."[9] North Korea possesses a large and diversified biological weapons stockpile as mentioned earlier.

A host of other public and customary international law, including, but not limited to, the following further cements the legal case against North Korea:

- The International Bill of Rights, consisting of the Universal Declaration of Human Rights (adopted 1948), the International Covenant on Civil and Political Rights (adopted 1966), and the International Covenant on Economic, Social and Cultural Rights (adopted 1966), all mentioned previously.

- Principles of *jus cogens* and *individual accountability*, which apply regardless of any lack of assent or adherence to orders, which may at most, mitigate not exonerate.

- While North Korea has not, South Korea has ratified the ***Rome Statute***[10] (also known as the Rome Treaty). Under the terms of the Rome Statute, jurisdiction is established over any party who commits an act in violation of the Rome Statute within the sovereign border of *any ratifying country*, such as South Korea. This treaty may apply more moving forward.

*   War crimes under the ***Geneva Convention***[11] and its progeny arguably apply to every transgression by North Korea since the start of the Korean War, which has never officially ended, a ceasefire agreement took place in 1953, but no treaty or other official end to the war ever followed.[12] More analysis will follow.

Notes

1   International Covenant on Civil and Political Rights, *opened for signature* Dec. 19, 1966, 999 U.N.T.S. 171 (entered into force Mar. 23, 1976).
2   See the Office of the High Commissioner for Human Rights website for the full text of this treaty: www.ohchr.org/EN/ProfessionalInterest/Pages/cescr.aspx.
3   Convention on the Rights of the Child, art. 38, *opened for signature* Nov. 20, 1989, 1577 U.N.T.S. 3 (*entered into force* Sept. 2, 1990).
4   Convention on the Elimination of All Forms of Discrimination Against Women, *entered into force* Dec. 18, 1979, 1249 U.N.T.S. 13.
5   Asia/Pacific Group on Money Laundering, www.apgml.org/ (last visited Aug. 30, 2014).
6   Korea JoongAng Daily, *North Korea Joins OECD Anti-money Laundering Group*, REG'L ANTI-CORRUPTION INITIATIVE (July 19, 2014) www.rai-see.org/news/world/4938-north-korea-joins-oecd-anti-money-laundering-group.html.
7   *Id.*
8   *Id.*
9   Convention on the Prohibition of the Development, Production and Stockpiling of Bacteriological (Biological) and Toxin Weapons and on their Destruction, arts. 1–4 & 9, *opened for signature* Apr. 10, 1972 (entered into force Mar. 26, 1975). The most recent Final Document of the Seventh Review Conference dated Jan. 13, 2012 is available at www.un.org/disarmament/WMD/Bio/.
10 *Rome Statute of the Int'l Crim. Ct.*, art.7, U.N. TREATY SOURCE, U.N. Doc. A/CONF.183/9, *available at* www.untreaty.un.org/cod/icc/statute/romefra.htm.
11 All the Geneva Conventions and their protocols can be found on the International Red Cross' website: www.icrc.org/eng/war-and-law/treaties-customary-law/geneva-conventions/.
12 *U.S.: N. Korea Boosting Guerrilla War Capabilities*, FOX NEWS, ASSOCIATED PRESS (June 23, 2009), www.foxnews.com/story/2009/06/23/us-n-korea-boosting-guerrilla-war-capabilities/.

8   The war that has not ended*

Scant attention in the legal literature has focused on the anomalous fact that the Korean War has never ended and that implications in international law follow. This chapter attempts to fill this void and demonstrate how international humanitarian law (IHL) applies to North Korea's continued hostilities and defiance on the Korean Peninsula and around the world. By analyzing the Korean Armistice Agreement, armistice law, and a few of the inter-Korean agreements over the last several decades, this chapter will explain how the Korean War continues.

It ventures to interpret the various sources of public international law, including international criminal and human rights tribunal case law, applicable treaties and conventions, customary international law and the laws of war, to find that IHL and facets of international human rights law directly apply to North Korea's continued hostilities toward South Korea and other states. It finds that not only has the DPRK perpetuated the Korean conflict through continued hostilities and belligerent behavior, but also that North Korea has perpetrated rampant violations of IHL principles. The armistice agreement itself presents the best starting point.

As mentioned in Chapter 1, in early 2013 the DPRK announced that it would no longer adhere to the armistice agreement, which it now considers void.[1] However, the armistice itself specifically prohibits such an announcement. Article IV, paragraph 62 states that "[t]he Articles and Paragraphs of this Armistice Agreement shall remain in effect until expressly superseded either by *mutually acceptable amendments and additions* or by provision in an appropriate agreement for *a peaceful settlement* at a political level between both sides." Unilateral withdrawal breaks its own terms and on its face, supersession—not violation or withdrawal— appears to be the only tool by which the armistice's precedent can come "undone". Further, the agreement specifically states that its provisions apply to *all* ground, naval, and air forces of both sides so that the DMZ and those territories under the military control of the other garner adequate respect. Not only must each military commander ensure that subordinates who violate the armistice are "adequately punished," the responsibility for such compliance and enforcement remains in the hands of the signatories and their successors. Moreover,

[t]he Commanders of the opposing sides shall establish within their respective commands all measures and procedures necessary to insure *complete*

compliance [emphasis added] with all of the provisions hereof by all elements of their commands. They shall actively cooperate with one another and with the Military Armistice Commission and the Neutral Nations Supervisory Commission in requiring observance of both the letter and the spirit of all of the provisions of this Armistice Agreement.[2]

As Chapter 1 demonstrated, such cooperation from the North has not transpired, and its defiance under this agreement commenced shortly after signing it.[3]

Additionally, the armistice clearly states its prohibitions of any acts of war by either side. Article I stresses that parties may not "execute any hostile act within, from, or against the Demilitarized Zone," and that no persons, military or civilian, may enter the DMZ, let alone cross it, "unless specifically authorized to do so by the Military Armistice Commission." Article II clarifies that a complete cessation of hostilities take place twelve hours after the signing of the Armistice Agreement, providing no exceptions for violations or encumbrances of the DMZ.[4] Neither a derogation clause nor other reserved right to withdraw or violate its provisions pending state emergency or other state interests exist.

Most importantly for our discussion, in addition to providing a comprehensive repatriation system for prisoners of war after the cessation of hostilities and the allowance of displaced civilians to temporarily cross the DMZ, Article IV of the agreement presents the building blocks of this chapter. Article IV had originally recommended that within three months of the signing of the armistice, a political conference would "be held by representatives appointed respectively to settle through negotiation the questions of the withdrawal of all foreign forces from Korea, the peaceful settlement of the Korean question, etc."[5] This peaceful settlement negotiation and treaty never materialized, exhibiting the fact that both sides remain at war because of the armistice's provisions.[6]

With the majority of scholars, the inquiry into international law and North Korea goes no further. However, some military scholars have discussed the significance of the armistice's application to the situation under customary international law and armistice law, and their insight weighs heavily on IHL's application to North Korea's actions since 1953. These scholars have pointed out that the armistice required a cessation of hostilities, but may not have brought an end to a state of war in the region.[7] An armistice, in sum, brings only a temporary peace. Quite simply, a peace treaty formalizes an end of a war.[8]

These author's concepts emanate from the Hague Conventions and the Law of Land Warfare and have attained customary international law status.[9] For example, Article 36 of the Hague Convention (No. II) with Respect to the Laws and Customs of War on Land explicitly states that

[a]n armistice *suspends* military operations by mutual agreement between the belligerent parties. If its duration is not fixed, the belligerent parties can resume operations *at any time*, provided always the enemy is warned within the time agreed upon, in accordance with the terms of the armistice.[10]

Although the Korean Armistice does not expressly allow for the recommencing of hostilities due to an intentional and serious breach of the agreement, Article 40 of this Hague Convention permits a belligerent party to denounce a serious violation of the armistice by another party and recommence hostilities immediately, if the situation presents any urgency.[11]

At least one scholar has traced this armistice law back to ancient Greece and Rome, where an armistice or truce (an *indutiae*) did not terminate the condition of war between parties like a treaty of peace (the *foedus*). Contemporary writers and modern military teachings have reflected this concept and such law has not substantially changed over the last sixty years.[12] Simon expresses the contrary view that the armistice and Korea's unique situation bypass this customary rule and that the provisions of the armistice have little application to the current military and political status of the peninsula.[13] However, this conclusion emerged at the beginning of continued provocations by North Korea in the region[14] and well before the contracting parties agreed to the numerous inter-Korean and other agreements mentioned in the introduction to this chapter.

Although North Korea's actions have expressed contempt for the armistice, "neither a new war nor a true peace has emerged to replace it."[15] Rather, the many concessions and agreements that North Korea has signed with various states support the contention that an international armed conflict still exists and that North Korea *knows* that this state of war continues intact.

For example, as explored in the next chapter, the second principle of unification as pronounced in the North–South Joint Statement of 1972 states that any unification would have to be achieved peacefully without the use of military force. North and South Korea expressly agreed that each side would implement measures to stop military provocations, which may lead to unintended armed conflicts.[16] Twenty years later, through the Agreement on Reconciliation, Non-Aggression and Exchanges and Cooperation between South and North, in February of 1992, the Koreas again wrote their concerns for peace on the peninsula. In addition to agreeing that the parties should refrain from acts of sabotage and insurrection by the terms of Article IV, Article V states that both the North and South would "together endeavor to transform the present state of armistice into a firm state of peace between the two sides and shall abide by the present Military Armistice Agreement until such a state of peace is realized." Articles 12 and 14 looked to establish a South–North Joint Military Commission and a South–North Military Sub-Committee, in order to achieve "phased reductions in armaments including the elimination of weapons of mass destruction and attack capabilities," as well as to help "remove the state of military confrontation" between the parties.[17]

In other words, North Korea understands the current state of war on the peninsula but chooses to disregard the legal ramifications. Even the more recent Inter-Korean Summit Agreement of October 2007 clearly restated this status. This agreement reiterated the same commitment by both sides—that each would work together to end military hostilities and tensions to guarantee peace; however, it also stated that

> [t]he South and the North *both recognize the need to end the current armistice regime and build a permanent peace regime.* The South and the North have also agreed to work together to advance the matter of having the leaders of the three or four parties directly concerned to convene on the Peninsula and *declare an end to the war.*[18] [emphasis added]

In 2011, even the U.S. Congress acknowledged the fact that the Korean conflict had not ended and that North Korea must abide by IHL standards, at least in terms of prisoners of war and abductees.[19] Yet only two years after the 2007 agreement, North Korea did not stop test-firing missiles but conducted yet another illegal nuclear test.[20]

Based on the provocations covered in Chapter 1 and as indicated by the North–South agreement and the Korean Armistice, the peninsula persists in a state of war. The question has remained whether this conflict has ended under the law of armed conflict or IHL, and at this juncture, other scholars have fallen short. A resounding "no" emerges to this question through this chapter's analysis—this established portion of international law accurately applies to North Korea's actions in many ways.

Although the laws of war have continued through thousands of years of armed conflict and find themselves fixed into the framework of customary international law, several treaties and conventions signed by the majority of the world's nations have codified the law in this area. This treaty law, particularly the Geneva Conventions, to which the DPRK itself agreed, constitutes a solid starting point for assessing whether such laws of war actually apply to the actions of the DPRK since signing the armistice and exactly what law applies.

The DPRK acceded to the four Geneva Conventions of 1949 on August 27, 1957, and the conventions' provisions came into effect on February 27, 1958.[21] Ironically, a mere week and a half earlier, North Korean agents hijacked a South Korean plane en route to Seoul.[22] North Korea later acceded to the conventions' first protocol on March 3, 1988, and its provisions came into effect on September 9, 1988.[23] The significance of these dates crystallizes when discussing these treaties' application to the DPRK's actions, but they demonstrate that North Korea acceded to each for quite some time and, hence, should remain cognizant of their applicability and relevance.

Our analysis starts with Common Article 2 of the Geneva Conventions; Article 2 of each convention states:

> In addition to the provisions which shall be implemented in peacetime, the present Convention shall apply to all cases of declared war or of any other armed conflict which may arise between two or more of the High Contracting Parties, even if the state of war is not recognized by one of them.[24]

Even though this language appears quite broad on its face, interpretation and applicability of its words have proved even broader. The Commentary to the Geneva Conventions clarifies how this article relates to the conventions' applicability in the context of armed conflicts:

There is no need for a formal declaration of war, or for recognition of the existence of a state of war, as preliminaries to the application of the Convention. The occurrence of de facto hostilities is sufficient ... *Any difference arising between two States and leading to the intervention of members of the armed forces is an armed conflict within the meaning of Article 2*, even if one of the Parties denies the existence of a state of war. It makes no difference how long the conflict lasts, or how much slaughter takes place. The respect due to the human person as such is not measured by the number of victims. Nor, incidentally, does the application of the Convention necessarily involve the intervention of cumbrous machinery.[25] [emphasis added]

The International Committee of the Red Cross (ICRC) reaffirmed this understanding of how a mere resort to arms by two states triggers an international armed conflict (IAC) as well as the conventions' applicability. Citing the conventions' commentary, the ICRC stated:

An IAC occurs when one or more States have recourse to armed force against another State, regardless of the reasons or the intensity of this confrontation. Relevant rules of IHL may be applicable even in the absence of open hostilities. Moreover, no formal declaration of war or recognition of the situation is required. The existence of an IAC, and as a consequence, the possibility to apply IHL to this situation, depends on what actually happens on the ground.

In fact, the ICRC adopted the more expansive opinion of the scholars D. Schindler and H.P. Gasser: that an international armed conflict comes into existence and triggers the conventions' applicability under this Article *as soon as one State employs any armed force against another.*[26]

North Korea has resorted to and instigated armed conflict with South Korea and other nations, most particularly the United States, on dozens of occasions, ranging from shooting down aircraft, infiltrating South Korea and killing its soldiers, government officials and citizens, sinking fishing and patrol boats, bombing military and civilian targets, and participating in gun battles at sea around the Korean Peninsula.[27] Therefore, under this definition, an international armed conflict still presently exists in Korea and applies to North Korea's actions.

The first Protocol to the Geneva Conventions offers similar applicability, suggesting that its added protections apply to North Korea's actions as well. Under Article 1, Protocol I supplements the Geneva Conventions and thus applies in every situation that falls under Common Article 2 as mentioned.[28] The Protocol's Commentary reinforces this interpretation as well by stating:

[H]umanitarian law also covers any dispute between two States involving the use of their armed forces. Neither the duration of the conflict, nor its intensity, play[s] a role: the law must be applied to the fullest extent required by the situation of the persons and the objects protected by it.[29]

Remember that North Korea acceded to Protocol I, as mentioned earlier, and therefore should be aware of Common Article 2 governing our analysis. In addition, South Korea also ratified Protocol I, making its provisions completely enforceable on both North and South Korea and any related hostilities between the two.[30]

However, Article 3 may arguably place a damper on the Protocol's applicability to the Korean situation. It reads: "The application of the Conventions and of this Protocol shall cease, in the territory of Parties to the conflict, on the general close of military operations."[31] One may interpret the Korean Armistice to represent a "general close of military operations" in the region, and, therefore, the provisions of the Protocol would not apply. In retrospect, the Commentary to this Article sheds light on the possible application to Korea:

> "Military operations" means the movements, manoeuvres and actions of any sort, carried out by the armed forces with a view to combat. "The general close of military operations" is the same expression as that used in Article 6 of the fourth Convention, which, according to the commentary thereon, may be deemed in principle to be at the time of a general armistice, capitulation or just when the occupation of the whole territory of a Party is completed, *accompanied by the effective cessation of all hostilities*, without the necessity of a legal instrument of any kind. When there are several States on one side or the other, the general close of military operations could mean the *complete cessation of hostilities between all belligerents*, at least in a particular theatre of war.[32] [emphasis added]

In effect, this language indicates that the Protocol's application ceases only when there is a complete or effective cessation of *all* hostilities among *all* belligerents.[33] This makes sense because "[the Protocol] is aimed, above all, at protecting individuals, and not at serving the interests of States."[34] Applicability of humanitarian law to protect individuals does not cease merely because parties think that hostilities will not continue after an armistice. Again, based on North Korea's continued military provocations, a complete cessation of hostilities has not transpired and, therefore, the DPRK's actions after 1988 would fall under the Protocol.

The opinion paper of the International Committee of the Red Cross analyzed earlier also presented the primary jurisprudence for its definition of an international armed conflict: *Prosecutor v. Tadic*.[35] In its maiden case, the International Criminal Tribunal for the Former Yugoslavia (ICTY) considered and defined the term "armed conflict" within the bounds of IHL. The Trial Chamber, in considering a Motion for Interlocutory Appeal on Jurisdiction, found that:

> an armed conflict exists whenever there is a resort to armed force between States or protracted armed violence between governmental authorities and organized armed groups or between such groups within a State. International humanitarian law applies from the initiation of such armed conflicts and extends beyond the cessation of hostilities until a general conclusion of peace

is reached … Until that moment, international humanitarian law continues to apply in the whole territory of the warring States[36]

The court recognized that determining whether an armed conflict exists is a crucial jurisdictional question for international criminal tribunals because IHL applies only within the duration of an armed conflict. However, IHL applies whether the armed conflict is international or non-international.[37] The Appellate Chamber affirmed this determination and added that an internal armed conflict can become international if another state intervenes with its own troops or if participants in the conflict act on behalf of an outside state.[38]

The establishment of the *Tadic* rule has been confirmed by reliance upon it in many subsequent cases. For example, in *Prosecutor v. Kupreskic*, the ICTY Trial Chamber stated again that "[a]n armed conflict can be said to exist whenever there is a resort to armed force between States."[39]

The ICTY has further clarified that a determination that an international armed conflict exists serves as a necessary predicate to application of Common Article 2 of the Geneva Conventions as a substantive element of a war crime. The Appeals Chamber in *Prosecutor v. Naletilic & Martinovich* did just this again in relation to grave breaches under the Geneva Conventions.[40] The Appellate Chamber in *Tadic* further ensconced the concept that the existence of an international armed conflict activates the grave breaches of provisions of the Geneva Conventions. Although this decision and precedent have proven controversial,[41] it has become a defining element in prosecuting defendants for war crimes and these breaches under the conventions.

Under this definition, the hundreds of armed skirmishes between North Korea and primarily South Korea compose a continuing "international armed conflict," especially considering their pattern through the decades. For example, in July 1997, fourteen North Korean soldiers intentionally crossed the DMZ and after repeated warnings to disengage, proceeded to start a twenty-three minute exchange of heavy gunfire with South Korean soldiers.[42] Accordingly, this analysis concludes that IHL would apply to these sorts of situations of armed attacks under *Tadic*, as part of an international armed conflict. In effect then, the application of the Geneva Convention's grave breaches provisions would also apply to North Korea's armed incursions, and liabilities may thereafter fall on the perpetrators.

Applying IHL and the Geneva Conventions

In addition to North Korea's proliferation mischief, its systematic hostilities toward South Korea, Japan, the United States, and other nations create greater culpability under applicable IHL treaties and conventions. Restrictions on the means of warfare (*jus in bello*) follow with the application of IHL. Note that *the DPRK signed or ratified every treaty and convention as indicated.* This treaty law will demonstrate that the DPRK's actions provide a solid basis for grave breaches of IHL and other international law.

Two of the 1949 Geneva Conventions rise to the level of primary concerns in our analysis: The Geneva Convention Relative to the Treatment of Prisoners of War of August 12, 1949 (Geneva Convention III) and the Geneva Convention Relative to the Protection of Civilian Persons in Time of War of August 12, 1949 (Geneva Convention IV). This chapter focuses on these two because the first two conventions apply to wounded, sick, and shipwrecked armed forces, classes of individuals that have not made up the primary classes of victims from North Korea's more current hostilities since 1958, when the DPRK became subject to the Geneva Conventions' provisions. Prisoners of war (POWs) and civilians have suffered more.

Geneva Convention III provides an extensive protective framework for prisoners of war in armed conflict. Article 12 makes it clear that states retain responsibility for these individuals' treatment, regardless of whom or what military unit captured them. The majority of Geneva III outlines the living conditions of POWs, who should receive humane treatment from the detaining power; murdering or endangering the health of a POW counts as a grave breach of the convention's provisions. Violence, intimidation, torture, experimentation, and discrimination against POWs run contrary to Geneva Convention III. From Article 21 to Article 130, Geneva Convention III lists and explains the necessary treatment of POWs by the detaining power, requiring everything from providing adequate food and proper living arrangements (i.e., basic necessities) to freedom of religion, reasonable payment for work performed while detained, and even periodic visits from the representatives of their home countries. In fact, POWs have allowances to participate in recreational activities, write to their families back home, and elect representatives from their camps! Article 129 requires parties to the convention to enact proper legislation to punish those individuals that violate such treatment requirements of POWs, while Article 131 specifies that parties cannot absolve themselves of "any liability incurred by itself or by another High Contracting Party in respect of [grave] breaches."[43]

South Korea's National Intelligence Service has reported in the recent past that 407 POWs still "resided" in North Korea, of which 268 were alive as of January of 2001 (eighty-three fewer than the previous September). It also reported that a total of sixteen POWs returned between 1994 and September of 2000, after years of hard labor and "re-education" in the DPRK.[44] Some estimates still place POW numbers as high as 560 (just for South Korean soldiers),[45] but with POW-MIAs operations at a stand-still for governments like the U.S.,[46] precise numbers remain elusive. The *U.S.S. Pueblo* incident gives an example of how North Korea has violated and continues to violate Geneva III in its treatment of POWs.

The *U.S.S. Pueblo* incident, as discussed in Chapter 1, demonstrates that North Korea does not treat POWs as required under Geneva Convention III. The psychological and mental torture to which the DPRK subjected them, along with inadequate living quarters, show that the DPRK committed grave breaches of this Convention in 1968.[47] Current POWs apparently have not had leave to write home to their families either, making it more difficult to assess their current treatment.[48] In every respect, North Korea retains culpability for these violations—from its actions in 1968 until the present date.

Geneva Convention IV has a similar objective to Geneva Convention III, but instead of protecting POWs, it seeks to protect civilians. Civilians under the Convention "are those who, at a given moment and in any manner whatsoever, find themselves, in case of a conflict or occupation, in the hands of a Party to the conflict or Occupying Power of which they are not nationals." These individuals, like POWs, must be granted respect and be free from all forms of violence or coercion. Article 34 clearly prohibits taking hostages, and under Articles 25 and 35, civilians may write to their families and possibly leave the country. As with Geneva III, states retain responsibility for the treatment of civilians regardless of individual responsibility. Even if civilians suffer confinement, standards in the convention grant humane treatment, adequate housing, food, water, clothing and health needs, freedom of religion and recreational opportunities, a complaint system and representation, and even an outlet for allowing family visits. Any internment must end once the necessity ends, and international humanitarian organizations must have access to these civilians. As with Geneva III, grave breaches include torture, inhumane treatment, murdering and other causing of suffering; parties *cannot* absolve themselves of liability from these grave breaches.[49]

Just a few examples illustrate that North Korea has also continuously violated Geneva Convention IV. In December of 1969, "North Korean agents hijacked a South Korean airliner YS-11 to Wonsan en route from Kangnung to Seoul with 51 persons aboard," of which twelve remained in custody as of January 2001. Kidnapping and hostage cases illustrate North Korea's actions contrary to Geneva IV: Kim Jong-Il ordered the kidnapping of South Korean actress Choi Eun-hee and her husband Shin Sang-ok in February 1978, and the DPRK abducted a South Korean teacher in June 1979, a South Korean student in August 1987, a pastor in July 1995, a South Korean businessman in September 1999, and a U.S. reverend in January 2000.[50] When North Korea seizes hostages in clear violation of Article 34,[51] it often does not allow them to write home to their families, to leave the country, or to accept visits from international organizations like the Red Cross. North Korea has not adopted as its *modus operandi* the disclosure of the precise location of these civilian prisoners to the protecting power (i.e., South Korea or the United States) or their families under Article 83, and at times does not release them under Article 132 after any supposed necessity for their internment has ended.[52] North Korea sometimes subjects these individuals to torture, not unlike what it inflicts upon the estimated 120,000–200,000 North Korean citizens still found in concentration camps scattered throughout the country.[53]

The Protocol Additional to the Geneva Conventions of 12 August 1949, and Relating to the Protection of Victims of International Armed Conflicts (Protocol I) creates several additional protections for POWs and civilians, and provides very clear humanitarian standards for armed conflict. For example, it protects POWs and civilians from medical experiments, a grave breach of the protocol. Under Articles 32, 33 and 34, contracting parties must inform families of their relatives' fates promptly and also to respect the remains of the dead and search for missing persons after the cessation of active hostilities.

The principle of distinction, memorialized in numerous articles, requires that attacks target only military personnel and military establishments rather than civilians and civilian structures. An indiscriminate attack does not aim for a specific military objective. This principle forbids military reprisals against the civilian population. Article 60 prohibits parties from extending "their military operations to zones on which they have conferred by agreement the status of demilitarized zone, if such extension is contrary to the terms of this agreement."[54] The best known DMZ globally, ironically the most militarized border in the world, divides the two Koreas and frequently sees skirmishes.

Article 75 provides a minimum human rights floor prohibiting all violence against a protected individual's health (i.e., murder, physical and mental torture, corporal punishment, and mutilation), humiliating and degrading treatment, forced prostitution, and any form of indecent assault; it also prohibits the taking of hostages, collective punishments, and threats of any such acts. Grave breaches include targeting civilians, launching indiscriminate attacks, making demilitarized zones the object of attack, and unjustifiable delay in the repatriation of POWs or civilians. These breaches constitute "war crimes" under Protocol 1. Most importantly, Article 91 summarizes responsibility: "A Party to the conflict which violates the provisions of the Conventions or of this Protocol shall ... be liable to pay compensation. It shall be responsible for all acts committed by persons forming part of its armed forces."[55]

All of these provisions of Protocol I point directly to numerous hostile acts that North Korea has committed after 1988, when it ratified this Protocol. For example, in April 1996, on three occasions, hundreds of armed North Koreans crossed into the DMZ at or near Panmunjom in clear violation of the armistice. Seven more crossed the DMZ the following month along with eleven ships clashing with South Korean forces on two separate occasions. Twenty-six more died doing the same that September while on a failed espionage/reconnaissance mission.[56] These incidents violate Article 60 as well as the grave breaches of provisions of the Protocol.

Additionally, consider the North Korean patrol boats that fired on a fishing vessel in May 1995, killing three fishermen and detaining five more for over six months in transgression of Article 51. In further violation of Article 51, North Korean agents poisoned Choi Duk-Keun, a South Korean diplomat, while in Russia, to "retaliate" for the above submarine espionage attack gone awry in September.[57]

In contravention to Articles 32 through 34, North Korea abducted over a dozen Japanese nationals in the 1970s and 1980s. In response to protests, the DPRK subsequently sent boxes of ashes to Japan: contrary to North Korea's claims, tests revealed that the boxes did not contain the remains of the kidnapped victims.[58] Such episodes have galvanized the Japanese populace against North Korea. An additional violation of Article 51 transpired on November 2010 when the North unleashed over 170 artillery rounds toward Yeonpyeong Island in the

Yellow Sea, killing two South Korean Marines and two civilians, injuring nineteen, and damaging several structures.[59]

Other key treaty law

The DPRK has signed several other conventions providing additional protections to certain classes of people and further limits its behavior pertaining to armed conflict. They include the Convention on the Prevention and Punishment of Crimes against Internationally Protected Persons, Including Diplomatic Agents (Diplomatic Agents Convention), the Convention on the Rights of the Child (Child Convention), the International Convention for the Suppression of the Financing of Terrorism (Terrorism Convention), the Convention on the Prevention and Punishment of the Crime of Genocide (Genocide Convention), and the Convention on the Non-applicability of Statutory Limitations to War Crimes and Crimes Against Humanity (War Crimes Convention).

North Korea acceded to the Diplomatic Agents Convention on December 1, 1982.[60] The convention's purpose is to prevent assassinations and assassination attempts of diplomats by requiring state parties to prohibit such acts in domestic law. Heads of state, as well as representatives or state officials or agents of international organizations, along with their immediate family members, receive protection. States agreeing to this convention must desist from murdering, kidnapping, attacking, or violently attacking the known premises of protected persons, as well as threatening to do so, attempting such acts, or even playing a part in such acts. Under the treaty, states should criminalize such actions, track down the perpetrators, and inform other states of the violator's whereabouts and circumstances if they have the proper knowledge.[61]

The timing of the DPRK's accession to this convention presents an irony because just four months prior, Canadian police uncovered a North Korean plot to assassinate then South Korean President Chun Doo Hwan during a visit to Canada. More ironically, North Korea attempted to assassinate the South Korean President again the following year in Myanmar—even after becoming a party to the convention.[62] North Korea evinces no respect for the concept of *pacta sunt servanda*.[63]

The Child Convention, the most ratified human rights treaty in the world, also applies to North Korea's actions. Article 38 requires that state parties "undertake to respect and to ensure respect for rules of IHL applicable to [children] in armed conflicts which are relevant to the child" and that "[p]arties take all feasible measures to ensure protection and care of children who are affected by an armed conflict."[64] The DPRK signed this convention in August 1990 and ratified it in September 1990.[65] Since that time, North Korea has failed to protect its own children in a time of ongoing war and famine on the peninsula.

> UNICEF has reported that each year some 40,000 North Korean children under five became 'acutely malnourished,' with 25,000 needing hospital treatment. The food security situation improved slightly from 2011 to 2012, but 28% of the population reportedly suffers from stunting.[66]

However, when looking at the money spent on its military, if North Korea effectively transferred this spending by approximately even 5 to 10 percent on agricultural infrastructure, for example, it could markedly ameliorate this situation.[67]

Similar to the Diplomatic Agents Convention, the Terrorism Convention seeks to eliminate and prevent acts of international terrorism around the world. Through its many articles, the convention requires state parties to illegalize terrorism, prosecute it, and prevent it, especially by suppressing funding.[68] North Korea signed the convention in November 2001.[69] Signing a convention marks a commitment not to contravene the object and purpose of that treaty. North Korea has a history of supporting terrorism financially and militarily[70]—abundant evidence exists to demonstrate that the DPRK has supported numerous terrorist organizations since 2001, including Syrian and Lebanese terrorists, the Tamil Tigers, and Hezbollah by helping them train in North Korea, building structures and bunkers, as well as selling missiles and chemical weapons.[71]

North Korea became a party to the Genocide Convention on January 31, 1989.[72] Parties, by signing the convention, according to the very first article of the treaty, explicitly "confirm that genocide, *whether committed in time of peace or in time of war*, is a crime under international law which they undertake to prevent and to punish" (emphasis added). Genocide is considered "any of the following acts committed with intent to destroy, in whole or in part, a national, ethnical, racial or religious group, as such" under Article II:

> *(a)* Killing members of the group; *(b)* Causing serious bodily or mental harm to members of the group; *(c)* Deliberately inflicting on the group conditions of life calculated to bring about its physical destruction in whole or in part; *(d)* Imposing measures intended to prevent births within the group; *(e)* Forcibly transferring children of the group to another group.

Article III forbids genocide, conspiracy to commit genocide, direct/public incitement to commit it, an attempt to commit it, and complicity in genocide.[73]

As explored in the previous chapters, North Korea has been engaging in genocide for decades. Numerous accounts have been recorded of infanticide policies involving Chinese and partially Chinese children.[74] The DPRK directly kills them by stabbing, shooting, suffocation, or intentional abandonment. North Korea also destroys them in the womb by severely beating the women or by other forced abortion techniques.[75] North Korea similarly targets Christians, who find themselves systematically imprisoned, tortured and executed.[76] Genocide has persisted as a crime against humanity since the International Military Tribunals of Nuremberg. Some scholars of international law consider it the ultimate crime.

The War Crimes Convention also intersects with North Korea's actions during armed conflicts. That convention seeks to extend any statutes of limitations for war crimes indefinitely. Such crimes (i.e., war crimes and crimes against humanity) include the aforementioned grave breaches regarding the Geneva Conventions (e.g., directly attacking civilians), apartheid, and genocide. In addition to specifically requiring state parties to abolish any statute of limitations on war crimes, it states that the convention applies directly "to representatives of the State authority and private individuals who ... participate in or who directly incite others to the commission of any of those crimes, or who conspire to commit them, irrespective of the degree of completion, and to representatives of the State authority who tolerate their commission."[77] North Korea acceded to the convention on November 8, 1984,[78] effectively placing culpability upon North Korea and directly exposing it to liability for war crimes and crimes against humanity for its numerous violations.

In addition to the NPT, North Korea also ratified two very important weapons treaties that play into our analysis of treaty law: the Protocol for the Prohibition of the Use of Asphyxiating, Poisonous or Other Gases, and of Bacteriological Methods of Warfare (Gas Protocol) and the Convention on the Prohibition of the Development, Production and Stockpiling of Bacteriological (Biological) and Toxin Weapons and on their Destruction (Biological Weapons Convention). The Gas Protocol prohibits the use of bacteriological warfare methods,[79] and the Biological Weapons Convention widely expands such prohibitions.

The Biological Weapons Convention prohibits parties from developing or manufacturing biological agents, toxins, and weapons for armed conflict, and must destroy such weapons or divert them to peaceful purposes within nine months of the convention entering into force. It also prohibits states from transferring such weapons to another state or assisting production of such weapons, as well as requiring parties to create necessary measures to prevent development or the retention of them. Parties have a duty to "continue negotiations *in good faith* with a view to reaching early agreement on effective measures for the prohibition of their development, production and stockpiling and for their destruction"[80] (emphasis added).

How has North Korea fared with this treaty? It has not fared well. Sources such as the Russian Federal Foreign Intelligence Service, the South Korean Ministry of Defense, and the Central Intelligence Agency (CIA), have reported that North Korea has developed biological weapons since the 1960s.[81] Some reports from South Korea claim that the DPRK could have up to thirteen biological agents and pathogens that the DPRK could easily "weaponize" (if it has not done so already) and use them in armed conflict or terrorist acts, including anthrax, cholera, the plague, yellow fever, and smallpox.[82] Simply having these capabilities ready to use for combat alone breaks the Biological Weapons Convention,[83] and North Korea's continued development after signing the Convention demonstrates yet another serious breach.[84]

Other applicable international law

Although the majority of the basis of customary international law in the field of armed conflict has been covered heretofore (e.g. North Korea having ratified the 1949 Geneva Conventions), a short analysis of two further principles follows, namely: (1) directly attacking demilitarized zones that have been agreed upon by the parties to be prohibited, and (2) the use of chemical weapons.

The International Committee of the Red Cross stands highly respected in the international community for its coverage, interpretation, and publications on IHL. It has documented dozens of rules of customary international law in IHL, based on decades of use by nations and dozens of international agreements, cases, and domestic law.[85] North Korea has manifested its defiance of such rules. It signs and ratifies treaties for tactical gain, not in good faith.

As noted by many scholars, the Geneva Conventions of 1949 and its Protocols replaced many of the Hague Conventions and other former IHL treaties.[86] As demonstrated, the Geneva Conventions stand in judgment over violations of IHL, like indiscriminate shelling of defenseless civilian towns and villages.[87] Similarly, the Red Cross's rules on demilitarized zones and chemical weapons have a similar function. North Korea's communication regarding its compliance with such rules is preposterous.

For example, in 1989, North Korea made a statement claiming that the country would not test, produce, store, or introduce from the outside any nuclear or chemical weapons, nor would it allow passage of such weapons through its territory: it also claimed in 1995 to oppose such weapons in principle.[88] However, the DPRK has tested, produced, and stored chemical weapons for many years in several locations around the North, some estimating that the nation has 2,500 to 5,000 metric tons of weapons, such as phosgene, hydrogen cyanide, mustard gas, and sarin.[89] North Korea has tested its chemical weapons on concentration camp prisoners in violation of this customary rule or established IHL.[90] When South Korea provided over 610,000 gas masks to its citizens after the bombing of Yeonpyeong Island, it did so to guard against a chemical weapons attack.[91] The second rule seeks to prevent attacks on civilians.

North Korea constantly breaks Rule 36 (the first rule mentioned) of these customary rules through its DMZ incursions. In 1996, the DPRK made accusations to the President of the U.N. Security Council that the Republic of Korea had overstepped the bounds of the armistice by building up military forces in the DMZ; in turn, it claimed the armistice no longer bound it in relation to the DMZ.[92] However, North Korea has breached the DMZ with infiltrators and armed attacks hundreds of times and for decades well before this 1996 date, and hundreds of times thereafter. In sum, even if North Korea had not signed the many IHL treaties, it would likely still retain liability for its hostilities in violating various principles of customary international law like the two presented.

The looming threat of responsibility

The International Criminal Court (ICC), after I urged prosecutors to do so, had commenced investigation of some of the DPRK's most recent hostilities against South Korea under the auspices of the Rome Statute. The Office of the Prosecutor had investigated whether it can charge DPRK nationals for war crimes regarding the sinking of the *Cheonan* and the shelling of Yeonpyeong Island. North Korea's original concern should have arisen from the fact that the ICC could have had jurisdiction under the Rome Statute to investigate and issue indictments for these incidents because South Korea remains a party to the Rome Statute and such acts concluded on South Korean territory.[93] Unfortunately, the Chief Prosecutor concluded in June of 2014 that these activities could not qualify as war crimes under the ICC Statute.[94] Regarding the *Cheonan*, the Prosecutor concluded "that the alleged attack was directed at a lawful military target and would not otherwise meet the definition of the war crime of perfidy as defined in the Rome Statute." As for Yeonpyeong Island, the information that was available on the incident was not enough to "provide a reasonable basis to believe that the attack was intentionally directed against civilian objects or that the civilian impact was expected to be clearly excessive in relation to the anticipated military advantage." This latter conclusion could be somewhat of a stretch, but both conclusions do tend to show the limitations of the ICC, as described further in this book. If anything positive came out of this unfortunate result, it is that the Prosecutor stressed that the ICC reserves the right to reopen the investigation if more information emerges contrary to these conclusions.[95]

Noting the *in absentia* indictment by the ICC of President Omar al-Bashir of Sudan,[96] who has never appeared before the Court, North Korea's leaders may fall within the ICC's grasp as well if such information of intentionality arises. The DPRK should remain cognizant of this risk, considering that the Prosecutor had been trying in vain to receive a response from the country for investigative purposes over the past several years. The ICC opened the investigation in December 2010.[97] If the Prosecutor finds a reasonable basis for the perpetration of war crimes committed under Article 8 of the Rome Statute based on more information in the future, the ICC can indict North Korean leaders for these crimes and try them individually.[98] Under Article 25, individuals can face criminal culpability for their actions and may have to pay reparations to victims of their crimes under Article 75.[99]

At this point, the better route would lie in the Prosecutor filing a *proprio motu* motion against the government of North Korea.[100] Given all of the resolutions against North Korea emanating from the Security Council, another possible option would be referral to the U.N. Security Council by the Prosecutor. I submit that either of these routes could prove more fruitful than jurisdiction based on violations in the territory of a Rome Treaty state, in this case South Korea. More about ICC prosecution and its feasibility will follow in the next chapter.

Additionally, the Geneva Conventions provide a means of chastising violations. Under Article 132 of Geneva III, a party to the conflict can inquire whether there have been transgressions of the Convention and work to put an immediate end to them.[101] Article 149 of Geneva Convention IV provides for the same.[102] Under Article 93 of Protocol I, any party to the conflict that violates the Conventions can be liable to pay compensation for such violations.[103] On top of all this, international criminal tribunals continue to use the Geneva Conventions and its Protocols to find individuals criminally liable for violations.[104]

A similar paradigm of liability exists with the Genocide Convention. Under Article VIII, any party to that convention can call upon U.N. organs to take any action necessary under the U.N. Charter to prevent or suppress acts of genocide. This means that states can call for action through a body like the Security Council to stop the genocide in North Korea by any means necessary without an objection by the DPRK—a signatory to the treaty.[105] The Biological Weapons Convention gives similar powers to the U.N. Security Council to investigate alleged violations via complaints of state parties, but it contains weaker language and delves less deeply regarding the enumerated powers of the Council as a U.N. organ.[106] These conventions have found individuals of state parties criminally liable.[107]

North Korea must also keep in mind the concept of universal jurisdiction. Certain egregious crimes rise to the level of *jus cogens* violations and can be redressed anywhere in the world with certain limits. Many of these (such as war crimes, genocide, and torture) have been addressed previously, and individuals may be subject to this jurisdiction when any one of the following crimes has been committed: piracy, slavery, war crimes, crimes against humanity, genocide, apartheid, and torture. Additionally, other crimes, such as hijacking airplanes, taking hostages, kidnapping, harming diplomatic agents, and forced disappearances, crimes that North Korea has committed as shown in Chapter 1, also coincide with universal jurisdiction. No separate criminal tribunal needs to award jurisdiction for some of the most heinous crimes if any nation that has an interest in the crime wants to prosecute North Korean individuals.[108] However, nations have exercised universal jurisdiction very sparingly—it remains very delicate and sensitive politically. Belgium, for example, is a nation that has ventured to use it more than others, but it too has pulled back due to backlash.

Conclusion

As seen from the continued hostilities on the Korean Peninsula and the increased tension between the DPRK and the rest of the world, we know that the Korean conflict has not yet ended. North Korea has admitted that fact on more than one occasion with its many agreements with South Korea and other interested nations. However, North Korea must remember that with this continuous armed conflict come consequences and certain international rules. International law, in its case precedents, conventions, and customary rules, provides the notion that the laws of international armed conflict still apply on the Korean Peninsula and that both North and South Korea as well as the United States and China remain bound by them.

A generally law-abiding nation could remain insouciant about these laws; North Korea, on the other hand, has egregiously defied these rules in nearly every turn of the conflict. Every infiltration of the DMZ, every plane hijacking, every murder and assassination, every kidnapping, every tortured POW, every illegal weapon, and every starving child speaks to North Korea's liability under this law. One day, ideally in the not-too-distant future, the leaders of North Korea will come to understand that they cannot hide their numerous violations of international law and blatant war crimes. For the sake of the DPRK's many victims, this author wishes that its attempts to mask, obfuscate, and distract from its heinous violations of international law will prove futile: justice demands it. Justice also requires redress, the subject of the next section.

Notes

* Kevin Zickterman proved indispensable as a co-author of this chapter; Michael Nealis assisted in the introduction of this section.

1 Hyung-Jin Kim & Foster Klug, *North Korea Says It Cancels 1953 Armistice*, CHI. DAILY LAW BULL. (Mar. 11, 2013), www.hosted2.ap.org/ILDLB/8ef5320729ce4298a befc1903704c7d5/Article_2013-03-11-Koreas-Tension/id-ef180ced68b746fb8 766b921b81eef4b?utm_source=subscriber&utm_medium=CDLBemail&utm_ content=APhed_North%20Korea%20says%20it%20cancels%201953%20 armistice&utm_campaign=headlines.

2 Agreement Between the Commander-In-Chief, United Nations Command, on the One Hand, and the Supreme Commander of the Korean People's Army and the Commander of the Chinese People's Volunteers, on the Other Hand, Concerning a Military Armistice in Korea, arts. II & IV, *opened for signature* July 27, 1953, 4 U.S.T. 234 (entered into force July 27, 1953) [hereinafter Korean Armistice].

3 Dick K. Nanto, Cong. Research Serv., RL30004, North Korea: Chronology of Provocations, 1950–2003 3 (2003) (detailing the hijacking of a South Korean airliner by North Korean agents less than five years after the signing of the armistice in February, 1958).

4 Korean Armistice, *supra* note 2, at arts. I & II.

5 *Id.* at arts. III & IV.

6 *See generally* Scott R. Morris, *America's Most Recent Prisoner of War: The Warrant Officer Bobby Hall Incident*, THE ARMY LAW., Sept. 1996, at 3–4.

7 *E.g.*, Ernest A. Simon, *The Operation of the Korean Armistice Agreement*, 47 MIL. L. REV. 105, 105 (1970) ("If the customary rules governing armistice are resorted to, the parties are technically still in a state of war, de facto and de jure, and the international law of war applies insofar as it is not displaced by the *Armistice Agreement* or the customary rules of armistice."); Morris, *supra* note 6, at 12 ("Within twelve hours of the signing of the Armistice Agreement at 1000, 27 July 1953, hostilities on the Korean peninsula were supposed to cease. However, that did not mean that the state of war on the peninsula ceased.").

8 Morris, *supra* note 6, at 13; Simon, *supra* note 7, at 108–09 ("The end in view is always the treaty of peace by means of which the relations between belligerent nations pass from a state of war to a state of peace."). Although a Vienna-style peace through a bilateral treaty would be preferred to permanently end the conflict, the objective of this chapter is not to discuss a preferred method of peace but to simply explore the means by which international humanitarian law can be applied to the North Korean situation.

9 Simon, *supra* note 7, at 109, 124–27.

10 Hague Convention No. II of July 29, 1899, with Respect to the Laws and Customs of War on Land, art. 36, 32 Stat. 1803, T.S. No. 403 [hereinafter Hague Convention II]; *see also Oxford Manuel for the Laws of War on Land*, art. 5, INT'L COMM. OF THE RED CROSS (Sept. 9, 1880), www.icrc.org/ihl.nsf/FULL/140?OpenDocument (last visited Mar. 17, 2013) ("Military conventions made between belligerents during the *continuance of war, such as armistices* and capitulations, must be scrupulously observed and respected." emphasis added).

11 Hague Convention II, *supra* note 10, at art. 40. These customary provisions found in the Hague Conventions were primarily and previously taken from Articles 47–52 of the Project of an International Declaration Concerning the Laws and Customs of War of Aug. 27, 1874, which can be found at the International Committee of the Red Cross website at www.icrc.org/ihl.nsf/FULL/135?OpenDocument.

12 Howard S. Levie, *The Nature and Scope of the Armistice Agreement*, 50 AM. J. INT'L L. 880, 884–85 (1956). Colonel Levie uses the United States Supreme Court's interpretation of the 1918 Armistice from World War I and a French Court of Cassation's 1944 case to demonstrate that courts around the time of the Korean Armistice interpreted armistice law consistent with the Greeks and Romans.

13 Simon, *supra* note 7, at 136–37 ("The customary rules of international law governing armistice status, insofar as they allow a resumption of hostilities, are no longer relevant to the present situation in Korea. This conclusion emerged from an analysis of the military and political conditions under which the armistice was concluded, the nature of the *Armistice Agreement*, the settlement of disputes arising during the armistice, and the practice of both sides in dealing with specific incidents.").

14 Latter parts of this chapter will highlight North Korea's pattern of hostilities, a pattern that is so widespread that over 124 provocations were recorded from the beginning of the Korean War to March 2003 and many more in the years to follow. *See generally* Nanto, *supra* note 3; Mark E. Manyin, Emma Chanlett-Avery & Helene Machart, Cong. Research Serv., RL32743, North Korea: A Chronology of Events, October 2002–December 2004 (2005); Emma Chanlett-Avery, Mark E. Manyin, & Hannah Fischer, Cong. Research Serv., RL33389, North Korea: A Chronology of Events in 2005 (2006).

15 Morris, *supra* note 6, at 887.

16 *July 4th 1972 North–South Joint Statement*, COLUMBIA LAW SCHOOL, www2.law.columbia.edu/course_00S_L9436_001/North%20Korea%20materials/74js-en.htm (last visited Mar. 8, 2013).

17 *Agreement on Reconciliation, Non-Aggression and Exchanges and Cooperation between South and North*, COLUMBIA LAW SCHOOL, www2.law.columbia.edu/course_00S_L9436_001/North%20Korea%20materials/coree91.html (last visited Mar. 13, 2013) (*entered into force* Feb. 19, 1992).

18 *Inter-Korean Summit Agreement*, DAILYNK PLUS, www.dailynk.com/english/db_info.php?db_name=October%204%20Inter-Korean%20Summit%20Agreement (last visited Mar. 8, 2013).

19 *See* H.R. 376, 112th Cong. (2011) ("Whereas 58 years have passed after the signing of the ceasefire agreement at Panmunjom on July 27, 1953, and the peninsula still technically remains in a state of war … encourages North Korea to repatriate any American and South Korean POWs to their home countries to reunite with their families under the International Humanitarian Law set forth in the Geneva Convention relative to the treatment of Prisoners of War … calls upon North Korea to agree to the family reunions and immediate repatriation of the abductees under the International Humanitarian Law set forth in the Geneva Convention relative to the Protection of Civilian Persons in Time of War.").

20 *A Timeline of North Korea's Nuclear Development*, THE PROGRAM IN ARMS CONTROL, DISARMAMENT, AND INT'L SEC., UNIV. OF ILL. AT URBANA-CHAMPAIGN, www.acdis.illinois.edu/resources/arms-control-quick-facts/timeline-of-north-koreas-nuclear-development.html (last visited Mar. 13, 2013) [hereinafter *A Timeline of North Korea's Nuclear Development*].

21 Geneva Conventions of 12 August 1949, INT'L COMM. OF THE RED CROSS, www.icrc.org/ihl.nsf/WebSign?ReadForm&id=375&ps=P (last visited Mar. 13, 2013); *Geneva Convention for the Amelioration of the Condition of the Wounded and Sick in Armed Forces in the Field*, U.N. TREATY COLLECTION, www.treaties.un.org/pages/showDetails.aspx?objid=080000028015847c (last visited Mar. 13, 2013).

22 Nanto, *supra* note 3, at 3. The hijacking took place on February 16, 1958. *This Week in USAF and PACAF History 16–22 February 2009*, PACIFIC AIR FORCES, U.S. AIR FORCE, www.pacaf.af.mil/shared/media/document/AFD-090218-081.pdf (last visited Mar.

13, 2013). This hijacking was separate from the hijacking that took place in December 1969.

23 Protocol Additional to the Geneva Conventions of 12 August 1949, and relating to the Protection of Victims of International Armed Conflicts (Protocol I), 8 June 1977, INT'L COMM. OF THE RED CROSS, www.icrc.org/ihl.nsf/WebSign? ReadForm&id=470&ps=P (last visited Mar. 13, 2013); *Protocol Additional to the Geneva Conventions of 12 August 1949, and relating to the protection of victims of international armed conflicts (Protocol I)*, U.N. TREATY COLLECTION, www.treaties.un.org/pages/ showDetails.aspx?objid=08000002800f3586 (last visited Mar. 13, 2013).

24 *E.g.*, Geneva Convention for the Amelioration of the Condition of the Wounded and Sick in Armed Forces in the Field of August 12, 1949, art.2, *opened for signature* Aug. 12, 1949, 75 U.N.T.S. 30 (entered into force Oct. 21, 1950) [hereinafter Geneva Convention I].

25 Commentary on Convention (II) for the Amelioration of the Condition of Wounded, Sick, and Shipwrecked Members of Armed Forces at Sea of August 12, 1949, INT'L COMM. OF THE RED CROSS, www.icrc.org/ihl.nsf/COM/370-580005?OpenDocument (last visited Mar. 14, 2013) [hereinafter Geneva II Commentary].

26 *How is the Term "Armed Conflict" Defined in International Humanitarian Law?*, INT'L COMM. OF THE RED CROSS, 1–2 (Mar. 2008), www.icrc.org/eng/assets/files/other/opinion- paper-armed-conflict.pdf [hereinafter ICRC Opinion Paper].

27 See, for example, the United States' Congressional Research Services' many sources for a timeline of all such provocations from 1950 to early 2007. Nanto, *supra* note 3, *passim*; Chanlett-Avery, Manyin, & Fischer, *supra* note 14, *passim*; Manyin, Chanlett- Avery & Machart, *supra* note 14, *passim*; Hannah Fischer, Cong. Research Serv., RL30004, North Korean Provocative Actions, 1950–2007, *passim* (2007).

28 Protocol Additional to the Geneva Conventions of 12 August 1949, and Relating to the Protection of Victims of International Armed Conflicts (Protocol I), art 2, *opened for signature* June 8, 1977, 1125 U.N.T.S. 3 (entered into force Dec. 7, 1978) [hereinafter Geneva Protocol I].

29 INT'L COMM. OF THE RED CROSS, COMMENTARY ON THE ADDITIONAL PROTOCOLS OF 8 JUNE 1977 TO THE GENEVA CONVENTIONS OF 12 AUGUST 1949, ¶1943 (Yves Sandoz et al. eds., 1987), *available at* www.loc.gov/rr/frd/Military_Law/pdf/Commentary_GC_ Protocols.pdf.

30 *Protocol Additional to the Geneva Conventions of 12 August 1949, and relating to the protection of victims of international armed conflicts (Protocol I)*, U.N. TREATY COLLECTION, www.treaties. un.org/pages/showDetails.aspx?objid=08000002800f3586 (last visited June 8, 2014).

31 Geneva Protocol I, *supra* note 28, at art. III.

32 Commentary on Protocol Additional to the Geneva Conventions of 12 August 1949, and relating to the Protection of Victims of International Armed Conflicts (Protocol I), 8 June 1977, INT'L COMM. OF THE RED CROSS, www.icrc.org/ihl.nsf/COM/470- 750006?OpenDocument (last visited Mar. 14, 2013).

33 More evidence of this meaning is found in the next paragraph of the commentary: "The general close of military operations may occur after the 'cessation of active hos- tilities' referred to in Article 118 of the Third Convention: although a ceasefire, even a tacit ceasefire, may be sufficient for that Convention, military operations can often continue after such a ceasefire, even without confrontations." *Id.*

34 Geneva II Commentary, *supra* note 25.

35 *Id.*

36 *Prosecutor v. Tadic*, Case No.IT-94-1-I, Decision on Defence Motion for Interlocutory Appeal on Jurisdiction, ¶70 (Int'l Crim. Trib. for the Former Yugoslavia Oct. 2, 1995).

37 *Id.*¶ 67.

38 *Prosecutor v. Tadic*, Case No.IT-94-1-A, Judgment, ¶84 (Int'l Crim. Trib. for the Former Yugoslavia, July 15, 1999).

39 *Prosecutor v. Kupreskic*, Case No.IT-95-16-T, Judgment, ¶545 (Int'l Crim. Trib. for the Former Yugoslavia, Jan. 14, 2000); *see also Prosecutor v. Boskoski & Tarculovski*, Case No. IT-04-82-T, Judgment, ¶175 (Int'l Crim. Trib. for the Former Yugoslavia, July 10, 2008).

40 *Prosecutor v. Naletilic & Martinovich*, Case No.IT-98-34-A, Judgment, ¶116–17 (Int'l Crim. Trib. for the Former Yugoslavia, May 3, 2006).

41 Bartram S. Brown, *Nationality and Internationality in International Humanitarian Law*, 34 STAN.J. INT'L L. 347, 376–77 (1998).

42 Nanto, *supra* note 3, at 23.

43 Geneva Convention Relative to the Treatment of Prisoners of War of August 12, 1949, arts. 12–17, 24–25, 34, 38, 60–67, 70, 79–81, 126, 129, 130 & 131, *opened for signature* Aug. 12, 1949, 75 U.N.T.S. 134 (entered into force Oct. 21, 1950) [hereinafter Geneva Convention III]. Crucial articles of the convention are found at Article 13 ("Prisoners of war must at all times be humanely treated. Any unlawful act or omission by the Detaining Power causing death or seriously endangering the health of a prisoner of war in its custody is prohibited, and will be regarded as a serious breach of the present Convention") and Article 129 ("The High Contracting Parties undertake to enact any legislation necessary to provide effective penal sanctions for persons committing, or ordering to be committed, any of the grave breaches of the present Convention defined in the following Article.").

44 *E.g.*, Nanto, *supra* note 3, at 5 & n. 10.

45 DEFENSE WHITE PAPER, Ministry of Defense, Republic of Korea, 157 (2008), *available at* WWW.MND.GO.KR/USER/MND_ENG/UPLOAD/PBLICTN/PBLICTNEBOOK_20130808070 3502930.pdf. THIS NUMBER IS SAID TO STILL BE AS HIGH AS 500 AS RECENTLY AS JUNE OF 2013. S. KOREAN LAWMAKERS URGE N. KOREA TO RETURN POWS, The Korea Herald (JUNE 24, 2013), www.koreaherald.com/view.php?ud=20130624001090.

46 Emma Chanlett-Avery & Ian E. Rinehart, Cong. Research Serv., R41259, North Korea: U.S. Relations, Nuclear Diplomacy, and Internal Situation (2014), *available at* www.fas.org/sgp/crs/nuke/R41259.pdf.

47 *See, e.g.*, Geneva Convention III, *supra* note 43, at arts. 17 & 130.

48 In fact, few non-citizens of the DPRK can find their way into the North. Even the Special Rapporteurs appointed by the U.N. Office of the High Commissioner for Human Rights have been disallowed from entering North Korea to investigate mass human rights abuses. *See, e.g.*, G.A. Res. 67/181, ¶1, U.N. Doc.A/RES/67/181 (Mar. 20, 2013) ("The continued refusal of the Government of the Democratic People's Republic of Korea to recognize the mandate of the Special Rapporteur on the situation of human rights in the Democratic People's Republic of Korea or to extend cooperation to him, despite the renewal of the mandate by the Human Rights Council in its resolutions 7/15, 10/16, 13/14, 16/8 and 19/13").

49 Geneva Convention Relative to the Protection of Civilian Persons in Time of War of August 12, 1949, arts. 4, 25, 27, 29, 31, 32, 34, 35, 37, 85, 89, 90, 92–94, 101–04, 116, 132, 142–43, 147 & 148, *opened for signature* Aug 12, 1949, 75 U.N.T.S. 286 (entered into force Oct. 21, 1950) [hereinafter Geneva Convention IV].

50 Nanto, *supra* note 3, at 5, 7, 10, 12, & 20.

51 A good definition of "hostage taking" that demonstrates North Korea is likely violating international law can be found in Article 1 of the International Convention Against the Taking of Hostages, a convention that unfortunately they are not a party to: "Any person who seizes or detains and threatens to kill, to injure or to continue to detain another person … in order to compel a third party, namely, a State, an international intergovernmental organization, a natural or juridical person, or a group of persons, to do or abstain from doing any act as an explicit or implicit condition for the release

of the hostage commits the offence of taking of hostages ('hostage taking') within the meaning of this Convention." International Convention Against the Taking of Hostages, art. 1, *opened for signature* Dec. 17, 1979, 1316 U.N.T.S. 1982 (*entered into force* June 3, 1983).

52 Geneva Convention IV, *supra* note 49, at arts. 83 ("The Detaining Power shall give the enemy Powers, through the intermediary of the Protecting Powers, all useful information regarding the geographical location of places of internment. Whenever military considerations permit, internment camps shall be indicated by the letters 1C, placed so as to be clearly visible in the daytime from the air. The Powers concerned may, however, agree upon any other system of marking. No place other than an internment camp shall be marked as such.") & 132 ("Each interned person shall be released by the Detaining Power as soon as the reasons which necessitated his internment no longer exist.").

53 *See, e.g.*, David Hawk, *Concentrations in Inhumanity*, U.S Comm. for Human Rights in N. Korea, 8(2003), *available at* www.freedomhouse.org/uploads/special_report/53.pdf (one of several of David Hawk's reports from defectors finding that up to 200,000 North Koreans are in such camps across the North).

54 Geneva Protocol I, *supra* note 28, at arts. 11, 32–34, 48, 51& 60.

55 *Id.* at arts. 75, 85 & 91.

56 Chanlett-Avery, Manyin & Fischer, *supra* note 14, at 12–13.

57 *Id.*

58 Chanlett-Avery, Manyin & Fischer, *supra* note 14, at 7.

59 Emma Chanlett-Avery & Ian E. Rinehart, Cong. Research Serv., R41259, North Korea: U.S. Relations, Nuclear Diplomacy, and Internal Situation 9 (2013).

60 *Convention on the Prevention and Punishment of Crimes against Internationally Protected Persons, including Diplomatic Agents*, U.N. Treaty Collection, www.treaties.un.org/Pages/ViewDetails.aspx?src=IND&mtdsg_no=XVIII-7&chapter=18&lang=en (last visited Apr. 2, 2013).

61 Convention on the Prevention and Punishment of Crimes against Internationally Protected Persons, Including Diplomatic Agents, arts. 1–3 & 5, *opened for signature* Dec. 14, 1973, 1035 *U.N.T.S.* 167 (entered into force Feb. 20, 1977) [hereinafter Diplomatic Agents Convention].

62 Chanlett-Avery, Manyin & Fischer, *supra* note 14, at 8–9.

63 Loosely translated, *pacta sunt servanda* means "treaty obligations must be met" or "kept" in Latin. Benjamin Neaderland, *Quandary on the Yalu: International Law, Politics, and China's North Korean Refugee Crisis*, 40 Stan. J. Int'l L. 143, 157 (2004).

64 Convention on the Rights of the Child, art. 38, *opened for signature* Nov. 20, 1989, 1577 U.N.T.S. 3 (*entered into force* Sept. 2, 1990) [hereinafter Child Convention].

65 *Convention on the Rights of the Child*, U.N. Treaty Collection, www.treaties.un.org/pages/ViewDetails.aspx?src=TREATY&mtdsg_no=IV-11&chapter=4&lang=en (last visited Apr. 4, 2013).

66 Chanlett-Avery, Manyin & Fischer, *supra* note 14, at 19.

67 Morse Tan, *The North Korean Nuclear Crisis: Past Failures and Present Solutions*, 50 St. Louis U. L.J. 517, 539 (2006).

68 International Convention for the Suppression of the Financing of Terrorism, Preamble & arts. 4–19, *opened for signature* Dec. 9, 1999, 2178 U.N.T.S. 179 (entered into force Apr. 10, 2002) [hereinafter Terrorism Convention].

69 *International Convention for the Suppression of the Financing of Terrorism*, U.N. Treaty Collection, www.treaties.un.org/pages/ViewDetails.aspx?src=TREATY&mtdsg_no=XVIII-11&chapter=18&lang=en (last visited Apr. 2, 2013).

70 *See generally* Bruce E. Bechtol, Jr., *North Korea and Support to Terrorism: An Evolving History*, 3 J. Strategic Security 45 (2010) (giving a history of North Korea's support

to terrorist and radical groups, including the Japanese Red Army and the Popular Front for the Liberation of Palestine); *see also* Chanlett-Avery, Manyin & Fischer, *supra* note 14, at 24 (describing the Scud missiles on their way to Yemen in 2002 found by allied forces in the Persian Gulf aboard a North Korean ship).

71 Bechtol, *supra* note 70, at 49–51 (giving a more recent history of North Korean terrorist financing and aid).

72 *Convention on the Prevention and Punishment of the Crime of Genocide*, U.N. TREATY COLLECTION, www.treaties.un.org/pages/ViewDetails.aspx?src=TREATY&mtdsg_no=IV-1&chapter=4&lang=en (last visited Apr. 3, 2013).

73 Convention on the Prevention and Punishment of the Crime of Genocide, arts. I–III, *opened for signature* Dec. 9, 1948, 78 U.N.T.S. 277 (entered into force Jan. 12, 1951) [hereinafter Genocide Convention].

74 *See, e.g.*, Morse H. Tan, *A State of Rightlessness: The Egregious Case of North Korea*, 80 MISS. L.J. 681, 699 (2010) (providing the testimony of a sixty-four-year-old grandmother witnessing the execution of half-Chinese infants).

75 *See* David Hawk's numerous articles of refugee and defector testimony on the brutal treatment and executions of these infants: David Hawk, *The Hidden Gulag: Exposing North Korea's Prison Camps*, U.S COMM. FOR HUMAN RIGHTS IN N. KOREA, *passim* (2003), *available at* www.hrnk.org/ HiddenGulag.pdf; David Hawk, *The Hidden Gulag: The Lives and Voices of "Those Who are Sent to the Mountains"* COMM. FOR HUMAN RIGHTS IN N. KOREA, *passim* (2012) *available at* www.davidrhawk.com/HRNK_HiddenGulag2_Web_5-18.pdf; *see also* Kook-shin Kim, et. al., *White Paper on Human Rights in North Korea*, KOREA INST. FOR NAT'L UNIFICATION, 513–20 (2011), *available at* www.kinu.or.kr/eng/pub/pub_04_01.jsp?page=1&num=32&mode=view&field=&text=&order=&dir=&bid=DATA04&ses=.

76 *See, e.g.*, Robert Park, *North Korea and the Genocide Movement*, HARV. INT'L REV. (Sept. 27, 2011), www.hir.harvard.edu/north-korea-and-the-genocide-movement.

77 Convention on the Non-applicability of Statutory Limitations to War Crimes and Crimes Against Humanity, Preamble & arts. I, II, & IV, *opened for signature* Nov. 26, 1968, 754 U.N.T.S. 73 (entered into force Nov. 11, 1970) [hereinafter War Crimes Convention].

78 *Convention on the Non-applicability of Statutory Limitations to War Crimes and Crimes Against Humanity*, U.N. TREATY COLLECTION, www.treaties.un.org/pages/ViewDetails. aspx? src=TREATY&mtdsg_no=IV-6&chapter=4&lang=en (last visited Apr. 3, 2013).

79 Protocol for the Prohibition of the Use of Asphyxiating, Poisonous or Other Gases, and of Bacteriological Methods of Warfare, Geneva, *opened for signature* June 17, 1925 (entered into force Feb. 8, 1928) [hereinafter Gas Protocol] ("That the High Contracting Parties … agree to extend this prohibition to the use of bacteriological methods of warfare").

80 Convention on the Prohibition of the Development, Production and Stockpiling of Bacteriological (Biological) and Toxin Weapons and on their Destruction, arts. 1–4 & 9, *opened for signature* Apr. 10, 1972 (entered into force Mar. 26, 1975) [hereinafter Biological Weapons Convention].

81 *Chemical and Biological Weapons: Possession and Program Past and Present*, JAMES MARTIN CTR. FOR NONPROLIFERATION STUDIES, MONTEREY INST. OF INT'L STUDIES, www.cns. miis.edu/cbw/possess.htm (last visited Mar. 30, 2013).

82 *North Korea: Biological*, NUCLEAR THREAT INITIATIVE, www.nti.org/country-profiles/north-korea/biological/ (last visited Mar. 30, 2013).

83 *See, e.g.*, John R. Bolton, U.S. Ambassador to the U.N., Beyond the Axis of Evil: Additional Threats from Weapons of Mass Destruction Lecture at the Heritage Foundation (May 6, 2002) (transcript available at www.heritage.org/research/lecture/beyond-the-axis-of-evil) ("North Korea has a dedicated, national-level effort to

achieve a BW capability and has developed and produced, and may have weaponized, BW agents in violation of the Convention.").

84 *States Party to the Following International Humanitarian Law and Other Related Treaties as of 15-Nov-2012*, INT'L COMM. OF THE RED CROSS, 9 (Nov. 15, 2012), www.icrc. org/IHL.nsf/(SPF)/party_main_treaties/$File/IHL_and_other_related_Treaties. pdf (showing that North Korea signed the Biological Weapons Convention on March 13, 1987); see also the U.S. Secretary of Defense's sources and investigations of North Korea's various chemical, biological, and nuclear capabilities at www. fas.org/nuke/guide/dprk/bw/index.html   and   http://www.fas.org/irp/threat/ prolif00.pdf.

85 *See generally* JEAN-MARIE HENCKAERTS & LOUISE DOSWALD-BECK, CUSTOMARY INTERNATIONAL HUMANITARIAN LAW, VOLUME I: RULES (2005) (providing the results of a study of the Red Cross regarding basic customary IHL Rules).

86 *See, e.g.,* J. Ashley Roach, *Certain Conventional Weapons Convention: Arms Control or Humanitarian Law?* 105 MIL. L. REV. 3, 35–36 ("The 1949 Conventions however 'replace,' 'complement,' or 'supplement' earlier Geneva and Hague Conventions in relations between powers who are bound by both.").

87 *See, e.g.,* Hague Convention No. VII Relating to the Conversion of Merchant Ships into War-Ships, 18 October 1907, arts. 1, 3, 5 & 6, 205 Consol. T.S. 319 (entered into force Jan. 26, 1910) (prohibiting naval bombardment of various civilian targets).

88 *Democratic People's Republic of Korea: Practice Relating to Rule 74. Chemical Weapons*, INT'L COMM. FOR THE RED CROSS, www.icrc.org/customary-ihl/eng/docs/v2_cou_kp_ rule74 (last visited Apr. 4, 2013).

89 *See North Korea: Chemical*, NUCLEAR THREAT INITIATIVE, www.nti.org/country-profiles/ north-korea/chemical/ (last visited Apr. 4, 2013); *DPRK: Chemical Weapons*, FED'N OF AM. SCIENTISTS, www.fas.org/nuke/guide/dprk/facility/cw.htm (last visited Apr. 4, 2013) ("North Korea has at least eight industrial facilities that can produce chemical agents, and probably nearly twice this many; however, the production rate and types of munitions are uncertain.").

90 See several of the Hague conventions and other conventions regarding the prohibition of the use of poisons and asphyxiating gas in warfare: Hague Convention No. II of July 29, 1899, with Respect to the Laws and Customs of War on Land, art. 23, 32 Stat. 1803, T.S. No. 403 (*entered into force* Sept. 4, 1900); Hague Convention No. IV Respecting the Laws and Customs of War on Land and its Annex: Regulations Concerning the Laws and Customs of War on Land, art. 23, Oct. 18, 1907, 36 Stat. 2277, 205 Consol. T.S. 277 (*entered into force* Sept. 4, 1900); Hague Convention IV, Declaration II- Concerning the Prohibition of the Use of Projectiles Diffusing Asphyxiating Gases, July 29, 1899, 26 Martens Nouveau Recueil (ser. 2) 998, 187 Consol. T.S. 453 (*entered into force* Sept. 4, 1900); Hague Convention No. VII of October 18, 1907, Relating to the Conversion of Merchant Ships into War-Ships, 205 Consol. T.S. 319 (entered into force Jan. 26, 1910); Project of an International Declaration concerning the Laws and Customs of War, art. 8, Brussels, 27 August 1874, *available at* www.icrc.org/ihl.nsf/FULL/135?OpenDocument; The Laws of War on Land, art. 8, Oxford, 9 September 1880, *available at* www.icrc.org/ihl.nsf/ FULL/140?OpenDocument.

91 *See North Korea: Chemical*, NUCLEAR THREAT INITIATIVE, *supra* note 89.

92 *Democratic People's Republic of Korea: Practice Relating to Rule 36. Demilitarized Zones*, INT'L COMM. FOR THE RED CROSS, www.icrc.org/customary-ihl/eng/docs/v2_cou_kp_ rule36 (last visited Apr. 4, 2013).

93 *Report on Preliminary Examination Activities 2012*, INT'L CRIMINAL CT., OFFICE OF THE PROSECUTOR, 15 (Nov. 2012), www.icc-cpi.int/NR/rdonlyres/C433C462- 7C4E-4358-8A72-8D99FD00E8CD/285209/OTP2012ReportonPreliminary Examinations22Nov2012.pdf.

94 *See, e.g., ICC Prosecutor Finds No Grounds to Investigate North Korea War Crime Allegations,* Jurist, www.jurist.org/paperchase/2014/06/icc-prosecutor-finds-no-grounds-to-investigate-north-korea-war-crime-allegations.php (June 25, 2014).

95 Press Release, Statement of the Prosecutor of the International Criminal Court, Fatou Bensouda, on the Conclusion of the Preliminary Examination of the Situation in the Republic of Korea, Int'l Criminal Court (June 23, 2014), *available at* www.icc-cpi.int/en_menus/icc/press%20and%20media/press%20releases/Pages/pr1019.aspx.

96 *E.g.,* Press Release, Office of the Prosecutor, Int'l Crim. Ct., ICC Prosecutor Presents Case Against Sudanese President, Hassan Ahmad AL BASHIR, for Genocide, Crimes Against Humanity and War Crimes in Darfur, Int'l Criminal Court (Jan. 11, 2012), *available at* www.icc-cpi.int/en_menus/icc/press%20and%20media/press%20releases/press%20releases%20(2008)/Pages/a.aspx.

97 *Report on Preliminary Examination Activities 2012,* Int'l Criminal Ct., Office of the Prosecutor, 15 (Nov. 2012), www.icc-cpi.int/NR/rdonlyres/C433C462-7C4E-4358-8A72-8D99FD00E8CD/285209/OTP2012ReportonPreliminary Examinations22Nov2012.pdf.

98 *See id.* at 15–17; art. 25.

99 *Rome Statute of the Int'l Crim. Ct.,* art.75, U.N. Treaty Source, U.N. Doc. A/CONF.183/9, *available at* www.untreaty.un.org/cod/icc/statute/romefra.htm.art ("The Court may make an order directly against a convicted person specifying appropriate reparations to, or in respect of, victims, including restitution, compensation and rehabilitation.").

100 *Pre-Trial Division,* Int'l Crim. Ct., www.icc-cpi.int/en_menus/icc/structure%20of%20the%20court/chambers/pre%20trial%20division/Pages/pre%20trial%20division.aspx (last visited Aug. 16, 2014).

101 Geneva Convention III, *supra* note 43, at art. 132.

102 Geneva Convention IV, *supra* note 49, at art. 149.

103 Geneva Protocol I, *supra* note 28, at 93.

104 *E.g., Prosecutor v. Naletilic & Martinovich,* Case No. IT-98-34-A, Judgment, ¶117 (Int'l Crim. Trib. for the Former Yugoslavia, May 3, 2006) (stating that the ICTY Statute gave the tribunal the jurisdiction to prosecute individuals for grave breaches of the Geneva Conventions of 1949).

105 Genocide Convention, *supra* note 73, at art. VIII.

106 Biological Weapons Convention, *supra* note 80, at art. VI.

107 *See, e.g.,* Press Release, U.N. Int'l Crim. Tribunal for the Former Yugoslavia, Radislav Krstic Becomes the First Person to be Convicted of Genocide at the ICTY and is Sentenced to 46 Years Imprisonment, U.N. Press Release OF/P.I.S./609e (Aug. 2, 2001), *available at* www.icty.org/sid/7964 (stating that Article 5 of the ICTY Statute defined genocide exactly the same as the Genocide Convention, which was used to convict Radislav Krstic of genocide on August 2, 2001).

108 *E.g.,* M. Cherif Bassiouni, *Universal Jurisdiction for International Crime: Historical Perspectives and Contemporary Practice,* 42 Va. J. Int'l L. 81, 106 (2001) ("As an *actio popularis,* universal jurisdiction may be exercised by a state without any jurisdictional connection or link between the place of commission, the perpetrator's nationality, the victim's nationality, and the enforcing state. The basis is, therefore, exclusively the nature of the crime and the purpose is exclusively to enhance world order by ensuring accountability for the perpetration of certain crimes.").

9 Nuclear defiance*

Trampling the NPT and ignoring the UNSC

In Chapter 8, we discussed North Korea's defiance in relation to the NPT. Supposed withdrawal from this proliferation agreement, continuous nuclear testing and satellite launching, withdrawing from the Six-Party Talks, etc. have played a large role in the DPRK's political charades over decades. With these startling events of brinkmanship, we begin the analysis of actually applying IHL to North Korea's actions.

One may ask why such acts involving the NPT bear any significance in relation to international armed conflict and international humanitarian law. There are two answers, namely: (1) by incorrectly withdrawing from the NPT and egregiously violating the treaty's provisions thereafter, North Korea has insistently defied international law, and (2) available jurisprudence suggests that such breaches and threats of nuclear violence violate the principles found in the U.N. Charter, and violate the general principles of international law applicable in armed conflict.

While North Korea often desires the obscurity of a dense fog, it has sometimes trumpeted its military focus and its production of nuclear weapons, eventually with international ballistic capabilities. North Korea remains the only state in history to attempt withdrawal from the NPT, an international treaty joined by 190 nations with the stated objective to prevent the spread of nuclear weapons and weapons technology, to promote cooperation in the peaceful uses of nuclear energy, and to further the goal of achieving nuclear disarmament.[1] North Korea ratified the NPT on December 12, 1985, but later provided official notice of its intent to withdraw on January 10, 2003. NPT Article X.1 requires a nation to provide ninety days' notice of its intent to withdraw before such withdrawal is officially accepted. On the eighty-ninth day after providing notice of its intent to withdraw, North Korea struck a deal with the United States known as the Agreed Framework and suspended its withdrawal notice.

Under the terms of the Agreed Framework, North Korea agreed to dismantle its one operable nuclear reactor power plant, as well as two then under construction. The United States sought this concession from North Korea since nuclear reactor plants can just as easily create weapons-grade enriched plutonium as they can function as an energy source. In exchange, North Korea would receive assistance from the United States to construct two light water reactor power plants, capable of providing an equitable amount of energy to the abandoned nuclear plants, as well as annual shipments of 500,000 tons of heavy oil to offset the energy deficit during the light water power plant construction.

In October 2002, North Korea's violation of the Agreed Framework by pursuing a secret uranium enrichment program was rebuked by the U.S., which suspended shipments of heavy oil to North Korea, and called for IAEA inspectors to conduct a thorough investigation. North Korea initially allowed the IAEA inspectors to begin their investigation, but after IAEA inspectors uncovered trace evidence of radiation and other markers consistent with uranium enrichment, North Korea quickly expelled the IAEA inspectors, destroyed their equipment, and, on January 10, 2003, announced that it officially ended the suspension of its prior notice of withdrawal from the NPT.[2] North Korea has since commenced a series of nuclear weapons tests, which began with an embarrassing nuclear fizzle in 2006,[3] thus blatantly violating the NPT. However, the world stopped laughing in 2009, when North Korea performed an unambiguously successful nuclear test, and, as an encore in 2013, set off a 1 km underground nuclear explosion coupled with claims that it had successfully miniaturized a nuclear warhead,[4] again blatantly violating the purpose and articles of the NPT.

Article X of the NPT states that parties may withdraw from the treaty if a state "decides that extraordinary events, related to the subject matter of this Treaty, have jeopardized the supreme interests of its country," further requiring the party to give notice of any withdrawal and the reasons for doing so to all contracting parties and the Security Council three months in advance.[5] North Korea simply did not satisfy these requirements, and thus the NPT still applies to its actions to date. When the DPRK first claimed its supreme interests were at stake, it highlighted two reasons: (1) South Korea's standard military exercises, and (2) the IAEA's biased nature toward inspections of nuclear facilities.[6] South Korea posed no nuclear threat to North Korea at this time—not having such capabilities—and the United States withdrew nuclear weapons in the region, albeit while retaining remote strike capabilities.[7]

Further, it strains credibility as to how any "biased" (so accused because it successfully uncovered illicit activity) IAEA special inspections regarding a small reprocessing plant posed any nuclear threat or other imminent threat to North Korea, or even amounted to an extraordinary event.[8] Indeed, the accurate analysis of the IAEA that circumvented the DPRK's attempts to hide its military nuclear program led to the DPRK's protest and ejection of IAEA inspectors and monitoring devices.[9] Additionally, the objections differed in the second notice of withdrawal, thereby destroying any legitimacy related to both supposed notices.[10]

Those parties that produced the NPT intended that the treaty's notice requirement help the Security Council and treaty members determine if valid reasons necessitating withdrawal exist based on a security threat to the withdrawing state, and whether to support, delay, or deny such withdrawal.[11] North Korea did not adequately allow this to happen and ignored the Council on several occasions when it concluded that no reason existed that necessitated withdrawal.[12]

Furthermore, North Korea cannot patch together notice time periods and get past the notice requirement by pulling out an antiquated withdrawal and reinstating it a decade in the future.[13] North Korea's approach ultimately frustrates the object and purpose of the treaty.

Additionally, IAEA safeguards and IAEA inspections should have continued during these withdrawal periods,[14] something not possible considering North Korea refused to allow inspectors into the few areas where it was likely producing nuclear weapons (i.e., the small reprocessing plant in Yongbyon)—well before a final supposed withdrawal in 2003.[15] In essence, North Korea's ineffective "withdrawal" keeps it *de jure* under the NPT. However, a compelling case has been made that even if North Korea had effectively withdrawn at its first attempt, the IAEA safeguards provisions still would have applied, resulting in a clear breach of the NPT's provisions.[16]

The NPT's application of its substantive provisions disallows the path that North Korea has pursued. Article II states that each party agrees "not to manufacture or otherwise acquire nuclear weapons or other nuclear explosive devices; and not to seek or receive any assistance in the manufacture of nuclear weapons or other nuclear explosive devices."[17] The DPRK has manufactured and tested nuclear weapons after acquiring nuclear centrifuge technology from Pakistan in return for medium-range ballistic missile technology.

Article III maintains that parties must accept IAEA safeguards and actions taken thereupon. North Korea essentially violated this article outright with its refusal to allow certain inspections in 1993 based on these safeguards, which ironically led to its attempted withdrawal from the treaty in the first place. Article VI requires parties

> to pursue negotiations in good faith on effective measures relating to cessation of the nuclear arms race at an early date and to nuclear disarmament, and on the treaty in general and complete disarmament under strict and effective international control.[18]

North Korea has repeatedly defied this principle in its outright condemnation and violations of many negotiated agreements related to nuclear proliferation and intentionally ignoring numerous Security Council resolutions, sometimes days after their promulgation. In short, North Korea has thoroughly violated the NPT.

Moreover, nuclear threats and any use of such weapons violate principles of international law even beyond the NPT. The International Court of Justice in its Legality of the Threat or Use of Nuclear Weapons Advisory Opinion (Nuclear Weapons Case) confirmed this notion. The Court unanimously concluded that "[a] threat or use of nuclear weapons should be compatible with the requirements of the international law applicable in armed conflict, particularly those of the principles and rules of international humanitarian law." The Court also found that an obligation exists "to pursue in good faith and bring to a conclusion negotiations leading to nuclear disarmament in all its aspects under strict and effective international control." With North Korea's repeated defiance of the NPT and the IAEA, as illustrated earlier, and the numerous inter-Korean and other agreements that it has signed to put an end to proliferation on the Korean Peninsula, good faith fails to fit North Korea's forcible reunification game. More importantly, a majority of the Court specified how these requirements fit together:

> [t]he threat or use of nuclear weapons would generally be contrary to the rules of international law applicable in armed conflict, and in particular the principles and rules of humanitarian law; [h]owever, in view of the current state of international law, and of the elements of fact at its disposal, the Court cannot conclude definitively whether the threat or use of nuclear weapons would be lawful or unlawful in an extreme circumstance of self-defence, in which the very survival of a State would be at stake.[19]

After the passing of the latest Security Council resolution on March 7, 2013, which strongly condemned North Korea's third nuclear test, the DPRK directly threatened a preemptive nuclear attack against the United States.[20] Just like the repeated threats directed to South Korea, in which the North has threatened to turn Seoul into a "sea of fire"[21], this reaction on March 7 included a statement by Army General Kang Pyo-Tolg Yong that long-range nuclear missiles would be launched against Washington, DC so that it would "be engulfed in a sea of fire."[22] These sorts of nuclear threats contravene the aforementioned International Court of Justice (ICJ) opinion. Additionally, North Korea does not make such threats out of self-defense, since neither aggression nor threat of aggression from any other state precipitated this highly inflammatory threat; conversely, it would be more appropriate under this standard for *South Korea* to put forth such threats—considering North Korea's systematic provocations and hostilities over the last fifty-five years against that state.

Furthermore, the ICJ also alluded that such nuclear threats violate certain aspects of customary international law. For example, the Court concluded in the Nuclear Weapons Case that "[a] threat or use of force by means of nuclear weapons that is contrary to Article 2, paragraph 4, of the United Nations Charter and that fails to meet all the requirements of Article 51, is unlawful."[23] Paragraph four indicates that U.N. members must refrain from using "threat or use of force against the territorial integrity or political independence of any state."[24] This paragraph and the Court's conclusion matter because North Korea ultimately aims to destroy the territorial integrity or political independence of South Korea and reunite the peninsula by force.[25] While previously not a member, the DPRK can now be found among the member states of the U.N. Furthermore, this principle may have risen to customary international law status.[26]

Keep in mind that all the while, in addition to violating international law by trampling on the NPT, the DPRK violated the U.N. Security Council's resolutions condemning North Korea's actions. For example, by conducting the nuclear test in February 2013, North Korea was essentially violating Resolutions 1695, 1718, 1874, and 2087. Since the first missile launch attempt in July 2006, every provocation related to proliferation thereafter violated a Security Council Resolution and, based on the strong wording of the latest resolution,[27] the Council may yet take more serious action against such defiance. More details of what the Council can do to curb these continued violations emerge in the latter chapters of this book.

No respect for agreement

In addition to the blatant breach of the Agreed Framework as described in Chapter 1, North Korea has a history of disrespecting the well-known tenet of *pacta sunt servanda* (i.e. generally agreements must be kept). At every turn, the DPRK violates its agreements with South Korea and the rest of the world. The North–South Joint Statement of 1972 states that any unification would have to be achieved peacefully without the use of military force. North and South Korea expressly agreed that each side would implement measures to stop military provocations that may lead to unintended armed conflicts. One concrete means to address this problem, still in use today even as North Korea proclaims to have voided the armistice, was to establish direct phone lines between Seoul and Pyongyang to prevent accidental military clashes.[28] As history has shown, this preventative measure has proven relatively unsuccessful, considering that less than two years later, in February 1974, North Korean patrol vessels sank two South Korean fishing boats and detained thirty fishermen. The agreement as a whole proved to be no more than empty words as six months after this incident, Park Chung Hee's wife (i.e., the Republic of Korea's First Lady at that time) was killed in an assassination attempt on her husband's life by an agent of a pro-North Korean group from Japan.[29] President Park's daughter serves as the current President of South Korea; the murder of her mother may still burn in her heart.

Twenty years later, through the Agreement on Reconciliation, Non-Aggression and Exchanges and Cooperation between South and North, in February 1992, the Koreas again wrote their concerns for the peninsula. In addition to agreeing that the parties should refrain from acts of sabotage and insurrection by the terms of Article IV, Article V states that both the North and South would "together endeavor to transform the present state of armistice into a firm state of peace between the two sides and shall abide by the present Military Armistice Agreement until such a state of peace is realized." The agreement continues to forbid armed aggression or force between the parties and requires peaceful resolution of disputes. Articles 12 and 14 looked to establish a South–North Joint Military Commission and a South–North Military Sub-Committee, in order to achieve "phased reductions in armaments including the elimination of weapons of mass destruction and attack capabilities," as well as to help "remove the state of military confrontation" between the parties.[30] However, not more than three months after these agreements, three agents of the DPRK in South Korean uniforms who charged across the DMZ were shot dead at Cholwon, Kangwondo.[31]

Also at this time, the Koreas signed the Joint Declaration of South and North Korea on the Denuclearization of the Korean Peninsula, which declared that neither Korea would use nuclear weapons and that nuclear capabilities would only be used for peaceful purposes.[32] In even more blatant defiance of these two agreements, a mere year after signing both, North Korea announced its first attempt at withdrawal from the NPT.[33]

The defiance continued. Five years after the June 2000 North–South Declaration, which capitalized upon each Korea's willingness to reunite families separated by the Korean conflict and settle unconverted long-term prisoners and other humanitarian issues,[34] the two Koreas signed the Joint Statement of the Fourth Round of the Six-Party Talks. This latter statement and the Six-Party Talks in general aimed to denuclearize the Korean Peninsula again through peaceful terms. Beyond the aforementioned denuclearization agreement in which the DPRK committed to abandoning all nuclear weapons and existing nuclear programs and returning to the NPT and IAEA safeguards, it also asseverated that the parties would "negotiate a permanent peace regime on the Korean Peninsula at an appropriate separate forum."[35] Yet even during the time between the North–South Declaration and these Six-Party Talks, North Korea still test-fired missiles.[36] Furthermore, just a year after this Six-Party Talk Joint Statement, North Korea attempted to test yet another long-range missile, prompting U.N. Security Council Resolution 1695, which condemned the tests.[37]

North Korea understands the current state of war on the peninsula and continues to utilize it to intimidate all parties involved. The Inter-Korean Summit Agreement of October 2007 clearly restated this state of war. This agreement reiterates the same commitment by both sides—that each would work together to end military hostilities and tensions to guarantee peace; however, it also stated that

> [t]he South and the North *both recognize the need to end the current armistice regime and build a permanent peace regime.* The South and the North have also agreed to work together to advance the matter of having the leaders of the three or four parties directly concerned to convene on the Peninsula and *declare an end to the war.*[38] [emphasis added]

Did the DPRK stop its provocations after this agreement? Unfortunately, the answer continues in the negative. Two years after this 2007 agreement, North Korea conducted yet another illegal nuclear test.[39] The vicious cycle continues to spin.

The intersection of IHL, international security, and human rights

As highlighted in previous chapters, North Korea has an atrocious human rights record. Although many scholars tend to differentiate the fields of international human rights law (IHR) and IHL, the two can fit together rather well, especially in characterizing North Korea's violations of international law and future liability. A few international courts have recognized this link, and their opinions tend to demonstrate that if North Korea's leaders were to be indicted and prosecuted under IHL, human rights law would appropriately find itself part of the proceedings.

One of the first courts to discuss the connection between these two major areas of international law was the ICJ in 2004. In the ICJ's *Legal Consequences of the Construction of a Wall in the Occupied Palestinian Territory* (Palestinian Case) Advisory Opinion, the court explained that protections offered by IHR conventions do not stop operating during an armed conflict. Derogation clauses, however, may apply. The Court said that although each of these areas of the law afford distinctive rights, areas of overlap also exist; accordingly, the Court said it had to look at both to determine whether rights had been violated in the occupied territory of Palestine. For example, the Court found that Article 2 of the Child Convention applied to the occupied territory in dispute, even though the events the Court addressed transpired in the midst of an international armed conflict.[40]

Additionally, other human rights courts have had similar thinking regarding applying IHL. For example, the Inter-American Court of Human Rights in the *Case of the Mapiripán Massacre v. Colombia* stated that it was necessary to analyze IHL principles to interpret the American Convention on Human Rights and find Colombia civilly liable for its paramilitary groups torturing and killing civilians in the town of Mapiripán.[41] Judge A. A. Cançado Trindade, in a separate opinion, not only agreed with the convergence of these areas of international law, he stated that the convergence clearly includes International Refugee Law as well.[42] The U.N. Commission on Human Rights has clearly recognized this link, providing guidance for states on internal displacement of refugees.[43]

The ICJ reaffirmed its commitment to utilizing both IHR and IHL when assessing civil liability of states in armed conflict. In *Armed Activities on the Territory of the Congo (Democratic Republic of the Congo v. Uganda)*, the court cited the Palestinian Case when finding that it should consider a number of IHR instruments and agreements in order to analyze whether the Uganda People's Defence Forces (UPDF) violated international law during the civil war in the Congo. After looking at both types of law, the court found that the UPDF had violated customary IHL (i.e., the Hague Regulations) and various principles of IHR law in its occupation of Ituri and fighting in Kisangani by indiscriminately attacking civilians, killing, torturing and inhumanely treating the Congolese civilian population, inciting ethnic conflict, and failing to take measures to put an end to the armed conflict.[44]

Another example comes from the Inter-American Commission on Human Rights. In a case regarding indiscriminate bombing during an internal conflict in Colombia, the Commission provided an *apropos* quotation in relation to North Korea and other states that abuse human rights in the midst of armed conflicts:

> The events of the present case are framed in the context of the internal armed conflict of Colombia, which does not exonerate the State from respecting and guaranteeing respect for basic human rights of individuals not directly involved, in accordance with the provisions of Common Article 3 of the Geneva Conventions. In this regard, the Commission considers that the State has general and special duties to protect the civilian population under its care, derived from international humanitarian law.[45]

These opinions demonstrate that if North Korea's leaders came before a tribunal or if North Korea as a nation-state stood before an international court, its human rights violations would substantially supplement its liability. This nexus should wax even clearer in what follows.

In addition to the case law regarding the application of IHL during armed conflict in the Korean context, ample case precedent from various international courts demonstrates that North Korea and its leaders could find themselves prosecuted for their continued hostilities and human rights abuses during the ongoing Korean conflict. North Korea's genocidal tendencies toward religious groups and Chinese (and even partially Chinese) children have generated grave concerns.

Genocide, a *jus cogens* norm, can yield even more serious consequences. For example, the International Criminal Tribunal for Rwanda (ICTR) has concluded that, at least under the ICTR's statute, incitement to commit genocide does not have to be public or even successful.[46] Specifically, the ICTR has stated that preventing births of an ethnic group, which North Korea has clearly done, qualifies as genocide.[47] In fact, the International Criminal Tribunal for the Former Yugoslavia (ICTY) has found that any act committed with intent to destroy a group in whole or part constitutes an act of genocide.[48] North Korea's leaders should take heed because the ICTY (prosecuting former President Milosevic) and the ICTR have asserted that heads of government have no immunity from any criminal liability for genocidal acts; they demonstrated this by convicting the former Prime Minister of Rwanda, Jean Kambanda, for genocide, ordering a life sentence.[49]

The DPRK should think twice before engaging in the torture of POWs, like those from the *U.S.S. Pueblo*, or its own people. As the Inter-American Court of Human Rights has pointed out, torture rises to the level of a *jus cogens* violation (like genocide) and its prohibition does not cease during wartime.[50] In addition, North Korea should desist from rape as the ICTY has pointed out that rape can qualify as a form of torture.[51] The Rome Statute, the constitutive treaty of the International Criminal Court, also counts rape as a crime against humanity.[52]

North Korea's military hostilities raise further concerns for liability. Courts like the European Court of Human Rights have found nations civilly liable for IHL violations like indiscriminate bombing and killing of civilians. Such bombings can violate the right to life under IHR law as well.[53] In other words, North Korea may yet incur legal culpability for shelling areas like Yeonpyeong Island.

Moreover, the DPRK must take note that even the well-worn defense of merely "following orders" does not immunize its military and civilian personnel for IHL and IHR law transgressions, although it may mitigate culpability.[54] So long as any accused exercised effective control over his or her subordinates when a crime was committed (i.e., *de jure* or *de facto* control), he or she can also be criminally liable for said crime.[55] It is "the failure of an official to fulfill his obligation to prevent or to punish criminal conduct" that incurs liability to everyone in the chain for the crimes committed.[56] Much of North Korea's military and governmental elite remain vulnerable in regards to IHL and IHR atrocities against their own people as well as those of other nations. This discussion provides a transition into the next chapter, analyzing North Korea's horrendous human rights situation under germane law.

Notes

* Kevin Zickterman assisted capably on this chapter.
1 *Treaty on the Non-Proliferation of Nuclear Weapons (NPT)*, UNITED NATIONS OFFICE FOR DISARMAMENT AFFAIRS, *available at* www.un.org/disarmament/WMD/Nuclear/NPT. shtml.
2 North Korea caused an international uproar by claiming NPT Article X.1 only required one more day's notice to effectuate an official withdrawal from the NPT, given its 89 days' notice, which it "suspended". Article X.1 only specifically requires a state to give three months' notice in total, and does not provide for other states to question a state's interpretation of "supreme interests of its country." While the IAEA Board of Governors and most countries rejected this interpretation, the Joint Statement of Sept. 19, 2005 issued at the conclusion of the Fourth Round of the Six-Party Talks called for North Korea to "return" to the NPT, implicitly acknowledging that it had withdrawn.
3 Graham P. Collins, *Kim's Big Fizzle*, SCIENTIFIC AMERICAN (Dec. 16, 2006) *available at* www.scientificamerican.com/article/kims-big-fizzle/.
4 Julian Borger, *North Korea's third test brings it closer to nuclear power status*, GUARDIAN (Feb. 12, 2013), www.theguardian.com/world/julian-borger-global-security-blog/2013/feb/12/north-korea-nuclear-test.
5 Treaty on the Non-Proliferation of Nuclear Weapons, art. X, *opened for signature* July 1, 1968, 729 U.N.T.S. 168 (entered into force Mar. 5, 1970) [hereinafter NPT].
6 George Bunn & Roland Timerbaev, *The Right to Withdraw from the Nuclear Non-Proliferation Treaty (NPT): The Views of Two NPT Negotiators*, YADERNY KONTROL (NUCLEAR CONTROL) DIG., Winter/Spring 2005, at 20, 21–22.
7 *Id.*; Morse Tan, *The North Korean Nuclear Crisis: Past Failures and Present Solutions*, 50 ST. LOUIS U. L.J. 517, 529 (2006).
8 *See* Bunn & Timerbaev, *supra* note 6, at 23.
9 JASPER BECKER, ROGUE REGIME: KIM JONG IL AND THE LOOMING THREAT OF NORTH KOREA 165–89 (2005).
10 *Id.* at 165–89 ("In North Korea's 2003 letter to NPT parties, it complained of President Bush's inclusion of it within his 'axis of evil' category and it maintained that the United States was targeting it for a preemptive strike. But, since it did not provide a new three-month withdrawal period, it had to have been relying on its 1993 notice of withdrawal as justification, and that notice did not contain these reasons.").
11 *Id.* at 22–23.
12 *See, e.g.*, S.C. Res. 2094, U.N. Doc. S/RES/2094 (Mar. 7, 2013) ("*Condemns* all the DPRK's ongoing nuclear activities, including its uranium enrichment, *notes* that all such activities are in violation of resolutions 1718 (2006), 1874 (2009) and 2087 (2013), *reaffirms* its decision that the DPRK shall abandon all nuclear weapons and existing nuclear programmes, in a complete, verifiable and irreversible manner and immediately cease all related activities and shall act strictly in accordance with the obligations applicable to parties under the NPT and the terms and conditions of the IAEA Safeguards Agreement (IAEA INFCIRC/403)").
13 *See* Bunn & Timerbaev, *supra* note 6, at 23 ("In North Korea's view, by its 2003 announcement and a one-day notice period, it had fulfilled the NPT's three-month notice requirement because it was relying on the 89 days that had gone by after the 1993 notice was given before North Korea announced that the 1993 notice was no longer in effect.").

14 *See, e.g.*, Antonio F. Perez, *Survival of Rights under the Nuclear Non-Proliferation Treaty: Withdrawal and the Continuing Right of International Atomic Energy Agency Safeguards*, 34 VA. J. INT'L L. 749 (1994). This Article persuasively argues that North Korea bears responsibility for its violations of the safeguards provisions while it remained under the NPT.

15 Bunn & Timerbaev, *supra* note 6, at 20–21; *A Timeline of North Korea's Nuclear Development*, THE PROGRAM IN ARMS CONTROL, DISARMAMENT, AND INT'L SEC., UNIV. OF ILL. AT URBANA-CHAMPAIGN, www.acdis.illinois.edu/resources/arms-control-quick-facts/timeline-of-north-koreas-nuclear-development.html (last visited Aug. 11, 2014) [hereinafter *A Timeline of North Korea's Nuclear Development*].

16 *See* Perez, *supra* note 14. Professor Perez presented a compelling argument on the subject: that the IAEA's right to safeguards based on the special investigation requested before North Korea's withdrawal from the NPT, in effect, survived the withdrawal, thereby making North Korea's refusal to allow inspections a continued breach of the NPT's provisions, which could have been justification for Security Council sanctions. *Id.*

17 NPT, *supra* note 5, at art. II.

18 *Id.* at arts. III & IV.

19 Legality of the Threat or Use of Nuclear Weapons, Advisory Opinion, 1996 I.C.J. 226, 266–67 (July 9, 1996) [hereinafter *Nuclear Weapons Case*].

20 Edith, M. Lederer & Hyung-Jin Kim, *UN Approves New Sanctions Against North Korea*, CHI. DAILY LAW BULL. (Mar. 7, 2013), www.hosted2.ap.org/ILDLB/8ef5320729ce4298abefc1903704c7d5/Article_2013-03-07-UN-North%20Korea/id-8a27f53d080146fc8257fa8aadecb074?utm_source=subscriber&utm_medium=CDLBemail&utm_content=APhed_UN%20approves%20new%20sanctions%20against%20North%20Korea&utm_campaign=headlines.

21 Dick K. Nanto, Cong. Research Serv., RL30004, North Korea: Chronology of Provocations, 1950 – 2003 12 (2003) (detailing the hijacking of a South Korean airliner by North Korean agents less than five years after the signing of the armistice in February, 1958) ("03/1994—For the first time in more than two decades, North Korea issued a threat of war in an inter-Korean meeting in Panmunjom. In response to Seoul's chief delegate mentioning the possibility of U.N. sanctions against the North for its refusal to accept full international nuclear inspections, Pyongyang's chief delegate reportedly replied: 'Seoul is not far away from here. If a war breaks out, Seoul will turn into a sea of fire.'").

22 Lederer & Kim, *supra* note 20.

23 *Nuclear Weapons Case*, *supra* note 19, at 266.

24 Charter of the United Nations: Chapter 1: Purposes and Principles, UNITED NATIONS WEBSITE, www.un.org/en/documents/charter/chapter1.shtml (last visited Mar. 24, 2013).

25 *See, e.g.*, Morse Tan, *The North Korean Nuclear Crisis: Past Failures and Present Solutions*, 50 ST. LOUIS U. L.J. 517, 519, 527, 533–34 (2006).

26 *See, e.g.*, Mary Ellen O'Connell & Maria Alevras-Chen, *The Ban on the Bomb – And Bombing: Iran, the U.S., And the International Law of Self-Defense*, 57 SYRACUSE L. REV. 497, 502–03 (2007).

27 S.C. Res. 2094, U.N. Doc. S/RES/2094 (Mar. 7, 2013) ("*Condemns* in the strongest terms the nuclear test conducted by the DPRK on 12 February 2013 (local time) in violation and flagrant disregard of the Council's relevant resolutions").

28 *July 4th 1972 North-South Joint Statement*, COLUMBIA LAW SCHOOL, www2.law.columbia.edu/course_00S_L9436_001/North%20Korea%20materials/74js-en.htm (last visited Mar. 8, 2013).

29 Nanto, *supra* note 21, at 6.

30 *Agreement on Reconciliation, Non-Aggression and Exchanges and Cooperation between South and North*, COLUMBIA LAW SCHOOL, www2.law.columbia.edu/course_00S_L9436_001/

North%20Korea%20materials/coree91.html (last visited Mar. 13, 2013) (entered into force Feb. 19, 1992).

31 Nanto, *supra* note 21, at 11.

32 Joint Declaration of the Denuclearization of the Korean Peninsula, N. Korea–S. Korea, Jan. 20, 1992, 33 I.L.M. 569, *available at* www.cns.miis.edu/inventory/pdfs/aptkoreanuc.pdf.

33 *IAEA-North Korea: Nuclear Safeguards and Inspections 1993*, MONTEREY INS. OF INT'L STUDIES, CTR. FOR NONPROLIFERATIONSTUDIES, www.cns.miis.edu/archive/country_ north_korea/nuc/iaea93.htm (last visited Mar. 13, 2013).

34 *South–North Joint Declaration*, U.S. INST. OF PEACE, www.usip.org/files/file/resources/ collections/peace_agreements/n_skorea06152000.pdf (last visited Mar. 8, 2013).

35 *Joint Statement of the Fourth Round of the Six-Party Talks*, MINISTRY OF FOREIGN AFFAIRS OF THE PEOPLE'S REPUBLIC OF CHINA (Sept. 19, 2005), www.fmprc.gov.cn/eng/zxxx/ t212707.htm.

36 Emma Chanlett-Avery, Mark E. Manyin, & Hannah Fischer, Cong. Research Serv., RL33389, North Korea: A Chronology of Events in 2005, 15 (2006).

37 *A Timeline of North Korea's Nuclear Development, supra* note 15.

38 *Inter-Korean Summit Agreement*, DAILYNK PLUS, www.dailynk.com/english/db_info. php?db_name=October%204%20Inter-Korean%20Summit%20Agreement (last visited Mar. 8, 2013).

39 *A Timeline of North Korea's Nuclear Development, supra* note 15.

40 Legal Consequences of the Construction of a Wall in the Occupied Palestinian Territory, Advisory Opinion, ¶¶106 & 113, 2004 I.C.J. 136 (July 9, 2004).

41 *Mapiripán Massacre v. Colombia*, Merits, Reparations and Costs, Judgment, Inter-Am. Ct. H.R. (ser. C) No. 134, ¶115 (Sept. 15, 2005).

42 *Id.* ¶43 (Separate Opinion of Judge A.A. Cancado Trindade).

43 *See Guiding Principles on Internal Displacement*, U.N. COMM'N ON HUMAN RIGHTS (Sept. 2001), *available at* www.brookings.edu/~/media/Projects/idp/GPEnglish.pdf.

44 *Armed Activities on the Territory of the Congo (Democratic Republic of the Congo v. Uganda)*, ¶¶215–17, 219 & 220, 2005 I.C.J. 168 (Dec. 19, 2005).

45 *Matino Lopez et al. (Operation Genesis) v. Colombia*, Case 12.573, Inter-Am. Comm'n H.R., Report No. 67/11, ¶¶215 & 240 (2011).

46 *Prosecutor v. Akayesu*, Case No.ICTR-96-4-A, Judgment, ¶¶417, 482–83 (June 1, 2001) ("Akayesu was individually responsible, under Article 6(1) of the Statute, for genocide, direct and public incitement to commit genocide, and crimes against humanity, all extremely serious crimes."); *see also* Jose E. Alvarez, *Lessons from the Akayesu Judgment*, ILSA J. INT'L & COMP. L. 5, 1991, 361 ("[T]he judges elaborate the controversial offense of incitement to genocide. They find that incitement need not be *direct* but can be *implicit*.").

47 Alvarez, *supra* note 46, at 362 ("The Akayesu judges note that, 'in patriarchal societies, where membership of a group is determined by the identity of the father, an example of a measure intended to prevent births within a group is the case where, during rape, a woman of the said group is deliberately impregnated by a man of another group, with the intent to have her give birth to a child who will consequently not belong to its mother's group.'") (quoting the *Akayesu* trial judgment).

48 *Prosecutor v. Krstic*, Case No.IT-98-33-A, Judgment (Int'l Crim. Trib. for the Former Yugoslavia, Apr. 19, 2004).

49 *See generally* Kingsley Chiedu Moghalu, *International Humanitarian Law from Nuremberg to Rome: The Weighty Precedents of the International Criminal Tribunal for Rwanda*, 14 PACE INT'L L. REV. 273, 289–93 (2002) (discussing the ICTR case of *Kambanda v. Prosecutor* in which Kambanda was convicted on all counts indicted against him, including genocide).

50 *See, e.g., Gladys Carol Espinoza Gonzales v. Peru*, Case 11.157, Inter-Am. Comm'n H.R., Report No. 67/11, ¶172 (2011) (citing numerous Inter-American Court of Human Rights cases stating this principle).

51 Alvarez, *supra* note 46, at 362 ("For this purpose, the judges affirm that rape when inflicted by or at the instigation of or with the consent or acquiescence of a public official or other person acting in an official capacity constitutes torture.") (citing the *Akayesu* trial court opinion).

52 *Rome Statute of the Int'l Crim. Ct.*, art.7, U.N. Treaty Source, U.N. Doc. A/CONF.183/9, *available at* www.untreaty.un.org/cod/icc/statute/romefra.htm (expressly including "Rape, sexual slavery, enforced prostitution, forced pregnancy, enforced sterilization, or any other form of sexual violence of comparable gravity" under subsection (g) of art. 7, the article that lists the terms included in the phrase "crimes of humanity" as defined by the court).

53 *E.g., Isayeva, Yusupova & Bazayeva v. Russia*, App. Nos. 57947/00, 57948/00 and 57949/00 Eur. Ct. H.R., ¶¶199–200 (2005) ("To sum up, even assuming that that the military were pursuing a legitimate aim in launching 12 S-24 non-guided air-to-ground missiles on 29 October 1999, the Court does not accept that the operation near the village of Shaami-Yurt was planned and executed with the requisite care for the lives of the civilian population. The Court finds that there has been a violation of Article 2 of the Convention in respect of the responding State's obligation to protect the right to life of the three applicants and of the two children of the first applicant, Ilona Isayeva and Said-Magomed Isayev."); *Esmukhambetov & Others v. Russia*, App. No. 23445/03 Eur. Ct. H.R., ¶¶150–51 (2011) ("In sum, the Court considers that the indiscriminate bombing of a village inhabited by civilians—women and children being among their number—was manifestly disproportionate to the achievement of the purpose under Article 2 § 2 (a) invoked by the Government … There has accordingly been a violation of Article 2 of the Convention on that account.").

54 *See generally* Matthew Lippman, *Humanitarian Law: The Uncertain Contours of Command Responsibility*, 9 Tulsa J. Comp. & Int'l L. 1 (discussing numerous ICTY and ICTR cases that convicted defendants based on command responsibility).

55 *E.g., Prosecutor v. Kajelijeli*, Case No. ICTR 98-44A-A, Judgment, ¶¶84–85 (May 23, 2005).

56 Lippman, *supra* note 54, at 72.

10 Prosecuting Hell's doorstep[*]

As illustrated in Chapter 3, one can liken the DPRK's prison camps to the doorstep of Hell. While international law and even the DPRK Criminal Code (to some lesser degree) require some due process and humane treatment of the accused, the reality reflects a broken system of gross, systematic injustice and impunity.[1] Where rights to due process, security of person, and freedom from torture represent just a handful of rights required under international law, the accused in the DPRK more realistically face arbitrary arrest, extrajudicial decisions, starvation and torture during interrogation, and sentencing without a (fair) trial—even before stepping into a prison camp. If life outside a concentration camp is already one large jail, and pre-sentence detainment and interrogation are egregious, strong enough words do not exist to accurately detail the sheer nightmare that prisoners witness and experience inside.[2]

As mentioned in Chapter 3, in February 2014, the Commission of Inquiry on Human Rights in the DPRK released a report of detailed findings that demonstrated North Korea's continuous human rights violations.[3] It detailed human rights violations by the systematic use of violence, arbitrary arrest, incommunicado detainment, deliberate disappearance, torture, starvation, and little or no judicial process.[4] The government has disregarded, circumvented, and contravened international law and the DPRK's own Criminal Code, leaving the accused without legal protection.[5] Based on the key human rights conventions that the DPRK has itself ratified and its own domestic law, the North Korean government stands without excuse for its massive violations.

When the government suspects political crimes, the process runs as follows: officials arrest and detain the accused;[6] the officials interrogate and torture the accused into confessing;[7] they convict and sentence the "defendants" without a fair judicial hearing, and then send them to concentration camps until their demise.[8]

The government of the DPRK still denies the existence of these concentration camps; however, as explained in Chapter 3, overwhelming evidence exists[9] that an extensive system of political prisons has been operating since the 1950s throughout the nation.[10] The government does, however, acknowledge ordinary prison camps and short-term labor camps, allowed under the DPRK Criminal Code, Article 31, in order to reform prisoners through labor.[11] However, the

DPRK government only acknowledges a fraction of the system and its prisoners,[12] showcasing only a comparatively pristine model that meets some humane standards, while the vast majority of prisoners do not have such guarantees.[13] Even the short term labor camps for minor offenders transgress international human rights standards by imposing unlawful sentences of forced labor without a court conviction obtained by due process.[14]

International law

Through every step of the process, the DPRK frequently violates international law and its own Criminal Code. International law affords an accused numerous rights, and DPRK law purports to afford some of the same rights—while falling far short in practice. The DPRK must uphold the right to life, freedom from torture, the right to liberty and security of persons, and the right to a fair trial under the International Covenant on Civil and Political Rights (ICCPR).[15] The DPRK has specifically ratified this treaty. For example, ICCPR Article 9(3) requires a prompt judicial hearing following arrest, whereas the DPRK Criminal Code provides for a prosecutor (a member of the executive branch of government) to oversee the issue of a warrant and oversight of the initial detention process.[16] Its practices fall far short of the standards.

The regime ignores DPRK provisions that appear to accord with international standards or carve out broad exceptions therefrom. For example, Article 183 of the DPRK Criminal Code requires notification of suspects' families of an arrest and the reason for it within forty-eight hours.[17] In reality, political prisoners disappear without any notification or reason given to them, let alone their families receiving notice.[18] According to Article 127 of the Code, the Provincial People's Courts have jurisdiction over all political crimes with a potential for life imprisonment,[19] yet most disappear without any due process and certainly no judicial hearing, in direct violation of ICCPR Article 14, which requires a fair and public trial.[20] The DPRK Code claims to grant the accused the right to state-appointed counsel; however, if the state appoints any counsel at all, he often stands silent or turns on the accused.[21] Further, illustrating the uselessness of written laws to protect the rights of its people, the Constitution requires that trials must remain open to the public.[22] The praxis, vis-à-vis broad exceptions under the Code, allow for closed trials when in the state's interest of avoiding "negative impact."[23] Forced disappearances without any semblance of due process also violate DPRK law; specifically, Article 252 of the Code forbids usurping sentencing powers of the judiciary.[24]

The Criminal Code supposedly provides additional provisions to protect the accused. Article 167 prohibits forced confessions.[25] Article 253 disallows torture during interrogation—even providing for victim compensation.[26] In reality, these provisions remain on the pages rather than coming alive in practice. As illustrated in numerous other chapters, DPRK agents regularly torture for the purposes of extracting forced confessions. Rotten with human rights violations, the concentration camps of the DPRK deliberately destroy anyone who dares to undermine in the least the Supreme Leader or any state authority.[27] These concentration camps engage in "re-engineering the social fabric of [sic] DPRK by purging groups of people."[28] A pattern of starvation during interrogation and then in prison is but one deliberate and systematic method employed to control an already oppressed people.[29]

The atrocities mentioned occur prior to a judicial hearing or trial and serve to obtain a confession.[30] After the SSD accepts a confession, the accused marks a written document with his fingerprint, swearing to the accuracy and vowing silence regarding the interrogation.[31] Whether the accused will have a scintilla of due process depends on the nature of the crime; it remains less likely for those accused of political and religious "crimes".[32]

The SSD orders execution or sends the accused to a concentration camp after consulting with provincial and national SSD headquarters.[33] Because the order does not come from a court or other politically independent decision-maker, and thereby deprives the accused of due process, it runs afoul of both international and DPRK law. Most often the SSD investigates political "crimes"; only those of medium severity receive a court pronouncement, normally in accordance with political predetermination.[34] The courts do not typically involve themselves in sentencing for serious political crimes; however, high profile cases provide an opportunity for the DPRK to use the court to set an example and sentence someone to death.[35] Minor offenses usually bypass the court; the MPS subjects the accused to additional interrogation.[36]

When the SSD handles a case, severe political crimes typically bypass the judiciary, and the accused find themselves in a concentration camp.[37] MPS handling of a severe crime devolves more to a court, which often pronounces a prison sentence or the death penalty.[38] Investigations of minor offenses often bypass the court and the accused are sent to a forced labor camp for up to two years, without any due process.[39] This short-circuiting of due process also violates tenets of customary international law and general principles of international law.

Short-term labor camp inmates enjoy some rights that other prisoners do not, such as family visits.[40] However, the prisoners in short-term camps also suffer some of the same violations as those in ordinary prisons, including starvation.[41] These camps routinely violate international law because sentencing occurs extrajudicially without due process at the hands of an executive law enforcement agency.[42] This amounts to arbitrary detention and forced labor, forbidden under international labor organization standards.[43]

Regular executions, both public and private, take place as a matter of public policy in the DPRK, even for the most arbitrary "crimes." Many examples of these executions found expression in Chapter 3. In addition to forcing various individuals (both prisoners and not) to observe such executions (a violation of the ICCPR in itself), the DPRK's Criminal Code goes well beyond what the ICCPR permits for capital punishment. The North Korean Criminal Code under Article 27 allows for capital punishment but does so against Article 6 of the ICCPR, such as for demonstrations with an "anti-state purpose." Article 6 of the ICCPR, on the other hand, requires that the state not take life arbitrarily. The state must reserve capital punishment for the most heinous crimes after a decision by a court, with the right to appeal.[44] For example, economic crimes and "disloyal destruction for anti-state purposes" do not constitute heinous crimes deserving execution, a far cry from ICCPR Article 6.[45]

The Articles 6 and 14 of the ICCPR grant the accused the opportunity to have their cases reviewed by a higher tribunal, with the option to seek pardon for a commuted sentence. The frequent executions on the spot within these concentration camps does not comport with these Articles.[46]

In 1946, the United Nations' Economic and Social Council (ECOSOC) established the Commission on Human Rights in accordance with Article 68 of the U.N. Charter.[47] Soon after, the committee completed a draft of the Universal Declaration of Human Rights. Although this document was unanimously adopted by the General Assembly in December 1948, it was not initially intended to have binding force, but was rather a "common standard of achievement for all peoples and all nations."[48]

After passage, the Assembly called on "[m]ember countries to publicize the text of the Declaration and to cause it to be disseminated, displayed, read, and expounded principally in schools and other educational institutions, without distinction based on the political status of countries or territories."[49] Even though the document was not binding, it was still a significant milestone in that it significantly advanced the actualization of human rights, and has been likened to widely hailed documents like the Magna Carta. The document took more than two years to draft and generated a multitude of debates. Each clause of the document resulted in over 1,400 votes from fifty-eight member states. In the end, it was unanimously adopted on December 10, 1948.[50] The Declaration has been translated into approximately 250 languages and is the most cited document on human rights in the world.[51] The Declaration has inspired more than sixty "legally binding treaties" designed to promote the protection of human rights. Unlike any other instrument of its type, the Universal Declaration holds a special normative place in the international community.[52]

The Declaration states, "[E]veryone is entitled to all rights and freedoms set forth in this Declaration … and to principles of equality." Nonetheless,

> [T]here were states that questioned the legally binding force of this declarational document which proposes human rigths [sic] guarantees. Because of this, the 21st UN General Assembly adopted the December 16, 1966, international human rights covenants in order to provide the necessary instruments to strengthen the binding force of the previous declaration and thereby address the problem.[53]

Over the next twenty-odd years came numerous international human rights covenants along with international agreements with binding force. North Korea is a party to the two primary covenants emerging in the wake of the Declaration and the U.N. Charter: the International Covenant on Economic, Social and Cultural Rights, and the Covenant on Civil and Political Rights.[54]

A number of legal scholars have argued for enhanced status for the Universal Declaration. These arguments include claims that the Universal Declaration (1) has achieved customary international law status, at least for certain rights,[55] (2) is binding as the legal exposition of U.N. Charter references to human rights,[56] or (3) is the authoritative statement of human rights in international law as a general principle of law.[57]

If an individual or group wishes to file a report regarding a human rights violation, they must follow the U.N. Human Rights Committee's Procedure 1503. When the Committee receives the report, it requires the accused state to reply and discuss the allegations in a closed session.

> [T]he committee may take actions such as examining the conditions wherein the human rights violation occured [sic], appointing special inspectors and proposing mechanisms for improvements by holding open discussions or setting up temporary special committees, sending in experts, publicizing the human rights violation, etc.

For failure to comply with the "requirement to reply," the report of the state's human rights violation gets publicized in the commission's annual report.[58] The negative publicity that can follow can pressure the state to amend the situation.

As a result of a report filed against North Korea for human rights violations, the U.N. assigned a special rapporteur to investigate the country and report the findings to the U.N. General Assembly and U.N. Commission on Human Rights (UNCHR). Vitit Muntarbhorn, a law professor from Southeast Asia, formerly fulfilled this role remotely as North Korea did not allow him to extend the investigation directly within its borders, similar to the latest commission's investigation.

Nevertheless, Professor Muntarbhorn did produce a report that diplomatically described the adverse human rights situation in the DPRK. Specifically, he reported the North Korean government's use of guilt by association to control its people, in addition to continuing violations of "guaranteed" freedoms of thought, religion, expression, and travel.[59] In his reports to the sixty-first and sixty-second meeting of the UNCHR, Professor Muntabhorn called for the following: (1) North Korea must fulfill the terms of all human rights treaties it has signed; (2) North Korea is encouraged to accommodate various recommendations contained in the special rapporteur's reports to the U.N. General Assembly; (3) South Korea should continue its support for the North Korean defectors; (4) the two Koreas should resolve the issue of abducted South Koreans; (5) North Korea should guarantee on-site observations of the distribution of humanitarian assistance materials; and (6) North Korea should include human rights improvement measures in its economic development plans.[60]

In response to the reporting of grave violations of human rights and the numerous practices of inhumane treatments such as tortures, beatings, rapes, starvation deaths, and murders of newborns, the UNHRC in its "concluding observations" strongly recommended North Korea allow onsite inspections of various correctional and detention facilities in North Korea by independent national and international teams. However, North Korea said it could do it itself, and refused this proposal.[61] No record of such internal investigation exists.

North Korea's massive campaign to rid the country of political dissent, censure speech and subject its citizens to labor camps and cruel punishment would clearly violate most of the provisions of the International Covenant on Civil and Political Rights.[62] Similarly, with North Korea's widespread religious persecution of Christians, withholding of basic necessities such as food, and horrendous working conditions for many, it would be violating a majority of articles under the International Covenant on Economic, Social and Cultural Rights.[63] North Korea's brutal treatment of many individuals, use of collective retribution and cultural oppression, much of which includes children and newborns, would violate nearly every article of the Convention on the Rights of the Child, which provides special protections to those under the age of 18.[64] Its horrendous treatment of pregnant women and its allowance of rampant human trafficking between China and Korea, the vast majority of which includes women and the sex trade, would violate substantial parts of the Convention on the Elimination of All Forms of Discrimination Against Women.[65]

To humanize these violations and how they transgress international law, I mention some here. Imagine the horror of a family sent to a concentration camp because their small child scribbled with a crayon on a portrait of Kim Jong-Il,[66] or the young woman imprisoned, beaten, and sexually abused for teaching other North Korean citizens a popular, South Korean song.[67] These examples not only implicate violations of *jus cogens* norms (with the torture and abuse of children and adults alike), but also would implicate violating several articles of the above treaties regarding free expression of adults (e.g. Article 19 of the International Covenant on Civil and Political Rights)[68] and children (e.g. Article 13 of the Convention on the Rights of the Child).[69]

As one digs deeper into the atrocities happening presently in North Korea, such crimes require some form of redress. As another example, consider a woman being forced to bury alive her own infants to comply with the DPRK's policy of killing infants of Chinese ancestry.[70] Or the eyewitness reports that between 150 and 200 individuals who escaped these prisons and camps across the North are repatriated each week to be to beaten, tortured, and killed in the same prisons.[71] These examples again demonstrate North Korea's numerous treaty and convention violations by ignoring the special rights and protections of pregnant women (Articles 11 and 12 of the Convention on the Elimination of All Forms of Discrimination Against Women),[72] the rights of child refugees (Article 22 of the Convention on the Rights of the Child),[73] and the rights of all its citizens to life and liberty (e.g. Articles 6 and 9 of the International Covenant on Civil and Political Rights).[74] Unfortunately, these examples merely represent everyday occurrences in North Korea and do not come close to constituting an exhaustive list.

Even absent the above conventions signed by North Korea and the country's constitution, the international community would still have recourse to customary international law and *jus cogens*. For example, in the preamble of every convention mentioned, there includes a sentence or paragraph that notes that the agreements accord with and recognize the Universal Declaration of Human Rights.[75] Consonant with the view that such rights under this declaration are already customary, this further shows that in signing these agreements, North Korea cannot escape the notion that their ratification recognizes these principles as law and gives significant evidence of *opinio juris*, one of the components of customary international law.[76] With its oppressive state action expressed earlier, North Korea has violated nearly every article of the declaration.[77] Moreover, this state action would defy established *jus cogens* (peremptory) norms.[78] The pervasive cruel and unusual punishment methods of countless citizens for any number of "offenses" or ideologies would fall under torture, not to mention that the labor camps likely qualify as institutions of slavery.[79] Its systematic persecution, imprisonment, torturing, and killing of religious dissidents (generally Christians) and infants of Chinese descent also amounts to genocide.[80] North Korea consistently and brazenly breaks the applicable treaties, conventions, and international principles and norms that apply to it, as well as its own domestic law.

Domestic law

Under Article 15 of the newest version of the constitution, the DPRK signaled intent to "champion the democratic, national rights of Koreans overseas and their rights recognized by the [sic] international law."[81] From this language alone, it appears that North Korea accepts its obligation to abide by international law, at least regarding citizens abroad. Considering that the DPRK has expressly stated in Articles 15 and 16 respectively of its latest Constitution that it would protect Koreans' rights under international law as well as even "guarantee the legal rights and interests of foreigners in its territory"[82] and has incorporated into its penal code punishments for important human rights crimes (e.g. child labor and torture, which the DPRK has itself violated), North Korea has integrated at least some human rights concepts into its domestic legal system.

Along these lines, a cursory examination of North Korea's constitution might insinuate that it gives various rights and freedoms. However, a closer reading reveals that these purported rights and freedoms prove illusory. All of these rights and freedoms are nullified by additional terms in this same constitution. This nullification takes place by subordinating all such rights and freedoms to the will of the Leader (i.e. one of the Kims) and the ruling party.

In its ongoing propaganda campaign, perhaps in response to rising international pressure to respect the human rights of its own people, North Korea revised its constitution in April 2009 and made it available to the public in late September 2009.[83] The new constitution purports to grant the people a right to elect and recall an assemblyman and declares that the people are the "masters of everything."[84] Of course, one should not ignore the rubber stamp legislature, the totalitarian dictatorship, and concentration camps full of slave labor when struggling to find any substantial meaning through actual praxis to these provisions.

The current constitution declares that the state shall respect and protect the human rights of the working people.[85] This provision has never appeared in any prior constitution of North Korea.[86] However, these new constitutional provisions merit a massive measure of skepticism.[87] Testimony has revealed public executions for "anti-regime" charges (e.g. a sergeant going AWOL), for economic crimes (e.g. theft of government property or theft of livestock), and for socially delinquent behaviors (e.g. streaking or disco-dancing).[88] Unfortunately, such extremely expansive utilizations of capital punishment report actual instances, not hypotheticals. So unless the government has engaged in a tectonic shift, a rather improbable prospect, comparable actions likely continue, notwithstanding the new language in the constitution.

The constitution purports to expand the already absolutist authority held by the Dear Leader, who serves as the chairman of the National Defense Commission (NDC), the head of the Workers' Party, and the Supreme Commander of the People's Army. Chapter VI Article 100 of the constitution pronounces the NDC chairman the Supreme Leader of the Democratic People's Republic of Korea (DPRK)—a reaffirmation of the already existing political structure. Moreover, a continued reading exposes these purported constitutional rights for the people of the DPRK as illusory since the NDC may "[r]escind the decisions and directives of state organs that run counter to the orders of the chairman of the DPRK."[89] In other words, the Kims' orders trump any right supposedly given by the constitution. While the new constitution may have revised some provisions, a grand canyon between the putative law and its implementation has persisted.

North Korea has revised its criminal code four times as of 1999, maintaining the heaviest penalties for those who injure the authority of the now three Kims.[90] In a report to Amnesty International, North Korea insisted that citizens enjoy equal rights and are "not discriminated against for reasons of race, color, sex, language, religion, political beliefs or opinions, national or social origin, property, birth or status." However, ample examples prove otherwise. For instance, the law "strictly classifies every individual by his or her family background (or class origin) and by the degree of loyalty to the regime."[91] This practice contradicts the assertions made in the report to Amnesty International.

The absence of an effective, politically independent judiciary also renders individuals' rights and freedoms unprotected. Furthermore, it is commonplace for those accused of political and certain economic crimes to lack due process of the law, such as the right to an attorney for their defense.[92] Even with an attorney, the role of attorneys in the North Korean criminal justice system is solely to protect the Workers' Party's policies instead of any particular individual's rights.[93] Trials often lead to summary sentencing without any semblance of a full judicial process, much less anything approximating a just result on the merits, as we saw earlier.

Notes

* Sarah Walsh and Kevin Zickterman aided me in this chapter.
1 *See*, U.N. Human Rights Council, Comm. of Inquiry on Human Rights in the Democratic People's Republic of Korea, Rep. of the Detailed Findings of the Comm., U.N. Doc. A/HRC/25/CRP.1 (Feb. 7, 2014) [hereinafter *H.R.C. Detailed Rep. 25*].

2 *See* U.N. Human Rights Council, Rep. of the Comm'n of Inquiry on Human Rights in the DPRK, Feb. 7, 2014, ¶693, U.N. Doc. A/HRC/25/63 (2014) [hereinafter *H.R.C. Rep.*].

3 *Id.*

4 *Id.* ¶¶56–63.

5 *Id.*

6 *Id.* ¶57.

7 *H.R.C. Rep., supra* note 2, ¶58.

8 *Id.* ¶59.

9 *Id.* ¶61.

10 *Id.* ¶733.

11 *Id.* ¶786.

12 *H.R.C. Rep., supra* note 2, ¶785.

13 *Id.* ¶787.

14 *Id.* ¶820

15 *Id.* ¶693.

16 *Id.* ¶694.

17 *H.R.C. Rep., supra* note 2, ¶697.

18 *Id.* ¶696.

19 *Id.* ¶721.

20 *Id.* ¶727.

21 *Id.* ¶796.

22 *H.R.C. Rep., supra* note 2, ¶797.

23 *Id.* ¶797.

24 *Id.*

25 *Id.* ¶705.

26 *Id.* ¶708.

27 *See H.R.C. Rep., supra* note 2, ¶682.

28 *Id.* ¶747.

29 *Id.* ¶¶681–82.

30 *Id.* ¶718.

31 *Id.* ¶718.

32 *H.R.C. Rep., supra* note 2, ¶720.

33 *Id.*

34 *Id.* ¶721.

35 *Id.* ¶¶721–22.

36 *Id.* ¶723.

37 *H.R.C. Rep., supra* note 2, ¶720.

38 *Id.* ¶725.

39 *Id.* ¶726.

40 *Id.* ¶821.

41 *Id.* ¶822.

42 *H.R.C. Rep, supra* note 2, ¶820.

43 *Id.* ¶801.

44 *Id.* ¶¶823–24.

45 *Id.* ¶¶825–26.

46 *Id.* ¶¶832.

47 Sung-Chul Choi, *Human Rights in North Korea in the Light of International Covenants, in* INTERNATIONAL COMMUNITY AND HUMAN RIGHTS IN NORTH KOREA 61 (Sung-Chul Choi ed., 1996).

48 Universal Declaration of Human Rights, Preamble, G.A. Res. 217 (III) A, U.N. Doc. A/RES/217(III) (Dec. 10, 1948), www.un.org/en/ documents/udhr/ (last visited Aug. 11, 2014).

49   *Id.*

50   Choi, *supra* note 47, at 62.

51   *A United Nations Priority: Universal Declaration of Human Rights*, UNITED NATIONS WEBSITE, www.un.org/rights/HRToday/declar.htm (last visited Aug. 11, 2014).

52   Peter Van Dijk, *The Universal Declaration is Legally Non-Binding: So What? in* REFLECTIONS ON THE UNIVERSAL DECLARATION OF HUMAN RIGHTS: A FIFTIETH ANNIVERSARY ANTHOLOGY, 108, 109 (Barend van der Heijden & Bahia Tahzib-Lie eds., 1998).

53   Choi, *supra* note 47, at 63, 65.

54   *Id.* at 65–66. The covenants include the following: International Covenant on Economic, Social and Cultural Rights, International Covenant on Civil and Political Rights, Optional Protocol to the International Covenant on Civil and Political Rights, Second Optional Protocol to the International Covenant on Civil and Political Rights Aimed at the Abolition of the Death Penalty, Covenant Against Torture and Other Cruel, Inhuman or Degrading Treatment or Punishment, Convention on the Elimination of All Forms of Discrimination against Women, Convention on the Rights of the Child, International Covenant on the Elimination of All Forms of Racial Discrimination and Convention on the Prevention and Punishment of the Crime of Genocide. *Id.*

55   RESTATEMENT (THIRD) OF THE FOREIGN RELATIONS LAW OF THE U.S. § 702 (1987). This source includes the following violations of human rights as customary international law without claiming comprehensiveness: murder or causing the disappearance of individuals, genocide, slavery, torture or other cruel inhuman or degrading treatment or punishment, prolonged arbitrary detention, systematic racial discrimination and consistent patterns of gross violations of internationally recognized human rights.

56   Thomas Buergenthal, *International Human Rights Law and Institutions: Accomplishments and Prospects*, 63 WASH. L. REV. 1, 10 (1988).

57   Bruno Simma & Philip Alston, *The Sources of Human Rights Law: Custom, Jus Cogens, and General Principles*, 12 AUSTL. Y.B. INT'L L. 82 (1992); *see also* Jonathan I. Charney, *Universal International Law*, 87 AM. J. INT'L L. 529, 549 (1993).

58   Choi, *supra* note 47, at 73–74.

59   David Hawk, *The Hidden Gulag: Exposing North Korea's Prison Camps*, U.S. COMM. FOR HUMAN RIGHTS IN N. KOREA 59, 77 (2003), *available at* www.hrnk.org/HiddenGulag. pdf.

60   Soo-am Kim et al., *White Paper on Human Rights in North Korea*, KOREA INST. FOR NAT'L UNIFICATION, 12 (2007), *available at* www.kinu.or.kr/kinu/sc/skin/kinu/data/file/ data04/data/hrn2007.pdf [hereinafter KINU 2007].

61   Lee Keum-Soon et al., *White Paper on Human Rights in North Korea*, KOREA INST. FOR NAT'L UNIFICATION, 107 (2004) [hereinafter KINU 2004].

62   International Convention on Civil and Political Rights, 999 U.N.T.S. 171 (entered into force Mar. 23, 1976). *See, e.g.*, arts. 1–3, 5–7, and 10–13 of this Convention.

63   International Covenant on Economic, Social, and Cultural Rights, 993 U.N.T.S. 3 (entered into force Jan. 3, 1976). *See, e.g.*, arts. 1, 2, 5–10, 12, 14, 15, 19–27 of this convention.

64   Convention on the Rights of the Child, art. 1, GA Res. 44/25 (Annex), U.N. GAOR, 44th Sess. Supp. No. 49, U.N. Doc. A/RES/44/49, at 166 (entered into force Sept. 2, 1990). *See, e.g.*, arts. 2, 3, 5–7, 9, 10, 12–17, 19–22, 24–32, 35–37, 39, and 40 of this pertinent convention.

65   Convention on the Elimination of All Forms of Discrimination Against Women, 1249 U.N.T.S. 13 (entered into force Dec. 18, 1979). *See, e.g.*, arts. 2, 5–12, 14–16 of this convention.

66   Hawk, *supra* note 59.

67   *Id.* at 46.

68   International Convention on Civil and Political Rights, *supra* note 62, 999 U.N.T.S. at 178.

69 GA Res. 44/25, *supra* note 64, at 168.

70 Hawk, *supra* note 59, at 61–62.

71 *Id.*

72 Convention on the Elimination of All Forms of Discrimination Against Women, *supra* note 65, 1249 U.N.T.S. at 18–19.

73 GA Res. 44/25, *supra* note 64, at 169.

74 International Convention on Civil and Political Rights, *supra* note 62, 999 U.N.T.S. at 174–76.

75 Convention on the Elimination of All Forms of Discrimination Against Women, *supra* note 65, 1249 U.N.T.S. at 14; International Convention on Civil and Political Rights, *supra* note 62, 999 U.N.T.S. at 173; International Covenant on Economic, Social, and Cultural Rights, *supra* note 63, 993 U.N.T.S. at 5; GA Res. 44/25, *supra* note 64, at 45.

76 For a general discussion regarding *opinio juris* as an element of customary international law, see Jo Lynn Slama, Note, *Opinio Juris in Customary International Law*, 15 OKLA. CITY U.L. REV. 603 (1990).

77 Universal Declaration of Human Rights, G.A. Res. 217 (III) A, U.N. Doc. A/RES/217(III) (Dec. 10, 1948). *See, e.g.,* arts. 2–15 and 17–29 of the declaration.

78 For an interesting discussion on *jus cogens* as peremptory norms in international law, see Andrea Bianchi, *Human Rights and the Magic of* Jus Cogens, 19 EUR. J. INT'L L. 491 (2008).

79 Torture in this context is clearly a *jus cogens* violation as many scholars point out. *See, e.g.,* Erika de Wet, *The Prohibition of Torture as an International Norm of* Jus Cogens *and Its Implications for National and Customary Law*, 15 EUR. J. INT'L L. 97 (2004).

80 Slavery and genocide are also undoubtedly *jus cogens* violations. *See, e.g.,* Evan J. Criddle & Evan Fox-Decent, *A Fiduciary Duty of* Jus Cogens, 34 YALE J. INT'L L. 331, 343 (2009) ("Although some peremptory norms such as the prohibitions against genocide and slavery are relatively uncontroversial across the international community of states").

81 The Democratic People's Republic of Korea Socialist Constitution Sept. 23, 2009, art. 15 (N. Kor.), *available at* www.servat.unibe.ch/icl/kn00000_.html. The alternative English translation previously cited is at www.asiamatters.blogspot.com/2009/10/north-korean-constitution-april-2009.html.

82 *Id.* at arts. 15–16 (N. Kor.).

83 Choe Sang-Hun, *New North Korean Constitution Bolsters Kim"s Power*, N.Y. TIMES, Sept. 29, 2009, at A12, *available at* www.nytimes.com/2009/09/29/ world/asia/29korea.html.

84 NORTHEAST ASIA MATTERS, www.asiamatters.blogspot.com (Oct. 8, 2009).

85 *Id.*

86 Choe Sang-Hun, *New North Korean Constitution Bolsters Kim"s Power*, N.Y. TIMES, Sept. 29, 2009, at A12, *available at* www.nytimes.com/2009/09/29/ world/asia/29korea.html.

87 KINU 2004, *supra* note 61, at 97

88 *Id.* at 85–89.

89 NORTHEAST ASIA MATTERS, *supra* note 84.

90 KINU 2004, *supra* note 61, at 108.

91 KINU 2007, *supra* note 15, at 111–12.

92 KINU 2004, *supra* note 60, at 116.

93 KINU 2007, *supra* note 15, at 111–12.

11 The plight of those in flight*

North Korea has one of the worst human rights records this planet has ever known.[1] Whether within the DPRK's gulags—the DPRK's political, concentration, and prison camps—or beyond the gulags' borders, the DPRK has habitually violated international law and its own constitution through its use of extermination, torture, crimes of association, and political and religious persecution of its own nationals.[2] Additionally, due to the combination of its isolationist regime and the drought and floods that ravaged the territory in the 1990s, North Korea suffered a severe famine, the effects of which continue to extend.[3] Although sources have differing numbers,[4] the extent of deaths caused by food shortages, malnourishment, and resulting starvation within North Korea since the beginning of the 1990s has grown to over two million people.[5] The caste system of North Korea further exacerbates the situation, as it affords decreasing rations to those in the lower categories, while reserving extra rations for the military and elite classes within the regime.[6] These unending human rights atrocities, political and religious persecutions, and food shortages have led to an exodus of North Koreans leaving their homeland, searching for the minimum necessities of life and human rights that have been denied them for so long.[7]

Whereas previous chapters expounded on the narrative of what has ultimately led to countless North Koreans leaving the DPRK—lack of food, avoidance of political and religious persecution, and human rights abuses, among others—this chapter will primarily focus on the illegal, unethical, and immoral treatment of the refugees by both North Korea and China. The first part of the chapter will detail the horrendous treatment by the DPRK toward either apprehended or repatriated refugees. The second part will focus on China's actions as a result of the North Koreans that took the risk of leaving their home state and entering into China, most commonly either to make a new life there, or as a springboard to enter South Korea, where they are welcomed as citizens.[8] If China refused to repatriate North Korean refugees, many of the DPRK's atrocities that befall the repatriated would not happen. Even by analyzing the documented facts in a light most favorable to both China and North Korea, both governments continue to violate many of their international obligations. Explaining these shortcomings lays the groundwork to address potential solutions to these gross violations of international law, which the final section of this book attempts.

North Korea's treatment of apprehended and repatriated refugees

North Korea's violations of freedom of movement and the right to work

To understand the treatment of North Korean refugees, the basic class structure (in a society purportedly against class) and laws of the DPRK need explanation. The DPRK classifies each national into one of three classes—core, wavering, or hostile.[9] The government then gives additional educational benefits to the core class, assigns preferable housing based on class, and provides greater rations to the core class.[10] Further, only the core class can live in the capital, Pyongyang,[11] where the best employment opportunities, best residences, and greatest abundance of food concentrate. Many laws and many procedures attempt to prevent the wavering and hostile classes from gaining information about the world beyond the DPRK's borders as well as to prevent realization of the extent of discrimination against the lower classes.[12]

Despite the state's constitution granting freedom of employment, only the Workers' Party of Korea has the exclusive right to assign all employment.[13] Moreover, the government assigns residences, often based near a person's work site.[14] More importantly, travel outside a citizen's own province requires travel permits issued by the government.[15] Anecdotal evidence suggests the difficulty of gaining clearance for visiting northern providences near China because of the DPRK's concern for citizens crossing into China without due authorization.[16] Finally, those that actually defect into China, regardless of whether this is for work, food, or asylum, commit a national crime tantamount to treason under North Korean law.[17] According to the 2004 Penal Code of North Korea, any person who betrays the fatherland by fleeing to another country shall be sentenced to five or more years in a correctional labor camp or labor training camp.[18] In extreme cases, the sentence can be increased to life in prison or even execution, as well as a confiscation of all personal property.[19]

Nevertheless, during the 1990s, crossing into China served as a solution to political persecution and starvation, and both the North Korean and Chinese governments had a relaxed stance on border control because of the famine.[20] Around the turn of the millennium, these attitudes changed because the DPRK began to demand that the Chinese send back any of the defectors for committing crimes against the state and the Chinese believed the influx of migrants would negatively impact the economy of the region.

These renewed restrictions on movement and employment violate the International Covenant on Civil and Political Rights (ICCPR)[21] and the International Covenant on Economic, Social, and Cultural Rights (ICESCR).[22] Article 12 of the ICCPR states that, "Everyone lawfully within the territory of a state shall, within that territory, have the right of liberty of movement and freedom to choose residence."[23] Further, "Everyone shall be free to leave any country, including his own."[24] Additionally, Article 6 of the ICESCR states that parties shall recognize the right to work, including "the opportunity to gain his living by work which he freely chooses and accepts."[25] Nevertheless, as explained, North Korea severely restricts or prohibits both moving and working either within the DPRK or into other countries.[26]

The government of North Korea may argue that its restrictions on travel and freedom of work that accompany free movement accord with the ICCPR because the restrictions protect national security, public order, public health and morals, or the rights and freedoms of others.[27] Nevertheless, this argument fails because restrictions that impair the essence of the right, reach disproportional extents to achieve their protective functions, or prevail as the norm and not the exception, fall outside the acceptable exceptions of Article 12(3).[28] While acceptable to have such restrictions placed near the Military Demarcation Line, where actions of citizens could escalate the ongoing Korean War, requiring travel permits to either Pyongyang or anywhere outside of the citizen's home province fails proportionality.[29] Finally, severe restrictions on these rights constitute the norm in the DPRK, as opposed to having exigent circumstances that might temporarily suspend or restrict movement. Thus, because the DPRK does not impose its restrictions on movement according to the applicable exception in ICCPR Article 12(3), the DPRK transgresses its international obligations under the ICCPR.

The DPRK's violations on freedom of movement and freedom of choosing place of work make it extraordinarily dangerous for a North Korean to even attempt to leave the country and seek refuge beyond the DPRK's borders. Not only does the government require travel permits, but permits to travel to the northern provinces near China are difficult to acquire. For the overwhelming majority of North Koreans, it is almost impossible to gain approval to leave the country.[30] Therefore, whether for refuge or employment, citizens have no choice but to illegally cross the border, usually into China.[31] Nevertheless, many do attempt to cross into China, as they find the risk of detention, torture, and even death outweighed by the promise of food and potential freedom.

The DPRK's failed obligations to the right to life regarding border control

Article 6 of the ICCPR states that all humans have an inherent right to life and that no one should be deprived of life arbitrarily.[32] However, the DPRK regularly breaks this international obligation through application of its border control policy. Soon after Kim Jong-Un came into power, he declared that border control needed tightening, resulting in not only potential lifelong imprisonment or execution of defectors, but also the same punishment for up to three generations of the family of the defectors.[33] Former security officials have even stated that it is policy that anyone trying to cross the border may be shot on sight, with the intent to kill.[34]

The Commission of Inquiry has stated that this shoot-to-kill policy violates international human rights laws, and, thus, fails as a legitimate means of controlling a country's borders.[35] As summarized, "The DPRK upholds a de facto total travel ban on ordinary citizens that violates international law and gives individuals no other option than to cross the border without authorization in order to exercise their human right to leave their own country."[36] The intentional taking of life simply to prevent an unauthorized border crossing is disproportionate and incongruous with upholding the right to life.[37] Moreover, the use of such lethal force may only prevent an immediate threat to another's life.[38]

However, the DPRK has never argued that its border control policy prevents imminent danger of a fatal nature to either North Korean or Chinese citizens. Even if the DPRK could prove that in rare instances killing a border crosser would prevent another's imminent death, it certainly would be unable to establish that a blanket shoot-to-kill policy harmonizes with international human rights law and the DPRK's obligations under the ICCPR. Thus, this border control policy proffers another example of how North Korea illegally treats potential and actual refugees.

North Korea's violations of the peremptory norm against torture

Although North Korea has not ratified the Convention Against Torture and Other Cruel, Inhuman or Degrading Treatment or Punishment (Torture Convention),[39] the prohibition of torture has reached a status of *jus cogens*.[40] As an international *jus cogens* norm, no state can derogate from the prohibition against torture under any condition, whether through treaty, custom, state-sanctioned or state-approved action, or any other means.[41] Thus, any state action—legislative, administrative, or judicial—that authorizes or tacitly allows torture to occur within the state crosses that state's international obligations to prohibit torture.[42] Yet it remains the most commonly violated customary international law.

To illustrate the horrific acts of torture by the DPRK against North Korean refugees, torture needs a definition. Article 1 of the Torture Convention defines torture as "any act by which severe pain or suffering, whether physical or mental, is intentionally inflicted on a person" for such purposes as obtaining information or confession, punishing an individual for committed or suspected acts, or intimidating or coercing for any reason based on discrimination.[43] A public official in his official capacity must perform the torturous act.[44] Examples include beating, burning, prolonged denial of rest or sleep, prolonged denial of food, and psychological suffering.[45]

There are four reasons why North Korean actions against repatriated nationals amount to torture. First, North Korea frequently employs torture as a means of control. The United Nations High Commissioner for Refugees (UNHCR) in 2004 and 2005 stated the serious apprehension the world community had regarding the use of torture on repatriated North Korean refugees.[46] More recently, the United Nations Human Rights Council Commission of Inquiry on Human Rights in the DPRK (Commission of Inquiry) confirmed that repatriated North Koreans suffer torture, arbitrary detention, summary execution, forced abortions, and sexual violations.[47] Second, repatriated refugees are subject to extreme sentencing. Correctional facilities require all prisoners to perform a minimum of ten hours of hard labor per day, while labor training camps average between twelve and fourteen hours of hard labor daily with minimal breaks, but only give prisoners one day off every fifteen days.[48] Third, the regime often reclassifies repatriated defectors as members of the hostile class, which leads to lower priority for food rations, increasing the chances of starvation and malnourishment.[49] This results in both severe physical and psychological suffering. Finally, many prisoners experience actions that amount to torture: severe beating to the point of permanent impairment of limbs,[50] burning using fire torture,[51] forced abortions by means of forced labor, beatings, or injections if found pregnant,[52] and public executions or forced witnessing of such executions.[53] Testimonies have also indicated that even at the interrogation stage—which may last many months—refugees receive food rations at a level designed to induce starvation, must perform forced labor without any criminal conviction, must silently sit or kneel in crowded cells without moving for many hours at a time, and must stay in inhumane conditions.[54] These actions of extreme sentencing combined with severe mental and physical pain and suffering fit squarely within the aforementioned definition of torture.

Repatriated women endure particular torture. Upon repatriation, every woman is detained, harshly interrogated, stripped of her clothing, and has her uterus physically searched by hand by either a female or male guard, often resulting in severe sexual violence.[55] Beyond the sexual violence abundant in the detention centers,[56] anyone found pregnant must have an abortion by beating, forced labor, or injection.[57] The severe emotional and physical pain that results perhaps qualifies these things as torture.

North Korea posits two failed arguments against these acts amounting to torture. First, the DPRK may argue that the prohibition of torture has not reached the level of *jus cogens*, and thus, the DPRK may continue to torture its repatriated citizens. However, as previously stated,[58] the U.N. Human Rights Committee and Inter-American Court of Human Rights have specifically held that there is a peremptory norm against torture. Furthermore, the Special Rapporteur on Torture has confirmed that "Torture is now absolutely and without any reservation prohibited under international law."[59] Even if not *jus cogens*, it qualifies at least as customary international law.

North Korea has also argued that it may do anything it wants to its nationals because the DPRK is a sovereign nation, subject to no other nation or organization.[60] However, because the DPRK joined the United Nations as a member, and has signed and ratified many treaties, the DPRK has bound itself to certain international law obligations despite its sovereignty. After joining and ratifying, North Korea cannot later argue that its sovereignty precludes actually adhering to the attendant obligations. Because both of the DPRK's arguments allowing torture fail, the DPRK remains severely deficient in its obligation to prohibit the torture of repatriated North Korean refugees.

The DPRK's illegal treatment regarding repatriated children

The DPRK's conduct toward both repatriated children and those who attempted to defect should deeply pain anyone with a heart. The DPRK has failed to meet its obligations as a party to the Convention on the Rights of the Child (Child Convention).[61] Children, as a particularly vulnerable class, call for special protection. The most notable rights violated include: the right to live and develop healthily,[62] the right to have parents help and guide their children,[63] the right to be protected from mistreatment and violence,[64] and the right to an adequate standard of living conditions to meet physical and mental development.[65]

Forced abortions and infanticide often occur with fetuses and children of North Korean defectors suspected of conceiving with Chinese males.[66] Further, in contravention of the right to parental assistance, a child suffers punishment if a parent assists him or her with work in the labor camps or even helps him or her to eat, which results in deprivation of rations.[67] Moreover, children begin hard labor in the camps as early as eight years of age,[68] and must witness public executions and violence at a very early age, all of which severely affects the children's mental and physical development. Finally, even children who remained in North Korea when a family member defected must go to labor camps.[69] These actions are just a few examples of North Korea's pervasive failure to adhere to its international obligations under the Child Convention.

China's illegal and immoral repatriation policy of North Korean refugees

Whereas North Korea's actions toward potential and actual North Korean defectors flout international law, China's policy to repatriate such individuals[70] also disregards international law. This section will specifically address how China has violated international law by repatriating these defectors, knowing that their return to North Korea often leads to hard labor in a gulag for defecting, and in some cases, even execution.

China's rationale for "legally" repatriating North Korean refugees

China has maintained that its repatriation of North Korean defectors does not run afoul of international law because it upholds its bilateral treaty obligations made with the DPRK. China contends that it has a secret agreement with the DPRK—the Escaped Criminals Reciprocal Extradition Treaty—made in the early 1960s, which requires that any North Koreans that illegally cross the DPRK–China border must be returned as criminals.[71] Furthermore, the Protocol between the PRC Ministry of Public Security and the DPRK Social Safety Ministry for Mutual Cooperation in Safeguarding National Security and Social Order in Border Areas describes mutual obligations regarding border control and repatriation of criminals.[72] Specifically, Article 4 of this Protocol states that both sides will prevent illegal border crossings and that, "Illegal border crossers will be returned to the other side with information on their identity and specific situation."[73] Finally, another protocol created in 1986 regarding security of the Chinese–North Korean border calls for further cooperation to prevent illegal border crossings as well as mutual extradition concerning defecting criminals.[74]

These three bilateral agreements between North Korea and China form the basis for the Chinese repatriation policies. China also has domestic laws that authorize such repatriation. Articles 29 and 30 of the Law of the People's Republic of China on Control of the Entry and Exit of Aliens empowers the government to fine or detain individuals who illegally enter or leave China, and if the circumstances are serious, China may even order persons to leave the country or to be expelled to another country.[75] Given the economic and political importance of keeping good relations with North Korea, along with maintaining its treaty obligations to the DPRK, it is not unreasonable to conclude that China considers all circumstances involving North Korean defectors serious enough to warrant repatriation under its laws. Therefore, assessing China's policy and actions regarding North Korean defectors using *only* the China–North Korea agreements and the aforementioned Chinese domestic law, it would appear that China does have the authority and obligation under international and domestic law to repatriate all defectors. However, as the remainder of this chapter will illustrate, by assessing the situation using all international law treaties and customs that China must follow, it follows that China should not repatriate North Koreans according to its current policy.

North Korean defectors' protection under refugee law

China is a party to the Convention Relating to the Status of Refugees,[76] which defines a refugee as a person who,

> owing to well-founded fear of being persecuted for reasons of race, religion, nationality, membership of a particular social group or political opinion, is outside the country of his nationality and is unable or, owing to such fear, is unwilling to avail himself of the protection of that country; or who, not having a nationality and being outside the country of his former habitual residence as a result of such events, is unable or, owing to such fear, is unwilling to return to it.[77]

Further, Article 33—also a non-derogable article—states:

> No Contracting State shall expel or return ('refouler') a refugee in any manner whatsoever to the frontiers of territories where his life or freedom would be threatened on account of his race, religion, nationality, [or] membership of a particular social group or political opinion.[78]

The principle of *non-refoulement* proclaimed in Article 33 seems to apply to North Korean defectors, thus prohibiting China from returning them to a country that will persecute them. However, China has forwarded two arguments against being bound by this obligation: (1) China's bilateral treaties with North Korea trump its obligations under the Refugee Convention;[79] and (2) the North Korean defectors do not fulfill the definition of refugees as defined by the Refugee Convention.[80]

China's argument that its border control treaties with the DPRK supersede China's obligations under the Refugee Convention fails for two reasons. First, Article 33 of the Refugee Convention is non-derogable,[81] meaning that upon ratification, China could put forth no rationale that would support repatriating a North Korean defector that China had cause to believe would be persecuted upon return due to membership in a particular religious, political, or social group.[82] Second, the UNHCR explicitly declared that *non-refoulement* has reached the status of customary international law, thus binding all states regardless of their status regarding the Refugee Convention or any other treaties.[83] When a state's extradition treaties conflict with its *non-refoulement* obligations, the bar "to surrender of an individual under international refugee and human rights law prevail over the obligation to extradite."[84] Further, no treaty can supersede the U.N. Charter,[85] and Articles 55(c) and 56 require states to take action to promote the universal respect and observance of human rights.[86] Thus, China cannot repatriate North Koreans because the customary international law principle of *non-refoulement* supersedes its other treaty obligations and domestic laws.[87]

China's second argument that the North Korean defectors do not qualify as refugees may have more merit, but ultimately fails after proper scrutiny. China avers that North Koreans who illegally cross into Chinese territory are properly characterized as economic migrants, rather than refugees.[88] An economic migrant is defined as a person who voluntarily leaves his or her country exclusively for economic reasons, and not for persecution as described in the Refugee Convention.[89] Because many North Koreans cross the China–DPRK border simply to avoid starvation, China contends that the motives of the defectors are entirely economic.[90] As such, China believes the defectors do not qualify as refugees protected by the Refugee Convention, and thus China may legally repatriate them.

However, the UNHCR has elaborated that if the underlying economic measures that drive an individual to leave the country result from racial, political, or religious bias of the home country, then the individual counts as a refugee, and not an economic migrant.[91] As previously explained, each North Korean pegs it citizens into three broad classes. The government gives preferential treatment to the core class in terms of education, housing, and food rations.[92] Furthermore, North Korea sometimes sends criminals, including defectors and family members associated with defectors, to remote, harsh mountainous regions,[93] thus making survival more difficult. Because the Refugee Convention protects individuals persecuted as members of a particular social group, and the government discriminates against North Koreans in the wavering or hostile classes, defectors of these classes should properly be protected by the Refugee Convention.[94] Therefore, it would appear that China has violated international law in relation to *at least some* of the individuals it has forcibly repatriated to North Korea.

Additionally, China has refused to allow the UNHCR near the border to determine the status of the North Koreans that cross into China.[95] This act, in and of itself, fails to heed the Protocol Relating to the Status of Refugees,[96] which compels China to cooperate with the UNHCR and facilitate the UNHCR's functions.[97] China even signed another agreement with the UNHCR in 1995, which obligates China to further cooperate with UNHCR requests and operations, as well as requiring implementation of a procedure for determining an individual's refugee status.[98] Nevertheless, China has neither created such a screening process nor allowed the UNHCR or anyone else to employ a system for determining defectors' refugee status.[99] Thus, China has continued to violate international law, both in its refusal to cooperate with the UNHCR and by actually repatriating individuals without determining their refugee status.

Finally, even if China could make the case that many of the people that illegally cross into China do so exclusively for economic reasons *not* caused by discrimination of a particular group or groups within North Korea, there remains a strong argument that those defectors have become refugees after arriving in China.[100] "A person becomes a refugee '*sur place*' due to circumstances arising in his country of origin during his absence."[101] Further, a person can become a *refugee sur place* by actions that the person commits after leaving the origin country, such as associating with other refugees or expressing political or religious views.[102]

Over the past few years, border control has increased. As with other "crimes", adverse consequences strike up to three generations of defector families.[103] Additionally, the government reclassifies many defectors as part of the hostile class, due to their ability to communicate information regarding life outside the DPRK.[104] Furthermore, the government interrogates those forcibly repatriated to deduce, among other things, whether the defectors have come into contact with Christians, which would make their sentencing more severe.[105] Therefore, because of potential actions and influences after defecting, a crackdown on the repatriated persons and their families, and a potential reclassification to the most discriminated class in North Korea, even economic migrants become refugees upon crossing the China–North Korean border. At that moment, despite the intentions of the defectors, China has a responsibility to protect these refugees; yet China has continually breached its international obligations under the Refugee Convention.

China's international violations relating to torture

Beyond the Refugee Convention, China cannot legally send defectors back to the DPRK due to ratifying the Torture Convention.[106] Clause 1 of Article 3 of the Torture Convention—the *non-refoulement* clause—states: "No State Party shall expel, return ('refouler') or extradite a person to another State where there are substantial grounds for believing that he would be in danger of being subjected to torture."[107] In order to determine substantial grounds to prevent repatriation, Clause 2 of Article 3 allows the relevant authorities to consider the totality of the circumstances, including a state's consistent pattern of gross, flagrant, or mass violations of human rights.[108] North Korea's consistent violation of human rights, as well as its propensity toward torture, particularly regarding North Korean defectors, results in China's repatriation contravening the Torture Convention and its *non-refoulement* principle. Whether through extreme sentencing, severe mental and physical suffering, forced labor before conviction, forced abortions and infanticide, or executions, North Korean refugees normally undergo torture after repatriation. Thus, China violates the Torture Convention each time it repatriates North Korean refugees.

China argues that it stays consistent with the Torture Convention because the Torture Convention does not protect against pain and suffering that arises from, or is incidental to, lawful sanctions.[109] China states that these acts, which would amount to torture in any other circumstance, follow as a direct penalty for the recognized criminal act of illegally crossing the border. Thus, China contends the acts do not fit within the Torture Convention's definition of torture. However, the only written penalty for illegal border crossing, according to the North Korean Penal Code itself, is the actual amount of time to be served within a correctional facility or labor camp. The beatings, the reclassification into the hostile class, the forced abortion policy, the public executions, and even the amount of labor hours worked within the camps[110] stretch far beyond the laws recognized in North Korea. Therefore, the torturous actions against North Korean refugees go much further than mental and physical pain and suffering resulting from purely lawful action. Thus, China's argument attenuates, and therefore, China's repatriation policy violates international law.

China's other international obligations, which may prevent repatriation of North Koreans

Although the Refugee Convention and the Torture Convention constitute the primary legal documents to evaluate China's repatriation policy of North Korean defectors, China also does not obey some of its other international obligations. First, China's actions fail to uphold its obligations under the Convention on the Elimination of All Forms of Discrimination Against Women.[111] Article 6 of this convention requires states to protect women from all forms of trafficking and prostitution.[112] In addition, Articles 11 and 12 afford women special protection from discrimination based on maternity or marriage.[113] Nevertheless, traffickers sell many women that cross over the border into China to Chinese men or to prostitution.[114] Although China does have strict rules against human trafficking, North Korean women often do not report it due to the fear of repatriation.[115] Moreover, DPRK officials force pregnant women to have abortions—all in contravention of the convention's protection of a woman's maternity.[116]

Additionally, China has failed to meet its obligations as a party to the Convention on the Rights of the Child.[117] China should know of the infanticide and forced abortions of those repatriated to North Korea.[118] Moreover, the DPRK has made it widely known that family members of defectors, including children, depart to prison camps,[119] where they must endure hard labor even at an early age.[120] Thus, China's repatriation leads to the violation of many guaranteed rights within the Child Convention.

China argues that it did not the cause these violations, and thus, it conforms with international law. However, *non-refoulement*, as customary international law, combines with the aforementioned treaties to say otherwise.

China also signed the ICCPR.[121] Because China did not ratify the ICCPR, China must only refrain from acting in contravention to the convention, to not frustrate its object and purpose. Nevertheless, China violates Article 7, which forbids torture or cruel, degrading, or inhuman treatment.[122] As previously mentioned, China subjects many people to the torturous acts of the North Korean government through its repatriation policy. China also violates Article 10 of the ICCPR, which states that all persons shall be treated with humanity and respect for the inherent dignity of humans.[123] As has been illustrated, repatriated North Koreans often undergo torture, starvation, death, and forced witnessing of public executions, all of which disrespect the dignity of a human. *Non-refoulement* must enter again in order to implicate China along these lines.

Finally, some of China's actions in actually repatriating North Koreans have abandoned its international obligations as party to the Vienna Convention on Diplomatic Relations (Diplomatic Convention) and the Vienna Convention on Consular Relations (Consular Convention).[124] Article 22 of the Diplomatic Convention indicates that the host state may not enter diplomatic property except with the consent of the head of the mission or diplomatic property.[125] Similarly, in Article 31 of the Consular Convention, the host state authorities shall not enter consular premises "used exclusively for the purpose of the work of the consular post except with the consent of the head of the consular post or of his designee or of the head of the diplomatic mission of the sending State."[126] Despite the required sovereignty and inviolability of the diplomatic property and consulates within China, in at least two cases Chinese police entered a diplomatic consulate area to retrieve North Koreans seeking asylum. On May 8, 2002, five North Korean refugees rushed into the Japanese consulate in Shenyang, China.[127] The police followed the refugees into the compound and dragged a woman and child outside of the gates, back into Chinese territory.[128] Just over one month later, on June 13, a North Korean man and his son entered into a South Korean consular office in Beijing using doctored identification.[129] Once the Chinese authorities ascertained their purpose—seeking asylum in South Korea—Chinese guards entered the office, began a physical altercation with multiple South Korean diplomats, and then removed the North Korean adult from the premises and into Chinese custody.[130] Fortunately, in both of the aforementioned situations, severe international criticism allowed these refugees safe passage to South Korea by indirect travel through a third country.[131] China's repatriation policy has resulted in actions of entering into the protected, sovereign ground of consulates, attacking diplomats within the consulates, and forcibly taking North Korean refugees back into Chinese territory, all of which manifestly transgress China's international obligations under the Consular Convention and Diplomatic Convention.

Political and public pressure regarding China's repatriation policy

China has refused to change its policy despite criticism also coming in the COI report.[132] China scapegoated the traffickers and lumped those helping the refugees together with the traffickers in its official response. However, worldwide public criticism has compelled China to forego repatriation in specific instances involving consulates, as already discussed. Actually, the scrutiny brought to bear on many of the embassy and consulate incidents regarding North Korean refugees have motivated China to enter into bilateral negotiations with the involved nations to create a way for the refugees to enter South Korea.[133] Further, governments such as the United States, have begun to enact legislation which increases recognition of the horrendous human rights situation in North Korea and accepts North Korean refugees.[134] Additionally, organizations and organs of the U.N., such as the U.N. Human Rights Council, can continue to publicly embarrass China for its ill-treatment of refugees and its cruel repatriation policy.[135] Finally, sovereign nations can impose sanctions on China for violating its international obligations and promoting human rights abuses. The world needs to continue to publicly castigate China's policies regarding North Korean refugees while simultaneously threatening and implementing economic sanctions for continuing forced repatriation. By doing this, China will soon realize that its interests relating to its other international relationships outweigh its interests in maintaining positive relations with North Korea. When this occurs, China will finally change its policy, and North Korean refugees will have a better chance at lasting freedom.

Hundreds of thousands of North Koreans have defected to China in an effort to survive and seek political refuge caused by the DPRK's human rights abuses and inability to provide for its nationals. North Korea's procedures regarding traveling within and outside its country, its shoot-to-kill border control policy, and its torture of the repatriated all contravene international law. China's implementation of a policy designed to forcibly repatriate these refugees with North Korea directly violates the Refugee Convention, the Torture Convention, the Diplomatic Convention, and the Consular Convention. Additionally, China may stand in violation of its responsibilities as a party to the Child Convention and the Convention on the Elimination of All Forms of Discrimination Against Women and as a signatory to the ICCPR, especially in conjunction with the customary law principle of *non-refoulement*.

Continually bringing both governments' failures before the public eye, having governments create laws that support the refugees, and employing sanctions against North Korea and China for their respective parts in the human rights abuses occurring to repatriate North Korean defectors, may remedy the situation. When China realizes the true economic impact of supporting the DPRK and continuously violating multiple international obligations, China may forego its policy, and North Korean defectors may have a brighter future. Additionally, this may, just may finally provide the turning point needed for North Korea to reconsider its policies regarding the plight of those in flight.

Notes

* Jeremy J. McCabe co-authored this chapter.
1 *See, e.g.*, Morse H. Tan, *A State of Rightlessness: The Egregious Case of North Korea*, 80 Miss. L.J. 681, 682 (2010) (citing various experts in the field).

2   *See generally id.* (discussing a multitude of human rights abuses committed by the DPRK).

3   *E.g.*, Benjamin Neaderland, Note, *Quandary on the Yalu: International Law, Politics, and China's North Korean Refugee Crisis*, 40 STAN J. INT'L L. 143, 146 (2004).

4   *See, e.g.*, Marcus Noland et al., *Famine in North Korea: Causes and Cures*, 49 ECON. DEV. & CULTURAL CHANGE 741, 741 (2001) (citing ranges of population lost due to famine from 220,000 by North Korea's official estimate to as high as three and a half million by NGOs).

5   Neaderland, *supra* note 3.

6   ROBERT COLLINS, COMM. FOR HUMAN RIGHTS IN N. KOR., MARKED FOR LIFE: SONGBUN, NORTH KOREA'S SOCIAL CLASSIFICATION SYSTEM 66–67 (2012) (explaining that the lower an individual's class designation, the less economic opportunity the individual has and the lower priority the state has in providing food rations to the individual).

7   *See* Albert Suh, Note, *First Steps Are Better than None: Distinguishing the Practical from the Rhetorical in the North Korean Human Rights Act of 2004*, 37 RUTGERS L.J. 585, 605 (2006).

8   Yeo Hoon Julie Park, Note, *China's "Way Out" of the North Korean Refugee Crisis: Developing a Legal Framework for the Deportation of North Korean Migrants*, 25 GEO. IMMIGR. L.J. 515, 526 (2011) (explaining that South Korea's law grants South Korean citizenship to anyone who is born to a parent who is a national of the Republic of Korea, which territory is defined as the entire Korean Peninsula, thus encapsulating North Korean citizens born in North Korea).

9   *E.g.*, Kyu Chang Lee, *Protection of North Korean Defectors in China and the Convention Against Torture*, 6 REGENT J. INT'L L. 139, 145–46 (2008).

10 *See id.* at 146.

11 U.N. Human Rights Council, Rep. of the Detailed Findings of the Comm'n of Inquiry on Human Rights in the DPRK, Feb. 7, 2014, ¶357, U.N. Doc. A/HRC/25/CRP.1 (2014) [hereinafter *H.R.C. Rep.*].

12 *See id.*

13 *Id.*¶359.

14 *Id.*

15 *H.R.C. Rep.*, *supra* note 11, ¶373.

16 *Id.*

17 Cho Jung-hyun, et al., *White Paper on Human Rights in North Korea*, KOREA INST. FOR NAT'L UNIFICATION 80 (2013) [hereinafter KINU 2013].

18 *Id.* at 478. Although illegal border crossing in and of itself only carries a two-year mandatory sentence, illegally crossing the border most often constitutes a crime of treason against the fatherland. *Id.* at 477–78.

19 *Id.* at 478.

20 Elisa Gahng, Note, *North Korean Border-Crossers in Yanibian: The Protection Gap Between the Economic Migrants and Refugee Regimes*, 24 GEO. IMMIGR. L.J. 361, 365–66 (2010).

21 International Covenant on Civil and Political Rights, *opened for signature* Dec. 19, 1966, 999 U.N.T.S. 171 (entered into force Mar. 23, 1976) [hereinafter ICCPR].

22 International Covenant on Economic, Social, and Cultural Rights, *opened for signature* Dec. 16, 1966, 993 U.N.T.S. 3 (entered into force Jan. 3, 1976) [hereinafter ICESCR].

23 ICCPR, *supra* note 21, at art. 12(1).

24 *Id.* at art. 12(2).

25 ICESCR, *supra* note 22, at art. 6(1).

26 *See H.R.C. Rep.*, *supra* note 11, ¶357.

27 *See* ICCPR, *supra* note 21, at art. 12(3) (indicating that reasonable restrictions on freedom of movement are not violative of this inherent right).

28 *See* U.N. Human Rights Comm., *CCPR General Comment No. 27: Article 12 (Freedom of Movement)*, ¶¶13–14, U.N. Doc. CCPR/C/21/Rev.1/Add.9 (Nov. 2, 1999).

29 *See H.R.C. Rep., supra* note 11, ¶379.

30 *Id.*¶382 (explaining that only those within a good class and with a spotless record may travel). Regardless of the record of the person approved, the officer who approves such travel may be responsible if the approved citizen later defects. *Id.* Thus, such travel permits are exceedingly difficult to acquire.

31 *Id.* ¶383.

32 ICCPR, *supra* note 21, at art. 6(1).

33 John M. Glionna, *North Korea's Kim Jong Un Wages Defector Crackdown*, L.A. TIMES (Jan. 5, 2012), www.latimesblogs.latimes.com/world_now/2012/01/kim-jong-il-death-new-north-korean-leader-kim-jong-un-crackdown-on-defectors.html (reporting on three North Koreans executed when attempting to cross into China).

34 *H.R.C. Rep., supra* note 11, ¶402.

35 *Id.* ¶403.

36 *H.R.C. Rep., supra* note 11, ¶403.

37 *Id.*

38 Special Rapporteur on Extrajudicial, Summary, or Arbitrary Executions, *Addendum: Study on Targeted Killings*, Human Rights Council, ¶32, U.N. Doc. A/HRC/14/24/Add.6 (May 10, 2010).

39 Convention Against Torture and Other Cruel, Inhuman or Degrading Treatment or Punishment, *opened for signature* Dec. 10, 1984, 1465 U.N.T.S. 85 (entered into force June 26, 1987) [hereinafter Torture Convention].

40 *See, e.g., Gladys Carol Espinoza Gonzales v. Peru*, Case 11.157, Inter-Am. Comm'n H.R., Report No. 67/11, ¶172 (2011) (citing Inter-American Court of Human Rights cases stating this norm); *Prosecutor v Furundzija*, Case No. IT-95-17/1-T, Judgment, n. 170 (Int'l Crim. Trib. For the Former Yugoslavia, Dec. 10, 1998) (citing the United Nations Human Rights Committee as having reported that the prohibition against torture has reached a peremptory norm).

41 *Furundzija*, Case No. IT-95-17/1-T, ¶¶153–55.

42 *See id.*¶155.

43 Torture Convention, *supra* note 39, at art. 1(1).

44 *Id.*

45 Special Rapporteur on Torture and Other Cruel, Inhuman or Degrading Treatment or Punishment, *First Rep. on Torture and Other Cruel, Inhuman or Degrading Treatment or Punishment*, Comm'n on Human Rights, ¶119, U.N. Doc. E/CN.4/1986/15 (Feb. 19, 1986) (by P. Kooijmans) [hereinafter *Report on Torture*].

46 Lee, *supra* note 9, at 153 (citing C.H.R. Res. 2004/13, U.N. Doc. E/CN.4/RES/2004/13 (Apr. 15, 2004) and C.H.R. Res. 2005/11, U.N. Doc. E/CN.4/RES/2005/11 (Apr. 14, 2005)).

47 *H.R.C. Rep., supra* note 11, ¶84.

48 KINU 2013, *supra* note 17, at 131–33; Robert Marquand, *North Korea's Hidden Labor Camps Exposed*, CHRISTIAN SCI. MONITOR (May 21, 2013), www.csmonitor.com/World/Asia-Pacific/2013/0521/North-Korea-s-hidden-labor-camps-exposed.

49 *See* Neaderland, *supra* note 3, at 159–60.

50 Lee, *supra* note 9, at 154–155 (giving an example of a person tortured until her legs were rendered useless).

51 *Id.; see also* KINU 2013, *supra* note 17, at 154.

52 KINU 2013, *supra* note 17, at 145.

53 Lee, *supra* note 9, at 155.

54 *H.R.C. Rep., supra* note 11, ¶¶411–12.

55 *See* KINU 2013, *supra* note 17, at 397–99.

56 *Id.* at 398–99.

57 *Id.* at 145–46.

58 *See supra* note 40–42 and accompanying text.

59　*Report on Torture*, *supra* note 45, ¶3. The Special Rapporteur went on to state that the prohibition on torture was *jus cogens*. *Id.*

60　*See* H.R.C. Rep., *supra* note 11, ¶1208. "Such a ridiculous attempt to infringe upon the sovereignty of the DPRK and do harm to its dignified socialist system by abusing human rights for a sinister political purpose is bound to meet a stern punishment by history." *Id.* (quoting *DPRK Foreign Ministry Spokesman Flays Hostile Forces' Adoption of "Human Rights Resolution" against DPRK*, KOREAN CENT. NEWS AGENCY (Nov. 20, 2013), www.kcna.co.jp/item/2013/201311/news20/20131120-21ee.html).

61　Convention on the Rights of the Child, *opened for signature* Nov. 20, 1989, 1577 U.N.T.S. 3 (entered into force Sept. 2, 1990) [hereinafter Child Convention].

62　*Id.* at art. 6.

63　*Id.* at art. 5.

64　*Id.* at art. 19.

65　*Id.* at art. 27.

66　YOONOK CHANG ET AL., U.S. COMM. FOR HUMAN RIGHTS IN N. KOR., THE NORTH KOREAN REFUGEE CRISIS: HUMAN RIGHTS AND INTERNATIONAL RESPONSE 24 (Stephen Haggard & Marcus Noland eds., 2006).

67　KINU 2013, *supra* note 17, at 157–58.

68　*See id.* at 158.

69　Glionna, *supra* note 33.

70　*See* H.R.C. Rep., *supra* note 11, ¶1197.

71　Kyu Chang Lee, *Protection of North Korean Defectors in China and the Convention Against Torture*, 6 REGENT J. INT'L L. 139, 139 (2008). The bilateral treaty is considered secret because there does not appear to be a complete copy available to the public; *see* Kevin Zickterman, *Worse than "Chinese Water Torture:" The Second Step in Straightening Out North Korea May Include Pressuring China to Stop Its Repatriation Campaign of North Korean Refugees*, 25 DCBA BRIEF 30, 31 (2013).

72　Protocol between the PRC Ministry of Public Security and the DPRK Social Safety Ministry for Mutual Cooperation in Safeguarding National Security and Social Order in Border Areas, June 9, 1964, China-N. Kor., P.R.C. Foreign Ministry Archive 106-01434-04, www.digitalarchive.wilsoncenter.org/document/115328.

73　*Id.* at art. 4(2).

74　Mutual Cooperation Protocol for the Work of Maintaining National Security and Social Order in the Border Areas, Aug. 12, 1986, arts. 4–5, China–N. Kor., www.nkfreedom.org/UploadedDocuments/NK-China-bilateral_treaty.pdf.

75　Law on Control of the Entry and Exit of Aliens (promulgated by the Standing Comm. Nat'l People's Cong., Nov. 22, 1985, effective Feb. 1, 1986), at arts. 29–30, www.english.gov.cn/2005-08/21/content_25035.htm.

76　Convention Relation to the Status of Refugees *opened for signature* July 28, 1951, 189 U.N.T.S. 150 (entered into force Apr. 22, 1954) [hereinafter Refugee Convention]; *see also* Neaderland, *supra* note 3, at 157 (stating that China ratified the Refugee Convention and its related protocol on Mar. 24, 1982).

77　*Id.* at art. 1(A)(2).

78　*Id.* at art. 33(1).

79　Gahng, *supra* note 20, at 370.

80　*Id.*

81　Refugee Convention, *supra* note 76, at art. 42 (stating that among others, both Articles 1 and 33 are non-derogable).

82　Although Article 33(2) of the Refugee Convention gives two narrowly tailored exceptions for refoulement—where the refugee poses a serious danger to the security of the country in which he currently occupies, or where the refugee is a danger to the community of the host country and has already been convicted of a very serious crime—China has never used either rationale as a basis for repatriating North Koreans. *See id.*

at art. 33(2). Even if China made such an argument, it would necessarily fail because this exception can only be applied after an individualized determination of national security and/or community danger, but China has a blanket repatriation policy regarding anyone crossing its border from North Korea. *See* U.N. High Comm'r for Refugees (UNHCR), *Guidance Note on Extradition and International Refugee Protection*, Apr. 2008, ¶¶15–16, *available at* www.refworld.org/docid/481ec7d92.html.

83 *Id.*¶8.
84 *Id.* ¶21.
85 "In the event of a conflict between the obligations of the Members of the United Nations under the present Charter and their obligations under any other international agreement, their obligations under the present Charter shall prevail." U.N. Charter art. 103.
86 U.N. Charter arts. 55(c), 56; Gahng, *supra* note 20, at 371.
87 Gahng, *supra* note 20, at 371.
88 *Id.* at 372.
89 *See* U.N. High Comm'r for Refugees (UNHCR), *Handbook on Procedures and Criteria for Determining Refugee Status under the 1951 Convention and the 1967 Protocol Relating to the Status of Refugees*, ¶62, U.N. Doc. HCR/IP/4/Eng/REV. (Jan. 1992) [hereinafter *Refugee Handbook*], *available at* www.refworld.org/docid/3ae6b3314.html.
90 Lee, *supra* note 9, at 145 (providing statistics indicating that more than half of the defectors fled the DPRK due to economic hardship).
91 *Refugee Handbook*, *supra* note 89, ¶63.
92 Lee, *supra* note 9, at 146.
93 *Id.*
94 *See id.*
95 Zickterman, *supra* note 71, at 34.
96 Protocol Relating to the Status of Refugees, *opened for signature* Jan. 31, 1967, 606 U.N.T.S. 237 (entered into force Oct. 4, 1967).
97 *Id.* at art. 2(1).
98 Zickterman, *supra* note 71, at 34.
99 Neaderland, *supra* note 3, at 158.
100 *See id.*
101 *Refugee Handbook*, *supra* note 89, ¶95.
102 *See id.* ¶96.
103 Glionna, *supra* note 33.
104 KINU 2013, *supra* note 17, at 464.
105 *Id.* at 482–83.
106 Torture Convention, *supra* note 39.
107 *Id.* at art. 3(1).
108 *Id.* at art. 3(2).
109 Torture Convention, *supra* note 39, at art. 1(1).
110 *See* KINU 2013, *supra* note 17, at 131 (explaining that art. 16 of the Socialist Labor Law and art. 36 of the Labor Protection Law define a work day as being eight hours in North Korea, while prisoners are forced to have a minimum of a ten-hour work day).
111 Convention on the Elimination of All Forms of Discrimination Against Women, *opened for signature* Dec. 18, 1979, 1249 U.N.T.S. 13 (*entered into force* Sept. 3, 1981). China ratified this convention on Nov. 4, 1980, even before the convention entered into force.
112 *Id.* at art. 6.
113 *Id.* at arts. 11–12.
114 Chang et al., *supra* note 66, at 23.
115 *See* KINU 2013, *supra* note 17, at 475.
116 *See* KINU 2013, *supra* note 17, at 145–46.

117   Child Convention, *supra* note 61.
118   Chang et al., *supra* note 66, at 24.
119   Glionna, *supra* note 33.
120   KINU 2013, *supra* note 17, at 158.
121   ICCPR, *supra* note 21.
122   *Id.* at art. 7.
123   *Id.* at art. 10.
124   Vienna Convention on Diplomatic Relations, *opened for signature* Apr. 18, 1961, 500 U.N.T.S. 95 (entered into force Apr. 24, 1964) [hereinafter Diplomatic Convention]; Vienna Convention on Consular Relations, *opened for signature* Apr. 24, 1963, 596 U.N.T.S. 261 (entered into force Mar. 19, 1967) [hereinafter Consular Convention].
125   Diplomatic Convention, *supra* note 124, at art. 22.
126   Consular Convention, *supra* note 124, at art. 31.
127   Neaderland, *supra* note 3, at 151; *see also* Elizabeth Rosenthal, *North Koreans Seek Asylum at Consulates in China*, N.Y. TIMES, May 9, 2012, www.nytimes.com/2002/05/09/world/north-koreans-seek-asylum-at-consulates-in-china.html.
128   Neaderland, *supra* note 3, at 151.
129   *Id.* at 152.
130   *Id.* at 152–53.
131   *Id.* at 152–54.
132   *E.g., H.R.C. Rep., supra* note 11, at Annex II: Correspondence with China (reproducing letters from China to the Commission of Inquiry which discount the Commission's legitimacy and reiterate that China's actions are in conformance with international and domestic law).
133   Zickterman, *supra* note 71, at 35.
134   *See* North Korean Human Rights Act, 22 U.S.C. §§ 7801–7845 (2006).
135   *UN Reports Horrific Human Rights Abuses in North Korea: Now What?* UN WATCH (Oct. 29, 2013), www.canadafreepress.com/index.php/article/58898 (calling for the U.N. Human Rights Council to publicly shame and pressure China into ending its repatriation policy).

12 Provisions for religious liberty*

North Korea's constitutional provisions for religious freedom

As examined in Chapter 5, North Korea flagrantly tramples upon religious freedom. Its persistent persecution of religious activity presents an incongruity with its own constitutional language that protects religious freedom for the people. The table below shows how some forms of religious freedom have appeared in the North Korean Constitution since its first iteration in 1948, all of which the regime has effectively ignored.

The changes in articles related to religion in the socialist constitution of North Korea[1]

Year of establishment and amendment	Articles related to religion
Adopted DPRK Constitution, September 8, 1948	Chapter 2. The fundamental rights and duties of citizens Article 14. Citizens have freedom of religion and religious worship.
Adopted DPRK Socialist Constitution, December 27, 1972	Chapter 4. The fundamental rights and duties of citizens Article 54. Citizens have freedom of religion and freedom from religious propaganda.
Revised DPRK Socialist Constitution, April 9, 1992	Chapter 5. The fundamental rights and duties of citizens Article 68. Public citizens have freedom of religion. This right is advocated to build religious buildings or permit religious services.
Revised DPRK Socialist Constitution, September 5, 1998 Revised DPRK Socialist Constitution, April 9, 2009 Revised DPRK Socialist Constitution, April 9, 2010 Revised DPRK Socialist Constitution, April 13, 2012	Chapter 5. The fundamental rights and duties of citizens Article 68. Citizens have freedom of religion. This guarantees the right to build religious buildings or hold religious services. Religion shall not be allowed to attract foreign intervention or disrupt the state's social order.

Though the state's constitution provides for religious freedom, the people of North Korea have yet to experience that freedom in practice. This blatant disregard of their written law fails any reasonable definition of rule of law. It manifests the cult of North Korea that coerces worship of the Supreme Leader (Kim Il-Sung, Kim Jong-Il, and Kim Jong-Un). Even the constitution bows to the Leader's thoughts and preferences:

> North Korea can be characterized as a charismatic society where the supreme, godlike leader's words and directives are the principal governing norms that supersede all else, including the law. His word is considered the quintessential source of enlightenment capable of dispensing justice … In other words, the Constitution in North Korea exists not for the protection of citizens' rights and interests, but merely as a tool to showcase the superiority of the State's system to its citizens and outside observers alike. In this regard, the mere existence of a provision for a fundamental right does not guarantee that right.[2]

Thus, the words and actions of the leader trump the Constitution—so the provisions for religious freedom prove illusory.

In practice, North Korea has the "One Thought" system based on Juche (roughly translated as "self-reliance"), which brooks no other system of thought and faith. The Korea Workers' Party has a general staff department that enforces the One Thought policy. The People's Grand Learning Center in Pyongyang demands that: "People have to dream of Kim, Jong-Un even when they sleep; people have to do what Kim, Jong-Un likes; and people have to walk to the routes that Kim, Jong-Un directs."[3]

The International Bill of Rights

However, North Korea still remains accountable, including under the applicable international law. Outside of North Korea's borders, and to a lesser extent within, the notion that people have a fundamental right to believe and practice their own religion remains ensconced. The Universal Declaration of Human Rights (UNDHR), written and promulgated in 1948 after the Second World War, stipulates in Article 18:

> Everyone has the right to freedom of thought, conscience and religion: this right includes freedom to change his religion or belief, and freedom, either alone or in community with others and in public or private, to manifest his religion or belief in teaching, practice, worship and observance.[4]

Though the UNDHR has no independent treaty status, it constitutes the seminal document of the International Bill of Rights. Several theories support its legal status and stature, as it is considered *the* text for international human rights, as mentioned above. The DPRK, though perhaps hard to believe, attained United

Nations member state status in September 1991. It should not turn a blind eye to the Universal Declaration.

One of many examples of how the DPRK violates Article 18 of the Universal Declaration includes the following account:

> In 1999, my town had a meeting for worship every Sunday. It was an underground church. The attendants were all caught and went to a political prison camp. I figured out later that the SSA sent one girl to attend this meeting. The person in charge of the meeting was an old lady and she loved the girl just like her own daughter, but the girl had a mission from the SSA. So, this girl denounced us and all were caught. Choi 00 went to a political prison camp, and her mother also went to a political prison camp.[5]

The DPRK, in its continued mistreatment of religious followers and as a U.N. member state, also defies a few key articles of the U.N. Charter. One mission of the various U.N. organs is to promote human rights in many different forms, including that of religious freedom. For example, Article 13 states that "[t]he General Assembly shall initiate studies and make recommendations for the purpose of ... assisting in the realization of human rights and fundamental freedoms for all without distinction as to race, sex, language, or religion."[6] It is no wonder then why the assembly continues to create rapporteurs and a commission to investigate, denounce and act upon North Korean defiance of the law. As a member state, the DPRK is also disregarding the actual purpose of U.N. member status and the role of the U.N. as an international organization with its religious discrimination. Article 55 reads:

> With a view to the creation of conditions of stability and well-being which are necessary for peaceful and friendly relations among nations based on respect for the principle of equal rights and self-determination of peoples, the United Nations shall promote ... universal respect for, and observance of, human rights and fundamental freedoms for all without distinction as to race, sex, language, or religion.[7]

In other words, North Korea's behavior directly contradicts its role as a member state altogether.

Further, the International Covenant on Civil and Political Rights, adopted by the U.N. General Assembly in 1966 and signed by North Korea, obligates the nation not to defeat its object and purpose, which includes freedom of religion in international law. Article 18 of the Covenant presents these broad rights of religious freedom:

> 1.   Everyone shall have the right to freedom of thought, conscience and religion. This right shall include freedom to have or to adopt a religion or belief of his choice, and freedom, either individually or in community

with others and in public or private, to manifest his religion or belief in worship, observance, practice, and teaching.

2. No one shall be subject to coercion, which would impair his freedom to have or to adopt a religion or belief of his choice.

3. Freedom to manifest one's religion or beliefs may be subject only to such limitations as are prescribed by law and are necessary to protect public safety, order, health, or morals or the fundamental rights and freedoms of others.

4. The States Parties to the present Covenant undertake to have respect for the liberty of parents and, when applicable, legal guardians to ensure the religious and moral education of their children in conformity with their own convictions.[8]

After 1981, when North Korea ratified the ICCPR, it has remained legally bound to provide these listed rights to its people, but it blatantly refuses to do so. North Korea even went so far in 1997 to state its wish to withdraw from the covenant, a quickly denied request since no withdrawal provisions exist in this treaty and such a withdrawal would have required approval by all member states, which the DPRK could not obtain. The following example illustrates North Korea's manifest disregard of its Article 18 obligations under the ICCPR:

> In 2005, I was forcibly returned to North Korea from China, and detained in the Onsung County SSA detention facility. The man who was in the next room was from 00 city. I heard that he sang a hymn. The SSA official made the man admit that he believes in Christianity, and the SSA official made him sing a hymn, and he sang. That night he disappeared … he was not sent to his town, but he got executed secretly.[9]

Commission of Inquiry

However, instead of complying post-1997, North Korea has blatantly ignored these commitments just as it disregards its own constitutional text except for the override provisions. The most recent report released in 2014 by the Commission of Inquiry on Human Rights in the Democratic People's Republic of Korea, widely cited through this book, stated the violation most definitively in two areas of its report:

> Freedom of religion and religious expression are guaranteed in articles 18 and 19 of the ICCPR, as well as articles 13 and 14 of the CRC. Both treaties not only call for State Parties to recognize these rights, but also to protect associated rights to freedom of association and peaceful assembly. Despite being a State Party to these treaties, the Commission finds that these protections are not afforded to DPRK citizens who are consequently unable to practise the religion of their choosing.
>
> [...]

Throughout the history of the Democratic People's Republic of Korea, among the most striking features of the state has been its claim to an absolute information monopoly and total control of organized social life. Based on witness testimonies, the Commission finds that there is almost complete denial of the right to freedom of thought, conscience, and religion as well as of the rights to freedom of opinion, expression, information, and association.[10]

These actions by the DPRK have merited public denunciation in the international community, but more vigorous action must follow to hold North Korea accountable for its blatant disregard of its fundamental international human rights obligations. These violations, as discussed in the final section of the book, could come before a hybrid tribunal.

In an analysis of 957 cases of religious persecution, religious activities underlie 45.6 percent (456) of them, the largest category. Possession of religious symbols accounts for 226 cases (23.6 percent) and form the second largest category. Spreading religion numbers 115 cases (12 percent) while contact with a missionary constitutes 5.3 percent (51).[11] These categories do not mutually exclude one another. In other words, a DPRK citizen may receive severe persecution for contact with a missionary, religious activities, as well as possession of newspapers with religious content.

International Religious Freedom Act

Under the International Religious Freedom Act, North Korea has consistently qualified as a Country of Particular Concern (CPC) as designated by the Secretary of State. The 2013 International Religious Freedom Report produced by the U.S. State Department provides specific reports for particular countries. The Executive Summary of the report for North Korea reads in part:

Although the constitution and other laws and policies provide for religious freedom, in practice, the government severely restricted religious activity, except for some officially recognized groups that it tightly supervised. Genuine religious freedom did not exist. Government practices continued to interfere with individuals' ability to choose and to manifest their religious beliefs. The government continued to repress the religious activities of unauthorized religious groups. Reports by refugees, defectors, missionaries, and nongovernment organizations (NGOs) indicated that religious persons who engaged in proselytizing and those who were in contact with foreigners or missionaries were arrested and subjected to extremely harsh penalties, including execution. South Korean media reported that North Koreans were executed for religious activities.[12]

Because North Korea has remained a CPC since 2001, the International Religious Freedom Act of 1998 requires the Secretary to continue imposing existing restrictions pursuant to sections 402(c)(5) and 409 of the Trade Act of 1974 (the Jackson-Vanik Amendment). The U.S. government has spoken out about religious freedom restrictions in the DPRK in multilateral fora and in bilateral talks with other governments, especially those with diplomatic relations with the country. The U.S. continues not to have diplomatic relations with North Korea. Addressing human rights, including religious liberty, would significantly improve prospects for closer ties between the two countries, as the U.S. government has expressed. U.S. government officials, such as representatives from the Office of International Religious Freedom and the special envoy for human rights in North Korea (a position created by the 2004 North Korea Human Rights Act), met with defectors and members of NGOs focused on North Korea.[13]

North Korea has amply deserved its designation as a CPC. It has engaged in severe and systematic persecution, especially against those in the border provinces. Though this section could cite a legion of cases, this border case represents many others:

> Seon 00 was a frequent border crosser. This person was sentenced to go to prison for five years, but lived only two years there because he was granted amnesty. But after he was released from prison, he was caught again because he brought back a Bible from China. Then he was sentenced to go to prison for ten years, but there was news that he died after only two years there. He might have died of malnutrition.[14]

In all the cases, the 00 occurs to preserve anonymity. Given North Korea's approach of extending persecution to friends and family members, the discretion is prudent; North Korea's crushing of religious liberty is not.

Notes

* Sonya Chung provided help with this chapter.
1 Cho Jung-hyun, et al., *White Paper on Human Rights in North Korea*, Korea Inst. for Nat'l Unification (2013).
2 Dae-Kyu Yoon, *The Constitution of North Korea: Its Changes and Implications*, 27 Fordham Int'l L. J. 1289 (2003).
3 Kim Soo-am et al., *White Paper on Human Rights in North Korea*, Korea Inst. for Nat'l Unification 312 (2012) [hereinafter KINU 2012].
4 Universal Declaration of Human Rights, art. 18, G.A. Res. 217 (III) A, U.N. Doc. A/RES/217(III) (Dec. 10, 1948).
5 KINU 2012, *supra* note 3.
6 U.N. Charter, art. 13, para.1.
7 U.N. Charter, art. 55.
8 International Covenant on Economic, Social, and Cultural Rights, art. 18, 993 U.N.T.S. 3 (entered into force Jan. 3, 1976).
9 KINU 2012, *supra* note 3, at 320.
10 U.N. Human Rights Council, Rep. of the Detailed Findings of the Comm'n of Inquiry on Human Rights in the DPRK, Feb. 7, 2014, ¶240, U.N. Doc. A/HRC/25/CRP.1 (2014).
11 KINU 2012, *supra* note 3, at 317–18.

12 *International Religious Freedom Report for 2013: Korea, Democratic People's Republic of,* U.S. DEP'T OF STATE, BUREAU OF DEMOCRACY, HUMAN RIGHTS AND LABOR, *available at* www. state.gov/documents/organization/222351.pdf.
13 *Id.*
14 KINU 2012, *supra* note 3.

Section Three

Constructive approaches and solutions

North Korea's gross and systematic violations of human rights and the laws of war have violated numerous tenets of international law, including contravention of the treaties that North Korea itself has ratified and signed. Nevertheless, a relative dearth of legal scholarship exists with respect to arguably the worst human rights and security situation in the world and what constructive approaches and solutions should apply.

This section will analyze possible tribunals and other options to provide a measure of redress for the victims of these heinous violations. It will provide context for the failed political solutions of the past involving the key international players in the Korean conflict, including China, Russia, the U.S., Japan, South Korea, and of course North Korea. It will provide a basis for new ways of looking at the Korean situation and provide hard-pressed solutions for the DPRK's continued defiance in the political arena. This section will explore concepts such as humanitarian intervention and the Responsibility to Protect, as well as provide implementation strategies for the best available options.

Essentially, it will suggest that to help prevent continuous military provocations and hostilities as perpetrated against South Korea and other nations by the DPRK, an immediate peace treaty needs to be signed and enforced with the critical concession that U.S. commitment remains. This must be done through multilateral as well as bilateral discussions, involving all the major players in the conflict and possibly the U.N. Secretary General and Security Council.

This section ventures to do so with a sober awareness of the difficulties and perils involved. The complexities present do not call for glib responses, but for serious research that wrestles with the real-life consequences and impact of the approaches and solutions considered. I humbly have attempted to do so.

13 Judicial justice*

Introduction

While contemplating other possibilities such as the International Criminal Court and South Korean courts after Korean reunification at the outset of this chapter, this chapter will eventually suggest a hybrid tribunal as the most promising forum for trying the alleged violations of human rights and war crimes by the DPRK. Since the inception of the ICC in July 2002, with currently over 100 signatories, certain shortcomings (notwithstanding its strengths) have surfaced. With problems such as insufficient staffing, limited resources and several jurisdictional hurdles, the ICC may not provide the best forum, although it may provide a rather good one, for addressing the egregious behavior of a criminal regime such as that of North Korea. Shortcomings in domestic law, sovereignty issues, and the perception of foreign influence among an ill-informed populace provide additional barriers to the legitimate working of an international court like the ICC.

The composition of a hybrid tribunal that combines aspects of international and domestic courts in an attempt to increase legitimacy in pursuing justice and to build the capacity of a renewed domestic system, while providing a workable and less expensive alternative to other, less effective international justice options comes as an intriguing solution. By combining the knowledge, expertise and work of both domestic and international personnel, hybrid tribunals can solve the problems of distance, access to witnesses and evidence, slow prosecution, and the high cost of the ad hoc tribunals of the past, while still achieving a comparable level of deterrence. Hybrids address the concomitant goals of respecting sovereignty, yet resolve to prosecute criminals *in situ* for violating universal norms.

Comparative analysis of prior precedents and cases from around the world will also strengthen the discussion. With a destroyed infrastructure and legal system, as well as the lack of a legitimate judiciary, a closer look at the former Yugoslavia provides insight into a possible Korea of tomorrow, one that might be recovering from a highly destructive conflict, although ideally that would not prove to be the case. A hybrid tribunal there attempted to correct Kosovo's devastated judiciary by incorporating domestic actors and aimed to increase legitimacy, decrease bias, and enhance capacity.

Cambodia, another Asian country that has suffered under the yoke of oppressive Communist dictators, has seen gross, systematic violations of human rights of its people, and provides another analogous situation. Similar to the widespread apathy regarding North Korea currently, the international community and the U.N. focused on Cambodia's sovereignty, while a farcical trial of the regime's leaders provided little redress for the Khmer Rouge's victims. Examples such as these provide the international community with lessons from antecedent hybrid tribunals regarding the most appropriate methods of implementing justice.

If the tragic climax of Korea's instability results in another full-blown war, then international participation in any sort of redress must avoid the substance and taint of "victor's justice". However, if the Koreas unite peacefully, the much preferred outcome, producing and utilizing any sort of tribunal so as to avoid an "imperialistic-looking" process would remain challenging at best. The end product should be a hybrid tribunal that would ideally combine the strengths of a domestic court with the contributions of an international court to enhance legitimacy, build domestic capacity, reduce costs, and help bring a measure of justice. As a lack of commitment by the international community has stymied the process of providing justice in many previous cases, we must stay committed to adequately providing a remedy that the victims of this criminal, totalitarian dictatorship so desperately need.

The International Criminal Court

North Korea stands next in line among the precedents set in the Nuremberg Trials and Tokyo Trials after World War II, the ad hoc tribunals for Rwanda and the former Yugoslavia, the hybrid tribunals concerning places such as Cambodia, Sierra Leone, East Timor, Bosnia and Herzegovina, and Kosovo, and the establishment of the ICC through the Rome Treaty. The magnitude, severity, and frequency of human rights violations in North Korea calls for the redress that such courts have sought to bring. Sufficient ratification of the Rome Treaty by enough countries established the ICC, the first permanent international criminal court based on a treaty,[1] and the start of analyzing possible redress options for the Korean Peninsula.

The negotiations for the ICC Statute, which entered into force on July 2, 2002, first began in Rome as early as 1998. Many parties to the Rome Statute house perpetrators of horrible human rights violations who could stand as possible defendants before the ICC. For example, Nigeria, Sierra Leone, as well as all former Yugoslav republics joined the ICC.[2] As of July 6, 2014, 122 countries, including Canada and a number of western European countries,[3] have ratified the Rome Treaty, while a total of 139 parties have signed it.[4] However, even those countries that have not ratified the Rome Treaty, like North Korea, may find themselves within the reach of the ICC. For example, the ICC has indicted president Omar al-Bashir despite Sudan's refusal to ratify the Rome Treaty.[5]

The recently completed investigation involves some of the most recent hostilities against South Korea under the auspices of the Rome Statute. The Office of the Prosecutor had been investigating whether it can charge DPRK nationals for war crimes regarding their sinking of the *Cheonan* and their shelling of Yeonpyeong Island. The ICC has jurisdiction under the Rome Statute to investigate and issue indictments for these incidents because South Korea remains a party to the Rome Statute and such acts concluded on South Korean territory.[6]

The Prosecutor has, unsurprisingly, been trying in vain to receive a response from the country for investigative purposes for the last several years.[7] If the Prosecutor finds a reasonable basis for prosecuting war crimes under Article 8 of the Rome Statute, the ICC can indict North Korean leaders for these crimes and try them individually.[8] Under Article 25, individuals can face criminal culpability for their actions and may have to pay reparations to victims of their crimes under Article 75.[9] The ICC can indict North Korea's leaders at virtually anytime, despite any political redress options and solutions on the table, so exploring ICC prosecution *before* attempting to offer political solutions and a local forum for such redress can provide negotiation leverage with a government that has responded positively only to forceful approaches.

Notwithstanding a country's willingness to engage in domestic prosecution, ICC prosecution can carry the advantage of an enhanced deterrent effect internationally. Prosecuting cases in the ICC can send a strong message to the rest of the world that certain types of behaviors will not be condoned and the international community will act to stop such behavior. When the cases pertain to heinous behavior by well-known offenders, or when the cases involve countries such as Sudan or North Korea, and where well-documented instances of terrible human rights violations exist, the resulting message would resound more widely. Therefore, Professor Milena Sterio thinks that prosecution at the ICC would result in a greater deterrent effect than prosecution in other tribunals.[10]

Professor Grace Kang wrote the definitive legal academic article on the case against the now deceased Kim Jong-Il before the International Criminal Court. In this article, she systematically and persuasively analyzes North Korean violations within the categorical rubric pertaining to the ICC.[11] However, this case for the prosecution of Kim Jong-Il in the ICC would have faced the considerable difficulty of his extradition. Similarly, an attempt at extradition of Kim Jong-Il's successor and son Kim Jong-Un might ignite another Korean conflagration, or it might succeed without such a consequence.

On the other hand, the ICC has limitations too:

> [T]he ICC cannot handle more than a tiny percentage of genocide, war crimes, and crimes against humanity cases as it faces many problems, including budgetary and staff deficiencies, jurisdictional hurdles, and a lack of political support from powerful countries such as the United States.[12]

In fact, the U.S. has remained quite outspoken about its preference for regional country-specific tribunals, such as the Special Court for Sierra Leone. In addition, the ICC has faced and still faces problems such as insufficient staffing needs, budgetary deficiencies and jurisdictional hurdles.[13] Consequently, the ICC can generally only prosecute a few of the top indicted individuals, which remains a serious limitation for the court. The limited resources of the ICC might not stretch to cover North Korean atrocities, although it arguably merits a place of priority among possible choices for ICC prosecution.

In part because of such limited resources, the ICC's principle of complementarity articulates the ICC's support of domestic primacy as well as its role in bolstering domestic law and systems:

> The design of the ICC, with the principle of complementarity as a key feature, recognizes that member states have the primary right and responsibility to prosecute crimes that fall under their jurisdiction, whether typical national offenses or grave violations of international criminal law. The hope was that the ICC would be "a catalyst for beefing up local systems to meet minimal international standards." The ICC would also strengthen international law generally by encouraging states to implement their ICC obligations through domestic legislation. Indeed, "a major success for the Court and the international community as a whole" would be a system where national institutions would respond so effectively so as to "obviate the need for trials before the ICC" altogether.[14]

Unfortunately, the world persists in a condition far removed from obviating the ICC. The complementarity principle of the ICC could remove the ICC regarding North Korea, if South Korea has sufficient means and abilities to provide the platform for North Korean prosecution in a reunified Korea. However, South Korea may not have the capacity to carry out the prosecution of North Korean human rights violations if North Korea attacked and devastated it.

The issue of bias or perceived bias might raise its head if South Korean judges and prosecutors engage in the prosecution. This issue could tilt in either direction: either for or against North Korean defendants. Sympathetic judges who identify strongly with North Koreans as fellow Koreans might incline favorably toward North Korean defendants. South Korean judges with memories of the Korean War and related hostilities might appear all too eager to convict North Korean defendants.

In this respect, the participation of international judges and attorneys could help defuse either actual or perceived bias. Although such international participants may bring biases of their own, a possible presumption of more impartiality given their comparative non-involvement with the Korean Peninsula might exist, unlike with its domestic participants.

Additional criticisms have come toward the ICC. The major criticisms are that the ICC has too many limits on its jurisdiction, its location usually removes it from the *situs* of the violations, and it cannot develop local legal facilities. Moreover, the ICC has a severe temporal restriction in that it cannot address any violations that occurred before 2002.[15]

With respect to North Korea, while a case existed for its jurisdiction over Kim Jong-Il, extradition may have proved difficult. However, the ICC could first indict

Kim Jong-Un before it had to worry about attempting extradition. The ICC probably would not contribute greatly to the development of local legal capacity in Korea, and it sits manifestly distant from the *locus* of the transgressions. Gross, systematic violations have taken place in North Korea prior to 2002, a period that the ICC cannot adjudicate.

Another problem with the ICC surfaces. The problem exists of international courts appearing as foreign impositions to the local populace. Like the problem of a body's immune system rejecting an organ transplant, a foreign court may find itself subject to a sense that it is "other", and therefore rejected on these grounds. As Laura Dickinson states it: "international courts such as the ICTY do face greater obstacles in establishing local legitimacy in the places from which the accused perpetrators come than they do in establishing legitimacy within broader international communities."[16]

Professor Diane Orentlicher also states that

> U.S. officials and other critics of the ICC assert that the Rome Statute violates basic tenets of international law regarding state sovereignty by allowing an international court to exercise jurisdiction over nationals of states that have not adhered to the court's statute.

Not only do critics feel that the ICC lacks democratic legitimacy in this way, they contend that the ICC does not maintain the checks and balances found in democratic states. Further, many think that "ICC judges will engage in expansive lawmaking from the bench by necessity since international crimes are defined with less precision than most national crimes."[17] The U.N. Security Council constructed the ICTY and ICTR under Chapter VII of the U.N. Charter before the formation of the ICC. Both the ICTY and ICTR had the authority to try defendants.[18] Some of the same criticisms leveled at the ICTY and ICTR have continued toward the ICC.

Considering the domestic option

Domestic prosecution presents another option. However, several complications may hinder efforts along this route. As one commentator put it, liabilities related to the structure and legitimacy of the domestic systems often hamper transitional justice efforts. Many times, the recent conflict destroys the physical and legal infrastructure of the nation, including the personnel needed for legal proceedings. The nation may even lack applicable domestic law or experience to prosecute such "egregious offenses", regardless of a sustained legal infrastructure. This structure goes to the heart of the legal system's legitimacy, which may also be completely lacking:

> The legitimacy of the domestic legal system is vital to any attempt at accountability, but may be absent either because it was employed as a mechanism for repression or because its personnel were complicit in the offenses committed.

> Transitional justice inherently implicates divisive political interests. Left to its own devices, a domestic legal system may not have the impetus to undertake such a daunting task. The temptation to condone, ignore and "forget", an often counter-productive strategy, is particularly strong when a widespread portion of the society was complicit in the atrocities.[19]

Allowing domestic prosecution also opens the door for a nation to purposely downplay its prosecutorial powers and limit its purported capability to address atrocities within its own ranks; the Indonesian Human Rights Courts could serve as Exhibit A.[20]

Applying these considerations, the horrors of another full-blown Korean war would likely obliterate the physical infrastructure of the legal system and possibly take the lives of too many civilian members of the legal profession. If enough survive, there would be a core of attorneys and judges who may adequately try the alleged violations. How to handle the North Korean issue has proven divisive in South Korea, in part because of the efficacy of North Korean propaganda in South Korea, partially due to the South Korean media's neglect in reporting violations by North Korea, partially due to a common ethnic identity, and in part due to partisan politics. A portion of the South Korean populace would likely try to condone or ignore North Korean atrocities.[21] All of these factors could militate against domestic proceedings.

Furthermore, North Korean domestic institutions, such as its judiciary, leave much to be desired in terms of political independence, the rule of law, due process, and many other concerns, as mentioned earlier in this volume.[22] In a future unified Korea, the legitimacy of the formerly South Korean institutions, such as the courts, would be stronger than its formerly Northern counterparts. Dickinson argues that even though the legitimacy of domestic institutions is often questionable in a post-conflict situation, the "precise nature of the legitimacy crisis varies and is inseparable from the unique history and culture of a given society." Dickinson has concerns that the judiciary would not only have suffered damage to its physical infrastructure, but also that the available personnel would be severely compromised:

> Judges and prosecutors from the prior regime—who failed to prosecute or convict murderers, torturers or ethnic cleansers—may remain in place, or alternatively, the new regime may have replaced the old personnel almost completely, resulting in an enormous skills and experience deficit, as well as the danger of show trials and overly zealous prosecution for past crimes.[23]

In the instance of Korea, South Korean legal personnel would not have the problem of association with the prior regime. The dramatic divergence and resulting contrast between South Korea and North Korea should clearly disassociate the two Koreas in most regards. The concern about show trials and overly zealous prosecution may still exist, but neither are insurmountable problems. Nonetheless, these concerns would yet remain in a solely domestic process.

Note that domestic courts could form the middle layer of a three-tiered approach. First, a hybrid tribunal can prosecute those most responsible for the most serious crimes. Second, a Truth and Reconciliation Commission could handle the least serious offenses and the least responsible offenders. The domestic courts could handle the middle tier. A hybrid tribunal would not obviate the role of domestic courts.

Further objections

Some scholars have also argued that the hybrid tribunals of Sierra Leone, Cambodia, and East Timor established just prior to the ICC "represent[ed] an attempt by states to reinsert themselves into the post-conflict legal process and reassert their sovereignty."[24] On the other hand, crimes pertaining to the ICC and other international courts frequently fall within *jus cogens* norms, usable to implement universal jurisdiction over many defendants—and therefore such courts do not require any assent to apply.[25] A recent empirical study of the perceptions of the International Criminal Tribunal for the former Yugoslavia (ICTY) within Bosnia and Herzegovina provides an applicable analogy with the ICC. The study showed that a wide cross-section of lawyers and judges from all ethnic groups were ill-informed regarding the efforts of the ICTY and were actually suspicious of the court's motive and results. The reasons for this lack of trust and legitimacy may have involved a variety of factors including:

> the location of the tribunal in the Netherlands, far from the local population, the failure of the ICTY to publicize its work within Bosnia, particularly within the legal community, the lack of participation of local actors, even as observers, and the use of predominantly common-law approaches to criminal justice that were unfamiliar to the local legal profession, which has been trained in a civil law tradition.[26]

Recall that the ICC and other international courts often carry out their functions far away from the countries involved in their cases, do not involve local actors, and must overcome suspicions about their work. Along these lines, Dickinson asserts that "[p]urely domestic and purely international institutions also often fail to promote local capacity-building. In post-conflict situations, the need to develop local capacity in the justice sector is often an urgent problem."[27] Such a problem would rise to acute levels if the country experienced the devastation of war. In Korea, a peaceful reunification would greatly diminish the need for local capacity building due to the existing capacity, especially in the former South Korea. Even in a peaceful reunification though, the north would still need a large infusion of capacity building.

Other international courts, such as the ICTY, can have limited effects of apparently brief durations: "For example, the efficacy of the Yugoslavia war crimes tribunal has frequently been called into question on the ground that the court has had little discernible impact on public attitudes in the former Yugoslavia relating to war crimes."[28] While such an assessment only looks at one aspect of effectiveness, it does raise a particular concern of its lack of impact on public attitudes. In fairness to the ICTY though, longer-term effects may yet germinate and blossom over time.

This concern materialized with respect to the Nuremberg trials as well as those of the ICTY. The impact of the Nuremberg trial was not seen on the German public until almost a generation later, when Germany began to prosecute Nazi criminals on its own initiative in the 1960s. It is just as likely that many citizens of the former Yugoslavia will initially resist the ICTY's lessons in individual responsibility, but the passage of time might bring about a different opinion. Already there is some evidence that the public in Serbia was impacted by the Slobodan Milosevic trial. Bogdan Ivanisevic, a Serbian staff member of Human Rights Watch, made the following observation one year after the trial of Milosevic had begun:

> Even though they have resistance to hearing non-Serb witnesses, people do take into consideration what they hear. The trial has caused reduced myth-making in Serbia. You don't hear, as you did prior to the trial … that [the massacre at] Srebrenica didn't happen or that the Muslims killed themselves. I wouldn't minimize this reduced space for rewriting history. As for acknowledgment of our side's crimes, it's a psychological barrier too difficult [to cross—admitting] that the policy we supported was criminal. It will take time. It may take a new generation that was not implicated.[29]

Decreasing the amount of revisionist history and the admittedly limited effect on the public, as modest as these gains may seem, do represent progress in a positive direction that can grow and mature over time. Reversing and ameliorating the effects of the totalitarian society in North Korea will take much time as well—such grievous wounds do not heal overnight. An appropriate tribunal can take some important steps in that direction that can substantially boost the process. As an Asian proverb states, "a journey of a 1000 miles begins with a single step."

There is also concern that prosecutions are an obstacle to peace. Proponents of punishment do not take into account that "[l]eaders with blood on their hands may cling more tenaciously to power if they cannot secure an airtight amnesty." Instead of promoting reconciliation, prosecutions might incite further grievances, so the objection runs.[30]

With respect to North Korea, such a prosecution would have a higher likelihood of taking place after Korea becomes reunited. Raising the prospect of prosecution *post* reunification in official interactions would decrease the danger embedded in this objection to prosecution. Whether raised or not with the leadership of North Korea, such a fear of prosecution can exist already due to other prosecutions around the world. Also, given that North Korea already has designs upon reunifying the peninsula by force and has already engaged in various types of belligerent behavior, it would be all too facile to scapegoat a possible tribunal for hostile actions that North Korea would have committed regardless of a possible tribunal.

On the other hand, moving forward with prosecution could serve as a catalyst for reunification. It could provide a lever to eject the Kim dynasty from North Korea.

Greater justice deepens a more rounded peace. Ignoring issues of justice cheapens the blood of those who have already experienced extreme violence at the hands of North Korean despotism. For victims of such horrendous suffering, it is the totalitarian regime that has already been anything but peaceful. The difficulties and possible peril involved in a tribunal do not mean that it should not be attempted. At the same time, the specifics of what, when, where, and how call for careful wisdom. As the North Koreans know all too well, the bulk of goods in a society may be swept away by injustice.

Lessons from the past

From a historical prospective, Cambodia provides an *apropos* analogy in a number of ways to North Korea. Both have been Communist regimes under oppressive dictators; both are in Asia; both have resorted to gross, systematic violations of human rights of their own people. Contemplating the Cambodian experience can provide lessons applicable to North Korea.

The Communist Party of Kampuchea (CPK), commonly known as the Khmer Rouge (KR), took control of Cambodia in 1975 and remained in power until Vietnamese forces drove most of the regime to the Cambodian–Thai border and largely out of power. Under the leadership of Pol Pot (Saloth Sar), the KR "strove to build a socially and ethnically homogeneous society by abolishing all preexisting economic, social, and cultural institutions, and transforming the population of Cambodia into a collective workforce." In the process, the regime displaced millions of Cambodians by subjecting them "to forced labor and inhumane living conditions, including physical exhaustion, starvation, and disease." In an effort to "purge perceived ideological enemies" throughout the country, the Khmer Rouge targeted "particular ethnic minorities, religious leaders, teachers, students, and other educated groups" to torture and subjected them to "extra-judicial executions."[31]

After their overthrow in 1979, the KR continued to fight the People's Republic of Kampuchea in certain parts of Cambodia and even retained enough power over sections of the country to obtain Cambodia's seat in the United Nations. This struggle continued until the 1990s:

> It was not until approximately 1993 that the Khmer Rouge ceased to be an active fighting force. Since that time, many Khmer Rouge members have returned to civilian life and now live freely in parts of Cambodia. The Cambodian government has integrated other members into the Cambodian national army and granted them immunity from prosecution under a 1994 Cambodian law that criminalized membership in the Khmer Rouge.[32]

What may be learned from the Cambodian experience for North Korea? First of all, the more aware and educated the world becomes about the grave human rights situation, the more traction may form for an eventual tribunal. NGOs, international organizations, and concerned individuals would likely continue to play leading roles in this regard as the bulk of national governments would unlikely lead in such an effort.

The decades following the overthrow of the KR wallowed in international apathy toward Cambodia, and the limited attention given concentrated on the establishment of a non-communist government rather than the adjudication of potential crimes.[33] Indeed, "[o]nly in 1997, after nearly two decades of relative inaction by the international community on the matter, did the United Nations (UN) and the Royal Government of Cambodia (RGC) begin to discuss establishing a tribunal to try the alleged perpetrators."[34] Regarding North Korea, much more attention comes from the international community regarding its nuclear weapons than the devastation already wrought through its extensive trampling upon the human rights of its own people.

Returning to the Cambodia example, once order was established, both the Cambodian government and the international community began to respond to the overthrow of the KR. Unfortunately, the Cambodian people did not derive a benefit from either of the responses, which has only produced more difficulties in bringing the former leaders of the KR to justice.[35]

Instead, Cambodia responded in 1979 with what is widely regarded as a farcical trial of both Pol Pot and Ieng Sary, the Standing Committee Member and Deputy Prime Minister for Foreign Affairs. The two leaders were tried in absentia without a defense counsel present, found guilty of the commission of genocide, and sentenced to death by a domestic tribunal.[36]

Many of the officers responsible for the KR atrocities were not and could not be punished because they died before the establishment of a proper tribunal, which emphasizes why a tribunal should be established as soon as possible.[37] As urgent as a tribunal for North Korea would be, it would not enhance the rule of law to engage in a similar breach of due process in trying Kim Jong-Un and his top officials. Any such trial should be full and fair, with built in protections of the criminal defendants. Otherwise, it would stoop to the sort of truncated pretense of a process that North Korea itself inflicts upon its own people.

North Korea's judiciary, as a mere tool for the ruling regime, lacks political independence and strength.[38] It certainly does not uphold human rights. Similarly, "the weakened state of the Cambodian judiciary from years of civil war and the international nature of the crimes to be prosecuted led the government to believe that international participation was necessary to ensure that the trials met international standards of justice."[39] As in Cambodia, international participation would greatly enhance the chances that the gross, systematic violations of human rights in North Korea would be addressed.

The description of the Cambodian human rights crisis analogizes well with North Korea in its severity and gravity, as well as the lack of response by the international community. For example, the U.N. Human Rights Commission's Sub-Commission on Prevention of Discrimination and Protection of Minorities produced a report on human rights issues in Cambodia in March 1979. The Sub-

Commission labeled the abuses that it recorded from the last four years as "'the most serious [human rights violations] that had occurred anywhere in the world since nazism,' concluding that they 'constituted nothing less than autogenocide.'" However, after the Vietnamese occupied Cambodia that same year, the U.N. ended its efforts to investigate the widespread atrocities. Even the International Conference on Kampuchea that met in New York soon after the report (in 1981) focused not on the human rights issues but "almost entirely on the Vietnamese involvement."[40]

Contemplate this lack of response:

> During the entire period of its rule, the Khmer Rouge occupied the Cambodian seat in the U.N., without even a single Western country voting against its retention. Perhaps more alarmingly, no country has invoked the Genocide Convention on behalf of the victims, brought a claim against Cambodia before the International Court of Justice, or extradited Khmer Rouge leaders for trial via universal jurisdiction.[41]

On the other hand, the international community did "take a prominent role in the multilateral Paris Peace Accords of 1991, which reinstituted the Cambodian government's full independence from Vietnam," and "on October 23, 1991, the Paris Conference on Cambodia signed a complex set of settlement accords." Surprisingly though, the mandate that originally established the conference did not even reference concepts like justice, human rights, or criminal tribunals. It appeared that Cambodian sovereignty stayed a higher priority for the international community than the blatant human rights issues, which were effectively cordoned off to the side. The international community prioritized Cambodian sovereignty and control, but would later need to undermine that control in order to lobby for an international tribunal. Unfortunately for many Cambodians, the U.N. subsequently rejected both an international criminal tribunal and a possible case before the International Court of Justice (the ICJ).[42]

The North Korean situation can run into future challenges involving the international community akin to those experienced in Cambodia. To help avoid similar complications, human rights redress should sit high on the agenda of any post-reunification scenario from the outset. If such redress takes a back seat early in the process, it will become that much more challenging for it to come to the foreground later.

The international community's approach toward Cambodia, emphasizing the Cambodian government's duty to human rights treaties and standards, includes an attempt to find an indirect route by addressing the human rights concerns in Articles 15 and 17 of the Paris Peace Accords. The approach contains implications of an approach that might apply to North Korea:

> Article 15 included several major human rights provisions: it stated that all Cambodians shall enjoy the rights and freedoms enumerated in the Universal Declaration of Human Rights and other international instruments; it imposed

on Cambodia an affirmative duty to protect human rights and institute preventive measures to ensure that the policies and practices of the Khmer Rouge era do not return; in an effort to eliminate the international neglect that prevailed during the Khmer Rouge era, Article 15 imposed corresponding obligations on other signatories; and Article 17 imposed on the U.N. Commission on Human Rights the obligation to monitor the human rights conditions in Cambodia. Professor Ratner best characterized the provisions as "viewed as best tackl[ing the problem] by obligating Cambodia to meet its commitments under the pertinent human rights instruments, especially the Genocide Convention."[43]

Given North Korea's ratification of a number of major human rights treaties,[44] a similar approach of applying these treaties to North Korea may transpire. Simply holding North Korea to its already existing commitments to international law can greatly help address the heinous crushing of its own people.

Similarly to the state of affairs in Cambodia, the international community has not paid sufficient attention to North Korea's human rights situation, although the tide has been turning in this regard. The experiences in Cambodia have taught the international community that its neglect over several decades has decreased the international community's ability to influence present attempts to create a tribunal. Attorney Luftglass states:

> As scholar of Cambodia Brian D. Tittemore observed: "The absence of timely intervention by the international community to prevent or punish Khmer Rouge atrocities significantly limited the United Nation's present-day ability to influence the creation of a Khmer Rouge tribunal or to ensure that any such tribunal is competent, impartial, and effective."

Luftglass went on to emphasize that past neglect creates concerns that the international community does not act in the best interests of Cambodia, and international action may end up doing more harm than good.[45]

Hybrid tribunals and their potential

As has been the case in Cambodia by way of a negative lesson, the sooner North Korea's human rights situation can receive greater attention and care from the international community, the better. Delay damages the prospects of timely and effective intervention, similarly to how delaying surgery in certain instances can harm a patient and worsen the prognosis.

A tribunal that would take place as soon as possible following reunification would appear as the most feasible approach. The International Criminal Court option, as attractive as it appears in some regards, closed its initial efforts. A *proprio motu* motion by the Prosecutor and Security Council referral are routes that remain. However, extradition of the inexperienced and untested Kim Jong-Un might prove much easier than it would have been to extradite his late father, Kim Jong-Il.

Indicting Kim Jong-Un, not a difficult step, would be a move in the right direction. If domestic prosecution does not or cannot provide a satisfactory resolution by itself, a hybrid tribunal appears to be the best option. In such a tribunal, corruption must be avoided; bias must be reduced as much as possible. The ECCC, the Cambodia hybrid, has been bogged down in corruption and politicized, improper influence. In addition, the tribunal must communicate well with the general public, and a sensible blend of domestic and international resources should be utilized with an eye toward aiding the domestic system long term.

A "third generation" of courts, hybrid tribunals, has emerged to address the challenges faced by purely international or domestic tribunals.[46] Hybrid courts, which combine aspects of international and domestic courts, attempt to increase legitimacy in pursuing justice, to build the capacity of a renewed domestic system while providing a workable and less expensive alternative to other, less effective international justice options. Not only does the hybrid tribunal provide legitimacy, which is crucial in itself, but a hybrid tribunal also provides expertise in the form of international judges and attorneys.[47]

Hybrid tribunals join international judges with local judges to apply amalgamated procedures and law that incorporate intrinsic domestic values as well as established international norms.[48] Local lawyers also work alongside their international counterparts in the process.[49] This hybridized tribunal acknowledges the importance of ideologically distancing the criminal court process from the perceptions of impropriety inherent in a prior local judicial system. Similarly, the hybrid court engages local stakeholders and incorporates them into the process.[50]

Hybrid tribunals have risen in response to the view that "solution[s] should be carefully tailored to the conflict and the needs and interests of the parties through an inclusive design process" instead of the assumption that "internationalized criminal courts are the best mechanisms for resolving every dispute."[51] Hybrids are a recent innovation in international justice, a next generation alternative that responds to specific criticisms of their ad hoc international tribunal predecessors: the 1993 ICTY and the 1994 International Criminal Tribunal for Rwanda (ICTR). These criticisms include the courts' vast distance from the countries in which violations took place, which disconnects them from the populace. The generally more proximate locations of hybrid tribunals provide readier access to testimony and evidence. The ad hoc tribunals have also received criticism for the slow pace of the trials and the massive expense of trying even only a handful of atrocity perpetrators.[52] In hybrids, by contrast, the dual goals of legitimacy and capacity building have fewer obstacles in some ways toward accomplishment while operating in a more cost-effective manner.[53] Given the foundational nature of justice in any society, establishing justice should constitute a high priority indeed, as injustice can destroy or remove most positive things. International participation in the prosecution also puts other dictators on notice that such egregious crimes against humanity can meet accountability.[54]

In 2000, the Special Court for Sierra Leone (SCSL)[55] came about as an autonomous court separate from the local court system through an agreement with the U.N. The SCSL coordinated its efforts with the Sierra Leone Truth Commission.

International judges held a majority against a minority of local judges in the tribunal. A hybrid with North Korea should also maintain an international majority to resist bias, corruption and illegitimacy.

In 2003, the Extraordinary Chambers in the Courts of Cambodia (ECCC) was formed through protracted negotiations with the U.N. It differs from the SCSL because it is part of the Cambodian court system, it applies both Cambodian and international law, and the tribunal consists of a narrow majority of local judges and a minority of international judges.[56] In 2000, East Timor and Kosovo tribunals were formed by domestic regulations, which created panels of international and national judges. In 2005, the War Crimes Chamber (WCC) of Bosnia and Herzegovina was created as a domestic institution functioning under national law. It was designed to facilitate the ICTY's exit strategy by prosecuting cases referred to it by the international tribunal.[57] Such prior hybrid tribunals provide predicate examples for contemplating a hybrid tribunal for North Korea's gross and systematic violations of human rights.

Even with only a handful of modern hybrid attempts under our collective and figurative belts, advantages to their employment appear to be greater legitimacy with the participants than other options, capacity building of the local legal systems, and infusing them with international norms, which can happen selectively.[58] Experience also tends to show that these tribunals more quickly indict individuals and bring them to trial.[59]

Hybrids contemplate the concomitant goals of respecting sovereignty while upholding universal standards—resolving to prosecute criminals domestically for violating universal norms.[60] As a result, the hybrid system represents the interests of all in the context of international justice.[61]

Hybrid courts have the potential to claim a stronger overall basis of legitimacy than the previous generations of either pure international or domestic processes.[62] The tribunal team linking national and international lawyers, judges, and other experts helps disarm challenges to legitimacy on imperialism grounds or domestic biases. Collaboration between international actors and regional partners further mitigates the possible perception that developed powers attempt to exact some arbitrary form of revenge on dictators. Overall, involving the local citizenry and their legal institutions may also increase the likelihood that hybrid tribunals "will bring a greater sense of reconciliation."[63]

Legitimacy concerns are a major hurdle for international judges in transitional justice proceedings where marginalized groups have been previously and violently oppressed by the dominant group. A residual lack of faith in legal processes may be borne into the post-conflict system, and special attention is needed to "resolve prior imbalances" and "recalibrate the equities" so as to craft a solid foundation into the new legal system.[64] A process that is not conceived as legitimate tends to alienate the local population and call into question the international community's commitment to genuine justice.[65] With respect to this factor in North Korea, it would depend on what circumstances exist when the tribunal is attempted. Pertinent factors would include whether Korea was unified or still divided; whether the resources of South Korea would be available or unavailable due to wartime devastation or another reason; whether qualified and sufficiently unbiased personnel could be drawn from North Korea (which, as demonstrated earlier, looks very dubious presently), etc.

Presumably, less biased and more disinterested international judges who consult with their local partners in joint decision-making processes can do much to increase public belief in and acceptance of the results. The result of judicial collaboration can be a standard of shared values defined by the integrated international and regional partnership.[66]

International judges benefit from proximity to the local population in hybrid models. The sensitivity to local issues, local culture, and local approaches to justice are more readily accessible when making decisions "on the ground" and in the conscious presence of the affected population.[67] The presence of these international actors may also enhance perceptions of judicial independence, especially important in transitional nations, which have a recent tradition of interference or overt control over the judiciary. In North Korea, no politically independent judiciary exists.[68] However, South Korea does have both judicial infrastructure and personnel who can contribute. National judges involved in the process receive the benefit of training, exposure to norms of international law, and skills useful for the long-term capacity building of the national judiciary for use at the termination of the tribunal's work.[69]

Similarly, international judges bring a level of impartiality in an environment that risks being highly politicized. The inclusion of international judges provides a layer of insulation against intimidation from local judges' own governments or other interference with the rule of law. When this hedge against improper interference is absent, the specter of illegitimacy may manifest itself and obstruct the process in some way. Tanaz Moghadam gives this example: the Iraqi High Tribunal (IHT), a pure domestic tribunal with foreign supervision, was barred from international judge participation and consequently lacked a sufficient level of quality in the proceedings. As a result, the trial of the ruthless Iraqi dictator Saddam Hussein was widely viewed as "lacking in legitimacy and fairness," citing vulnerability to political interference and government manipulation.[70]

However, one issue regarding international participation in Korea involves language. If international personnel take part and the Korean community is to perceive the proceedings as legitimate (or at all for that matter), this matter would have to be addressed. Similar to tribunals in the past, a Korean hybrid tribunal would have to utilize both Korean, the native language of the peninsula, and English, the *de facto* international language. Although this could be seen as a challenge to any Korean hybrid tribunal, successfully integrating both languages into the proceedings would strengthen the institution's legitimacy and acceptance with the local population. As an analogy, the Inter-American Court of Human Rights employs both Spanish and English.

Hendler suggests that permitting a newly awakened nation access to the results of the judicial process is not a matter for curiosity alone: "Apart from its socializing function through the education of the people, there is the legitimating function that comes from the acceptance of the law as a body of rules to be followed."

In fact, he continues, it is a necessary first step for ensuring that the rule of law is adopted by a transitional community or else it will supplant its own formal mechanisms of justice like an overflowing river pouring over its banks:

> Societal opinion will always find a channel; it may be chaotic, as is the case with lynching, assemblies cheering and hooting judges, or street demonstrations calling for television broadcasts, or it may be in the form of institutionalized answers, like juries, lay magistrates, popular councils of advisers or any similar variation … There is no need to explain how uncontrollable the pressure of public opinion can become in cases of spontaneous response like the one described above.[71]

Community participation begins with community awareness. To cultivate community awareness, intervening actors must ensure the public has access to recordings and court declarations of the proceedings. Such materials can then be broadcast to the entire nation through the news outlets. As a collection of records comes to light throughout the process, the documentation of the previous regime's actions may help alleviate the tension surrounding what may be thought of by some as international intrusion and further justify the grounds for collaboration by local legal experts.[72]

The diffusion of norms into societies afflicted by institutionalized atrocities may be accomplished to an extent by integrating international standards of justice and human rights into domestic law. This takes place in the hybrid tribunal environment through applying the principles uniformly in practice and by showcasing the interaction between elite actors throughout the process.[73] Judges, law experts, secretaries, police officers, local news outlets, and anyone from the community who has contact with the hybrid court may adopt the normative values. This is especially important when there is an opportunity for domestic or international interference in the national reconstruction process by individuals or groups that supported the abuses of the previous regime. Individuals who view the fruits of the tribunals first-hand can resist notions of impropriety and assist in the establishment of the post-regime judicial system.

National institutions in post-conflict countries often find themselves destroyed physically through warfare and political neglect or through judicial corruption and intervention by the former regimes. The judicial systems themselves may lack physical infrastructure, competent personnel, and public confidence. Entire groups may have been denied access to education or professional choice under the old regime.[74] "In the wake of mass violence, there may be very few trustworthy leaders left in the afflicted society, not to mention the society's physical infrastructure, which may have been completely destroyed."[75]

The hybrid judicial process allows society to transition toward stability and security in the new system, while acknowledging the atrocities committed by the former regime.[76] It also helps to rebuild domestic judicial systems by providing judicial training for these systems, while serving as an institution of justice.[77] Sharing the responsibilities of administration of justice between local and international actors aids in establishing the legitimacy of the judicial process, while simultaneously strengthening the domestic capacity for administering justice in a post-regime environment.[78]

The ICC explicitly incorporates a spirit of "complementarity" from its own statute, accepting that member states may receive jurisdiction to prosecute criminal cases on their own. Reasons for this include the fact that international tribunals require a large amount of resources and veteran judges to try individuals higher up on the chain of command who are more directly responsible for causing atrocities:

> [I]t is important to let national courts prosecute lesser offenders. National jurisdictions, especially in war-torn countries, have to grow, so that allowing them to prosecute offenders of important crimes might help them rebuild their criminal codes and their judiciary. Prosecutions might also be necessary as part of the country's healing process, and prosecutions in the country that suffered a civil war are going to be a lot more effective than ICC prosecutions taking place at [T]he Hague. [T]he advantages of prosecution in the home country include: the proximity of the evidence and the witnesses; the judges' awareness of the nature of the conflict that occurred; the government's cooperation; as well as the fact that such national prosecutions might be part of the home country's healing process.[79]

A hybrid tribunal for North Korea can try the most responsible defendants, leaving the prosecution of those less responsible to the reconstituted domestic system.

The effectiveness of norm diffusion also depends on the availability of a legal system that is willing to accept universal norms. While tribunals may play a part in holding accountable those who grossly violate and abuse their citizenry, international standards and practices alone may not overcome normative beliefs cultivated through accumulated decades of brutal oppression and propaganda, such as in North Korea.[80]

Regardless, Moghadam posits that the hybrid methodology can adapt for any state. She states that hybrid tribunals help enhance the interpretation of national law by conforming it to international standards.[81] Such a benefit assumes of course that the international standards would actually be an improvement over the domestic ones, a more likely scenario in a situation of gross, systematic violations of human rights as in the DPRK.

Hybrid tribunals also have the effect of strengthening the network of normative accountability across domestic and international borders. Also, fair conduct of tribunals can demonstrate the uniform application of law that stands reasonably independent of political intrusion. This role plays a large part in regenerating faith in legal institutions, which were previously tools of oppression. Moghadam also indicates the positive impact hybrids can have on building regional capacities that reinforce international norms and local traditions.[82] Each of these benefits would immensely benefit a society such as North Korea, which has suffered too long from pernicious injustice.

The complexity of post-regime systems requires a flexible approach to rebuilding that seeks to repair the nation.[83] While such flexibility can constitute a major advantage of hybrid tribunals, it requires careful analysis and application as to the specifics that emerge for that context.

Flexibility is a keystone of the hybrid model, as evidenced by the varying approaches and contexts in which hybrids have previously occurred. Hybrids can meet the needs and particularities of each participating society.[84] While retaining universal norms, a hybrid for North Korea should consider the specifics regarding North Korea, rather than a cookie-cutter hybrid mold, which stuffs the Korean scenario into its pre-existing dimensions. Many of these specifics would call for analysis if and when a hybrid tribunal comes together.

Ad hoc tribunals have proven costly to administer. The hybrid courts implemented in Kosovo, East Timor, and Sierra Leone function as less expensive alternatives.[85] Simply put, hybrid tribunals usually have a lower economic cost.[86] Promoting speedier case resolution not only diminishes financial costs, it surely would lower the psychological costs that people pay when they must wait years for slowly emerging verdicts.[87]

Although hybrid tribunals cost less relative to their ad hoc predecessors,[88] the cost of running a potentially multi-year judicial proceeding requires considerable support. Without such support, the ability of the court to produce uniform justice and accountability may diminish. Decreases in legitimacy, capacity building, and norm diffusion may follow.[89]

The Special Court of Sierra Leone ran on fewer budgeted dollars as the project went on. Fiscal year 2003/04 had a budget of $34 million, which was reduced to $29.9 million in 2004/05. At the time, experts recognized the decreasing funds as a natural function of the process and projected the amounts to further decrease to $25.5 million in the following fiscal cycle.[90]

Hybrid tribunals also come with their challenges and caveats. On paper, it sounds simple enough to combine the expertise of the international actors with the legitimacy of the local community but, unsurprisingly, difficulties lurk in the details. Hybrid tribunals, at their worst, run the risk of unleashing the worst of both worlds with the external interference of international actors and the weakness of local institutions that facilitated the atrocities to begin with.[91] Another challenge is that hybrid tribunals need to establish a body of both substantive and procedural law.[92]

Conflict and tension between old and new political, economic, and ethnic systems will likely persist despite any success by the tribunal. Long-term commitment of investment and political capital helps prevent backsliding.[93] Fatigue and the resulting erosion in commitment can contribute to deterioration of the nascent, reformed domestic system.

Despite the choice of a hybrid tribunal, problems may persist. Witness protection, evidence gathering, persistent bias in local judges, lack of training, uncooperative national government entities, coercion or corruption through bribery or other means, perceptions of victor's justice against "heroes" of the nation, and the visible discrepancy between the treatment of perpetrators of atrocities who are held in air-conditioned buildings and receive better food and medical treatment than the local population, may all emerge as challenges to achieving the desired goals of transitional justice.[94]

Transitional justice through a hybrid court is inherently complex and difficult. No amount of expertise, effort, and good intentions in the courtroom can ultimately resolve all the difficulties facing the injured populace. Consideration must be given to the rule of law in a particular state, as well as the "sincerity of the government in creating a free and fair process."[95] The best that a model can seek to do is to craft the most effective approach at mitigating and providing redress for the damage done by the atrocities.[96]

The hybrid model offers one mechanism for boosting local legal development, but the process of holding atrocity perpetrators accountable and incorporating domestic experts may not, *ipso facto*, be enough to expect the post-regime legal system to take flight on its own. A lack of time and sustained resources may even limit the ability of hybrids to assist in redress for domestic legal development to a helpful level.[97] Personnel and infrastructure difficulties in East Timor and Kosovo, and funding and delay in Sierra Leone are just a few examples of this phenomenon.[98] "A lack of commitment by the international community has stymied the process of providing justice"[99] in many of these cases.

Certainly, post-regime nations lacking basic public infrastructure, economic venues, political mechanisms, and medicine[100] would also benefit from international assistance in their own right and by the appropriate contributing agency, but that is not the role of a legal accountability system. However, without these necessary institutions and an established legal culture to support a "rule of law," hybrid tribunals are even more difficult to construct.[101]

Sterio mentions the U.N. judicial panels set up in Kosovo to try war criminals and suggests that the mixed panel may be a starting point for Kosovar capacity building. Eventually, the international judges would not be needed once the local judges receive field training and education. Sterio is correct in stating that international judges will not be needed for a hybrid criminal tribunal indefinitely. As a model for local judges steering the helm of a domestic criminal tribunal, local authorities in Croatia report to the ICTY prosecutor per Rule 11 *bis* of the ICTY Rules of Procedure and Evidence.[102] To the extent matters may be tilted toward the domestic side of the spectrum without unduly sacrificing important objectives, such an approach has potential advantages in terms of domestic ownership, longer-term sustainability, and cost.

Yet Moghadam maintains that the very presence of the international judges with experience working in tandem with domestic judges in applying international standards serves as a better approach by demonstrating the efficacy of "reviving faith in rule of law" where such consistency has been the exception, not the norm.[103] In a place such as North Korea that does not have rule of law, a revival of faith in, and the actual practice of the rule of law are precious purposes indeed.

The precise contours of what would constitute the most legitimate hybrid tribunal would depend on the context from which it emerges. If it emerges

on the heels of a war, then legitimacy would be burnished by the participation of international judges and prosecutors not from the victorious countries.
Otherwise, the accusations of "victor's justice" could vitiate the process. Such a
tribunal would more likely be subject to the criticism that it is merely a vindictive
instrument rather than a means of attaining a greater measure of justice. It would
be more vulnerable to the claim of being an imposed, imperialistic institution
rather than an aid to the emerging domestic system. These caveats do not imply
that there may not be *any* participation from those on the victorious side, but
that such participation, if it exists, should be mingled with participation from
those who might be considered less biased, more impartial, and therefore more
legitimate.

If such a tribunal emerges after a peaceful reunification of Korea, the aforementioned issues would become less pronounced. The concern exists though that
the possibility of such a tribunal might be taken to be a perverse incentive for those
in North Korea *not* to relinquish power peacefully and to fight to the bitter end.
Such diplomatic concerns must be handled with great sensitivity and skill. At the
same time, these concerns should not entirely overshadow the overwhelming call
for justice in light of the gross, systematic violations of human rights.

The local people and many of the opposing parties that survive the collapse of
the previous regime may "suddenly find themselves in a war zone" of conflict-
ing and confusing ideologies. International actors seeking to inject themselves
into the judicial process may be seen as the natural outlet for the expression of
turmoil and frustration by the domestic population.[104] Indeed, the weight of
domestic North Korean ideology is geared toward rejecting the validity of other
nationals, with the partial exception of their sibling state South Korea, which
North Korean propaganda claims is under the imperialistic yoke of the United
States. For this reason, South Koreans must play a genuinely important role in
the hybrid tribunal or it runs the risk of its delegitimization as a tool of "foreign
devils".

Recognizing the critical fusion of domestic and international elements, it is
thus conceivable that at some point in the process, a hybrid tribunal could be
structured to phase into a domestic tribunal at the achievement of a series of
pre-conceived milestones in the criminal trials. A former Sierra Leone prosecutor
suggests that the ideal length of a hybrid tribunal is five years.[105] In that way, a
majority of international judges can be gradually replaced by a majority of domestic judges as judicial capacity is built on the ground—as long as such substitutions
do not abandon important purposes.[106] These characteristics begin to outline a
potential timeline around which to build this framework.

As the availability of skilled Korean judges eventually grows out of the partnership between South Korean and international judges, a hybrid tribunal may serve
to pool judicial development resources while simultaneously trying the criminals
who destroyed this capacity to begin with. A well-calibrated hybrid tribunal may
make major progress in bringing a greater respect for human rights in this state of
rightlessness, and justice for those who have suffered terribly at the hands of the
North Korean government.

Reunification and what it means for the peninsula

Words of reunification have emanated from the lips of Koreans everywhere since the armistice agreement and the commencement of the Geneva Conference of 1954.[107] Korea had been a unified country for the bulk of multiple millennia prior to the division against its will along the 38th parallel, now the most heavily fortified border in the world. What is difficult, however, is bringing these same people together who have subsequently diverged dramatically in most every way over the last sixty years.[108] While one may find it difficult to prognosticate about what may take place after over a half century of separation, a sketch of two general scenarios may help as possible backdrops for a future tribunal to redress the despicable treatment of the North Korean people.

The joint declaration and understanding by North and South Korea in June 2000 fanned a spark for future reunification, a longed-for outcome by the people of both Koreas.[109] Since that time, many commentators have started to outline the possibilities for the reunification of Korea and put forth their own strategies of how to attempt such a restoration.[110] Although the precise form of such unification remains uncertain, a peaceful unification would provide the preferable yet politically precarious platform for a tribunal addressing the atrocities of North Korea.

The vast majority of commentators and analysts have proposed the foundation of a feasible unification strategy based on a gradualist approach.[111] Estimates calculate that a *gradual* unification of the peninsula as one Korean state could cut government expenditures in half,[112] a factor to take into account when considering the high cost of international criminal tribunals. It is even easier to understand that no viable nation would stand quietly while another state absorbed it so quickly, especially a criminal government such as in North Korea. Such a gradual, peaceful integration of the nations could also allow North Korea to slowly integrate with South Korea's legal and economic structure, an important possibility for retaining the necessary capital and infrastructure for a hybrid tribunal as outlined later.[113]

Even peaceful unification, however, comes with additional issues. Dissolving North Korea into South Korea could mean new nuclear problems and a dissolving of the past non-proliferation treaties under the Vienna Convention on Succession of States in Respect of Treaties.[114] Combining and reconciling each of the nations' constitutions, as well as economic, employment, and transportation infrastructures would prove demanding.[115] The costs of reunification look staggering even by lower estimates,[116] making the amount of money and capital needed for a criminal tribunal look miniscule in comparison. Yet the costs of peaceful reunification look much better when compared to the devastating costs of preparing for and fighting a full-scale war.

Until the actual reunification does occur, and depending on which method brings it to peaceful fruition, it remains difficult to determine precisely how the post-unification process will impact the creation of this new tribunal. Sufficient political will to redress the atrocities that North Korea has inflicted on its own people will prove a critical factor.

If the greatly preferred peaceful unification of the Korean Peninsula does not transpire, the terrible specter of reunification by war broods over the peninsula. The instigation of such a war would likely emanate from North Korea. North Korea has built up the fourth largest military in the world, including large stockpiles of biological and chemical weapons as well as up to a dozen nuclear weapons or so that it can utilize toward its ultimate objective of reunification through force.[117] Such a full-blown war would likely result in catastrophic consequences. Rough estimates put a casualty total of over one million, horrendous for any nation involved.[118] North Korea's nuclear testing, aggressive military assaults, and abandonment of the Six-Party Talks have exacerbated the tensions on the peninsula.[119]

The United States may play a significant role in any successful reunification in the region, similarly to how it would play a potentially major role in any diplomatic solutions to the current situation.[120] The United States' Congress enacted the North Korean Human Rights Act of 2004 seeking to promote human rights in North Korea and move toward peaceful reunification. The U.S. has remained a key player in the regional negotiation processes and should continue to do so.

Unification through war might present surmountable yet difficult challenges in establishing a tribunal. Infrastructure, capital (and human capital), and other resources could be scant, possibly meaning a heavy reliance on the U.N. or other international funding. A relatively neutral location outside the war zone (which could be a distance depending on the extent of the war) would have to be found and agreed upon.

Without knowledge of the method of unification employed or the existence of a legal infrastructure after such unification, it remains speculative to contemplate a particular location for a tribunal. However, based on the preposterous legal system—if it rightfully deserves such an appellation—that allows for the systematic human rights abuses currently found in North Korea,[121] two likely options for a location surface: South Korea or an external location such as China.

If a peaceful unification emerges for the peninsula, it would be *apropos* for justice to be pursued in a Korean courtroom with, of course, Korean plaintiffs and defendants. While North Koreans might object to the criminal tribunal proceedings taking place south of the 38th parallel, the DPRK's substandard judicial system and infrastructure make it more suitable to limit such procedures to a courtroom in the South. This conclusion finds its premises not only on the shortcomings of a legal system plagued by injustice and corrupt politicization in the North, but also on the better court facilities in terms of more advanced technology, facilities, and the knowledgeable personnel of the South.[122] In other words, it is likely that the South's facilities would require far less upgrading, conserving resources for impending prosecution. If the Supreme Court of South Korea, for example, remains intact, it could serve as a fitting site for the proposed hybrid tribunal.

On the other hand, a violent unification of the peninsula may eliminate the possibility of the tribunal taking place in Seoul. With both North Korea's and South Korea's infrastructure demolished by large-scale war, an external location would have to be utilized for a criminal tribunal of this magnitude. The decision for the *locus* of a hybrid tribunal should consider the availability of witnesses, court personnel, judges, and appropriate facilities.[123] North Korean defendants and the people in general would find locations like Japan and the United States quite objectionable due to the past colonization by Japan of Korea, and the fact that the U.S. spearheaded U.N. efforts against North Korea in the Korean War.[124] So then a magnanimous choice on behalf of the defendants might be China, North Korea's closest ally and the host of the Six-Party Talks. China might also be the only forum to which formerly North Korean leaders would agree. Although leaders would not necessarily have to come to an agreement in this respect, especially those leaders that may be indicted, a more agreeable location would undoubtedly limit the perception of "victor's justice," bias or other legitimacy concerns. Finally, China's geographic proximity to Korea via Korea's large northern border could make it the most sensible external venue that would diminish the charges of "victor's justice."

Judges, attorneys, and court personnel constitute the *sine qua non* to make the proposed tribunal operational. Under a hybrid tribunal system, judges, attorneys, and other court personnel emerge from both the domestic as well as international contexts.[125] Domestically, formerly South Korean judges and prosecutors would be less biased participants to adjudicate the human rights violations of North Korean leaders against the North Korean people than North Korean judges and prosecutors. Similar to the defendant judges that appeared before the Nuremburg Tribunal in the late 1940s, North Korean judges would likely participate as either witnesses or defendants.[126] Defense attorneys could possibly be drawn from among North Korean attorneys who are not defendants or witnesses. Even if these attorneys were determined to be unfit for this task, international co-counsel could be assigned to aid and monitor their work. However, North Korean judges serve as mere functionaries of Kim Jong-Un's dictatorship as his close affiliates in the Workers' Party of Korea, and thus would have biases to disqualify them from serving as judges. Ideally, excellent judges and attorneys from a wide array of nations, especially from nations who played no role in a Korean conflict to enhance the perception of neutrality, would also emerge from the international community.

If Korea does not unite peacefully, Kosovo may provide apt lessons. The mass atrocities committed in Kosovo did not leave any fully functioning domestic institutions standing after the conflict ended. This dearth of domestic institutions led the international community and large segments of the local population to establish an interim transitional administration, run by the United Nations. Its purpose was to restore peace and stability and to develop the democratic institutions, including a fully-functioning judiciary, necessary to pave the way for self-governance. Transitional help can prove critical to plant new institutions afresh. "Moreover, if the lack of formal institutional legitimacy is difficult to confer on a fledgling justice system, the establishment of informal legitimacy—broad societal acceptance of institutions—is even more difficult to establish."[127]

The conflict in Kosovo severely damaged more than the physical infrastructure of the legal system. The legitimacy of the system remained in question because it bore the taint of the former oppressive regime. The legal system did not have the confidence of the public in part due to the prior systematic exclusion of the ethnic Albanians by the Serbs, the former administrators of the justice system. Not only were court buildings, prisons, and equipment destroyed, but the need for human resources was immense. This was because

> [i]n Kosovo, only Serbs had the experience and training to work as judges and prosecutors, yet these Serbs often refused to work in the new system because doing so would constitute a betrayal of their ethnic heritage. Albanians had some training but little experience, as they had been excluded from the system for many years.[128]

With respect to North Korea, the analogy with Kosovo would vary depending upon the conditions on the Korean Peninsula when such a tribunal might be attempted. Another Korean war could wreak mass destruction on not just the physical infrastructure,[129] but could also decimate judges and attorneys in South Korea, who would be the best prospects domestically for stepping into a tribunal regarding North Korea. North Korea has threatened before to turn Seoul, which stands not far from the 38th parallel, into a "sea of fire" or "lake of fire,"[130] and has the military means to do so;[131] thus, this possible destruction caused by war presents itself as a valid concern.

On the contrary, if the two Koreas reunite peacefully, the physical infrastructure and members of the legal profession would remain. In such an instance, a united Korea would have much more ample resources to hold a tribunal. However, one might question whether sufficient political will exists to hold such a tribunal. A peacefully united Korea may not require as much international support, and a substantial portion of such legal proceedings could move forward domestically. Choice of law and domestic fora for such proceedings would prove challenging to resolve. If the tribunal used international law, it would likely require more international support and involvement.

Bias and legitimacy remain important problems to consider in constructing a tribunal. Sometimes local systems carry so much "baggage" of bias and illegitimacy that more international involvement can help to relieve this. Turning again to Kosovo, there is evidence that the establishment of a new local system and the over-correction of the imbalances create new problems instead of solving old ones. For instance, it was initially easier to appoint ethnic Albanian judges than ethnic Serb judges. Only a few Serb judges were willing to serve, and even those who were appointed subsequently stepped down in response to pressure from Belgrade. Yet without representation of Serbs within the judiciary, the independence of the decision-making, a key to legitimacy among the entire local population, was severely in question. Under these circumstances, there was little ability for the local justice system to deliver verdicts perceived to be legitimate in trials of those suspected of committing mass atrocities.[132]

As discussed previously, North Korean judges would have similar susceptibility to claims of illegitimacy and bias. Given the already existing lack of judicial independence from illegitimate political control, judges in North Korea should be disqualified from judging.[133] As among the few in North Korea that reaped benefits from the former Kim Jong-Il regime, charges of bias would likely stick.

In this sort of instance of domestic bias and illegitimacy, hybrid tribunals, as Kosovo has shown, can prove to be helpful alternatives to either purely domestic or purely international courts by increasing legitimacy, decreasing bias, and enhancing capacity.

> The sharing of responsibilities among international and local actors in the administration of justice, particularly with respect to accountability for serious human rights crimes, helps to establish the legitimacy of the process as well as strengthen the capacity of local actors.

Such amelioration in regards to impartiality, legitimacy, and expertise enhanced matters in Kosovo and can potentially aid in similar ways regarding bringing a measure of justice for the people of North Korea.[134] In Korea though, there would likely be pronounced sensitivity toward anything that smacked of foreign imperialism. Additionally, a hybrid tribunal must try to save the face of Koreans as much as possible throughout such a process. Such considerations of culture would be critical to the success of a hybrid tribunal regarding North Korea.

Although it seems that international attention to human rights in North Korea has been increasing, sometimes it has been submerged under important geopolitical and strategic concerns. In this way, the situation in North Korea finds itself analogous to the Cambodian situation.

Conclusion

A situation as complex as the current North Korean crisis requires an understanding of history[135] and context, a consideration of options and ideas from various angles (including legal), and courageous yet not foolhardy implementation. The stakes could rise as high as not only another Korean War, but at worst, even World War III, if countries such as China, Russia, Japan, the United States and their allies all enter the fray.

On the other hand, a successful resolution can build a bridge toward peaceful reunification, which could help considerably in stabilizing the region, stimulating growth and cooperation, and averting a horrendous cataclysm. If the thoughts in this chapter help move the situation toward greater understanding and resolution through implementation in even a small way, it will have fulfilled its primary *raison d'etre*. If it at least gives more clarity to the issues involved so that all concerned may see more sharply, then it was not written in vain. While at best a work in progress as the actual situation continues to unfold, it aims to provide constructive insight into a very precarious, real-life situation that cries out to be understood and addressed—rather than ignored.

But even when the dust settles on the Korean Peninsula, ideally after a peaceful unification, the work does not stop there. Building on the prior chapters, this chapter also offers a possible means to address the state of rightlessness, the egregious case of North Korea. This solution, a hybrid tribunal, would ideally combine the strengths of a domestic court with the contributions of an international court to enhance legitimacy, build domestic capacity, reduce costs, and help bring a measure of justice. Such a court must carefully contextualize itself to the particulars of Korea and avoid the pitfalls of imperialism, corruption, and strong bias.

Such a hybrid tribunal and the aspiration to strengthen Korea's domestic legal system can also contribute momentum toward the eventual formation of an Asian system of human rights.[136] Drawing from the lessons of already existing regional systems of human rights in Europe, the Americas, and Africa, such a system could serve as a more permanent bulwark to fortify respect for human rights in Asia.[137] It could in time reduce, and perhaps someday obviate, the need for the sorts of hybrid tribunals discussed herein.

Until there is an establishment of such a system of human rights for the most populous continent in the world, however, a means such as a hybrid tribunal can serve as a stopgap measure to address the hemorrhaging in places such as North Korea. The unspeakable suffering of so many under Pyongyang's steel boot should not be met with passive indifference. Whether through the ICC, domestic prosecution, or a hybrid tribunal, impunity and oppression should not be allowed to reign unchecked. The healing of the Land of the Morning Calm, the stability of the region, and the sizable ramifications around our deeply interconnected world all hang in the balance. This egregious case of gross, systematic violations of human rights in North Korea demands redress. A hybrid tribunal may provide the best path forward to address this criminal regime.

Notes

* Kevin Zickterman aided me in this chapter.

1 Milena Sterio, *Seeking the Best Forum to Prosecute International War Crimes: Proposed Paradigms and Solutions*, 18 FLA. J. INT'L L. 887, 895 (2006).

2 *Id.*

3 International Criminal Court, *Frequently Asked Questions*, www.icc-cpi.int/en_menus/icc/about%20the%20court/frequently%20asked%20questions/pages/faq.aspx (last visited June 21, 2014).

4 United Nations, *Rome Statute of the International Criminal Court*, Ch. XVIII §10 (1998), *available at* www.treaties.un.org/Pages/ViewDetails.aspx?src=TREATY&mtdsg_no=XVIII-10&chapter=18&lang=en (last viewed June 7, 2014).

5 *See* Jaya Ramji-Nogales, *Designing Bespoke Transnational Justice: A Pluralistic Process Approach*, MICH. J. INT'L L., Fall 2010, at 1, 45–46.

6 *Report on Preliminary Examination Activities 2012*, INT'L CRIMINAL CT., OFFICE OF THE PROSECUTOR, 15 (Nov. 2012), www.icc-cpi.int/NR/rdonlyres/C433C462-7C4E-4358-8A72-8D99FD00E8CD/285209/OTP2012ReportonPreliminaryExaminations22Nov2012.pdf.

7 *Id.* at 15.

8 *See id.* at 15–17; Rome Statute of the International Criminal Court, art. 25, U.N. Doc. A/CONF.183/9, *available at* www.icc-cpi.int/nr/rdonlyres/ea9aeff7-5752-4f84-be94-0a655eb30e16/0/rome_statute_english.pdf.

9 *Id.* at art. 75 ("The Court may make an order directly against a convicted person specifying appropriate reparations to, or in respect of, victims, including restitution, compensation and rehabilitation.").

10 *See* Sterio, *supra* note 1, at 903.

11 *See generally* Grace M. Kang, *A Case for the Prosecution of Kim Jong Il for Crimes Against Humanity, Genocide, and War Crimes,* 38 COLUM. HUM. RTS. L. REV. 51 (2006).

12 Sterio, *supra* note 1, at 895–96. The United States has not ratified the Rome Statute, has been an outspoken opponent of the ICC, and prefers regional tribunals like that of the Special Court for Sierra Leone.

13 *Id.* at 895–96.

14 Tanaz Moghadam, Comment, *Revitalizing Universal Jurisdiction: Lessons from Hybrid Tribunals Applied to the Case of Hissene Habre,* 39 COLUM. HUM. RTS. L. REV. 471, 515–17 (2008).

15 *See generally* John Dermody, Note, *Beyond Good Intentions: Can Hybrid Tribunals Work After Unilateral Intervention?* 30 HASTINGS INT'L & COMP. L. REV. 77, 81 (2006).

16 Laura Dickinson, *The Relationship Between Hybrid Courts and International Courts: The Case of Kosovo,* 37 NEW ENG. L. REV. 1059, 1067–68 (2003). The government of Rwanda actually rejected the construction of the ICTR for several reasons, one of which was the distant location of the tribunal in Arusha, Tanzania; the Rwandan government claimed that this distant location would contribute to the loss of the tribunal's deterrent effect on the local populace. STEVEN D. ROPER & LILIAN A. BARRIA, DESIGNING CRIMINAL TRIBUNALS: SOVEREIGNTY AND INTERNATIONAL CONCERNS IN THE PROTECTION OF HUMAN RIGHTS 23–24 (2006).

17 Diane Orentlicher, *Judging Global Justice: Assessing the International Criminal Court,* 21 WIS. INT'L L.J. 495, 509–11 (2003).

18 Roper & Barria, *supra* note 16, at 25. The *Tadic* case was the first trial under the ICTY and expressly held that the ICTY's establishment under Chapter VII was legal and had the authority to try defendants. *Id.* However, acquiring defendants from neighboring countries remains a challenge for hybrid tribunals like the SCSL.

19 *Id.* at 82.

20 Roper & Barria, *supra* note 16, at 52. For example, the Attorney General of Indonesia argued that he could not prosecute crimes against humanity because these crimes were not found in the domestic legal system and in turn severely limited his own human rights investigations.

21 *See* Morse Tan, *The North Korean Nuclear Crisis: Past Failures and Present Solutions,* 50 ST. LOUIS U. L.J. 517, 525–27, 543–46 (2006).

22 *See e.g.,* Patricia Goedde, *Law "of Our Own Style": The Evolution and Challenges of the North Korean Legal System,* 27 FORDHAM INT'L L.J. 1265, 1287–88 (2004) ("The current predicament concerns the creation of a viable legal regime for foreign investors, one that is reliable, fair, and transparent, without intrusive State involvement.").

23 Dickinson, *supra* note 16, at 1059, 1064–65, 1067.

24 *Id.* at 30.

25 *See* Moghadam, *supra* note 14, at 477 ("Universal jurisdiction now covers the narrow range of jus cogens crimes that are at the core of customary international law, such as torture, genocide, war crimes, and crimes against humanity.").

26 Dickinson, *supra* note 16, at 1067.

27 *Id.* at 1068.

28 Orentlicher, *supra* note 17, at 501.

29 *Id.* at 502–03

30 *Id.* at 500.

31 Brian Tittemore, *Khmer Rouge Crimes: The Elusive Search for Justice,* HUM. RTS. BR., Fall 1999, at 3, 3.

32 *Id.*

33 Scott Luftglass, Note, *Crossroads in Cambodia: The United Nation's Responsibility to Withdraw Involvement from the Establishment of a Cambodian Tribunal to Prosecute the Khmer Rouge,* 90 VA. L. REV. 893, 901–02 (2004).

34 Kelly Whitley, *History of the Khmer Rouge Tribunal: Origins, Negotiations, and Establishment, in* THE KHMER ROUGE TRIBUNAL 29 (John D. Ciociari ed., 2006).

35 *Id.* at 30–31.

36 *Id.* These trials emerged as problematic and procedurally unfair: "The international community refuses to recognize these trials as legitimate for several reasons. First, the two leaders were tried in absentia, a violation of the International Covenant on Civil and Political Rights (ICCPR). Second, the Decree Law establishing the 'People's Revolutionary Tribunal' contained language denouncing the two defendants, functionally assuming their guilt, a violation of the international norm of the 'presumption of innocence.' Third, the definition of genocide used at the trial did not comport with the internationally accepted definition, and it was crafted to virtually ensure the guilt of the defendants. The definition of genocide included: planned massacres of groups of innocent people; expulsion of inhabitants of cities and villages in order to concentrate them and force them to do hard labor in conditions leading to their physical and mental destruction; wiping out religion; [and] destroying political, cultural and social structures and family and social relations. On balance, the People's Revolutionary Tribunal was neither normatively fair nor in conformity with prevailing international law. The international community was predominantly focused on ensuring Cambodian territorial sovereignty and stability, at the expense of a thorough and adequate investigation and prosecution of those responsible for the atrocities. The U.N. was involved in the settlement agreements terminating the Khmer Rouge leadership and establishing transitional Vietnamese occupation." Luftglass, *supra* note 33, at 902–03. *See also* Roper & Barria, *supra* note 16, at 38.

37 THE KHMER ROUGE TRIBUNAL 12–13 (John D. Ciociari ed., 2006).

38 *See e.g.,* Goedde, *supra* note 22, at 1287. ("Creating an independent judiciary, devolving power to the people, applying civil liberties fairly—these are all counterintuitive processes in the Party-conscious hierarchy of North Korea.").

39 Lindsey Raub, *Positioning Hybrid Tribunals in International Criminal Justice,* 41 N.Y. U. INT'L L. & POL. 1013, 1033 (2009). The experts that assessed the human rights abuses in Cambodia suggested a tribunal similar to the ICTR and ICTY because of the various independency problems in local judiciary. Roper & Barria, *supra* note 16, at 39. But after a Sen-staged coup, the Cambodian government rejected the assessment and wanted instead to construct a hybrid tribunal.

40 Luftglass, *supra* note 33, at 903.

41 *Id.* at 904.

42 *Id.* "Professor Steven R. Ratner, who represented the United States during the negotiations at the Paris Conference, stated: 'Although all the participants believed that human rights should be mentioned, it was harder to reach consensus on how to … punish Khmer Rouge officials responsible for the atrocities and to prevent the repetition of these acts. As a result, the human rights obligations at times appear opaque.'" *Id.* at 904–05.

43 *Id.* at 905.

44 North Korea has signed both the International Covenant on Economic, Social and Cultural Rights, and the Covenant on Civil and Political Rights. Morse H. Tan, *A State of Rightlessness: The Egregious Case of North Korea,* 80 MISS. L. J. 681, 689 (2010).

45 Luftglass, *supra* note 33, at 905–06.

46 Etelle Higonnet, *Restructuring Hybrid Courts: Local Empowerment and National Criminal Justice Reform,* 23 ARIZ. J. INT'L & COMP. L. 347, 352–56 (2006).

47 Dermody, *supra* note 15, at 83–84.

48 Moghadam, *supra* note 14, at 490–91; *see also* Roper & Barria, *supra* note 16, at 36 ("[T]he legal basis provided of the SCSL and the ECC provided the governments much more involvement and control over the final institution.").

49 Dermody, *supra* note 15, at 82.

50 Higonnet, *supra* note 46.

51 Ramji-Nogales, *supra* note 5, at 4.

52 Moghadam, *supra* note 14, at 490–91. The tribunals were plagued with other issues as well. For example, "[t]he ICTY's greatest difficulty early on was securing the apprehension of indictees," especially that of high ranking officials. Roper & Barria, *supra* note 16, at 24–25. The ICTR, for example, was experiencing problems with the concurrent jurisdiction of the national court and the international tribunal. *Id.* at 25–26.

53 Higonnet, *supra* note 46.

54 Sterio, *supra* note 1, at 903–04.

55 There is a discussion of how the SCSL is better than its predecessors in Raub, *supra* note 39, at 1037.

56 Moghadam, *supra* note 14, at 492–93; Roper & Barria, *supra* note 16, at 42–43. The court also maintains investigating judges, co-prosecutors, and an expansive jurisdiction, but it still has had the problem of finding and effectively prosecuting high ranking officials. *Id.*

57 Moghadam, *supra* note 14, at 492–94.

58 Dermody, *supra* note 15, at 83.

59 Roper & Barria, *supra* note 16, at 93.

60 "One advantage is that the hybrid tribunal is located in the locus delicti. Therefore, through public stigmatization and just retributions, local trials can expose those responsible for atrocities to the local population, which can aid gradual reconciliation and is a cathartic process." *See* Raub, *supra* note 39, at 1042.

61 Moghadam, *supra* note 14, at 491–92.

62 Dickinson, *supra* note 16, at 1064.

63 ROPER & BARRIA, *supra* note 16, at 93.

64 Moghadam, *supra* note 14, at 513–14.

65 Roper & Barria, *supra* note 16, at 94.

66 *See* Moghadam, *supra* note 14, at 513–14, 519–21.

67 "The incorporation of local perspectives through population surveys, studies of traditions, and participation of moral authorities should increase the legitimacy of the source from, and process through, which" hybrid courts are created. Ramji-Nogales, *supra* note 5, at 66.

68 Goedde, *supra* note 22, at 1287.

69 Moghadam, *supra* note 14, at 513–14, 491–92. Roper and Barria agree with Ramji-Nogales in that hybrid tribunals have created greater educational and training programs than international tribunals. Roper & Barria, *supra* note 16, at 93.

70 Moghadam, *supra* note 14, at 511–12.

71 Edmundo Hendler, *Lay Participation in Argentina: Old History, Recent Experience*, 15 Sw. J. L. & TRADE AM. 1, 4, 18–19 (2008).

72 Dermody, *supra* note 15, at 80–81.

73 *Id.* at 100.

74 *See generally* Moghadam, *supra* note 14, at 521–25.

75 Ramji-Nogales, *supra* note 5, at 67.

76 Dermody, *supra* note 15, at 80–81.

77 Roper & Barria, *supra* note 16, at 93.

78 Dickinson, *supra* note 16, at 1068–69.

79 Sterio, *supra* note 1, at 903–05

80 Dermody, *supra* note 15, at 100–01.

81 Moghadam, *supra* note 14, at 523–24.
82 *Id.* at 521–25.
83 Dermody, *supra* note 15, at 102.
84 Moghadam, *supra* note 14, at 491–93.
85 Dermody, *supra* note 15, at 82. This may be partly attributed to the fact that many countries that maintain hybrid tribunals, like Cambodia, also contribute to their operating and other costs. Roper & Barria, *supra* note 16, at 40; *see also id.* at 61–62 (stating that "the evidence is clear that for some states, the creation of hybrid tribunals and the termination of Chapter VII tribunals is a cost saving measure" and presenting tables with contribution amounts for each tribunal).
86 Raub, *supra* note 39, at 1045–46.
87 Richard Lempert, *Citizen Participation in Judicial Decision Making: Juries, Lay Judges and Japan*, 2001 St. Louis-Warsaw Transatlantic L.J. 1, 6–7 (2001–02).
88 Hybrid tribunals located in the locus delicti provide proximity to witnesses and immediate access to evidence, which could reduce the cost. Raub, *supra* note 39, at 1042.
89 Dermody, *supra* note 15, at 83, 92–93.
90 *Id.* at 92–93
91 *Id.* at 82.
92 Raub, *supra* note 39, at 1044.
93 *See id.* at 1045.
94 Sterio, *supra* note 1, at 897–98. Because most hybrid tribunals are not established with the authority of Chapter VII, jurisdiction over many defendants is another problem. Roper & Barria, *supra* note 16, at 93–94.
95 Roper & Barria, *supra* note 16, at 94.
96 *See* Dermody, *supra* note 15, at 100.
97 *Id.; see also* Roper & Barria, *supra* note 16, at 94.
98 Dermody, *supra* note 15, at 83. For example, the Special Crimes Panel for East Timor had a collection of personnel and logistical problems that led to questions of legitimacy and impartiality, including a shortage of court personnel, management inefficiency leading to longer trials, inexperienced judges, immense language barriers, and the inability to retrieve defendants from Indonesia. Roper & Barria, *supra* note 16, at 55–56.
99 Dermody, *supra* note 15, at 94.
100 Sterio, *supra* note 1, at 902.
101 Roper & Barria, *supra* note 16, at 93. Cambodia is the perfect example of this problem considering that the rule of law is being addressed in part by the former perpetrators under the old Khmer Rouge regime. *Id.*
102 *Id.*
103 Moghadam, *supra* note 14, at 521–25.
104 Dermody, *supra* note 15, at 88.
105 *Id.* at 92.
106 However, the international community must be wary of leaving such matters solely to domestic judges. For example, the Indonesian Human Rights Courts appointed both career and "ad hoc" judges (typically highly inexperienced lawyers) that contributed greatly to a lack of convictions, a flawed appeals process, a lack of professionalism in the judiciary, incompetent prosecutors, and a lack of coordination and political will overall. Roper & Barria, *supra* note 16, at 54, 56–58.
107 *See generally* Jin Lee, *A Millennium Hope for Korea: Lessons from German Unification*, 9 MSU-DCL J. Int'l L. 453, 456–462 (2000) (outlining unification efforts from the 1950s to the end of the Millennium).
108 *See* Tan, *supra* note 21, at 505, 520–22.
109 *Id.* at 453.
110 Cecilia Y. Oh, Comment, *The Effect of Reunification of North and South Korea on Treaty*

Status, 16 EMORY INT'L L. REV. 311, 316–48 (2002) (outlining state succession law and the effects of unification on Korean treaties); Curtis J. Milhaupt, *Privatization and Corporate Governance in a Unified Korea,* 26 J. CORP. L. 199 (2001) (presenting a comprehensive privatization plan for North Korean state-run industries to integrate the two Korean economies).

111 *See, e.g.,* Lee, *supra* note 107, at 502 ("Ideally, a unification method based on two state's consensus would be finalized by the result of long negotiations, compromises, and agreements between the two Koreas.").

112 Oh, *supra* note 110, at 342–43 (stating further that a quick merging of the nations could cost up to $800 billion over ten years).

113 Lisa Blomgren Bingham et al., *Participatory Governance in South Korea: Legal Infrastructure, Economic Development, and Dispute Resolution,* 19 PAC. MCGEORGE GLOBAL BUS. & DEV. L.J. 375, 398 (2007).

114 Oh, *supra* note 110, at 337–348.

115 Lee, *supra* note 107, at 508–511, 518–20.

116 *See* Oh, *supra* note 110, at 342 ("According to a South Korean think-tank, a sudden and unplanned reunification of North and South Korea ... would cost approximately $800 billion over a span of ten years.").

117 Lee, *supra* note 107, at 262–63.

118 Tan, *supra* note 21, at 525–26.

119 *See* Lee, *supra* note 107, 279–84.

120 *See* Albert Suh, *First Steps Are Better than None: Distinguishing the Practical from the Rhetorical in the North Korean Human Rights Act of 2004,* 37 RUTGERS L.J. 585, 591–93, 599 (2006).

121 *See generally* Goedde, *supra* note 23.

122 *See generally* Kuk Cho, *The Ongoing Reconstruction of the Korean Criminal Justice System,* 5 SANTA CLARA J. INT'L L. 100 (2006) (outlining South Korea's legal system and highlighting its recent promising legal reforms).

123 Dermody, *supra* note 15, at 81–82 (explaining how hybrid tribunals combine domestic and international court personnel).

124 *See* Tan, *supra* note 21, at 521.

125 *See* Dermody, *supra* note 15, at 81–82.

126 *See* Douglas O. Linder, *Journeying Through the Valley of Evil,* 71 N.C. L. REV. 1111, 1118 (1993).

127 Dickinson, *supra* note 16, at 1065.

128 *Id.* at 1065, 1068.

129 *See generally* Tan, *supra* note 21, at 525–27.

130 Paul Richter, *Two-War Strategy Faces Test,* L.A. TIMES Feb. 13, 2003, at A1.

131 Tan, *supra* note 21, at 527–28.

132 *See* Dickinson, *supra* note 16, at 1066–67. "In fact, due to concerns about lack of due process and insufficient evidence, several judgments imposed against Serb defendants by panels of ethnic Albanian judges were later thrown out by panels that included international judges."

133 *See e.g.,* Goedde, *supra* note 22, at 1271–72 (explaining how state coercion in the "rule of law" is legitimized in North Korea and other socialist countries).

134 *Id.* at 1068–70.

135 For more about how the two Koreas developed during their first thirty years as separate nations, see JOUNGWON ALEXANDER KIM, DIVIDED KOREA: THE POLITICS OF DEVELOPMENT, 1945–1972 (1975). For a more far-ranging historical perspective, see B. K. GILLS, KOREA VERSUS KOREA: A CASE OF CONTESTED LEGITIMACY (Michael Liefer ed., 1996).

136 One effort may well be under way with the formation of the Asian Human Rights Commission. For a discussion on the Commission and its potential future problems, see Bina D'Costa, *Challenges for an Independent Asian Human Rights Commission,* 4 ILSA J

INT'L & COMP. L. 615 (1998). See also the Commission's website to read a draft document of the proposed Asian Human Rights Charter *at* www.material.ahrchk.net/charter/mainfile.php/draft_charter/.

137 For a general discussion on the human rights systems in Europe, Africa, and especially the Inter-American Human Rights Commission, see Richard J. Wilson, *Researching the Jurisprudence of the Inter-American Commission on Human Rights: A Litigator's Perspective*, AM. U. J. INT'L L. & POL'Y, Fall 1994, at 1.

14 Diplomacy with a criminal regime*

The deterrence factor

North Korea's behavior, at least regarding nuclear weapons, has led many American sources—ranging from scholars and politicians to comedians and talk show hosts—to suggest that North Korea acts and speaks in a crazy and irrational manner.[1] While it may be correct to speak about North Korea in this fashion if one incorporates a moral dimension to those statements, it is inaccurate in terms of whether or not North Korea's behavior and speech is logically connected with its own goals and objectives.

As we discussed in previous chapters, North Korean officials have multiple objectives: to hold on to power, remove American involvement in the peninsula, reunify Korea by force, and wrest benefits from other countries through the use of threats and coercion. Perhaps the single biggest mistake made by the United States and South Korea in past dealings with North Korea has been to ignore or misinterpret its goals and pattern. This section of the chapter analyzes past dealings in four major areas—military, political, economic, and ethnic—to show that past responses to North Korea have proven inadequate or wrong-headed. Then it recommends better solutions for handling each of these four areas before launching into full-scale redress options.

As the preceding chapters made clear, North Korea's most obvious—and, for the world dangerous—goals are militaristic: holding on to power in its totalitarian dictatorship, reunifying Korea by force, proliferation, and extracting benefits from other countries through the use of threats and coercion.[2] North Korea has doggedly continued with its belligerent and hostile actions toward the United States and South Korea since the cease-fire—whether through naval battles with South Korea, frequent border skirmishes, or intentional incursions into South Korea with thousands of agents, both armed and possibly unarmed.[3] These actions have extended to Japan as well.[4] Time after time, North Korea has persistently sought these aforementioned objectives, often in overtly hostile ways.

Because North Korea aims to unify Korea by force, drawdowns in military assets would move in the wrong direction. For example, one devious way in which North Korea may seek to start a war is by having its own soldiers dress in South Korean military uniforms and pretend to invade North Korea; in response to this phony incursion, North Korea would then attack South Korea with the justifica-tion of having been "attacked" first. Indeed, North Korea has actually engaged in military exercises practicing such a subterfuge.[5]

Therefore, it makes sense to bolster the defensive capabilities against North Korean aggression. The South Korean military should remain ever-ready because the belligerent rhetoric of North Korea has many times escalated into combat. Importantly, South Korea needs to have enough of a deterrent—especially in terms of defensive measures—readily at hand.[6] Such measures should discourage the outbreak of war and send a clear message to North Korea that it would meet vigorous resistance and ultimately find defeat if it instigates another war.

Japan's recent investment in its military to defend, among other things, against the North Korean threat, should motivate China to persuade North Korea to disarm.[7] In recent years, Japan has taken a harder line toward North Korea, and has increased more of its defensive capabilities.[8]

The U.S. has sent greater defensive reinforcements, such as more Patriot missile batteries, which my earlier scholarship recommended.[9] An emphasis on defense forecloses reasonable pretexts for North Korea to attack preemptively by consid-ering buildup of offensive capabilities as an indicator of imminent U.S. attack. Otherwise, North Korea might try to claim that America is building up its military forces in and around the peninsula in order to attack North Korea: Pyongyang could, for example, draw analogies with the military buildup in Iraq prior to the Persian Gulf wars.[10] However, primarily defensive reinforcements would at once take away such an excuse while preparing for a possible attack by North Korea.

The North Korean pattern of brinkmanship or "negotiating on the edge"—as Scott Snyder has put it in his book by that title, and as shown in a recent book on North Korean negotiation strategy—takes place in five steps: (1) escalate the crisis; (2) use it to gain bargaining leverage to get the desired parties (most particularly the United States) to the table; (3) as a result of the crisis, come to an agreement, which (4) gives North Korea benefits, which it swallows; and then (5) not abide by its promises, break the agreement, and create another crisis—thus starting this cycle again.[11]

In terms of a solution, we must always remember that deception and the breaking of its word have been the norm, not the exception, for North Korea. In addition to deceiving the international community, North Korea pumps a steady stream of lies to its own populace. Its propaganda repeatedly disseminates notions such as: that South Korea suffers much worse economic conditions than North Korea; purveying the outlandish deification of the Kim dictators; sounding the alarm on the supposedly ever present threat of attack from South Korea and the U.S.; and hammering home the false promise that a communist utopia will come about if the populace just perseveres a little bit longer.[12] Also, North Korea levels a steady stream of wild accusations against South Korea and the United States that describe North Korea's actions and position better than what either South Korea or the United States have done vis-à-vis North Korea.[13]

One recurring problem involves North Korean efforts to negotiate directly with the U.S. while sidelining South Korea.[14] Given the continuing North Korean policy that fails to officially recognize or engage in official diplomacy with South Korea,[15] and continues on the path of seeking forceful reunification,[16] there exist continuing tensions about how to conduct multilateral negotiations.[17]

Secretary of State Condoleeza Rice responded to North Korean accusations that the United States is hostile toward North Korea and is about to wage war and attack North Korea. Secretary Rice called such rhetoric ridiculous—that the United States has no war plans against North Korea presently.[18] These accusations amounted to nothing more than the continued spewing of the North Korean propaganda machine and the lineup of lies that it regularly puts forth to its populace.[19]

Although these actions by Secretary Rice indicated an awareness of North Korean tactics, other parts of our government seemed overly optimistic. Pronouncements by U.S. Representative Curt Weldon, who was at one point part of a Congressional delegation to North Korea, appeared so. Shortly after his return, Weldon claimed that North Korea anticipated denuclearizing.[20] Not long after that press conference—within a matter of weeks—North Korea announced unabashedly to the world that it possessed nuclear weapons.[21] Thereafter, U.S. Rep. Tom Lantos, the ranking democratic foreign relations committee member, in a speech at John Hopkins' School of Advanced International Studies, drew a parallel to the example of Libya's reaping economic and political benefits after it voluntarily disarmed its arsenal of weapons of mass destruction.[22] As we have seen, however, such a prospect does not reflect North Korea's past patterns of behavior.[23]

While Lantos acknowledged that it is a "long shot" that North Korea would follow the path of Libya,[24] his words nonetheless indicated that members of Congress may have wanted to take a softer approach. The insistence on Six-Party Talks, rather than only bilateral negotiations directly with North Korea, helped to counter North Korea's attempt to go over the head of South Korea—and for that matter, over the heads of its regional neighbors—to directly negotiate with the United States.[25] Such bilateral talks, which led to the 1994 Agreed Framework, not only failed, but also gave additional time for North Korea to become more dangerous and to reap benefits without meeting its obligations.[26] The multilateral approach with built-in bilateral components avoids a false dichotomy as well as blackmail.

Lantos did parlay a tactic that might help the United States politically, although it may have helped even more had the speaker come from outside the United States. Lantos had spoken to leaders in China and indicated that it was in China's interest to see that North Korea disarm its weapons of mass destruction because of the possibility of Japan's rearming to defend and deter North Korean potential aggression with such weapons.[27] Given the history of hostilities that historically had transpired between China and Japan, China would not want Japan to rearm. Thus, Lantos used the approach that former Secretary of State George Schultz had suggested would be an effective way to motivate China to step in to help disarm North Korea.[28] As Japan continues to grow its military, China may rein in North Korea more. The U.S. has key military bases in Japan, and while Japan has largely aligned itself with the U.S., concerns exist regarding the present Japanese administration.

If North Korea merely diminished its military spending by approximately 5–10 percent, then it could potentially feed its starving populace by investing in its agricultural infrastructure, for example; yet, it refuses to do so.[29] It has preferred artillery, tanks, and fighter planes to rice, kimchi (Korean fermented vegetables), and kalbi (Korean-style marinated short ribs)—thus deciding to be armed to the teeth while turning its populace into ragged skeletons. Along these lines, the current American administration has repeated the line, "Feed your people first!"

The Six-Party Talks and the need for continual deterrence

A relatively recent U.S. bipartisan congressional delegation claimed some success in speaking with the North Korean government.[30] Apparently, in an attempt to defuse the North Korean nuclear deterrent reasoning for its nuclear weapons program, the U.S. delegation indicated that Washington did not seek regime change nor plan a preemptive attack.[31] During this visit, the beleaguered North Korea reportedly offered to become a "friend" of the United States if Washington did not make inflammatory remarks about Kim Jong-Il's regime (this visit having been before Kim Jong-Il's death). The North Korean government also stated its desire to resume "substantive discussions" according to Rep. Curt Weldon with no option "off the table," including an end result of "giving up their nuclear capability."[32]

One should view this claim in light of North Korea's history of mendacity, its obsessive effort to keep a grip on power, its past reaping of benefits without corresponding adherence to the obligations that it agrees to, and its continued goal to remove the United States from the picture on the peninsula. Even the day after this meeting, the official, government-controlled newspaper (*Nodohng Shinmuhn*, a more accurate transliteration than the more common *Rodong*) continued its usual anti-American tirades, calling the U.S. a "nuclear criminal."[33] The North Korean newspaper, given the history of what has transpired thus far, appears more representative of Pyongyang's actual stance. While speaking against the "inflammatory" language of the U.S., it frequently resorts to inflammatory anti-American language itself. One strains to see evidence of substantial policy changes under Kim Jong-Un.

Although there have been multilateral talks in Beijing, they have largely consisted of recitations of each country's positions, with no real progress toward an agreement. The United States, North and South Korea, China, Japan, and Russia attempted for months to set up a fourth meeting to pressure Pyongyang to abandon its nuclear weapons, a development that all the other countries *sans* North Korea claim to seek.[34] The Six-Party Talks failed to make much substantive progress in resolving the current crisis on the peninsula. For the most part, the delegates from each country reiterated their positions and stood their ground. Minor agreements as to the setting up of sub-committees that would address issues resulted; however, no breakthroughs have yet emerged. North Korea indefinitely suspended the Six-Party Talks in 2005 while giving conditions for it to return to these multilateral talks.[35]

The effort to encourage North Korea to continue in the multilateral talks, however, is still a better one than bilateral talks alone because it includes North Korea's regional neighbors and applies international pressure upon North Korea to disarm. However, Russia has thus far taken a less than tenacious stance toward North Korea and its nuclear weapons.[36] China's hand in drafting the last U.N. Security Council Resolution may mark a watershed. The U.S. has repeatedly let each country know that applying such pressure to North Korea would be desirable.[37]

Notwithstanding its shortcomings, indefinite suspension by North Korea, and the absence of a breakthrough, this multilateral approach is better than the U.S. appearing to engage in unilateral efforts. Accordingly, the Bush administration did a fine job of resisting the brinkmanship blackmail that North Korea again attempted to perpetrate. The Obama administration has had somewhat similar success. Allowing North Korea to go straight to the United States, over the head of South Korea, seriously undermines South Korea. Concurrent bilateral action should first and foremost be between South Korea and North Korea, who after all live on the same peninsula in question, not North Korea and the U.S.

As explored in Chapter 6, China's role could prove critical in resolving the crisis. As North Korea's best ally in the world, China's strong insistence that North Korea denuclearize the peninsula would carry the most weight.

Russia, which has recently renewed its ties with North Korea, while not as influential as China, might have some sway with North Korea. North Korea still owes a sizable monetary debt to Russia.[38] Russia could offer a measure of debt forgiveness as an incentive for North Korea to relinquish its nuclear weapons program. However, because of the U.S.'s recent clashes with Russia regarding the Ukraine situation, and Putin's past burnishing of North Korea's reputation, Russia may very well not take this step.

Japan has aligned itself with South Korea and the United States. It takes a firm stance that North Korea must get rid of its nuclear arms. Given North Korea's abduction of Japanese citizens and the sending of fraudulent ashes when the issue arose, some 70 percent of the Japanese public supports the levying of sanctions against North Korea.[39]

These multi-party talks might benefit from outside assistance. The U.N. Secretary General, currently Ban-Ki Moon (Korean himself), could use his office as a mediator for multi-party talks. Passive attempts to make the Secretary General office available, as well as attempts to diminish tensions by visiting the respective countries, South and North Korea, have not helped in the past. Yet, when all U.S. attempts failed, the Secretary General used his office to negotiate the release of captured U.S. airmen after the Korean War.[40] A role as mediator for an existing multi-party framework may help drive the talks, especially because Ban-Ki Moon may be able to relate better to the ongoing Korean tensions as a Korean that remembers the perils of the Korean War.

North Korea has stated, however, that it does not consider the U.N. a neutral party. The argument stems from the U.N.'s condemnation, and subsequent military action against the North Korean aggression that started the Korean War.[41] It conveniently ignores the aid that U.N. organizations have rendered to North Korea.[42]

Hwang Jang-Yop also indicated that Kim Jong-Il was a coward, and capriciously changed his decisions based on his mood.[43] Kim Jong-Il reportedly chose his third son Kim Jong-Un because this son most resembled him. If so, it is possible that a course of diplomacy that incrementally increases the pressure on North Korea to the point of actively going in and disarming their military at the last stage of this process might turn out as the best approach—to call North Korea's bluff and see whether or not Kim Jong-Un proves to be as courageous as Saddam Hussein was—darting from spider hole to spider hole and offering very little resistance to U.S. forces notwithstanding his inflated rhetoric.

However, this would not be the first or even most desirable step in the process—it should come only if prior efforts fail. A call for continued multilateral pressure from other countries and international organizations, with resort to international law, should continue—whether or not North Korea returns to the Six-Party Talks. Additionally, invitations to North Korea to engage in negotiations either through the good offices of the U.N. Secretary General and/or through multilateral Six-Party Talks should be extended to Pyongyang again. The recent Security Council Resolutions also urge North Korea to return to the Six-Party Talks.

Step by step, the heat can be turned up on North Korea, and as the heat rises, the drive for accountable ways (also known as complete, verifiable, and irreversible dismantlement, or CVID)[44] in which North Korea could indeed be disarmed can be pursued. After the heat increases sufficiently, giving some positive incentives for North Korea to comply could increase the likelihood of a peaceful resolution.[45] Both sticks and carrots (but sticks first[46]) can be incrementally ratcheted up, step by step, stage by stage, to the point where if none of these things work, only then would it be time for a very proactive international effort to disarm North Korea, such as through international humanitarian intervention discussed later. Such an approach may be the best means of dealing with the North Korean crisis because softer approaches have clearly failed repeatedly in the past. As Chuck Downs, a former senior Pentagon official, puts it:

> The experience with North Korea is that they never respond positively to favorable treatment. They abuse people who give them favorable opportunities. Unfortunately, the only way you can get them to do what you want them to do is by pressure and force. That's the way they treat their people and that's the only way they understand foreign policy ... The North Korean government will abuse any opportunity you give them. They'll take it and run.[47]

Giving positive incentives and a soft landing or a soft way out after turning up the heat and pressure might be much more persuasive to a regime that operates on the basis of fear and intimidation of its own people, as well as its regional neighbors, and indeed, the world.[48] Along the lines of this incremental ratcheting up, it could include an agreement with specific resort upon noncompliance to the

U.N. Security Council, the ICC and the ICJ, and whatever is maximally possible through the IAEA.[49]

Along these lines, it could then help to have U.N. Security Council resolutions (for example, through Article VI of the U.N. Charter)[50] or other assertive action.[51] The basis for such resolutions and possible sanctions can lie squarely on the multiple instruments of international law that North Korea has violated. Consider that it has broken every single major agreement that it has made, whether with other countries or international organizations, including the biological weapons convention, the cease-fire agreement after the initial Korean War, the 1991–92 agreements with South Korea, the 2000 agreement after the summit between the leaders of South and North Korea, the 1994 Agreed Framework, the IAEA dictates, and the NPT.[52] Hwang Jang-Yop explains how North Korea only enters into such agreements for tactical gain—not with any intention to restrict itself based on legal instruments.[53]

There is an interesting secondary role that the General Assembly can play if the U.N. Security Council is paralyzed by the abuse of a veto by, for example, Russia, who would seem the most likely to veto actions, including resolutions or sanctions against North Korea. It can take the initiative to recommend action by the U.N. Security Council in such situations while passing resolutions of its own.[54]

There should also be international, not just U.S., verification of North Korea's disarmament. Furthermore, there should be international assurance that North Korea complies with international organizations such as the IAEA, rather than ejecting the IAEA inspectors as it did in the past.[55] Otherwise, the acceptability and impunity of nuclear proliferation would be a message learned by other potentially dangerous regimes. Ideally, it would be best if North Korea returns to the NPT—given that it was the first country in history to attempt withdrawal from it and disavow it in 2003.[56] Regardless of North Korea's purported withdrawal from the NPT, there remains little doubt that it breached it while still a party to it.[57]

Again, it is worth stressing that South Korean and U.S. military forces ought to put in place as many defensive measures as possible to deter North Korean aggression. The United States must reaffirm a strong determination to defend South Korea. What North Korea would perceive as U.S. weakness or anticipated non-involvement could prove catastrophic for the peninsula.

In this whole process of external pressure, North Korea could come closer and closer to an internal collapse,[58] in which case the possibility for reunification exists. On the other hand, the threat of China perhaps stepping in and grabbing North Korea would then be a distinct possibility. China, however, denies a desire in this direction.[59]

The U.S. nuclear presence in Korea has steadily dwindled to none. In 1967, the United States had 2,600 nuclear weapons in Korea and Okinawa.[60] The number of nuclear weapons in Korea decreased to 151 by 1985,[61] and in 1991, the United States removed all of its nuclear weapons from Korea.[62] However, because the United States has long-range delivery systems, the presence of nuclear weapons in Korea—or even Asia—carries less significance than if the United States had only mid-range or short-range delivery abilities.[63]

The U.S. Army has had about 20,000–40,000 troops stationed in South Korea.[64] These troops have ample equipment, such as Apache helicopters and Patriot missile batteries.[65] The largest forward-deployed fleet of the Navy, the Seventh Fleet, rests not far from the shores of North Korea.[66] Around 200 aircraft, 40 to 50 ships, and some 20,000 Navy and Marine personnel constitute the Seventh Fleet.[67] Air Force deployment in the Pacific numbers 45,000 military and civilian personnel—with about 300 fighter and attack aircraft under its control.[68] The Seventh Air Force perches in Korea with the Fifth in Japan.[69]

These forces in the Pacific, some in and around Korea and Japan, can respond rapidly to an outbreak of hostilities. At the same time, the ability to quickly deploy additional military resources enables rapid reinforcement of the present numbers. The U.S. commitment to South Korea constitutes the greatest deterrent to North Korean aggression.

U.S. involvement

The United States must continue its involvement in the region. The stability of the region depends upon it. The critical theme of U.S. involvement emerges from the mass of scholarship.

The other side of the coin may be to continue sanctions, or, as another scholar has suggested, to try new types of sanctions, those that can be directed at the regime and not the people. The Security Council Resolutions do so by sanctioning military and luxury goods, but not humanitarian aid. The U.S. has continued with its humanitarian aid, even as it continues maximal sanctions. On a different note, the use of the Internet and technological sanctions in this technological age is a fresh idea to contemplate.[70]

South Korea, as an ally, must also play a large part in any diplomatic solution. Deep historic ties exist between South Korea and the U.S., given that South Korea and the U.S. have stayed close allies over the past half-century. In fact, the development of the two Koreas is intimately linked to the influence of other nations. Just as North Korea is an exaggerated version of Maoist China and Stalinist Soviet Union, through U.S. protection and investment, South Korea has developed into a much more free-enterprise, democratic, and open society than its northern counterpart[71]—so extensive social, economic, political, religious, educational, and cultural ties between the U.S. and South Korea continue.

These ties ought not be taken for granted or subsumed under the anti-U.S. rhetoric barrage tilting the culture. A solution would be for those in power in South Korea, and those in the media sympathetic to U.S.–South Korean ties, to promote the affinities between the two nations. South Korea must learn that all it has received back from North Korea after it has provided extensive aid and economic investments has been continued hostility and an unrelenting aggressive stance against it. South Koreans need to know that they may be helping to sustain a failed regime, stoking the dying embers of that society. If South Korea did not subsidize North Korea to the extent that it has, perhaps North Korea would have collapsed already. South Korea may be unwittingly delaying the peaceful unification of the Korean Peninsula by virtue of what it has done to prop up a malignant, totalitarian dictatorship. For example, a South Korean president handing half a billion dollars to Kim Jong-Il with no strings attached did not solve or improve anything.

The potential for internal collapse

The Korea Institute for National Unification (KINU) published an interesting empirical study that takes the factors used by Zbigniew Brezizinski, formerly National Security Advisor in the Carter administration, one of President Obama's main advisors on foreign politics, and a scholar in the field of international relations. Brezizinski examined various factors to measure the degree of crisis within regimes in Eastern Europe to help to predict whether they would experience impending collapse, transformation, regime change, and other similar events. KINU took the Brezizinski factors, added some of its own that it deemed appropriate to the North Korean context, and measured to what extent the North Korean regime is in crisis and the probability that it would implode. KINU's conclusion, after analysis of political, social, economic, cultural, and other factors, was that even through 1995—when the measurements ended—North Korea had already entered a crisis level. Many of those factors were on a downward trend, potentially leading to regime transformation or regime change if the trends were not reversed.[72]

Twenty years later, if one presumes that at least the majority of those factors have grown worse, which may not actually be the case, then North Korea has grown closer to possibly imploding. The initial implementation of economic free-enterprise zones may have helped to start to reverse its economic woes, but more likely, a greater factor in helping sustain North Korea, as was mentioned earlier, is increased trade and aid, most particularly from South Korea. Two-way trade between South and North Korea had risen to over $1.97 billion by 2013, much of it owed primarily to the continued inter-Korean industrial projects like the Gaeseong Industrial Complex.[73] Predominantly, the amount flowing from North Korea to South Korea was miniscule, but the numbers have increased dramatically since that time.[74]

The head of Hyundai, one of the two giant conglomerates in Korea, has been funding various projects, including the Mount Kumgang Tourist Region (which halted after a North Korean soldier shot and killed a South Korean tourist), as well as an entire industrial zone, various donations, and funds for infrastructure.[75] That type of aid from various South Korean sources has been increasing, and increasing dramatically.[76] China is another major source of aid and trade, but Russia has diminished its aid to North Korea due to its own economic woes.[77] North Korea only engages the international community to the extent that it thinks it can benefit from such interaction while continuing to pursue its own inimical goals. While North Korea may have taken certain steps to increase its diplomatic relationships,[78] the depth of those relationships extends no further than the instrumental pursuit of its own interests at best.

North Korea claims that if it just gets sufficient humanitarian aid, then it would be sustained thereby.[79] The root problem is more foundational, though: its economic system has failed.[80] North Korea, however, has experimented with economic free enterprise zones, a step in the right direction as far as increasing production.[81] Kim Jong-Un, however, fears extending them further lest it undermine or end his reign.

To help free the society and the economy, North Korea should implement reforms that move toward a more free-market, capitalistic direction that rewards industriousness, productivity, and enterprise. China-style reform would be a great leap forward. It has made slight steps in that direction as mentioned, and trade, especially with South Korea, has increased dramatically[82]—even as it has evaporated with almost the entire rest of the world. But North Korean so-called "trade" is more charity than anything else, where South Korea is helping North Korea, and getting little to nothing in return, except the continued animosity and hostility of the Pyongyang regime.[83]

Continued containment and deterrence remains necessary. Along these lines, nations such as Japan and the United States—and especially South Korea—take the path of patiently waiting, and perhaps in some ways accelerating, an internal implosion or transformation: leading to the demise of North Korea as it currently exists. Reinforcing this terrible regime, one that has miserably failed its people, would delay the day that it falls. Providing humanitarian aid without propping up the regime strikes the balance.

One can argue that even if North Korea will collapse, it is better for it to collapse with better economic conditions in order to alleviate the burden of South Korea, as well as other nations and organizations that would help. However, it seems that given the determination of Kim Jong-Un and his regime to hold on to power at all costs, and to orient the whole regime to maintaining a grip on power rather than serving the common good of the populace, it is highly likely that aid to North Korea would only tend to increase the grip that Kim Jong-Un and his cronies have on the country, especially given the diversion of aid to government and military personnel rather than to the peasants who need it most.[84] Savvy means of giving aid, such as giving food the elite scorn to eat and that spoil too quickly to enter storage as emergency war rations, increases the chances that the aid reaches the people.

China and Russia, among others, have urged appeasement of North Korea's repeated demands for a bilateral security agreement with the United States.[85] Such a move would be inadvisable if it removed the U.S. commitment to protect South Korea. Hwang Jang-Yop, the highest-level defector from North Korea that we mentioned in prior chapters, indicated that North Korea still is intent on taking over South Korea and the whole peninsula (unification by force is the official North Korean policy still), and in order to do so, it seeks to take the U.S. out of the picture.[86] The U.S. commitment to defend South Korea is the principal impediment for North Korea not to take over the peninsula—after all, it was the U.S. forces, along with the United Nations and South Korean forces, which pushed back North Korean aggression during the Korean War. Thus, it would be a mistake to take Pyongyang's insistence upon the security agreement with the United States as simply the paranoid delusions of a regime that anticipates U.S. aggression to dismantle the regime. Rather, if Hwang Jang-Yop's diagnosis is correct, and he had the best and highest inside view of the regime available, it is a very calculated effort for the North Koreans to take the United States out of the picture as far as defending South Korea on the peninsula.[87] Yet an agreement that ends the Korean War but does not diminish the U.S. commitment to South Korea could help. However, the DPRK might reject such a peace treaty.

Notes

* Kevin Zickterman aided me in organizing this chapter.
1 *See, e.g.,* Sung-Yoon Lee, *Global Pressure Point: Nuclear Diplomacy vis-à-vis the DPRK: A Dead-End Street,* 27 FLETCHER F. WORLD AFF. 151, 155–58 (2003). David Letterman, host of The Late Show, when discussing North Korea, frequently refers to Kim Jong-Il and his son "Menta Lee Il (Mentally Ill)." James Brooke, *Pop Culture Takes Aim at North Korea's Kim,* INT'L HERALD TRIB., June 1, 2005, at 2. The movie *Team America: World Police* portrayed an ego-maniacal Kim Jong-Il as the primary villain.
2 Lee, *supra* note 1.
3 *See* JOSEPH S. BERMUDEZ, JR., TERRORISM: THE NORTH KOREAN CONNECTION 24–54 (1990); SANG-WOO RHEE, SECURITY AND UNIFICATION OF KOREA 210 (1983).
4 *See* Bermudez, *supra* note 3, at 146–54. North Korean agents kidnapped at least thirteen Japanese nationals, forcing them to teach Japanese language and culture while using their identities to infiltrate South Korea and Japan. Robert J. Lundin III, Note, *International Justice: Who Should be Held Responsible for the Kidnapping of Thirteen Japanese Citizens?* 13 TRANSNAT'L L. & CONTEMP. PROBS. 699, 700–01 (2003).
5 *See* Barry A. Feinstein & Justus Reid Weiner, *Israel's Security Barrier: An International Comparative Analysis and Legal Evaluation,* 37 GEO. WASH. INT'L. L. REV. 309, 331 (2005).
6 *See* Bermudez, *supra* note 3, at 24–54 (describing extensive North Korean acts of terrorism and violence); JAMES E. HOARE & SUSAN PARES, CONFLICT IN KOREA: AN ENCYCLOPEDIA xxiii (1999).
7 *See* CHARLES M. PERRY & TOSHI YOSHIHARA, THE U.S.-JAPAN ALLIANCE 47, 81, 130 (2003).
8 Richard P. Cronin, *The North Korean Nuclear Threat and the U.S.-Japan Security Alliance: Perceived Interests, Approaches, and Prospects,* 29 FLETCHER F. WORLD AFF. 51, 53–54 (2005); *see also* CHRISTOPHER W. HUGHES, JAPAN-NORTH KOREA RELATIONS: OBSTACLES TO A BREAKTHROUGH, IN COOPERATION AND REFORM ON THE KOREAN PENINSULA 28, 35–36 (James M. Lister et al. eds., 2002).
9 *Cf.* JONG CHUL PARK, KOREA'S ENGAGEMENT POLICY TOWARD NORTH KOREA AND ITS IMPLICATIONS TO THE U.S. 14–16 (2001) (suggesting that the United States simultaneously pursue missile defense and negotiations); Perry & Yoshihara, *supra* note 7, at 138–46 (suggesting that the United States pursue missile defense).
10 *See* William M. Drennan, *Nuclear Weapons and North Korea: Who's Coercing Whom?* in THE UNITED STATES AND COERCIVE DIPLOMACY 157, 190 (Robert J. Art & Patrick M. Cronin eds., 2003). The U.S.–South Korean alliance has been and will continue to be a primary deterrent against North Korean aggression, so these two nations must not only continue but also must strengthen their ties. Stephen W. Bosworth, *U.S.-Korean Relations After the Summit,* 25 FLETCHER F. WORLD AFF. 25, 27 (2001).
11 SCOTT SNYDER, NEGOTIATING ON THE EDGE: NORTH KOREAN NEGOTIATING BEHAVIOR 68–96 (1999); Hyun Joon Chon, *Characteristics of North Korea's South Korean Policy,* in KINU Research Abstracts '02, at 39, 40–41 (2003); *see* ROBERT S. LITWAK, ROGUE

STATES AND U.S. FOREIGN POLICY: CONTAINMENT AFTER THE COLD WAR 226 (2000) (quoting a former North Korean theoretician: "[North Korean officials] understand that there is no alternative to brinkmanship.").

12 *See, e.g.*, KIM IL SUNG, FOR THE INDEPENDENT PEACEFUL REUNIFICATION OF KOREA (1975); Li Jong Mok, Speeches to the United Nations (Oct. 21, 27, 29, 1975), in On the Question of Korea: Speeches of Representatives at the 30th Session of the U.N. General Assembly 1, 1–25 (1976); Park Chung Hee, Speech, North Korean Communists' Deceptive Double Tactics (January 14, 1975), in TOWARD PEACEFUL UNIFICATION 110 (1976); Park Chung Hee, Speech, Peace Propaganda and Warlike Provocations (July 4, 1975), in TOWARD PEACEFUL UNIFICATION, *supra*, at 116.

13 *See* Sung, *supra* note 12; Kim Il Sung, Speech at Pyongyang Mass Meeting (June 23, 1973), in KOREAN UNIFICATION: SOURCE MATERIALS WITH AN INTRODUCTION 340 (Se-Jin Kim ed., 1976). Kim Il Sung refers to "the U.S. imperialist occupation of south Korea," and accuses the United States of engaging in "machinations," and "double-dealing tactics." *Id.* at 341–42.

14 Lee, *supra* note 1, at 151–52.

15 The 2000 Summit remains an insubstantial anomaly that achieved greater support from South Korea to North Korea while ultimately giving South Korea very little; North Korea lost next to nothing by agreeing to the reunion of families, its largest "concession." See generally Mark E. Manyin, *North-South Korean Relations: A Chronology of the "New" Dialogue* 1–2 (2001), www.fas.org/man/crs/RL30811.pdf.

16 *See* Lee, *supra* note 1, at 155–58.

17 For a more thorough discussion of the need for all six nations to be involved, and why no single nation should predominate, see ILPYONG J. KIM, THE MAJOR POWERS AND THE KOREAN TRIANGLE, IN TWO KOREAS—ONE FUTURE?; A REPORT PREPARED FOR THE AMERICAN FRIENDS SERVICE COMMITTEE 119 (John Sullivan & Roberta Foss eds., 1987) [hereinafter TWO KOREAS—ONE FUTURE?].

18 Joel Brinkley & Steven R. Weisman, *Visiting Korea Base, Rice Sends Forceful Reminder to the North*, N.Y. TIMES, Mar. 20, 2005, at 11.

19 *See* Daniel A. Pinkston et al., Special Report on the North Korean Nuclear Weapons Statement, CTR. FOR NONPROLIFERATION STUDIES, MONTEREY INST. OF INT'L STUDIES, (2005), *available at* www.cns.miis.edu/pubs/week/050211.htm. For years, Pyongyang has expressed its desire to improve relations with the United States, while paradoxically issuing belligerent statements toward Washington. For example, on February 2, 2005, the North Korean media broadcast a statement by a North Korean Air Force officer declaring that the North Korean military would turn U.S. military bases into a "sea of fire" if the United State attacked the DPRK; *see also* Glenn Kessler, *Three Little Words Matter to N. Korea: Bush Has Avoided "No Hostile Intent,"* WASH. POST, Feb. 22, 2005, at A10 (reporting that the Bush administration repeatedly states that it has no intention to invade North Korea, but backs away from the Clinton-era phrase "no hostile intent").

20 Glenn Kessler, *N. Korea Talks May Hinge on Bush: Lawmaker Advises Bush to Choose His Words Carefully*, WASH. POST, Jan. 28, 2005, at A23; Jason Motlagh, *North Korea: Denuclearization is Final Goal*, THE WASH. TIMES ONLINE (Jan. 19, 2005), www.washtimes.com/upi-breaking/20050119-102012-8082r.htm.

21 Motlagh, *supra* note 20; *see also* Michael Duffy, *What Does North Korea Want?* TIME, Feb. 21, 2005, at 23 (reporting the North Korea's February 2005 announcement).

22 Congressman Tom Lantos, Speech at the Paul H. Nitze School of Advanced International Studies, Is Libya the Future of North Korea? (Feb. 14, 2005), www.sais-jhu.edu/pubaffairs/SAISarticles05/Lantos_Speech.pdf [hereinafter Lantos Speech].

23 *See id.*; *see also* Henry Sokolski, *The Qaddafi Precedent*, WKLY. STANDARD, Jan. 26, 2004, at 12, *available at* www.npec-web.org/Frameset.asp?PageType=Writings; Adam Wolfe, *U.S. Attempts to Make an Example Out of Libya Will Fail*, PINR.COM (Apr. 24, 2004), www.pinr.com/report.php?ac=view_report&report_id=163&language_id=1.

24 Lantos Speech, *supra* note 22.
25 *Id.* U.S. Ambassador to the Republic of Korea Stephen W. Bosworth notes the advantage of multi-party talks over bilateral negotiations because the former builds broad regional consensus that supports dialogue and cooperation between North and South Korea. See Bosworth, *supra* note 10, at 25.
26 *See* Erik Raines, Note, *North Korea: Analyzing the "New" Nuclear Threat*, 12 Cardozo J. Int'l & Comp. L. 349, 359–62 (2004).
27 Lantos Speech, *supra* note 22.
28 *See* Steven Kamara, *Schultz '42 Discusses Solutions to Nuclear Threat from North Korea*, Daily Princetonian Online (Apr. 14, 2003), www.dailyprincetonian.com/archives/2003/04/14/news/7921.shtml.
29 *See N. Korea: Starving for Missiles*, CBSNews.com (Aug. 13, 1999), www.cbsnews.com/stories/1999/08/13/eveningnews/main58131.shtml.
30 *See* Sang-Hun Choe, *North Korea Back to Usual Line, Calls U.S. a 'Nuclear Criminal,'* Chicago Sun-Times, Jan. 16, 2005, at 30.
31 Andrew Salmon, *N. Korea Will Return to Nuclear Discussions Six-Party Talks May Resume Within Weeks, U.S. Says*, Int'l Herald Tribune, Jan. 15, 2005, at 1.
32 Choe, *supra* note 30, at 30.
33 *Id.*
34 *Id.*
35 See James Brooke & David E. Sanger, *North Koreans Say They Hold Nuclear Arms*, N.Y. Times, Feb. 11, 2005, at A1.
36 *See id.*
37 Tatiana Zakaurtseva, North Korean Nuclear Issue and Some Ways of Its Settlement from the Russian Point of View, International Symposium on Peace and Prosperity in Northeast Asia 123, 130–34 (Jan. 13, 2005) (on file with author); Yunling Zhang, Ending Confrontation in the Korean Peninsula: The Way Out, International Symposium on Peace and Prosperity in Northeast Asia 145 (Jan. 13, 2005) (on file with author).
38 *Id.*
39 Akio Miyajima, Some Thoughts and Comments on [the] North Korean Nuclear Issue, International Symposium on Peace and Prosperity in Northeast Asia 165, 165, 168 (Jan. 13, 2005) (on file with author).
40 Chi Young Pak, Korea and the United Nations 99, 103, 106–07, (2000).
41 See *id.* at 101–02 (describing the justification of Secretary General Trygve Lie's "bold action" in response to the Korean crisis).
42 *See, e.g.*, Maggie Farley, *U.N. Rejects North Korea's Assertion That It Can Do Without Food Aid*, L.A. Times, Sept. 24, 2005, at A6 (describing U.N. efforts to increase humanitarian aid to North Korea).
43 Morse Tan, *The North Korean Nuclear Crisis: Past Failures and Present Solutions*, 50 St. Louis U. L.J. 517, 550 (2006). (Hwang Jang-Yop is the highest level government official to ever defect from North Korea.)
44 Zakaurtseva, *supra* note 37, at 136.
45 *See* Robert J. Art, *Coercive Diplomacy: What Do We Know?* in The United States and Coercive Diplomacy, *supra* note 10, at 359, 402.
46 The United States and Coercive Diplomacy, *supra* note 10, culls several lessons from the history of U.S. coercive diplomacy. It seems that in this incremental ratcheting up, the stakes can be made more and more serious for North Korea, and as that pressure is being applied, perhaps a way out, including positive incentives for verifiable disarmament could look increasingly attractive.
47 Interview by Mike Kim, May 31, 2007.
48 *But see* Drennan, *supra* note 10, at 193–96 (suggesting that the Clinton administration's reliance on incentives encouraged Kim Il Sung's brinkmanship tactics almost to the

point that he finally crossed the only real limit the U.S. had—the development of nuclear weapons).

49 A weakness of the IAEA is that it does not provide for resort to the ICJ. *See id.* at 164 ("The IAEA … lacks both the mandate and the means to enforce compliance with the terms of IAEA and [Non-Proliferation Treaty] membership.").

50 Zakaurtseva, *supra* note 37, at 142–43, recommends an in camera meeting of the Security Council.

51 A reason to think that U.N. Security Council action could help is that during the early 1990s, North Korea backed down from its initial threats to withdraw from the Non-Proliferation Treaty following an IAEA appeal to the U.N. Security Council. Pak, *supra* note 40, at 135.

52 *See* Anna Fifield, *Asia-Pacific: Pyongyang is Stepping Up its Nuclear Might, Seoul Claims*, FIN. TIMES, USA, Feb. 5, 2005, at 2; Pak, *supra* note 40, at 84; B. K. GILLS, KOREA VERSUS KOREA: A CASE OF CONTESTED LEGITIMACY 233–34 (Michael Liefer, ed., 1996); Cecilia Y. Oh, *Comment, The Effect of Reunification of North and South Korea on Treaty Status*, 16 EMORY INT'L L. REV. 311, 314–15 (2002);– Pak, *supra* note 40, at 145.

53 *Defector Warns of North Korea War Plans, Despite Economic Plight, No Near-Term Collapse*, KOREAUPDATE, July 21, 1997, at 1–2.

54 Pak, *supra* note 40, at 110–11, 141–42. This role for the General Assembly emerged out of the Uniting for Peace resolution precedent. See *id.* at 109–14 for a fine delineation of the Uniting for Peace resolution in the context of the U.N. Charter arts. 10, 11, 12, and 24, and their historic interpretation

55 *See* Gills, *supra* note 52, at 236.

56 Harold Hongju Koh, *On American Exceptionalism*, 55 STAN. L. REV. 1479, 1493 (2003).

57 *See, e.g.*, Drennan, *supra* note 10, at 165 (documenting U.S. intelligence indicating North Korea secretly developed nuclear military capabilities in 1989).

58 See Sung Chull Kim et al., North Korea in Crisis: An Assessment of Regime Sustainability 7 (1997).

59 Yunling Zhang, Ending Confrontation in the Korean Peninsula: The Way Out, International Symposium on Peace and Prosperity in Northeast Asia 145, 151–52 (Jan. 13, 2005) (on file with author).

60 Robert S. Norris et al., *Where They Were*, 55 BULL. ATOMIC SCIENTISTS 26, 26–35 (1999), *available at* www.thebulletin.org/print.php?art_ ofn=nd99norris_024. See generally *A History of U.S. Nuclear Weapons in South Korea*, THE NUCLEAR INFORMATION PROJECT (Sept. 28, 2005), www.nukestrat.com/korea/koreahistory.htm.

61 Robert S. Norris & William M. Arkin, *Nuclear Notebook: U.S. Nuclear Weapons Locations, 1995*, 51 BULL. ATOMIC SCIENTISTS 74, 74–75 (1995), *available at* www.thebulletin.org/issues/nukenotes/nd95nukenote.html.

62 See Benjamin Friedman, *Fact Sheet: North Korea's Nuclear Weapons Program*, Jan. 23, 2003, www.cdi.org/nuclear/nk-fact-sheet-pr.cfm. South Korea was the last forward nuclear base for the United States in the Pacific. See Norris et al., *supra* note 60.

63 *See* CHARLES J. MOXLEY, JR., NUCLEAR WEAPONS AND INTERNATIONAL LAW IN THE POST COLD WAR WORLD 501–14 (2000).

64 Friedman, *supra* note 62.

65 *U.S. Forces Order of Battle*, GLOBAL SECURITY.ORG, www.globalsecurity.org/military/ops/korea-orbat.htm (last visited Nov. 1, 2005).

66 *Seventh Fleet-Forward Presence*, www.c7f.navy.mil/New/Pages/Forward%20presence.html (last visited Oct. 3, 2005).

67 *Id.* The ships typically include three to five Aegis guided-missile cruisers, five to ten destroyers and frigates, and one to two aircraft carriers. Eighteen of these ships use Japan and Guam as their bases.

68 United States Air Force Factsheet: Pacific Air Forces, www.osan.af.mil/Facts/Pacific%20Air%20Forces.htm (last visited Oct. 3, 2005).

69 *The United States Security Strategy for the East Asia-Pacific Region*, U.S. EMBASSY IN THAILAND, www.bangkok.usembassy.gov/services/docs/reports/ussec1.htm (last visited Oct. 14, 2005). The Seventh Air Force includes the Fifty-first and Eighth Fighter Wings, with a combined 117 planes and 8,300 air force personnel. *See 7th Air Force*, OSAN AIR BASE, www.osan.af.mil/7th%20Air%20Force.htm (April 2003). The Fifty-first uses A-10 aircraft as well as squadrons of F-16 fighter aircraft. *See 51st Fighter Wing Osan AB, Korea*, OSAN AIR BASE, www.osan.af.mil/ (last visited Nov. 12, 2005).

70 *See generally* Benjamin Brockman-Hawe, *Using Internet "Borders" to Coerce or Punish: The DPRK as an Example of the Potential Utility of Internet Sanctions*, 25 B.U. INT'L L.J. 163 (2007).

71 Gregory Henderson, *The Politics of Korea*, in TWO KOREAS—ONE FUTURE? *supra* note 17, at 95, 108–12 (stating that North Korea "rules through exceedingly concerted and consistent propaganda and socialization programs in an isolated polity").

72 SUNG CHULL KIM ET AL., NORTH KOREA IN CRISIS: AN ASSESSMENT OF REGIME SUSTAINABILITY iii, 9, 124, 126 (1997).

73 *See e.g.*, Christine Kim, *North Korea Posts 2nd Successive Year of Growth-Bank of Korea*, REUTERS (July 11, 2013) www.reuters.com/article/2013/07/12/korea-north-econ-omy-idUSL4N0FI0EG20130712; *North Korean Economy Records Positive Growth for Two Consecutive Years*, THE INSTITUTE FOR FAR EASTERN STUDIES (July 17, 2013), www.ifes. kyungnam.ac.kr/eng/FRM/FRM_0101V.aspx?code=FRM130717_0001; *but see* Aiden Foster-Carter, *How Seoul Distorts Pyongyang's Trade Statistics*, KOREA REALTIME (May 30, 2014), www.blogs.wsj.com/korearealtime/2014/05/30/how-seoul-distorts-pyongyangs-trade-statistics/.

74 In a historic move, North Korea actually shipped shirts to South Korea in 2005. B. J. Lee, *An Oasis of Capitalism: South Korea Companies Explore the Possibilities of Outsourcing to the North, in a New Economic Zone*, NEWSWEEK INT'L, Sept. 19, 2005, at 51.

75 Young Whan Kihl, *The DPRK and its Relations with the ROK*, in KOREA BRIEFING 1997–1999, at 123, 139 (Kongdan Oh ed., 2000); James Brooke, *An Industrial Park in North Korea Nears a Growth Spurt*, N.Y. TIMES, Feb. 28, 2006, at C5.

76 *See* Sung Chul Yang, *South Korea's Sunshine Policy: Progress and Predicaments*, 25 FLETCHER F. WORLD AFF. 31, 33–34 (2001).

77 Perry & Yoshihara, *supra* note 7, at 78–87.

78 *See* U.S. Dep't of State, Bureau of East Asian and Pacific Affairs, Background Note: North Korea (2005), www.state.gov/r/pa/ei/bgn/2792.htm. North Korea has sought to broaden its formal diplomatic relationships. In July 2000, North Korea began participating in the ASEAN Regional Forum (ARF), with Foreign Minister Paek Nam Sun attending the ARF ministerial meeting in Bangkok. The DPRK also expanded its bilateral diplomatic ties in that year, establishing diplomatic relations with Italy, Australia, and the Philippines. The U.K., Germany, and many other European countries have established diplomatic relations with the North, as have Australia and Canada.

79 *See* Joseph Kahn, *North Korea Says It Will Abandon Nuclear Efforts*, N.Y. TIMES, Sept. 19, 2005, at A1.

80 *See* Yang, *supra* 76, at 32 (comparing the 1999 per capita incomes and total trade of the two nations, when North Korea was at $714 per person and $1.48 billion in trade, while South Korea stood at $8,581 and $263.5 billion respectively).

81 *See* Brooke, *supra* note 75.

82 Yang, *supra* note 76, at 33.

83 *Id.*; Bosworth, *supra* note 10, at 28 (arguing that the large cost of reconstructing North Korea's collapsed economic infrastructure "will have to be carried, in effect, on the balance sheets of South Korea's government, South Korea's corporations, and, ultimately, South Korea's households").

84 Kongdan Oh calls those who favor trade, "the engagement school," while those who think that economic aid to North Korea is not a good idea, "the confrontation school." KONGDAN OH, THE PROBLEM AND PROMISE OF ECONOMIC COOPERATION, IN KOREA

BRIEFING: TOWARD REUNIFICATION (David R. McCann ed., 1997). Oh suggests that economic dealing with North Korea will help only North Korea in the short term, but that eventually South Korea will need to expand and integrate to sustain its growth. *Id.* at 46–47.

85 Zakaurtseva, *supra* note 37.
86 *See* Lee Wha Rang, *North Korea's Hwang Jang Yop Saga Continues*, KOREA WEB WEEKLY, www.kimsoft.com/korea/nk-whang.htm#how (last visited Mar. 17, 2006); Hwang Jang-Yop, *Letter to Intellectuals of the World: Mankind Must Head to Democracy*, DAILY NK (June 5, 2005), www.dailynk.com/english/read.php?cataID=nk02200&num=166.
87 Morse Tan, *The North Korean Nuclear Crisis: Past Failures and Present Solutions*, 50 ST. LOUIS U. L.J. 517, 550 (2006) ("Provided that the South Korea-US alliance remains strong, we can say that South Korea is superior to North Korea militarily.").

15 China's potential to solve the puzzle*

A history of failed diplomacy

Over the past twenty-five years of nuclear diplomacy, the United States has tried military exercises, economic sanctions, and political isolation to pressure the North Korean leadership to behave more responsibly. But today, the Obama administration and the U.S. Congress find themselves in the same place as their predecessors—with policy decisions resulting only in stalemated negotiation, a consistent pattern of broken promises by Pyongyang, a plethora of ongoing human rights violations, and a burgeoning nuclear weapons and missile program. In the wake of North Korea's third nuclear test in February 2013, its reckless threats to nuke Japan and the U.S., the continued provocation of South Korea and its decision to throw out the armistice that ended the Korean War, as well as the unwanted attention brought to China's forced repatriation of North Korean refugees by the U.N. Commission of Inquiry, it appears that China stands poised to wield its massive influence over North Korea with coercive diplomacy and progressively harsher and more consistent punishments that aim to steer North Korea toward a better path.

In just the first six months of 2014, North Korea fired eight missiles, eighty-five short-range rockets, and 560 artillery shells in waters around the Korean Peninsula.[1] It is likely that Pyongyang will soon conduct a fourth nuclear test, if it has not already done so by the time this book is published. To rein in North Korea, one need only look to North Korea's historical "protector" along the country's northern border for an answer. In a meeting with the South Korean Ambassador to the U.S., he told me that he thought China held the most potential to successfully address North Korea. As North Korea becomes increasingly isolated worldwide because of its actions, the Kim regime has depended more and more on the People's Republic of China for economic survival.[2] China is North Korea's closest ally, most significant trade partner, and largest provider of food, fuel, and industrial machinery. China has the most ability to wield influence in North Korea's capital, Pyongyang.[3]

Furthermore, China's own internal policies are changing to reflect a more concerned attitude toward international human rights norms. Beijing's support for North Korea's ruthless, bloody regime that attacks its neighbors and brutalizes its own people only draws attention to China's own human rights failings, and undermines China's soft power.[4]

So can we count on China to use its enormous influence to rein in this murdering, torturing, and dangerous regime? Has it sanctioned or punished North Korea for its blatant opposition to international nuclear armament controls? And to what extent would China interfere with the sovereignty of another nation going forward—something Beijing and current president Xi Xinping has vocally opposed. These issues will form the focus of this section, intended to outline a China lead or co-lead approach to tackling both nuclear diplomacy and the multitude of human rights violations within North Korea.

Beijing's shifting policy on North Korea

For years, Chinese diplomats have stuck to a carefully worded script when discussing tensions between North and South Korea and the U.S. "All parties should engage in dialogue," reads a typical quote. "China wants to preserve peace and stability on the Korean Peninsula," reads another.[5] But recently, China's Communist leaders have deviated from their list of stock phrases, allowing their apparent frustration with Pyongyang to seep into public view. In early April 2013 and subsequent to North Korea's third nuclear test, China's new president, Xi Jinping, delivered the rhetorical equivalent of a rap on the knuckles to Pyongyang. "No one should be allowed to throw a region and even the whole world into chaos for selfish gains," Mr. Xi warned during a speech at the Boao forum on the Chinese island of Hainan. The Chinese president did not mention any country by name, but it is widely believed that his words targeted Pyongyang.[6]

China's new leadership and a changing North Korea policy

The recent change in China's leadership has yet to show a paradigmatic shift in its policy toward North Korea. However, a number of significant indicators show that China may increase its tightening measures on North Korea because of its belligerent, threatening, and globally unpopular behavior. For example, following North Korea's most recent nuclear test in early 2013, Chinese President Xi Jinping told South Korean President Park Geun-hye that "he understands Park's thoughts [on bringing North Korea to a dialogue] well and he will continue trying to persuade the North, although it is difficult."[7] Even more recently, and almost a year and half after North Korea's 2013 nuclear test, President Xi met with President Park during an unprecedented two-day trip to Seoul in an effort to establish solidarity over the North Korea nuclear issue as well as bolster an already booming trade relationship between China and South Korea. After their talks, South Korean President Park told reporters that she and President Xi agreed on the need to rid North Korea of nuclear weapons and would resolutely oppose any more nuclear tests. Xi also called for negotiations to end the North's nuclear program and the uncertainty that lingers on the Korean Peninsula.[8]

North Korea, meanwhile, welcomed the leader of its only major ally and main source of fuel and food to the Korean Peninsula with a flurry of rocket and missile tests, some aimed in the direction of South Korea, the most recent tests occurring only a day before President Xi's visit to that country. The tests, as well as a vow by North Korea's military to conduct more, may express the North's anger at China for ignoring it in favor of its archrival. North Korea may possess roughly six to twelve crude nuclear weapons and has conducted three atomic tests since 2006, the most recent in 2013.[9]

Beijing, entangled in hostile territorial disputes across Asia, may see an opportunity to boost its influence with the rare neighbor that feels generally positive about China, while also further driving a wedge between U.S. allies, Seoul and Tokyo.[10] China, the world's second-largest economy, and South Korea, the fourth-biggest economy in Asia have a booming trade relationship. China is South Korea's largest trading partner, and Seoul reported that two-way trade topped $220 billion last year—an amount greater than the combined value of South Korea's trade with the U.S. and Japan.[11]

Managing security matters, and more specifically North Korea's possession and proliferation of nuclear weapons and development of the long-range missiles to carry them, has always been trickier. China has unusual leverage with hard-to-read North Korea and is often pressed to do more to force change. Recently, North Korea has repeatedly looked to China for diplomatic cover when the U.N. has taken serious issue with North Korean nuclear and missile tests and its much-criticized human rights record.[12] The shared regional concern about North Korea has helped draw Seoul and Beijing together. Officials in Seoul now expect China to take strong action over future provocations, especially if North Korea conducts another nuclear test as it moves toward building an arsenal of nuclear-tipped missiles that could reach the U.S.[13] Still, it does not seem likely that Xi will abandon North Korea entirely as long as Seoul remains loyal to an alliance with Washington that has shielded the South from North Korean aggression and allowed it to build its impressive economy.

Not just another North Korean execution: China loses an ally

In a move that took observers and experts of the Hermit Kingdom by surprise, Kim Jong-Un dramatically removed his uncle from office as the second most powerful leader in North Korea, and then had him publicly executed. State media claimed that Kim removed Jang Song-thaek and his faction from office and executed him for "attempting to overthrow the state by all sorts of intrigues and despicable methods with a wild ambition to grab supreme power."[14] North Korea's brutal purge and execution of Kim Jong-Un's uncle raised international fears of instability in a state with an active nuclear weapons program and a willingness to ratchet up regional tensions without provocation.[15] Jang held responsibility for economic relations with China, by far North Korea's largest trading partner, including the establishment of special economic zones on the border between the two countries. The brother-in-law of Kim Jong-Il, who died in 2011,

Jang married Kim Kyong-hui, Kim Jong-Il's only sister.[16] He accompanied Kim Jong-Il on three trips to China in 2010 and 2011 that focused on implementing Chinese-style pro-market restructuring. Jang made a further trip to China in 2012 to meet with Chinese leaders on economic policy.

The announcement of Jang's removal from office, carried by North Korea's official Korean Central News Agency (KCNA), said that he was responsible for throwing the state financial management system into confusion after committing such acts of treachery as selling off precious resources of the country at cheap prices. Accordingly, North Korea issued a directive to any North Korean citizens in China to return home, a move targeted at punishing anyone with connections to Jang.[17] While the highly unusual public humiliation and execution indicates the possibility of a power struggle within the secretive government, a much more complex and nuanced account of the events have emerged. According to the South Korean intelligence service, the execution was less about Jang's attempt to usurp his nephew's power and more about Jang's provocation of the North Korean elite by dominating lucrative business deals.[18]

The story pieced together by South Korean and American intelligence officials points to a clash of elite factions over who would profit from North Korea's most lucrative exports (coal, crabs, and clams) to China, the country's only major trade partner. For years, the profits from fishing grounds, coal mines, and the output from munitions factories and trading companies went directly to the North Korean military, helping it feed its troops, and enabling its top officers to send cash gifts to the Kim family. When Mr. Kim succeeded his father two years ago, he took away some of the military's fishing and trading rights and handed them to his cabinet, which he designated as the main agency to revive the economy. Mr. Jang was believed to have been a leading proponent of this policy of curtailing the military's economic power.[19]

Mr. Jang appears to have consolidated many of those trading rights under his own control—meaning that profits from the coal, crabs, and clams went into his accounts, or those of state institutions under his control, including the administrative department of the ruling Workers' Party of Korea, which he headed.[20]

Accusations of factionalism and scheming within the North Korean elite are not news. Approximately six or seven key families control most of North Korea's trading companies. The most surprising and unprecedented thing is not that someone was planning to overthrow the state, it is the implication that Jang had a substantial number of followers. The first-ever official admission of significant disunity in North Korea could signal more elite infighting to come.[21] Kim's two predecessors, Kim Il-Sung and Kim Jong-Il, his grandfather and father respectively, both managed the internal factions without drawing massive public attention to the issue. Whether this recent decision by North Korea to execute Kim's uncle indicates faltering leadership and an all-out war between various family interests remains uncertain.[22]

Given the opaqueness of the country's inner circle of elites, many details of the struggle between Kim Jong-Un and his uncle remain unclear. However, what is known suggests that while Kim has eliminated a potential rival, it has been at the enormous cost of revealing a massive fracture inside North Korea's elite over who pockets the foreign currency—mostly Chinese Renminbi—from the few nonmilitary exports the country produces.[23]

China and human rights: Shifting priorities

China's own internal policies are changing to reflect a more concerned attitude toward human rights norms. China is a great power that is increasingly concerned with its standing in the world, and with cultivating "soft power." Beijing's support for North Korea's ruthless, bloody regime that attacks its neighbors and brutalizes its own people only draws attention to China's own human rights failings, and undermines China's soft power.[24] Recent evidence of China's increasing concern with its standing in the world and with cultivating soft power was when China ran for, and was elected in November 2013 to the U.N. Human Rights Council for a period of three years.[25] Three days later, on November 14, 2013, the Chinese government announced it would ease its one-child family restrictions and also abolish "re-education through labor" camps, significantly curtailing two policies that have defined China's authoritarian control over its people and that human rights advocates have strongly opposed.[26] According to a scholar from Human Rights Watch, this marked "an important step to do away with a system that not only profoundly violated human rights, but was also standing in the way of any further legal reform."[27]

Unwelcome accountability: China and the U.N. Commission of Inquiry Report

While China is making at least outward efforts to increase its human rights standing on the national stage, the recent United Nations Human Rights Council's report on North Korea trained a harsh spotlight on China's rigorous and unsettling policy of forcibly repatriating citizens of North Korea who flee the country. North Korea imposes a virtually absolute ban on ordinary citizens travelling abroad, thereby violating their human right to leave the country according to the Universal Declaration of Human Rights and the International Covenant on Civil and Political Rights.[28] Despite the enforcement of this ban through strict border controls, North Korean nationals still take the risk of fleeing, mainly to China. When forcibly repatriated and returned to North Korea, officials there systematically subject them to persecution, torture, prolonged arbitrary detention, and, in some cases, sexual violence. Repatriated women who are pregnant are regularly subjected to forced abortions, and babies born to repatriated women are often killed. Persons found to have been in contact with officials from South Korea or with Christian churches are forcibly "disappeared" into political prison camps, imprisoned in ordinary prisons, or summarily executed.[29] The earlier refugee chapters, Chapters 4 and 11, treat this subject in more depth.

In a letter directed to the Commission of Inquiry, China simultaneously emphasized that it did not support the establishment of the Commission of Inquiry on Human Rights in North Korea and made clear its continued position that DPRK citizens who have entered China illegally do it for economic reasons. Therefore, China does not consider them refugees.[30] However, when U.N. investigators told China that it might be aiding and abetting crimes against humanity by sending migrants and defectors back to North Korea to face torture or execution, this charge prompted an immediate yet predictable response from Beijing.[31] According to Beijing's official response, China "could not accept this unreasonable criticism," and "believes that politicizing human rights issues is not conducive toward improving a country's human rights." It also stated that "taking human rights issues to the International Criminal Court is not helpful to improving a country's human rights situation."[32] According to the Commission of Inquiry Report, in forcibly returning North Korean nationals, China also violates its obligation to respect the principle of *non-refoulement* under international refugee and human rights law. In some cases, Chinese officials also appear to provide information on those apprehended to their counterparts in the DPRK.[33]

The U.N. Commission of Inquiry on Human Rights in the DPRK conducted official visits to South Korea, Japan, Thailand, the U.K., and the U.S. during its investigation. On multiple occasions the commission sought access to China in order to conduct inquiries and to consult with government officials and local experts along the shared China–North Korea border. China eventually responded that given its position on country-specific mandates, especially on the Korean Peninsula, it would not extend an invitation to the commission.[34] This refusal presented an obstacle to collecting substantive refugee data from within China. In fact, until the Commission of Inquiry (COI) released its report on North Korea, reports written by previous U.N. rapporteurs treaded too cautiously about extending their reach beyond North Korea, and feared that China might rescind its support for the process if they did.[35] The COI report was the first to not only call China out publicly on the issue, but to record in detail the many dimensions of the issue—forced repatriation, human trafficking, sexual abuse, and the status of children born to North Korean–Chinese couples. Unfortunately, observers remain skeptical that China will substantially alter its policies. On the other hand, a cluster of Chinese academics, as well as a growing tech-savvy population through social media, have started to question official arguments providing possible domestic, economic, or political rationale.[36]

How will China's shifting priorities impact its relationship with North Korea?

In the past, China has been willing to use certain resources in its control to gain economic or political advantage over North Korea. For example, Beijing has used its exports of oil to the DPRK to apply pressure to Pyongyang in matters of policy. In 2003 and 2006, China temporarily cut off the supply of petroleum to the DPRK in response to North Korea's nuclear and missile tests.[37] In December 2010, China again temporarily cut off North Korea's oil supply to dissuade Pyongyang from retaliating against South Korea for conducting live-fire exercises after the North's artillery shelling of Yeonpyeong Island.[38]

More recent evidence showing China's willingness to use coercive diplomacy with harsher repercussions is Beijing's signing on to U.N. sanctions against North Korea and initiating sanctions of its own.[39] After the latest nuclear test in February 2013, the Chinese government took unprecedented measures to implement sanctions against North Korea. Among the most prominent steps, the state-run bank of China halted business with North Korea's main foreign exchange bank. Additionally, the central government instructed local governments to implement U.N. Resolution 2094, which has led to more rigorous inspections of North Korea-bound cargo.[40] The Chinese government also tightened customs inspections in Dandong and Dallan resulting in a significant decrease in North Korea shipping traffic. North Korea relies on most of its sea transportation through this route. Additionally, China froze assets in two North Korean banks not even listed by UNSCR 2087 and 2094.[41]

The Chinese have enormous leverage over North Korea in many respects. But the question remains, can China exercise that leverage to a much greater extent without destabilizing the region? Will China do it? The answer may well turn out "yes" to both questions. With growing economic dependency of North Korea on China, along with a coalescing worldview against human rights violations, and China's increasing focus on its own global reputation, China would clearly benefit from leading a global effort to improve human rights in North Korea.

China's main focus as it relates to North Korea is maintaining stability on the peninsula. With North Korea getting closer and closer to causing regional instability both from a human rights perspective and an international security perspective with its increasing nuclear capabilities, China must find other alternatives to managing the relationship than those of the past. China's goal of maintaining stability on the peninsula may fall in jeopardy unless Beijing diverges from its current role of acquiescing to much of North Korea's belligerent behavior and instead gradually implements an approach based on coercive diplomacy and punishments.[42]

Increasingly aggressive tactics could include the threat of signing on to future United Nations resolutions that would further isolate North Korea, reducing its oil supply to North Korea for a prolonged period, or decreasing the export of consumer goods to the country. However, the use of these coercive diplomacy and pressure tactics does not mean that China will discontinue all of its cooperative economic development efforts, subsidies, or trade, etc. with North Korea. These joint projects boost China's poor northeast provinces, but also act as a softer tool to gradually induce economic reform in North Korea.[43]

China and the nuclear "threat" next door

North Korea has conducted three nuclear tests since 2006, demonstrating its ability to at least produce crude nuclear devices. North Korea has a sizable arsenal of short and medium-range missiles, and it is developing longer-range missiles. A recent assessment by the Pentagon's Defense Intelligence Agency has concluded with "moderate confidence" that the North now knows how to make a nuclear device small enough to be delivered by a ballistic missile.[44] North Korea conducted underground nuclear tests in 2006, 2009, and most recently 2013. The most recent was the largest, though it was estimated to be less powerful than the first bomb the United States dropped on Hiroshima, Japan, in 1945.[45] North Korea's third nuclear test came two months after the country launched a rocket that put its first satellite into orbit. The United States and its allies widely consider the rocket launch as a cover for North Korea to develop intercontinental ballistic missiles that could reach North America. The U.N. Security Council condemned the launching as a violation of resolutions that barred the North from testing technology used for ballistic missiles, and adopted tightened sanctions against the country.[46]

As the North's missile technology has gained more sophistication, the launching of longer-range missiles has evoked more international concern. In 1998, when the North launched a Taepodong that flew over Japan, Japan temporarily cut off its contribution toward a North Korean energy project.[47] In July 2006, when the North launched another missile, various countries began imposing sanctions, while the U.N. Security Council began adding to economic sanctions. In April 2009, when the North's efforts to launch a three-stage Unha-2 rocket failed, the Security Council said it would strengthen punitive measures. It did so after the North conducted a nuclear test the next month. In April 2012, the U.S. canceled planned food aid when the North tried to launch a more advanced missile, the Unha-3. That launching failed, but another in December succeeded in lifting a small satellite into orbit. The Security Council tightened sanctions yet again. After the North's nuclear test in February 2013, China, North Korea's longtime protector, participated in writing painful new sanctions aimed at North Korean banking, trade, and travel.[48]

What international sanctions already exist?

The U.N. Security Council has passed four resolutions since 2006 aimed at penalizing North Korea for its nuclear weapons program. In addition, the U.S. has imposed its own regimen of strict economic sanctions. The combined effects have severely squeezed North Korea's economy.[49] Under Resolutions 1718 (2006), 1874 (2009), 2087 (2013), and 2094 (2013), the United Nations has prohibited the North from conducting nuclear tests or launching ballistic missiles, requested that it abandon all future efforts to pursue more nuclear weapons, and urged it to return to negotiations with China, Japan, Russia, South Korea, and the United States, previously referred to as the Six-Party Talks.[50] The resolutions have also imposed embargos on large-scale arms, weapons-related research and development materials, and luxury goods, banned many types of financial transactions including transfers of cash, placed new restrictions on diplomats, and created monitoring mechanisms for enforcement.[51]

The U.S. has adopted sanctions that freeze all North Korean property interests in the U.S., ban most imports of goods and services from the North, and prohibit American dealings with any names on a blacklist of North Korean businesses and individuals suspected of illicit activities including money laundering, counterfeiting, currency smuggling, and narcotics trafficking.[52]

What is North Korea trying to accomplish?

In the past, U.S. administrations and South Korean governments managed to tamp down periodic heightened tensions with North Korea by offering concessions, including much-needed aid, in return for the North's promising to end its nuclear weapons programs. Pyongyang has always reneged on those promises after receiving aid.[53] Many analysts believe that North Korea again seeks aid and other concessions. The North Korean government highlights supposed threats from abroad as a favorite tool to enhance internal cohesion in an impoverished country that has experienced enormous deprivation, including devastating famine as well as continuing and pervasive hunger.[54]

North Korea's latest behavior has rattled nerves more than previous episodes because of the youth and inexperience of the North's new leader, Kim Jong-Un. South Korea and the U.S. have said the provocation appears to follow a familiar script, but the new Kim does not have an extensive track record.[55] For that reason, the U.S. has mounted an unusually muscular display of deterrence, sending a guided-missile destroyer and B-2 stealth bombers to the Korean Peninsula—all to send a message that it will defend its allies in the region, namely South Korea and Japan.[56] South Korea's new president, Park Geun-hye, has also recently pledged a robust response to any attack. China, which has long frustrated the West with its unwillingness to curb the North, recently began growing publicly impatient with Mr. Kim. With no shortage of fanfare and publicity, President Xi Jinping met with President Park during an unprecedented July 2014 trip to Seoul in an effort to celebrate and reaffirm the significant trade relationship between China and South Korea, as well as to establish solidarity over the North Korea nuclear issue.[57] Much to the chagrin of Pyongyang, South Korea's Park told reporters that she and President Xi agreed on the need to rid North Korea of nuclear weapons and would resolutely oppose any additional nuclear tests. President Xi publicly called for a re-start of negotiations to end the North's nuclear program and the uncertainty that lingers on the Korean Peninsula.[58]

The tipping point in China's tolerance for North Korea's nuclear weapons program seems to lie with the delicate power balance in Asia. If North Korea ever genuinely provoked the U.S., South Korea, or Japan in a believable way, China would wake up and take serious action. As China's numerous priorities shift, so too will its stake in achieving results from the North Korean nuclear negotiations it continues to advocate.

Economic development: A prerequisite to stability

Taken to its logical end, brushing over human rights considerations in favor of economic success should merit censure, not celebration. The legitimacy of any state must be measured more by its just human rights concerns than its economic performance. Yet economic growth and enjoyment of rights correlate positively, a reason for nurturing North Korea's feeble economy.[59] For years, China has urged the ever-resistant Pyongyang to follow its development pattern of reform that has led to its own successful economic growth. Despite China's urging, the Kim regime has always remained hesitant to taking any steps to reform the economy because it might lead to a loosening of its straightjacket-like grip on society.[60] However, the economic development strategy that has emerged in North Korea nevertheless appears to benefit both countries.

The first major step in this budding economic development strategy is the Rason industrial complex, launched officially in May 2011 and located near the two North Korean towns of Rajin and Sonbong. The Chinese plan provides guidance for the project, with Chinese companies managing the investments and operations. The development plan calls for building or upgrading roads and port facilities, establishing international freight brokerage, export processing, and financial institutions, as well as investing in generating electricity, coal mining, oil refineries, manufacturing, and tourism. The Rason complex operates as a Chinese project, and Chinese companies hire North Korean workers.[61] One Chinese company, the Sangdi Guanqun Investment Company, has signed a memorandum of understanding with Pyongyang's Investment and Development Group in which the company agrees to construct a coal-fired power plant for the DPRK in exchange for the right to build an oil refinery. The refinery will represent a $2 billion investment and will refine crude oil imported from the Middle East and Russia and be sold to China and other countries.[62]

Another area of development is a free-trade zone to be established on the Whwa and Huangjinbing Islands in the Yalu River separating the Chinese city of Dandong and the North Korean city of Sinuiju. China has reportedly negotiated a 100-year lease on the two islands and intends to invest $800 million there for industrial development. The goal is to build an industrial park on the islands similar to the Gaesong industrial complex on the border between North Korea and South Korea. This would provide an enormous boost to the economy in China's poor northeastern region.[63] Given the size of the planned investments in the Rason and Sinuiju projects, it seems that China's direct investment in North Korea may increase dramatically.

While North Korea continues to make it increasingly difficult for the Chinese to do business there because of the regional and global chaos Pyongyang instigates, secretive actions by this bellicose regime indicates North Korea's desire to cultivate its own economy by attracting new investment from its most meaningful benefactor. Evidence of North Korea's recent commitment to economic development occurred after the execution of Jang Song-Thaek, uncle to Kim Jong-Un and known for spearheading Chinese–North Korean business partnerships. According to diplomatic sources, in February 2013, Pyongyang sent North Korea's chairman of the State Commission for Economic Development, Kim Ki-Sok, to visit China and other areas of Asia seeking to firm up economic ties.[64] Kim made a stop in China's capital city Beijing, but also visited Shenzhen, a southern Chinese city that is the home to a successful special economic zone. While there, Kim met with businesses with expertise in such zones that could help North Korea develop its own. In October 2012, North Korea launched a commission that planned for fourteen special economic zones around the country. The sources said that Kim's efforts were for the most part fruitless, and he returned to North Korea without any solid leads.[65]

Jang Song-Thaek was one of the biggest North Korean business liaisons with China, and had spent several years building his network of contacts, initially under previous leader Kim Jong-Il. After Kim Jong-Il's passing in late 2011, Jang was kept as a top advisor to Kim Jong-Un. However, as mentioned earlier in this chapter, analysts suspect that Jang's close economic ties to China, which are key to North Korean industrial and agricultural resources, threatened the new leader, ultimately leading to Jang's execution.[66] According to diplomatic sources from inside Beijing speaking to the South Korean Newspaper *The Chosun Ilbo*, the agenda for China's upcoming annual parliamentary meeting, the National People's Congress, will include forming an action group to look into China's direct investment in North Korea now that Jang and his associates have been removed from office. Some watchers predict that either Prime Minister Pak Pong-Ju or deputy department chief of the DPRK's Workers' Party Ri Su-Yong will also make a visit to China soon and will likely be replacing some of the positions previously held by Jang's associates.[67]

While many scholars criticize Kim Jong-Un for abandoning any form of economic development under his regime, countervailing indications also appear to point otherwise. In addition to sending delegations to attract investment (as detailed earlier), North Korea has recently consolidated its Joint Venture Investment Committee and the State Economic Development Committee into a new ministry, which some analysts interpret as an effort to make economic development more manageable, attract foreign investment, and promote trade. The country has also placed more of an emphasis on special economic zones as well as microeconomic reforms.[68] Moreover, to some extent the young North Korean has tied the legitimacy of his own rule to being able to deliver improvements in the general economic situation of the country. Kim Jong-Un has done this on multiple instances by making public commitments (domestic and international) to give more attention and priority to economic development.[69] This is important because it shows Kim Jong-Un has a powerful political incentive to find a way to improve the economy. Although North Korea's economic development aspirations seem in certain respects to be growing, the critical question is whether the Kim regime is willing to develop policies that will integrate its own economy with regional and international economies—a move necessary for increasing trade and investment. It remains to be seen in which direction Kim Jong-Un decisively moves regarding the economic future of North Korea.

A China-led approach to North Korea: Addressing dual global concerns

In the past, China has been fundamentally risk-averse in its approach to North Korea, both with regard to human rights violations and nuclear proliferation. However, due to a number of shifting priorities that were mentioned previously in this chapter, China appears to be "shaping" its neighbor gradually from various angles rather than employing drastic measures stemming from drastic policy changes or direct military force.[70] Where China previously maintained a one-dimensional policy with North Korea based on a "friendship sealed in blood," Beijing's approach is evolving to a multi-dimensional policy focused on risk minimization instead of risk aversion.[71] This multi-dimensional approach will likely utilize diverse strategies, including coercive diplomacy and punishments, as well as economic development initiatives, to manage different types of risks surrounding the Korean Peninsula.

Some experts argue that links between the two countries failed to recover after the death of Kim Jong-Il. It is widely believed that when Kim Jong-Un came to power he failed to pay his respects to the leaders in Beijing, who were providing his regime with the majority of North Korea's food and fuel aid.[72] According to Cheng Xiaohe, Deputy Director at the Center for China's International Strategic Studies at Renmin University in Beijing, in comparison with his grandfather and his father, China has minimal contact with the young leader. "When this young guy came to power, he tried to show his tough face to the U.S. and South Korea, but also to China."[73] Recently, some academics and journalists in China are openly pushing Beijing to rethink its policy on North Korea. In a 2013 *Financial Times* newspaper op-ed titled "China Should Abandon North Korea," Deng Yuwen, the editor of an influential Chinese Communist Party journal, argued that Beijing should support Korean reunification. He was later dismissed from his job after the Chinese foreign ministry called to complain about the article.[74]

International pressure can help politically isolate China from North Korea by forcing China to publically separate itself from North Korea. In a similar way to North Korea seeking a treaty with the U.S. so it can attack South Korea without fearing an immediate, automatic retaliation by the U.S., North Korea will be left vulnerable to defend itself, legally and/or militarily, absent support from China. Momentum is already gathering in this direction. For instance, when the U.S. enacted the North Korean Human Rights Act of 2004,[75] the U.S. Congress officially stated that:

> North Korea is a dictatorship in which there is no freedom of speech, expression, or of the press; the government tortures political prisoners; and many people starve each year due to failed centralized agricultural policies ... *[and this bill also seeks to encourage] China to stop returning refugees to North Korea, where they face torture or death* [emphasis added].

By taking this one step further, the United Nations can issue formal charges against China for violating the Convention and Protocol Relating to the Status of Refugees.[76]

Many prominent Chinese government officials want Beijing to maintain the status quo with North Korea, for all the usual reasons: millions of North Korean refugees could pour across China's borders if the Kim regime collapsed, creating additional economic pressures for Beijing. Traditional rationale from China–North Korea policy experts also cites the prospect that a unified Korea might align with Washington, leaving China with a U.S. ally right on its border. At the same time, China is busy with its own domestic troubles and Beijing's own regional tensions in the South and East China Seas, and increased troubles from Pyongyang are undoubtedly an unwelcome distraction.[77]

As mentioned previously, Chinese diplomats are attempting to defuse the North Korea problem by embracing strongly worded diplomacy and U.N. sanctions to keep Pyongyang in line. If that fails, more direct action might be taken by reducing fuel or economic aid, as Beijing has done in the past. With little notice or effort, Beijing could decimate North Korea's flimsy economy by limiting trade between the two countries.[78] While trade between China and North Korea is rising, it continues to remain extremely unbalanced. Recent figures estimate China accounts for 70 percent of North Korea's trade. North Korea accounts for less than 1 percent of Chinese trade. A steep drop in business with North Korea would affect China's northeastern Jilin province, but few other regions would notice a change.[79] If China were to decide to impose an economic embargo on North Korea, it would be absolutely crippling to North Korea and would essentially be unnoticeable to the Chinese economy. Even more importantly, North Korea's fuel needs are serviced by China. According to Marcus Noland, Senior Fellow and Director of Studies at the Peterson Institute for International Economics in Washington D.C., "If you turn off the oil pipeline, and there is literally a pipeline, the North Koreans freeze pretty quickly."[80] China has reduced oil shipments to North Korea in the past. Following a missile test by the North in 2003, China temporarily cut off oil shipments through its pipeline, though it blamed technical problems for the suspension.[81] Still, the decision to limit trade or aid with North Korea again should not be taken lightly. Average people in North Korea would certainly feel the effects of Beijing's wrath before Pyongyang's political elite. Also, Beijing would have to carefully consider any option that could lead to the collapse of the North Korean state, a possibility that could lead to millions of North Korean refugees pouring into China.

Whether China's changing policy toward North Korea is a long-term trend will depend on China continuing a progressively hardline approach with North Korea. One clear indictor of a long-term trend would be consistent and additional implementation of U.N. sanctions. Another indicator would be whether China and the U.S. could form a cooperative relationship based on the mutual need to manage risk on the Korean Peninsula. Still another indication would be the further tightening of Chinese export controls and sanctions at its borders of key material and technology related to North Korea's nuclear program. To its credit, China has recently banned a long list of items that could potentially be used for nuclear armament purposes.[82]

China, the United States, and coercive diplomacy tactics

In the wake of North Korea's third nuclear test in February 2013, its continued reckless threats to nuke Japan and the United States, its continued provocation of South Korea and its decision to throw out the armistice that ended the Korean

War, as well as the unwanted attention brought to China's forced repatriation of North Korean refugees by the U.N. Commission of Inquiry, it appears that China is finally poised to wield its massive influence over North Korea with coercive diplomacy and punishments that are progressively harsher and more consistent.

Should China decide to take the lead on curbing North Korea's worst indiscretions, the solutions to solving both the human rights situation in North Korea and managing risks created by the country's nuclear proliferation lie tightly intertwined with the willingness of China to do two things: (1) join and eventually lead an international effort to curb North Korea's human rights abuses and violations, including collaboration with the U.S. and South Korea; and (2) actively lead an international coalition utilizing coercive diplomatic tactics to pressure and sanction North Korea with regard to its nuclear proliferation and overt threats of force. While both the U.S. and China seem to have similar goals with respect to stabilizing the security threat posed by North Korea, the two nations have rarely worked together to craft mutually satisfying approaches to the threats the country poses to the world. If both China and the United States establish and pursue an engagement strategy that includes a blend of coercion and enticement, that may overturn the *status quo* in the DPRK.

In recent years, China has shown considerable discomfort regarding the North Korean nuclear and missile programs.[83] Nuclear proliferation on the Korean Peninsula does not appear to serve the interests of China. The possession of nuclear weapons by North Korea could act as a catalyst for the pursuit of nuclear weapons by Japan and even South Korea. The resulting potential arms race in East Asia, nuclear or otherwise, does not redound to China's interest.[84] The tipping point in China's tolerance for North Korea unfortunately seems to rest with the delicate power balance in Asia, specifically North Korea's nuclear weapons program and constant overt threats of force in China's backyard. If North Korea ever actually threatened the stability in Asia by seriously provoking a major actor in the region, friend or foe, whether it is the U.S., South Korea, or Japan, chances are high China will take serious action. While North Korea's plethora of human rights violations have begun to seep into China's public image, it presently does not look likely it will support "interference" by the International Criminal Court in "another state's internal affairs," or participate in U.N. efforts to expose and find a solution to this crisis as long as it involves another country's human rights issues. China's recent decision to address some of its own most visible human rights failings does lead to the possibility of some type of action to at least partially address its forced repatriation of all refugees fleeing North Korea. The highly publicized U.N. Commission of Inquiry report continues to bring a significant amount of public attention to China's forced repatriation, which often results in the torture and/or execution of those returned to the brutal North Korean regime. The U.N. may continue to pressure China to make some policy changes.

While it is difficult to say exactly what specific policies, punishments, and enticements Beijing may continue to use to address the plethora of globally concerning issues occurring in North Korea, China possesses a unique and singular advantage over any other country in dealing with Pyongyang. By increasing engagement with the U.S. on North Korea-related issues, maintaining current progress in adopting and aligning itself with U.N. resolutions and sanctions, as well as utilizing its own substantial economic contributions and global authority, Beijing is uniquely positioned to force the Kim regime to address both its multitude of human rights violations as well as North Korea's nuclear proliferation. China may significantly, albeit gradually, shape North Korean policy in a way no other individual nation can accomplish on its own.

Notes

* Weston Sedgwick co-authored this chapter. He is an expert in international trade and policy, a former economic advisor to Indiana Governor Mitch Daniels, and a Juris Doctor candidate at Northern Illinois University College of Law with a focus in international law.

1 *Ballistic Missile Test Firing by North Korea Unlikely to Raise Risk of Regional Conflict*, IHS JANE'S 360 (March 25, 2014), www.janes.com/article/35970/ballistic-missile-test-firing-by-north-korea-unlikely-to-raise-risk-of-regional-conflict.

2 Dick Nanto, *Increasing Dependency: North Korea's Economic Relations with China*, KOREA ECONOMIC INST. OF AM. 77 (2011), www.keia.org/publication/increasing-dependency-north-korea's-economic-relations-china.

3 *Id.*

4 Jennifer Lind, *Will China Finally 'Bite' North Korea?* CNN.COM (March 14, 2013), www.cnn.com/2013/03/11/opinion/lind-north-korea/.

5 Celia Hatton, *Is China Ready to Abandon North Korea*, BBC NEWS (April 12, 2013), www.bbc.com/news/world-asia-china-22062589.

6 *Id.*

7 Ser Myo-ja, *Xi Offers his Support for Park's Policy on the North*, KOREA JOONGANG DAILY (March 21, 2013), www.koreajoongangdaily.joins.com/news/article/article.aspx?aid=2968915.

8 Kim Hyung-jin, *China Leader Snubs North Korea in Visit to Seoul*, WASH. POST (July 3, 2014), www.washingtonpost.com/business/with-seoul-visit-china-leader-sends-message-north/2014/07/02/c057efcc-0257-11e4-8bb2-6b921949ecfa_story.html.

9 *Id.*

10 Simon Denyer, *China's Rise and Asian Tensions Send U.S. Relations into Downward Spiral*, WASH. POST (July 7, 2014), www.washingtonpost.com/world/asia_pacific/chinas-rise-and-asian-tensions-send-us-relations-into-downward-spiral/2014/07/07/f371cfaa-d5cd-4dd2-925c-246c099f04ed_story.html?wpisrc=nl%5Feve.

11 *SKorea, China to Hold Free Trade Negotiations*, THE HONG KONG STANDARD (July 10, 2014), www.thestandard.com.hk/breaking_news_detail.asp?id=51603&icid=1&d_str=.

12 Kim, *supra* note 8.

13 *Id.*

14 Zachary Keck and Ankit Panda, *North Korea Executes Leader's Uncle*, THE DIPLOMAT (Dec. 13, 2013), www.thediplomat.com/2013/12/north-korea-executes-leaders-uncle/.

15 Tania Branigan, *Execution of Kim Jong-un's Uncle Raises Fears of Instability in North Korea*, GUARDIAN (Dec. 13, 2013), www.theguardian.com/world/2013/dec/13/execution-kim-jong-un-uncle-instability-north-korea.

16 Peter Symonds, *Signs of China-North Korea Tensions After Jang Song-Thaek's Execution*, WSWS.ORG (Dec.16, 2013), www.wsws.org/en/articles/2013/12/16/kore-d16.html.

17 Michelle FlorCruz, *North Korean Businessmen in China Called Back by Pyongyang Following Jang Song Thaek Execution*, INTL. BUS. TIMES (Dec. 16, 2013), www.ibtimes.com/north-korean-businessmen-china-called-back-pyongyang-following-jang-song-thaek-execution-1510326.

18 Branigan, *supra* note 15.
19 Choe Sang-hun & David E. Sanger, *Korea Execution is Tied to Clash Over Businesses*, N.Y. Times, (Dec. 23, 2013), www.nytimes.com/2013/12/24/world/asia/north-korea-purge.html?pagewanted=all&_r=0.
20 *Id.*
21 Branigan, *supra* note 15.
22 *Id.*
23 Choe & Sanger, *supra* note 19.
24 Lind, *supra* note 4.
25 Sangwon Yoon, *Saudis, China, Russia Elected to UN Human Rights Council*, Bloomberg (Nov. 12, 2013), www.bloomberg.com/news/2013-11-12/saudis-china-russia-elected-to-un-human-rights-council.html.
26 Chris Buckley, *China to Ease Longtime Policy of 1-Child Limit*, N.Y. Times, (Nov. 15, 2013), www.nytimes.com/2013/11/16/world/asia/china-to-loosen-its-one-child-policy.html.
27 *Id.*
28 U.N. Human Rights Council, Rep. of the Comm'n of Inquiry on Human Rights in the DPRK, U.N. Doc. A/HRC/25/63, ¶¶42–44 (Feb. 7, 2014).
29 *Id.*
30 *Id.* at 33.
31 Staff Report, *Beijing Rejects UN's "Unreasonable" Criticism in North Korea Report*, South China Morning Post (Feb. 18, 2014), www.scmp.com/news/china/article/1430315/beijing-rejects-uns-unreasonable-criticism-north-korea-report.
32 Ben Blanchard, *China Rejects U.N. Criticism in North Korea Report, No Comment on Veto*, Reuters.com (Feb. 18, 2014), www.reuters.com/article/2014/02/18/us-china-korea-north-idUSBREA1H0E220140218.
33 U.N. Human Rights Council, *supra* note 28.
34 *Id.* ¶¶16–17.
35 Stephan Haggard, *Chinese Repatriation of North Korean Refugees*, North Korea: Witness to Transformation Blog, Peterson Institute for International Economics (July 7, 2014), www.blogs.piie.com/nk/?p=13287.
36 *Id.*
37 Nanto, *supra* note 2 at 77–83, 75.
38 *Id.*
39 Bonnie S. Glaser, *A New Type of Major Power Relations on North Korea*, Center for Strategic & Int'l Stud. (Sept. 2013), 1–4, 1, www.csis.org/publication/thoughts-chairman-new-type-major-power-relations-north-korea.
40 *Id.*
41 Jenny Jun, *Dealing with a Sore Lip: Parsing China's "Recalculation" of North Korea Policy*, 38 North Blog (March 29, 2013), www.38north.org/2013/03/jjun032913/.
42 Lind, *supra* note 4.
43 *Id.*
44 Thom Shanker, David E. Sanger & Eric Schmitt, *Pentagon Finds Nuclear Strides by North Korea*, N.Y. Times, (April 11, 2013), www.nytimes.com/2013/04/12/world/asia/north-korea-may-have-nuclear-missile-capability-us-agency-says.html?pagewanted=all&_r=0.
45 *Id.*
46 *In Focus: North Korea's Nuclear Threats*, NY Times (Apr. 16, 2013), www.nytimes.com/interactive/2013/04/12/world/asia/north-korea-questions.html?_r=0.
47 *Id.*
48 *Id.*
49 Colum Lynch & Joby Warrick, *U.N. Security Council Approves New Sanctions Against North Korea*, Wash. Post (Mar. 7, 2013), www.washingtonpost.com/world/asia_pacific/

north-korea-threatens-nuclear-strike-against-aggressors/2013/03/07/1a1e1ada-8726-11e2-999e-5f8e0410cb9d_story.html.

50 *Id.*

51 UNITED NATIONS SECURITY COUNCIL WEBSITE, www.un.org/en/sc/documents/resolutions/index.shtml.

52 Office of Foreign Assets Control, U.S. Dep't of the Treasury, *An Overview of Sanctions With Respect to North Korea,* (May 6, 2011), www.treasury.gov/resource-center/sanctions/Programs/Documents/nkorea.txt.

53 *In Focus: North Korea's Nuclear Threats, supra* note 46.

54 *Id.*

55 *Id.*

56 Jim Miklaszewski and Courtney Kube, *U.S. Navy Shifts Destroyer in Wake of North Korea Missile Threats,* NBCNEWS.COM (March 31, 2013), www.worldnews.nbcnews.com/_news/2013/03/31/17543980-us-navy-shifts-destroyer-in-wake-of-north-korea-missile-threats?lite.

57 Kim, *supra* note 8.

58 *Id.*

59 DAVID ALTON & ROB CHIDLEY, BUILDING BRIDGES: IS THERE HOPE FOR NORTH KOREA 172–4 (2013).

60 Nanto, *supra* note 2 at 77–83, 79.

61 *Id.* at 80.

62 *Id.*

63 *Id.*

64 Staff Report, *N. Korean Official Secretly Courts Chinese Investments,* THE CHOSUN ILBO (Feb. 26, 2014), www.english.chosun.com/site/data/html_dir/2014/02/26/2014022601787.html.

65 *Id.*

66 Michelle FlorCruz, *North Korea Still Courting Chinese Business Partners After Execution of Jang Song-Thaek,* INTL. BUS. TIMES (Feb. 27, 2014), www.ibtimes.com/north-korea-still-courting-chinese-business-partners-after-execution-jang-song-thaek-1558316.

67 *N. Korean Official Secretly Courts Chinese Investments, supra* note 64.

68 Phebe Kim, *Babson: N. Korean Leadership Needs Developed Financial System,* NK NEWS (July 7, 2014), www.nknews.org/2014/07/babson-n-korean-leadership-needs-developed-financial-system/.

69 *Id.*

70 Jun, *supra* note 41.

71 *Id.*

72 Hatton, *supra* note 5.

73 *Id.*

74 *Chinese Editor Fired over Call to Abandon N. Korea,* THE CHOSUN ILBO (Apr. 1, 2013), www.english.chosun.com/site/data/html_dir/2013/04/01/2013040101039.html.

75 *See* www.gpo.gov/fdsys/pkg/PLAW-108publ333/pdf/PLAW-108publ333.pdf.

76 *See* www.unhcr.org/3b66c2aa10.html (emphasis added).

77 William Wan. *While China's Territorial Disputes Drag On, Xi Jinping Tells Others to Seek Peace,* WASH. POST (June 28, 2014), www.washingtonpost.com/world/asia_pacific/while-defending-territorial-disputes-chinas-president-tells-others-to-pursue-peace/2014/06/28/00f0dab2-feca-11e3-932c-0a55b81f48ce_story.html.

78 Celia Hatton, *China's Delicate Balancing Act with North Korea,* BBC NEWS (Feb. 13, 2013), www.bbc.com/news/world-asia-china-21441917.

79 *Id.*

80 Stephen Haggard & Marcus Noland, *What to Do About North Korea: Will Sanctions Work?* PETERSON INSTITUTE FOR INTERNATIONAL ECONOMICS (July 3, 2009), www.iie.com/publications/opeds/print.cfm?ResearchId=1254&doc=pub.

81 *Id.*

82 Jane Perlez, *China Bans Items for Export to North Korea, Fearing Their Use in Weapons*, N.Y. TIMES, (Sep. 24, 2013), www.nytimes.com/2013/09/25/ world/asia/china-bans-certain-north-korean-exports-for-fear-of-weapons-use.html?_r=0.

83 Ranjit Dhawan, *China and its Peripheries: Contentious Relations with North Korea*, INSTITUTE OF PEACE AND CONFLICT STUDIES (2014), www.ipcs.org/issue-brief/china/china-and-its-peripheries-contentious-relations-with-north-korea-231.html.

84 *Id.*

16 U.S. and U.N. remedial actions*

For many years, the bulk of media coverage and discussion of North Korea has focused on security issues and nuclear proliferation. Over time though, the human rights crisis in North Korea has increasingly stirred the attention of the international community and continues to gain momentum. In 2004, the U.S. government enacted the North Korean Human Rights Act, bringing the human rights aspect of North Korea into the spotlight. Section 101 of the Act states: "It is the sense of Congress that the human rights of North Koreans should remain a key element in future negotiations between the United States, North Korea, and other concerned parties in Northeast Asia." In addition, the Act expresses that assistance should be linked to substantial progress in human rights in North Korea. Section 202(b)(2) specifies areas for progress:

- basic human rights, including freedom of religion;
- family reunification between North Koreans and their descendants and relatives in the U.S.;
- information regarding Japanese and South Koreans abducted by North Korea and allowing them and their families to leave North Korea;
- reform of the North Korean prison and labor camp system and allowing independent monitoring of it; and
- decriminalization of political expression and activity.[1]

The act also created the Special Envoy for North Korean Human Rights Issues within the U.S. Department of State to "coordinate and promote efforts to improve respect for the fundamental human rights of the people of North Korea."[2]

The U.S. government can help in these efforts in addition to legislation. Though the U.S. currently has limited diplomatic relations with North Korea, the U.S. has continued to involve itself in human rights matters, especially regarding religious freedoms.

The U.S. government raised concerns about religious freedom in the country in multilateral forums and in bilateral discussions with other governments, particularly those with diplomatic relations with the country. The United States has made clear that addressing human rights, including religious freedom, would significantly improve prospects for closer ties between the two countries.[3]

In addition to the recommendations given by the Commission of Inquiry to the international community, the U.S. Commission on International Religious Freedom (USCIRF) in its 2014 Annual Report adds:

- Coordinate efforts with regional allies, particularly Japan and South Korea, to raise human rights and humanitarian concerns and press for improvements, including closure of the infamous penal labor camps;
- Encourage Chinese support for addressing the most egregious human rights violations in North Korea, and raise regularly with the government of China the need to uphold its international obligations to protect North Korean asylum seekers in China, including by allowing the UN High Commissioner for Refugees (UNHCR) and international humanitarian organizations to assist them and ensuring that any repatriations to North Korea do not violate the 1951 Refugee Convention, its 1967 Protocol, or the Convention Against Torture; and
- Implement fully the provisions of the North Korean Human Rights Act of 2012, and use authorized funds to increase access to information and news media inside North Korea, increase the capacity of NGOs to promote democracy and human rights, protect and resettle refugees, and monitor deliveries of humanitarian aid.[4]

Further U.N. action, especially through the U.N. Security Council, could come at just about any time. The U.N. Security Council could pursue further action against North Korea in the near future and it appears in the last few years that it inches ever closer to doing so. The DPRK has been violating the Council's resolutions involving various restrictions on North Korea's activities, especially regarding nuclear proliferation, for a number of years now, and it should take heed for at least several reasons. First and foremost, it should bear in mind that the Security Council assembled the original military coalition forces to repel North Korea's attack of the South in 1950 and remains technically in control of such forces, with the armistice the primary agreement in place and the peninsula still at war. Second, under the same Chapter VII powers that the Council used to assemble these forces, the Council can carry out other military actions to restore international peace and security if North Korea's hostilities and threats continue in the region.[5] Third, the Council can continue to cripple North Korea in other respects through additional sanctions that could contribute to its collapse.[6]

Additionally, China's support for North Korea has waned, as seen with its involvement in the drafting of the latest resolution; China's support for further action against North Korea could deliver a large blow to the DPRK—as China remains its biggest lifeline.[7] China has the potential to exert more influence over the DPRK than any other nation—if it chooses to do so.

In addition to the continued threat of a re-opening of ICC prosecution, North Korea must also remember that disobeying these various Security Council resolutions violates international law and could lead to any one of the three aforementioned actions by the Council (which it has several times in the past). For example, North Korea recently threatened to restart its nuclear facilities in direct violation of the latest Security Council resolution,[8] moved a long-range missile to its east coast,[9] and refused to allow South Korean workers into its industrial zone to work.[10] In looking at all angles of the issues and the recent, harshly-worded Security Council resolution,[11] even miscues or miscalculations could quickly escalate into a conflagration.[12] Consistent with its pattern of brinkmanship, nearly two months after its initial threat to reopen its nuclear facilities, North Korea approached the U.S. to resume talks.[13]

In 2004, the U.N. Commission on Human Rights established the Special Rapporteur on the situation of human rights in North Korea. The Special Rapporteur must investigate and report on the human rights situation in North Korea and whether the state complies with obligatory international human rights law.[14] The Special Rapporteurs have pointed out various human rights violations and have urged the international community to take note and action:

> The former Special Rapporteur asked the UN to consider "whether the issue of violations in [the DPRK] will be taken up at some stage at the pinnacle of the system, within the totality of the United Nations framework", and has recommended that the international community must "mobilise the totality of the United Nations to promote and protect human rights in the country; support processes which concretise [sic] responsibility and accountability for human rights violations, and an end to impunity."[15]

Moreover, in light of these developments and reports of the rapporteur, the U.N. Human Rights Council recently created the U.N. Commission of Inquiry on North Korea; the Commission held its first official meeting on July 5, 2013 in Geneva and looked in-depth at the internal human rights situation in the North.[16] The members of the Commission included Michael Donald Kirby (Australia), Sonja Biserko (Serbia), and Marzuki Darusman (Indonesia, U.N. Special Rapporteur on the situation of human rights in the DPRK). This Commission performed a large-scale investigation into the systemic violations of human rights in North Korea and confirmed and detailed many of the atrocious human rights violations provided earlier in this book.

On February 7, 2014, the Commission released a 372-page report on "[a] wide array of crimes against humanity" that "have been committed and continue to take place in the Democratic People's Republic of Korea."[17] Despite the Commission's lack of access to the DPRK and important sections of China, over 240 witnesses were interviewed revealing abundant crimes against humanity: everything from extermination, murder, enslavement and torture to forced abortions, enforced disappearances, and prolonged starvation.[18] Although this report comes as no surprise, this Commission perhaps will ultimately serve to more widely disseminate knowledge about North Korea's crimes, and may also serve as a springboard for further action. In fact, a primary result of the Commission's work is its recommendation to refer the situation to the ICC for further action.[19]

The Commission of Inquiry also provided concrete starting points for advancing human rights within North Korea. A synopsis of these points can be found near the end of the report, and they include many suggestions involving the Commission, Rapporteur, Security Council, ICC, and humanitarian aid:

(a) The Security Council should refer the situation in the Democratic People's Republic of Korea to the International Criminal Court for action in accordance with that court's jurisdiction. The Security Council should also adopt targeted sanctions against those who appear to be most responsible for crimes against humanity. In the light of the dire social and economic situation of the general population, the Commission does not support sanctions imposed by the Security Council or introduced bilaterally that are targeted against the population or the economy as a whole.

(b) The General Assembly and the Human Rights Council should extend the country-specific human rights monitoring and reporting mechanisms on the Democratic People's Republic of Korea that pre-date the establishment of the Commission. These include the periodic reports of the Secretary-General and the High Commissioner for Human Rights, as well as the mandate of the Special Rapporteur on the situation of human rights in the Democratic People's Republic of Korea. Such mechanisms should be mandated to focus on ensuring accountability, in particular for crimes against humanity, and should report on the implementation of the Commission's recommendations.

(c) The United Nations High Commissioner for Human Rights, with full support from the Human Rights Council and the General Assembly, should establish a structure to help to ensure accountability for human rights violations in the Democratic People's Republic of Korea, in particular where such violations amount to crimes against humanity. The structure should build on the collection of evidence and documentation work of the Commission, and further expand its database. It should be field-based, supported by adequate personnel deployed to the region so as to enjoy sustained access to victims and witnesses. In addition to informing the work of human rights reporting mechanisms and serving as a secure archive for information provided by relevant stakeholders, the work of such a structure should facilitate United Nations efforts to prosecute, or otherwise render accountable, those most responsible for crimes against humanity.

(d) The High Commissioner for Human Rights should continue the OHCHR's engagement with the Democratic People's Republic of Korea, offering technical assistance and enhancing advocacy initiatives. The High Commissioner for Human Rights should facilitate the implementation of a strategy led by the Special Rapporteur and involving all concerned human rights mechanisms of the United Nations system, to address, coherently and without delay, the special issue of international abductions and enforced disappearances and related matters described in this report. Member states should afford full cooperation to ensure the implementation of such a strategy.

(e) The High Commissioner should periodically report to the Human Rights Council and other appropriate United Nations organs on the implementation of the recommendations contained in the Commission's report.

(f) The Human Rights Council should ensure that the conclusions and recommendations of the Commission do not pass from the active attention of the international community. Where so much suffering has occurred, and is still occurring, action is the shared responsibility of the entire international community.

(g) The United Nations Secretariat and agencies should urgently adopt and implement a common "Rights up Front" strategy to ensure that all engagement with the Democratic People's Republic of Korea effectively takes into account, and addresses, human rights concerns including those collected in this report. The United Nations should immediately apply this strategy to help prevent the recurrence or continuation of crimes against humanity in the Democratic People's Republic of Korea. The strategy should contemplate the possibility of the Secretary-General referring the situation to the Security Council.

(h) States that have historically friendly ties with the Democratic People's Republic of Korea, major donors and potential donors, as well as those states already engaged with the Democratic People's Republic of Korea in the framework of the Six-Party Talks, should form a human rights contact group to raise concerns about the situation of human rights in the Democratic People's Republic of Korea and to provide support for initiatives to improve the situation.

(i) States should not use the provision of food and other essential humanitarian assistance to impose economic or political pressure on the Democratic People's Republic of Korea. Humanitarian assistance should be provided in accordance with humanitarian and human rights principles, including the principle of non-discrimination. Aid should only be curbed to the extent that unimpeded international humanitarian access and related monitoring is not adequately guaranteed. Bilateral and multilateral providers of assistance should coordinate their efforts to ensure that adequate conditions of humanitarian access and related monitoring are provided by the Democratic People's Republic of Korea.

(j) Without prejudice to all the obligations under international law that the Democratic People's Republic of Korea must immediately implement, the United Nations and the states that were parties to the Korean War should take steps to convene a high-level political conference.

Participants in that conference should consider and, if agreed, ratify a final peaceful settlement of the war that commits all parties to the principles of the Charter of the United Nations, including respect for human rights and fundamental freedoms. States of the region should intensify their cooperation and consider following such examples as the Helsinki Process.[20]

These recommendations will take both extensive time and effort, but they demonstrate that many of the potential solutions we have and will discuss in this book have been contemplated and disseminated by the Commission. Many of these remedial actions presented earlier can provide the international community with numerous meaningful starting points to address the worst human rights situation in the world.

Notes

* Kevin Zickterman played a vital role in this chapter.

1 North Korean Human Rights Act of 2004, §202(b)(2), 22 U.S.C. § 7801 *et seq.* (2006).

2 *Office of the Special Envoy for Human Rights in North Korea*, U.S. DEP'T OF STATE, www.state. gov/s/senk/ (last visited Aug. 13, 2014).

3 *International Religious Freedom Report for 2013: Korea, Democratic People's Republic of*, U.S. DEP'T OF STATE, BUREAU OF DEMOCRACY, HUMAN RIGHTS AND LABOR, *available at* www. state.gov/documents/organization/222351.pdf.

4 *Annual Report 2014: North Korea*, U.S. COMM'N ON INT' RELIGIOUS FREEDOM, *available at* www.uscirf.gov/sites/default/files/North%20Korea%202014.pdf.

5 *See generally* U.N. Charter, arts. 39–51 (composing the articles of Chapter VII titled "Action With Respect To Threats To The Peace, Breaches Of The Peace, And Acts Of Aggression").

6 *See, e.g.*, U.N. Charter, art.41 ("The Security Council may decide what measures not involving the use of armed force are to be employed to give effect to its decisions, and it may call upon the Members of the United Nations to apply such measures. *These may include complete or partial interruption of economic relations and of rail, sea, air, postal, telegraphic, radio, and other means of communication, and the severance of diplomatic relations.*" (emphasis added)).

7 China had a hand in drafting the latest Security Council resolution against North Korea's third nuclear test, even though it has been the biggest supporter of North Korea since the fall of the Soviet Union. Edith M. Lederer And Hyung-Jin Kim, *UN OKs new sanctions against North Korea*, Associated Press, Mar. 7, 2013, www.lubbock-online.com/filed-online/2013-03-07/un-oks-new-sanctions-against-north-korea#. VH7825hhvdk; *see also China and North Korea: Comrades Forever?*, INT'L CRISIS GRP. (Feb. 1, 2006), www.crisisgroup.org/~/media/Files/asia/north-east-asia/north-korea/112_china_and_north_korea_comrades_forever.pdf (providing one overview of China's continuous support to North Korea since the early 1990s).

8 Hyung-Jin Kim & Foster Klug, *North Korea Vows to Restart Nuclear Facilities*, CHI. DAILY LAW BULL. (Apr. 2, 2013), www.hosted2.ap.org/ILDLB/8ef5320729ce4298abefc19 03704c7d5/Article_2013-04-02-Koreas-Tension/id-bc8e0b66e98847aaa671c0c2da f845c0?utm_source=subscriber&utm_medium=CDLBemail&utm_content=APhed_North%20Korea%20vows%20to%20restart%20nuclear%20facilities&utm_campaign=headlines.

9 Sam King & Hyung-Jin Kim, *S Korea: North Korea Moved Missile to East Coast*, CHI. DAILY LAW BULL. (Apr. 4, 2013), www.hosted2.ap.org/ILDLB/8ef5320729ce4298abefc1903

704c7d5/Article_2013-04-04-AS-Koreas-Tension/id-321f37e1cea34537a8760b5666 57cd8c?utm_source=subscriber&utm_medium=CDLBemail&utm_content=APhed_ SKorea:%20North%20Korea%20moved%20missile%20to%20east%20coast&utm_ campaign=headlines.

10 Kim Yong-Ho & Ahn Young-Joon, *N Korea Refuses to Let S Koreans Enter Joint Factory*, CHI. DAILY LAW BULL. (Apr. 3, 2013), www.hosted2.ap.org/ILDLB/8ef5320729ce 4298abefc1903704c7d5/Article_2013-04-03-Koreas-Tension/id-9b3c2ce629d047 878efdedb6edd7b342?utm_source=subscriber&utm_medium=CDLBemail&utm_ content=APhed_NKorea%20refuses%20to%20let%20SKoreans%20enter%20 joint%20factory&utm_campaign=headlines.

11 S.C. Res. 2094, U.N. Doc. S/RES/2094 (Mar. 7, 2013) ("*Condemns* in the strongest terms the nuclear test conducted by the DPRK on 12 February 2013 (local time) in violation and flagrant disregard of the Council's relevant resolutions").

12 Interview with Young-jin Choi, Ambassador of the Republic of Kor. to the U.S., *in Washington, D.C.*, April 5, 2013.

13 Jean H. Lee, *North Korea Changes Tack and Tells US: Let's Talk*, CHI. DAILY LAW BULL. (June 17, 2013), www.hosted2.ap.org/ILDLB/8ef5320729ce4298abefc1903704c7d5/ Article_2013-06-17-Koreas-Tension/id-9ced508002944327b0c888ca6cc1815e?utm_ source=subscriber&utm_medium=CDLBemail&utm_content=APhed_North%20 Korea%20changes%20tack%20and%20tells%20US:%20Let's%20talk&utm_ campaign=headlines.

14 *Special Rapporteur on the Situation of Human Rights in the Democratic People's Republic of Korea*, U.N. OFFICE OF THE HIGH COMM'R FOR HUMAN RIGHTS, www.ohchr.org/EN/ HRBodies/SP/CountriesMandates/KP/Pages/SRDPRKorea.aspx (last visited Aug. 13, 2014).

15 Written statement submitted by the Jubilee Campaign to the U.N. Human Rights Council, 20th Session, Agenda Item 4, A/HRC/20/NGO/15, June 7, 2012 (quoting a report of the DPRK's Special Rapporteur from August of 2007).

16 *UN Commission of Inquiry on North Korea Begins Operations*, U.N. OFFICE OF THE HIGH COMM'R FOR HUMAN RIGHTS, Jul. 5, 2013, www.ohchr.org/EN/NewsEvents/Pages/ DisplayNews.aspx?NewsID=13508&LangID=E.

17 *North Korea: UN Commission Documents Wide-ranging and Ongoing Crimes Against Humanity, Urges Referral to ICC*, U.N. OFFICE OF THE HIGH COMM'R FOR HUMAN RIGHTS (Feb. 17, 2014), www.ohchr.org/EN/NewsEvents/Pages/DisplayNews. aspx?NewsID=14255&LangID=E.

18 U.N. Human Rights Coun., Report of the Commission of Inquiry on Human Rights in the Democratic People's Republic of Korea, U.N. Doc. A/HRC/25/63, 25th Sess., Agenda Item 4 (Feb. 7, 2014), *available at* www.ohchr.org/Documents/HRBodies/ HRCouncil/CoIDPRK/Report/A.HRC.25.63.doc. The full report of the commission can be found here: www.ohchr.org/Documents/HRBodies/HRCouncil/ CoIDPRK/Report/A.HRC.25.CRP.1_ENG.doc. This report is used extensively in other chapters.

19 Office of the High Commissioner of Human Rights, Statement by Mr. Michael Kirby Chair of the Commission of Inquiry on Human Rights in the Democratic People's Republic of Korea to the 25th session of the Human Rights Council, Geneva (Mar. 17, 2014), www.ohchr.org/EN/NewsEvents/Pages/DisplayNews. aspx?NewsID=14385&LangID=E.

20 U.N. Human Rights Coun., *supra* note 18.

17 International humanitarian intervention and the responsibility to protect*

Along these lines, North Korea must also be cautious in its extreme political and military moves because of a key doctrine that the U.N. and the Security Council may use to solve the problems on the peninsula. North Korea's mass human rights violations and disregard of its non-proliferation agreements most certainly meet the criteria under the doctrine of humanitarian intervention to justify international action in North Korea. The primary focus here will not be on the prudence of actually following through with armed humanitarian intervention. Rather, it illustrates the doctrine's applicability to further emphasize North Korea's gross disrespect for human rights and to advocate that the international community proactively seeks relief and justice for the North Korean people. The strongest possible diplomacy may make use of them. However, based on the theme of this chapter, humanitarian intervention is technically an option for a solution and potential redress.

We begin our analysis by examining one potential basis for the doctrine of international humanitarian intervention (IHI). International humanitarian intervention is the "threat or use of force by a state, group of states, or international organization primarily for the purpose of protecting the nationals of the target state from widespread deprivations of internationally recognized human rights," even if the target state does not consent to such intervention.[1]

Although there are varying interpretations of the applicability of humanitarian intervention, the most recognized approach is intervening after gaining authorization by the U.N. Security Council. Chapter VII of the U.N. Charter gives the Security Council broad powers to prevent aggravation of any threat or breach of the peace.[2] An expansive interpretation of "threat to the peace" not only includes threats of one nation toward another, but also severe human rights violations against a state's own nationals.[3] First, under Article 41, the Security Council may authorize measures that do not utilize armed forces to ameliorate breaches of peace, including passing resolutions that may sanction the offending state in an effort to bring the state back into compliance. If these sanctions prove ineffective, Articles 42 and 43 may then be imposed, which allow for armed military intervention to restore international peace and security.[4] These three articles form the basis for IHI through the Security Council. The dire situation in North Korea serves as a paradigmatic instance of when the doctrine of humanitarian intervention aptly applies.

Non-forcible and forcible intervention

We continue our analysis by drawing a distinction between non-forcible and for-cible intervention. Non-forcible intervention includes actions, such as economic sanctions or diplomatic action, taken by an outside state or a group of outside states in an effort to get an offending state to rectify its human rights abuses. Non-forcible actions could also include an outside state taking action to rescue its own citizens who find themselves under the custody of the offending state.[5]

In contrast, forcible intervention, the more controversial form of humanitarian intervention, constitutes the threat or use of force by a state or group of states against an offending state without the offending state's permission. At the heart of both non-forcible and forcible forms of intervention, foreign states take action in a sovereign state without that state's permission because of the massive human rights violations occurring or about to occur in the state. The action is taken in order to protect its citizens' human rights and stop the violations.[6]

In order to assess whether humanitarian intervention, particularly forcible intervention, applies to North Korea, the following international humanitarian principles apply: just cause, last resort, good over harm, proportionality, right intention, and reasonable prospect.[7] Just cause means that intervention is only justified in cases of gross human rights violations or human suffering. Just cause as a criterion limits instances of intervention in order to avoid states interven-ing over minor violations by reserving intervention to the most extreme cases.[8] Intervention in North Korea meets the criterion of just cause because North Korea has one of, if not *the* worst records of human rights in the world, both in terms of the range of rights trampled as well as the percentage of its population thus oppressed.

North Korea's leaders have perpetrated gross and systematic violations of human rights statewide, violating obligations pertaining to treating its own nation-als with minimum human rights standards. As stated in Chapter 10, North Korea has arguably violated the Convention on the Rights of the Child by diverting humanitarian aid to its military during famine, resulting in the malnourishment and stunting of a large percentage of its children. Further, North Korea has violated the Genocide Convention through its brutal infanticide policies against Chinese or partially Chinese offspring as well as through its systematic extermina-tion of Christians. Additionally, the DPRK engages in widespread imprisonment and torture of its citizens, often for minor crimes, political crimes, or crimes of association. The ICC refers to genocide as manifestly unlawful and persecutions of political and religious groups as crimes against humanity, one of the worst crimes attributable to a state.[9] Combining these extreme human rights violations with North Korea's general refusal to allow humanitarian aid within its borders, North Korea easily clears the just cause bar of humanitarian intervention, with ample space to spare.

Tied specifically to forcible intervention, last resort refers to exhaust-ing non-force options before resorting to force. The reasoning behind last resort is similar to that of just cause, in that exhausting non-force options limits instances of states forcibly intervening for minor abuses.[10] In the case of North Korea, the major players and the U.N. have expended extensive diplomatic efforts, donated much humanitarian aid and levied considerable sanctions against the DPRK. The U.N. resolutions and economic sanctions against North Korea have focused on the threat posed by North Korea after it has launched missiles and tested nuclear devices—not in response to human rights violations.[11]

Recently, members of the international community have taken some steps to shed light on the human rights abuses occurring in North Korea with the desire that raising awareness of the human rights abuses will inspire action, such as U.N. resolutions that specifically address North Korea's grave human rights violations.[12] The efforts extended to address North Korea's security threat in concert with the growing attempts to expose its gross, systematic infringements of human rights, add weight to the contention that they have satisfied the last resort criterion. Even if one argues that last resort has not been satisfied, intervention is sufficiently legitimate so long as several of the criteria have been met. So whether a particular criterion fails or not, the overall assessment tips toward a legal mandate for forcible intervention in North Korea. At the same time, the potential cost in casualties alone can caution otherwise, which transitions the discussion to proportionality.

Proportionality, which is also often tied to good over harm, weighs issues such as the military action necessary to achieve the goal of ending the human rights violations in light of rights of the citizens of the offending country. Proportionality also weighs factors such as the cost of human life from force as compared to the cost under the current abuse and ensures that the harm of the force used to achieve the goal does not exceed the harm from the current abuses. Like just cause and last resort, considering proportionality also seeks to exhaust non-force intervention before resorting to forcible intervention and seeks to minimize the amount of force used in intervention.[13] Given the DPRK's ability to fulfill its threat to turn Seoul, one of the most populous cities in the world, into a "lake of fire" by *conventional* weapons alone (not to even factor in nuclear, chemical, or biological weapons), the cost of forcible IHI may prove quite high indeed. Add the possibility of a nuclear attack on Tokyo, also among the most populous cities in the world, and the scales of proportionality may very well tilt against forcible intervention.

Not intervening increases the time that North Korea has to develop intercontinental ballistic missiles, the ability to miniaturize a nuclear device into a nuclear warhead if it has not done so already, further proliferate its arms to other criminal and terrorist states, allow it to add to its massive human rights abuses, as well as otherwise increase the damage and potential damage that the DPRK may inflict. While a peaceful resolution would be greatly preferred, fear of forcible intervention may only compound the considerable problems and delay an eventual solution.

Intention of the intervening state refers to the idea that by invoking humanitarian intervention, the intervening state's primary motivation must be of a humanitarian nature. Although states will most likely have additional reasons to intervene outside of humanitarian purposes, the primary motive should be a humanitarian one to ensure that states minimize force and focus on ending the human rights abuses.[14]

Another factor that must be analyzed is right intention, or the motivations of the intervener for applying humanitarian intervention. Under this criterion, if the motives of the intervener are not primarily for the promotion of human rights or security, then the intervention is not legitimate. *Ex post* reasoning can wane in credibility and appear more as rationalization. If the humanitarian motivations impel the intervention *ab initio*, and are announced in clarion fashion at that time, then legitimacy rises accordingly.

Nevertheless, this criterion is controversial, as many scholars have opined that motives are irrelevant while results are supreme. If the intervention actually results in protecting human rights, then it is legitimate. This author does not subscribe to the view that motives are irrelevant—they matter profoundly in assessing the justice of an intervention. Regardless of the stance taken though, most states intervening in North Korea would likely have two primary objectives: preventing the proliferation of weapons and military knowledge to terrorist/rogue states and preventing further human rights atrocities. Both of these motivations could constitute the requisite motivation individually and in tandem.

Finally, reasonable prospect looks to the likelihood that the military intervention will be effective in ending the human rights abuses and protecting vulnerable citizens.[15] If the intervention is ultimately repelled, then this may result in a war-torn state that has no means of supporting its citizens, but continues with even more severe oppression. Additionally, this factor also includes the length of time needed before the intervening states can remove themselves from the offending state without human rights abuses resuming. Because North Korea is a military-first regime and has the fourth largest number of military units in the world, the casualties for both sides could prove catastrophic. Nevertheless, with a united set of forces, the intervening states, under the existing projections, would most likely prove ultimately successful in ending the human rights atrocities. However, the only way to guarantee such violations will not continue after leaving North Korea is to completely replace the North Korean leadership as well as set up a new government that respects the rights of its people. North Korea may become a right-respecting democracy simply through reunification with the South under South Korea's government. Therefore, although the principle of reasonable prospect favors intervening, it may cost painfully much in human lives, resources, and time.

Using these principles as criteria for humanitarian intervention acknowledges several of the fears associated with humanitarian intervention, such as imperialist motivations and infringement upon the sovereignty of the offending state, and ensures that ending the human rights abuses occurring in the offending state remain the focal point of the action. Even so, with such atrocious abuses occurring in North Korea, it is difficult to argue against at least most of the principles favoring armed humanitarian intervention.

At the same time, if resolution can yet be achieved through non-forcible intervention, all the better. After proper publicity has been shed on the DPRK's human rights abuses by the U.N. Commission of Inquiry on North Korea, and all other non-forcible interventions have failed to resolve the situation, then and only then should the world seriously contemplate resort to armed humanitarian intervention. Before then, the looming possibility of forcible intervention may serve as the sort of motivation that the DPRK needs to cease and desist from its atrocities and metastasized militarization. At the same time, it should be kept in mind that delay in performing necessary surgery to remove cancer can allow that cancer to grow and spread further.

The responsibility to protect

Next, we need to build on the discussion of the doctrine of IHI by applying a variation of the doctrine, known as the Responsibility to Protect (R2P), to the human rights crisis in North Korea.[16] In contrast to the IHI doctrine, the R2P directly addresses the issues of authority and sovereignty, which are key criticisms of the IHI doctrine. While classic IHI lacks a central decision-making body and decision-making process to determine when intervention (whether non-forcible or forcible) is warranted, the R2P emanated from the U.N., thereby providing a decision-making body to determine when the international community should intervene in another state.

Further, through its promulgation, the U.N. has developed criteria to evaluate whether or not to intervene. Uniquely, the R2P is couched in terms of sovereignty. By framing sovereignty as a duty of states to protect the peoples within its borders, the R2P reinforces a major *raison d'etre* of sovereignty, and thus of a legitimate government. This forms a critical distinction from the standard IHI doctrine, which some have criticized for its potential to serve as a pretext for developed states to jeopardize developing nations' sovereignty. Because the R2P is based on state sovereignty and emanates from the U.N., it may prove to be the best method for addressing North Korea's human rights abuses—as it directly and intentionally challenges North Korea's misguided use of sovereignty as a cloak attempting to cover its failure to protect its own people and for its gross, systematic human rights abuses against them.

In response to growing international debate regarding the IHI doctrine and its use or non-use in intra-state conflicts involving mass human rights violations, the R2P was first presented by the International Commission on Intervention and State Sovereignty (ICISS) in 2001.[17] The ICISS's 2001 Report on the Responsibility to Protect focused on intervention by the international community that "is taken against a state or its leaders, without its or their consent."[18] In the case of North Korea, Kim Jong-Un and his totalitarian state would constitute the target. Such a doctrine clearly contravenes consensualist theories of international law but not necessarily higher law theories.

Central to the controversy regarding the IHI doctrine lay the competing interests of sovereignty and human protection, which stand at odds with one another.[19]

In his Millennium Report, then U.N. Secretary General Kofi Annan's challenge to the General Assembly illustrates the dilemma between the competing interests: "if humanitarian intervention is, indeed an unacceptable assault on sovereignty, how should we respond to ... gross and systematic violations of human rights that offend every precept of our common humanity?"[20]

The R2P purports to reconcile the interests of sovereignty with human protection. Although the R2P acknowledges that sovereignty includes an obligation of states to respect other states' sovereignty, the R2P also recognizes that sovereignty involves a responsibility. This responsibility includes a duty on the part of an individual sovereign state to protect the human rights of people within its own borders and a duty of outside nations to react to "situations of compelling need for human protection."[21] This duty to react includes actions by the international community ranging from "political, economic, or judicial measures,"[22] and in selected cases, military action. The duty to react flows from a state's membership in the U.N. Upon voluntarily signing the U.N. Charter, the state assumes a responsibility to uphold human rights.[23] The Universal Declaration of Human Rights, with the International Convention on Civil and Political Rights and the International Convention on Economic, Social and Cultural Rights, the "International Bill of Rights," provides the cornerstone of states' obligation to protect human rights both outside and within its borders.[24] North Korea has ostensibly failed on both counts.

The United Nations and its member states adopted the R2P at the 2005 World Summit.[25] Under the 2005 World Summit document, member states and their leaders agreed that "[e]ach individual State has the responsibility to protect its populations from genocide, war crimes, ethnic cleansing, and crimes against humanity."[26] These categories correspond closely with those of the Rome Treaty that established the ICC. Additionally, the international community has the duty to protect populations from human rights abuses and assist states in upholding their responsibility to their own populations through the U.N.[27] The international community's duty, exercised through the U.N., to encourage states to uphold their responsibility includes using "diplomatic, humanitarian and other peaceful means ... to help protect populations from" human rights abuses.[28] The list of "diplomatic, humanitarian and other peaceful means" extended to North Korea is legion, although many of them have focused more on security issues than human rights abuses. The Security Council Resolutions have addressed security issues but have yet to broach human rights abuses.

In the event that peaceful means fail, the international community agreed to act "in a timely and decisive manner, through the UN Security Council." The 2005 World Summit Outcome specifically authorizes the U.N. Security Council to determine when forcible intervention is warranted.[29] The 2005 World Summit Outcome further articulates that forceful methods are appropriate when "national authorities manifestly fail to protect their populations" from human rights abuses.[30] In North Korea, the government has not only failed to protect its people from human rights abuses that include torture, mass imprisonment, and denial of rights such as free speech, but the government itself has intentionally perpetrated these mass human rights abuses.

The then-nascent U.N. Security Council denounced North Korea's aggressive war against South Korea, leading to a U.S.-led U.N. Coalition that eventually restored the original line of demarcation. North Korea should take note that the same body could again authorize forcible intervention. While the Soviet Union's boycott of the Security Council meetings deciding to denounce North Korea's invasion of South Korea did not constitute a veto, present-day Russia and China both retain veto power, which they may wield. However, China not only has not vetoed the Security Council Resolutions against North Korea, it helped to draft the most recent Resolution, perhaps marking an important watershed that could augur yet more vigorous action from the Security Council.

Following the 2005 World Summit, U.N. Secretary General Ban-Ki Moon[31] presented a report in 2009 on the Responsibility to Protect. In his 2009 report, the Secretary General articulated the three pillars of the R2P. These three pillars are: (1) the protection responsibilities of the state, (2) international assistance and capacity building, and (3) timely and decisive response.[32]

The first pillar represents each individual state's responsibility to its own population. This duty is owed to all peoples within a nation's borders, whether the individuals are citizens or not. The key to Pillar One is the idea that "prevention begins at home,"[33] meaning that the duty to prevent human rights abuses remains foremost with the individual state as a responsible sovereign. A state's sovereign responsibility to its people includes taking steps to ease tensions that give rise to human rights abuses. Such efforts entail encouraging diversity through "non-discrimination and the equal enjoyment of rights," fostering inclusion through institutions and programs that educate individuals about diversity, and actively protecting the rights of minorities, the poor, and women.[34]

North Korea, a state of rightlessness, has sought to redefine rights beyond recognition. The state has a "right" to extirpate its enemies, even to the point of eliminating three generations of family, whether through executions or concentration camps. In this way, North Korea assigns largely unprecedented degrees of collective guilt upon its populace. In no way can such an approach satisfy Pillar One of the R2P.[35]

A state's failure to meet Pillar One triggers the international community's responsibility to assist a non-complying state to meet its responsibility under Pillar Two. Prevention remains the lodestar of Pillar Two. Pillar Two seeks to equip a state that "lacks the capacity to protect its population effectively"[36] to meet its responsibility, thereby preventing human rights abuses that might eventually trigger forcible intervention. Pillar Two relies on international cooperation, particularly on the "institutional strengths and comparative advantages of the United Nations systems."[37] By working through the United Nations, Pillar Two utilizes diplomacy, cooperation (especially on a regional level) and foreign policy. Non-complying states actively participate in the process through mutual diplomacy and cooperation in order to develop the policies and programs necessary to meet their responsibilities.[38]

North Korea has not allowed Special Rapporteurs entry into the country to investigate, previously ejected the U.N. World Food Program from the country when it insisted on preventing illicit diversions of the aid as well as proper crediting of the food sources, removed monitoring equipment and personnel from the International Atomic Energy Association, and regularly violates the treaties it has ratified. It seeks to hide and deny the existence of its concentration camps. It limits what visitors are permitted to see by giving them elaborately pretentious "tours" of the country, which include views of Pyongyang made of building facades that literally have no building behind them: they are like movie sets. These tours, replete with false propaganda, try to claim that North Korea respects human rights. For example, in an effort to claim that it respects religious liberty, Party members pretend to conduct worship services in sham churches that put on a show when visitors come. In sum, North Korea has largely rejected efforts to support or ameliorate its atrocious human rights situation, predominantly making a mockery of Pillar Two.[39]

In general, efforts by the international community to equip states include educational programs, training, and providing assistance to the state and its leadership. Further, those states that are seeking to commit crimes against humanity may be deterred through diplomatic efforts that emphasize the costs of committing crimes against humanity. These costs include economic loss, loss of international standing, high societal loss, and huge setbacks in development. Moreover, in such cases, emphasizing the benefits of preventing human rights abuses include assistance from the international community, through educational and developmental efforts.[40]

North Korea has plunged recklessly ahead with its ongoing human rights transgressions notwithstanding the heavy sanctions levied against it—both by individual countries as well as through the U.N. Security Council. It has become one of the most isolated, pariah states in the world. Its reputation deservedly remains abysmal; arguably, its reputation must worsen further to come closer to corresponding with the hellish realities found within.

At the same time, North Korea has accepted aid of various kinds. It has accepted large amounts of food aid; it has allowed some external input in seeking to build its agricultural infrastructure. Yet it has emphatically rejected external efforts to improve its human rights situation. Pillar Two, while tried in many ways, has remained difficult at best and largely unsuccessful.

Finally, Pillar Three outlines the international community's responsibility to act in a "timely and decisive manner" when a state has failed to uphold its responsibility to protect its population, and efforts to assist the state in meeting its responsibility by the international community have failed.[41] Thus a state's failure to comply with Pillars One and Two triggers Pillar Three.

While Pillars One and Two focus on prevention, Pillar Three focuses on early action and flexibility. Early action is more than a military response; rather when possible, other forms of early action, such as "on-site investigations and fact-finding missions" should be taken before military action.[42] However, North Korea has not allowed on-site investigations and fact-finding missions.

Other non-military actions include diplomatic sanctions, such as sanctions against travel, luxury goods, financial transfers, and military goods.[43] All of these have found their way into U.N. Security Council Resolutions regarding North Korea.

Fact-finding missions and diplomatic embargos demonstrate a flexible approach to communicating to a state that its failure to fulfill its responsibility is unacceptable. Such actions, when taken early enough, may also avoid military action. Nevertheless, these non-military actions are initial steps that do not substitute "timely and decisive action." However, when military response is required, the U.N. lacks a "rapid-response military." The U.N., therefore, relies on commitment and support from the international community when military action is required, which corresponds with the international community's duties under its acceptance of the R2P.[44] North Korea should wonder whether, how, and when it may collide further with Pillar Three.

As has been outlined, the R2P doctrine gives clear guidance on when and with what authority states may forcefully intervene due to another state's failure of the first two pillars. Nevertheless, R2P is a rather new wrinkle on the longer standing international humanitarian intervention doctrine, and thus, has yet to be extensively tested.[45] However, being based on general IHI principles, along with strong support of it in the U.N.,[46] one may accord it a presumption of legitimacy. Therefore, the greatest concern is not R2P's legitimacy, but rather how and by whom the doctrine should be enforced—particularly regarding Pillar Three's forceful intervention. It remains to be seen which state(s) will take up the R2P banner against North Korea, knowing the costs will possibly be great for all involved. Although precise method, timing, and means remain unspecified, the R2P doctrine authorizes and demands further action against North Korea.

As a last resort, the doctrine of IHI, with its recent R2P variation, may provide sufficient enough shock to bring the DPRK leadership to its senses. If the credible possibility of intervention fails, the actual application of it, if prudential judgment permits, waits in the wings. The cry of the North Korean people for their liberation from massive injustices must ring out for all the world to hear. A just peace must replace the ongoing war between the Koreas as well as the lesser-known war North Korea wages against its own people.

Notes

* Amanda Beveroth and Jeremy McCabe aided me on this chapter.
1 Young Sok Kim, *Responsibility to Protect, Humanitarian Intervention in North Korea*, 5 J. Int'l Bus. & L. 74, 74–75 (2006).
2 U.N. Charter art. 39.
3 J. L. Holzgrefe, *The Humanitarian Intervention Debate, in* Humanitarian Intervention, Ethical, Legal, and Political Dilemmas 15, 18 (J. L. Holzgrefe & Robert O. Keohane eds., 2003).
4 U.N. Charter arts. 41–43.
5 Holzgrefe, *supra* note 3, at 40–41.
6 *Id.*
7 Nicholas J. Wheeler, *Legitimating Humanitarian Intervention: Principles and Procedures*, 2 Melb. J. Int'l. L. 550, 554–60 (2001); Eric A. Heinze, *Humanitarian Intervention and the*

War in Iraq: Norms, Discourse, and State Practice, 36 PARAMETERS: US ARMY WAR C. Q. 20, 22–29 (2006).

8 Heinze, *supra* note 7, at 24.

9 *Rome Statute of the Int'l Crim. Ct.*, arts.7 & 33, U.N. TREATY SOURCE, U.N. Doc. A/CONF.183/9, *available at* www.untreaty.un.org/cod/icc/statute/romefra.htm.

10 *See* Heinze, *supra* note 7, at 26; Wheeler, *supra* note 7, at 556.

11 *See generally* S.C. Res. 2094, U.N. Doc. S/RES/2094 (Mar. 7, 2013) (defining the multitude of most recent sanctions placed upon North Korea and focusing mostly on nuclear proliferation).

12 *See, e.g.*, Human Rights Council Res. 22/13, Situation of Human Rights in the Democratic People's Republic of Korea, 22d Sess., Feb. 25–Mar. 22, 2013, U.N. GAOR, 68th Sess., A/HRC/Res/22/13 (Mar. 21, 2013) (creating a Commission of Inquiry to investigate the systematic, widespread and grave violations of human rights in the Democratic People's Republic of Korea, with a view to ensuring full accountability, in particular for violations which may amount to crimes against humanity).

13 *See* Heinze, *supra* note 7, at 28–29; Wheeler, *supra* note 7, at 556–58.

14 *See* Heinze, *supra* note 7, at 22–23; Wheeler, *supra* note 7, at 558–60.

15 *See* Heinze, *supra* note 7, at 27–28; Wheeler, *supra* note 7, at 560.

16 INTERNATIONAL COMMISSION ON INTERVENTION AND STATE SOVEREIGNTY, THE RESPONSIBILITY TO PROTECT, vii (2001) [hereinafter ICISS REPORT].

17 *Id.* at ii. In 2000, the Canadian government established the ICISS with the mandate to develop a system of action through the United Nations in response to human rights violations.

18 *Id.* at viii. Human purposes includes mass murder, rape, and starvation.

19 The Report discusses the controversial nature of both action and inaction relating to the Doctrine of Humanitarian Intervention. For example, in Rwanda, where inaction took place, the international community's inaction raised questions about the true universality of human rights and whether each life is of equal value. In contrast, action did take place in Kosovo. The international community's action in Kosovo resulted in questions of legitimacy, particularly in the bypassing of the U.N. and whether intervention was politically motivated. *See id.* at 1. The two cases of Rwanda and Kosovo further illustrate the consequences of the tension between human protection and sovereignty. Where intervention occurs, sovereignty is often seen to be eroded, while lack of action often results in large scale loss of human life. Both results are often viewed as failures on the part of the international community. *See id.*

20 ICISS REPORT, *supra* note 16, at 2 (quoting Secretary General Kofi Annan).

21 *Id.* at 13, 29.

22 *Id.* at 13, 29.

23 *Id.* at 13, 29.

24 *Id.* at 13–14; Universal Declaration of Human Rights, G.A. Res. 217 (III) A, U.N. Doc. A/RES/217(III) (Dec. 10, 1948); International Convention on Civil and Political Rights, *opened for signature* Dec. 16, 1966, 999 U.N.T.S. 171 (entering into force Mar. 23, 1976); International Convention on Economic, Social, and Cultural Rights, *opened for signature* Dec. 16, 1966, 993 U.N.T.S. 3 (entered into force Jan. 3, 1976).

25 Importantly, the R2P was developed through the United Nations and adopted by the United Nations. This lends a level of legitimacy and authority to the R2P that may not exist in certain variations of the Doctrine of Humanitarian Intervention.

26 U.N. GAOR, 16th Sess., 8th mtg. at 30, U.N. Doc. A/RES/60/1 (Oct. 24, 2005).

27 2005 World Summit Outcome, G.A. Res. 60/1, ¶¶ 138–39, U.N. Doc. A/60/L.1 (Sept. 15, 2005) [hereinafter 2005 World Summit Outcome].

28 *Id.* (in accordance with Chs. 6 & 8 of the Charter).

29 2005 World Summit Outcome, *supra* note 25, at ¶ 139 (on a case-by-case basis and in accordance with Ch. 7 of the Charter).

30 *Id.*
31 This author avers that it is more than coincidental that this report was created by the U.N. Secretary General, a South Korean, at a time when South Korea's position relative to North Korea has become increasingly perilous. *See North Korea Threatens to Turn South into "Ashes"*, N.Y. Times, www.nytimes.com/2008/03/30/world/asia/30iht-korea.1.11529498.html?_r=0 (last visited Feb. 5, 2014). (North Korea reiterated that Seoul will be reduced to ashes, and not simply a sea of fire. This was in response toward South Korea's harsher stance regarding entering into military conflict with North Korea if the DPRK initiated a nuclear strike.)
32 U.N. Secretary-General, *Implementing the Responsibility to Protect*, 2, U.N. Doc. A/63/677 (Jan. 12, 2009) [hereinafter 2009 Report].
33 *Id.* at 2, 10.
34 *Id.* at 2, 10.
35 *Id.* at 10–14.
36 *Id.* at 9, 15.
37 *Id.* at 9, 15.
38 *Id.* at 9, 15.
39 *See* 2009 Report, *supra* note 30, at 15–22.
40 *Id.* at 15.
41 *Id.* at 9 (any intervention must be in accordance with Chs. VI, VII & VIII of the U.N. Charter).
42 *Id.* at 9, 23 (such action must comply with art. 34 of the U.N. Charter).
43 2009 Report, *supra* note 30, at 23 (any action must be in accordance with arts. 41 & 53 of the U.N. Charter and the decision to act must be made the Security Council).
44 *Id.* at 9, 23, 27–28.
45 *See generally id.* (explaining the broad steps necessary to operationalize the doctrine).
46 *See* S.C. Res. 1674, U.N. Doc. S/RES/1674 (Apr. 28, 2006) (U.N. Security Council unanimously adopts resolution 1674, which reaffirms the responsibility to protect doctrine).

18 Sundry solutions and constructive approaches*

Information infiltration

The old adage that "knowledge is power" can apply powerfully in North Korea by providing knowledge that overcomes the web of deceit. Despite Kim Jong-Un's best efforts to the contrary, there are a growing number of ways by which information can be carried or sent into North Korea that can be successful. Google has, for instance, used weather balloons to physically drop pamphlets from the sky. The North Korea Intelligence Solidarity, a group of North Korean intellectual defectors, have sought to collaborate with Google in this way. Cleverly,

> one South Korean NGO is sending in a single sheet of information of true history and true facts about the death and destruction the regime has caused. The information is written across a photo of Kim Jong-Il, which means no one from North Korea can destroy the pamphlet because it is a crime against the regime to deface a photo of Kim Jong-Il. We know that these pamphlets are having a tremendous impact because in meetings between North and South Korea, the North Koreans have complained bitterly to the South Korean government about these balloon projects and the information that is being sent into North Korea. North Korean delegations have actually brought to talks with the South these orange pamphlets and demanded that this propaganda be stopped. So we know the regime is feeling the impact of it.[1]

More recently, the Human Rights Foundation organized an event in San Francisco, CA, dubbed "Hack North Korea" that was attended by roughly 100 computer scientists and engineers who spent a weekend working in small groups to create working prototypes of ideas to promote information infiltration into North Korea.[2] The winning team, a pair of teenage siblings, developed a prototype that could allow North Korean citizens to receive real-time information by using micro-radio or satellite-television devices about the size of credit cards that could easily be dropped by balloons or smuggled into the country.[3] With these devices, North Koreans could access radio transmissions transmitted into North Korea, as well as pick up satellite television broadcasts aimed at China, since those transmissions pass over North Korean airspace.[4]

Furthermore, a natural by-product of encouraging more of these cutting-edge information infiltration campaigns is media attention and public education on North Korea's defiance. The mainstream media may see these campaigns' "wow factor" as a way to gain readership or viewership by reporting them as feature news stories. This, in turn, may help stir the global conscience into finally taking action to address the human rights and security crises of North Korea.

Short-wave and other radio broadcasts, such as Radio Free Asia and Free North Korea Radio, make their way into North Korea. Cell phone usage has increased. A Samsung think tank scholar spoke to me of flooding North Korea with cell phones as a deliberate strategy. In a conversation I had with a North Korean defector in South Korea, she claimed that accessing forbidden media has become commonplace in North Korea, notwithstanding its illegality.

Exchanges

I am in favor of maximizing exchanges. First of all, I refer to opportunities for family members and friends separated across the DMZ to meet and communicate with each other. The more this happens, the better.

I also think positively about cultural exchanges. For example, I consider the New York Philharmonic playing in Pyongyang as a positive step along these lines. Sports teams from and to North Korea can help too. Educational exchanges of students and professors would help to reverse the widespread dehumanization and alienation endemic in North Korea. Journalists can also engage in exchanges, which happened, for example, between German and North Korean journalists. The improvement of interpersonal relationships through cultural exchanges may have surprising ripple effects.

Educational footholds

The Yanbian University of Science and Technology (YUST) and the Pyongyang University of Science and Technology (PUST) have done amazing work near and inside North Korea respectively. My wife Sarah and I have known various people involved with these institutions, which have had a tremendous impact for good by influencing a strategic segment of North Korea.

Friends of Sarah who helped develop curriculum for PUST told us that they intentionally sought to exclude knowledge that North Korea could use for military purposes. The government so desires scientific and technological expertise that it has accommodated these institutions, even one in its capital.

I had the opportunity to meet President Dr. James Kim of both institutions. A remarkable man, he spent time in prison, but with his buoyant, visionary leadership, one might not surmise it. He has recruited highly credentialed and unusually committed professors to teach at both institutions.

The story told by Lord David Alton, the leading member of the British Parliament engaged with the North Korean situation, provides a fitting conclusion to this final chapter:

Dr Kim has a remarkable story of his own, which only adds to the symbolic power of PUST. In 1950, at the outbreak of the Korean War, James Kim was just 15 years old when he enlisted and fought for the South against the North. One night on the battlefield, after reading John's gospel, he promised "to God to work *with* the Chinese and the North Koreans, our enemies ... I would devote my life to their service, to peace and to reconciliation". Of 800 men in his unit, so he says, just he and 16 others survived.

Between the end of the war and the start of the 1980s, Kim travelled the world. He moved between Europe, America, and South Korea, working, studying and starting businesses, but he never forgot his promise. When the time was right, he sold his businesses and his home in order to finance the setting up of a university college in South Korea. The project was a success, and by 1992 he was ready to export his model of education to China. There he established Yanbian University of Science and Technology (YUST), which was the country's first foreign joint-venture university. It was to become a model for his university in Pyongyang.

Before PUST could become a reality, Dr. Kim had to return to North Korea. When he did so he was promptly arrested, accused of being an American spy, and sent to jail to await execution. When ordered to write a will, he told his captors that they could have his body parts for medical research. Stripped as he was of all possessions and property, this was the closest he could come at the time to fulfilling his vow to give everything in the service of the North Korean people.

In his will and testament, he wrote to the US government: "I died doing things I love at my own will. Revenge will only bring more revenge and it will be an endless cycle of bitter hatred. Today, it will stop here and the hate will not see a victory. I am dying 'for the love of my country and my people'. If you take any actions for my death then my death would truly have been for nothing and for no reason."

In explaining what then occurred, James Kim told me that "the North Korean government was moved and allowed me to return to my home in China". He made no public complaint about what had happened and, only two years later, they invited him back to North Korea and "asked whether I would forget our differences and build a university for them like the one I had established in China".

He said yes, but with certain conditions. He was to choose the site of the university; be given full ownership of the land; be allowed to bring in foreign professors to teach; and be authorized to establish a research and development centre.

His demands were all met and, by unbelievable coincidence or yet another miracle, the site he chose later proved to have extraordinary significance for Korea. On that site had once stood the church built to commemorate the work of the Welsh missionary Robert Jermain Thomas, who, as we have seen, was central to the story of Christianity in Korea. The church, which pre-dated the tragic division of the two Koreas, was destroyed by the

Japanese during their occupation and was symbolic in many ways of Korean suffering. Dr. Kim believes it was "the hand of God bringing two histories together".

Dr. Kim believes his own experience is evidence that the Korean situation can ultimately be transformed through education—which "has the power to transcend nationalistic boundaries and promote cross-cultural understanding and respect". Dr. Kim recognizes that change will not happen overnight and "peace comes with a price". As a childhood friend said of him, "He is neither foolish nor naïve but rather shrewd, precise, resourceful and witty. His appetite and thirst are generated from his ideals and sense of justice."[5]

YUST and PUST, as led by Dr. Kim, have made a remarkable impact, and provide an emblematic example of hope and inspiration for North Korea, the notes with which I would like to conclude this book.

Notes

* Michael Nealis contributed to this chapter.
1 Mike Kim interview with Suzanne Scholte, May 15, 2007.
2 Jonathan Cheng, *Silicone Valley Takes on North Korea*, WALL STREET JOURNAL Aug. 5, 2014, www.blogs.wsj.com/korearealtime/2014/08/05/silicon-valley-hackers-take-on-north-korea/.
3 *Id.*
4 *Id.*
5 DAVID ALTON & ROB CHIDLEY, BUILDING BRIDGES: IS THERE HOPE FOR NORTH KOREA? 204–06 (2013).

19 Conclusion

Hope for the people of North Korea and the world!

The question is not *whether* North Korea will fall; the questions are *when* and *how*. The days are numbered for such a thoroughly unjust regime. While the fall of North Korea may occur in my lifetime, generations more may suffer before the end comes. However, in the grand sweep of history, by historical proportions, North Korea must transform dramatically from within in order not to find itself swept into the dustbin of history. On its current course of gross and thoroughgoing injustice, it cannot stand for long by broad historical measures.

Currently on its third totalitarian dictatorship, the denouement and conclusion of the DPRK might come suddenly, not unlike the Warsaw Pact countries of Eastern Europe, or Burma more recently. The paths of peace and justice beckon it, but will the government heed the call?

The challenge and crisis of North Korea to the world must rank among the gravest in our slice of history. When future generations look back on our era, whether we rose to the occasion regarding North Korea will color how we are judged. I yearn for a positive verdict.

Clear-minded knowledge and courageous compassion can together dissipate apathy, passivity, and ignorance toward the DPRK. Whether directly or indirectly (such as through the organizations listed in Appendix Two), each of us can play an impactful part in the ongoing story of North Korea. The cumulative weight of all the constructive action will, at some point, reach a tipping point. May that day come sooner rather than later, for the sake of the North Korean people and the world!

When that day comes, North Korea can turn from its state of rightlessness to honoring the rights of its people, perhaps in a peacefully reunited Korea. The concentration camps can close; the borders can open; the reign of a just rule of law can shine; true liberty can rise to enable human flourishing; the cult of the Kims can collapse; the economic, political, and legal systems can transform; free exercise of religion can return. From the thawing of a deep winter of injustice, a Korean spring can emerge for the North Korean people.

I am under no illusion that such a change would happen easily. The difficulties that would mark the road of reunification run deep. The wounds that cry out for healing would not do so overnight. The dramatic divergence that has come to characterize the two Koreas would ideally, over time, fuse back together like the mending of a broken bone, possibly to emerging stronger. Yet the traumas attendant to such a transition might also produce fresh fractures and fissures. The people of North Korea though, cannot withstand much more extensive hemorrhaging than they already have.

The security risks for the region of the world remain real, both with respect to North Korea's advancing military capabilities as well as its proliferation of military equipment and know-how to terrorist and outlaw states. Full implementation of the Security Council resolutions regarding North Korea would diminish the expanding risks. Deterrence through U.N. and U.S. commitments to defend South Korea must continue, as they have remained the most important safeguards for peace on the peninsula. Without such commitments, the path toward North Korean reunification of Korea by force, its ultimate goal, opens much more widely. The specter of a larger war involving the biggest militaries in the world, such as China, the U.S., Russia and North Korea, hangs over the peninsula. World War III is not out of the question, neither are further terrorist strikes. Both remain distinctly undesirable, to understate the matter.

However, full-blown war does not have to destroy the peninsula again. Ample reasons exist for taking the road of sanity and peace. The efforts of countries like China, the U.S., South Korea, and Japan can steer North Korea more in this direction. NGOs and international organizations can ameliorate the ravages of a criminal regime. I have a dream that someday, peace and justice will embrace in a reunified Korea. For the sake of the people of North Korea and all impacted by its government, may that day come soon!

Appendix I North Korean Human Rights Bill

(Sponsored by Representative Hwang Jinha)

(Unofficially translated by Barbara Russell; no official translation exists; this translated bill may be used for reference, but may not reflect the most current version of the Korean legislation.)

Bill Number   152

Date Introduced: 6/15/2012
Sponsored By: Hwang Jinha, Kim Taewon, Nam Gyeongpil
                     Jeong Gapyun, I Uhyeon, Yu Jeongbok
                     I Inje, Song Yeonggeun, Kim Yeongu
                     Gwon Seongdong, Jeong Suseong, Kim Seongcheon
                     Ha Taegyeong, Kim Jaegyeong, An Hyudae
                     Kim Myeongyang, Jeong Munheon, Kim Jonghun
                     I Jaegyun, Representative Hwang Uyeong
                     (20 People)

Purpose of This Initiative

Even though human rights are a universal value guaranteed to all, the North Korean people are not only suffering a situation that is a severe violation of human rights due to excessive punishment, but also a shortage of food and medical supplies that especially threatens the health and life of the elderly and infirm. Many of the North Korean people are deserting to escape this, but fleeing North Koreans cannot get legal protection, and they continue a life of endless wandering and human rights abuses under constant surveillance.

Therefore, we begin to offer humanitarian aid to North Korea as food or medical supplies, and ensure transparency in the distribution process so that the aid must be distributed to North Korean people according to need, while at the same time installing institutional arrangements such as the construction of a cooperative international system in order to increase the security of the North Korean people in their right to live and improve their civil liberties.

Principal Contents

A) This country identifies that the North Korean people have the right to human worth, dignity, and to pursue happiness, and will make all efforts to promote human rights in all areas, including political, economic, social, and cultural (Article 3).

B) The North Korean Human Rights Advisory Committee shall consult on North Korean Human Rights related issues with the Ministry of Unification, and the Minister of Unification shall create a plan for North Korean human rights every three years in consultation with the heads of central government agencies and the Committee, all of which is to be reported to the National Assembly without delay (Article 5 and Article 6). (This is the edited version.)

C) Require monitoring of North Korean authorities or government agencies providing humanitarian assistance to the North Korean people in order to ensure compliance with internationally recognized standards for transmission, distribution, and oversight (Article 8).

D) Promote communication between people in international associations, non-governmental organizations, and foreign governments in order to promote the human rights of the North Korean people, and to alert the international community to North Korean human rights issues (Article 9).

E) Investigate the human rights situation in North Korea, develop policy and conduct research to improve human rights in North Korea, and establish a foundation for North Korean human rights to implement domestic and international programs to improve human rights in North Korea (Article 11).

F) Investigate violations of North Korean human rights, and systematically collect, record, and preserve data for the Justice Department's North Korean human rights records archives (Article 12).

G) Take measures to establish and implement national education and promotion of the North Korean human rights situation and improvement of human rights, inclusion of matters related to North Korean human rights in the unified education plan, reflecting these efforts in elementary and middle school curricula (Article 14). (This is the edited version.)

H) Enable active support through the Foundation for private organization activities promoting North Korean human rights, and allow assisting private organizations with expenses necessary for aid (Article 16).

XXXth Law

North Korean Human Rights Bill

Article 1 – (Purpose):

The purpose of this Act is to promote human rights through humanitarian aid to North Korean citizens and by defining details necessary to the protection of human rights and the basic right to live.

Article 2 – (Definitions):

In this Act "North Korean citizens" are people who live in the area north of the Military Demarcation Line (hereinafter "North Korea"), based on their address, immediate family, spouse, employment, etcetera.

Article 3 – (Basic Principles and The Nation's Obligation):

The Nation must make every effort to promote human rights in politics, economics, society, culture, and all aspects of life, and affirms that all North Korean citizens have human dignity, worth, and the right to seek happiness.

Article 4 – (Priority):

This Act takes precedence over other laws regarding human rights.

Article 5 – (North Korean Human Rights Advisory Committee):

§ 1 Places the North Korean Human Rights Advisory Committee (hereinafter the "Committee") in the Ministry of Unification in order to consult on policies related to North Korean human rights.

§ 2 The Committee shall be composed of no more than ten members including one Chairperson.

§ 3 The Chairperson shall be elected from among the members, and one out of two of the members shall be appointed by the Minister of Unification from among the plentiful civilian experts with knowledge and experience concerning North Korean human rights.

§ 4 Additional requirements for the Committee's operation and configuration will be determined by Presidential Decree.

Article 6 – (North Korean Human Rights Master Plan and Implementation Plan):

§ 1 The Minister of Unification, in consultation with heads of relevant central government agencies, shall establish a North Korean Human Rights Plan (hereinafter the "Plan") every three years after consulting with the Committee, which includes the following matters:

1. Humanitarian aid to North Korean citizens
2. Plan to promote the human rights of North Korean citizens
3. International and domestic education and promotion regarding the North Korean human rights situation
4. International cooperation to improve North Korean human rights
5. Additional matters concerning humanitarian aid to North Korean citizens and promotion of North Korean human rights as determined by Presidential Decree

§ 2 The Minister of Unification shall establish an executive plan for the promotion of human rights (hereinafter the "Executive Plan") each year after consulting the committee in accordance with the basic Plan.

§ 3 The Minister of Unification shall report the basic Plan and Executive Plan to the National Assembly when established without delay.

Article 7 – (North Korean Human Rights Policy Ambassador):

§ 1 The government can establish a North Korean Human Rights Foreign Ambassador (hereinafter the "North Korean Human Rights Ambassador") in the Ministry of Foreign Affairs and Trade in order to effectively carry out government policy and cooperate and consult with the international community for promoting human rights on matters related to North Korean human rights.

§ 2 The North Korean Human Rights Ambassador's duties and required qualifications are determined by Presidential Decree.

Article 8 – (Humanitarian Aid):

§ 1 The Nation must strive to ensure compliance with the following when providing humanitarian aid to North Korean citizens, the North Korean government, or North Korean institutions.

1. Monitoring of delivery and distribution in accordance with internationally accepted delivery standards
2. Delivery to North Korean citizens who need support
3. North Korean citizens who receive support will be able to know who provided the support
4. Prevent humanitarian aid from being used for other purposes, such as for military purposes

§ 2 In addition to §1 above, the Nation shall strive to ensure private organizations that provide humanitarian aid also comply with the requirements of §1.

§ 3 The Nation must ensure North Korean citizens become able to meet their own basic needs through systematic humanitarian aid.

§ 4 The Minister of Unification adjusts roles between domestic organizations and institutions engaged in humanitarian operations or activities.

Article 9 – (International Cooperation for North Korean Human Rights):

The Nation must strive for exchanges of personnel and information in conjunction with international institutions, international organizations, and foreign governments in order to promote North Korean human rights and provide humanitarian aid to North Korean citizens, and strive to increase the attention of the international community to North Korean human rights issues.

Article 10 – (Establishment of the North Korean Human Rights Foundation):

§ 1 The government shall establish the North Korean Human Rights Foundation (hereinafter the "Foundation") to investigate the North Korean human rights situation and develop research and policy related to improving North Korean human rights, and to perform activities domestically and internationally to improve North Korean human rights.

§ 2 The Foundation is a corporation, and will be established by registering the location of the principal office.

§ 3 The Foundation performs each of the following functions.

1. Survey and research the human rights situation in North Korea
2. Development of policy alternatives to resolve North Korean human rights problems and government policy
3. Support for Non-Governmental Organizations for North Korean human rights
4. North Korean human rights promotion, education, publication, and dissemination

    5. Inter-Korean contact and cooperation for North Korean human rights

    6. International exchange and cooperation activities for North Korean human rights

    7. Other projects as designated by the Minister of Unification

§ 4 Other requirements to establish the Foundation are determined by Presidential Decree.

Article 11 – (Foundation Operation):

§ 1 The Foundation will operate with the following funding:

    1. Government grants and contributions

    2. Other revenue

§ 2 The Foundation can solicit donations with the approval of the Minister of Unification in accordance with applicable law.

§ 3 The Minister of Unification will oversee and provide guidance to the Foundation.

§ 4 Minister of Unification can request that officials at the head of related agencies be sent to the Foundation when necessary to achieve the Foundation's objectives.

§ 5 Except as specified in this act, corresponding civil law provisions apply to the Foundation.

§ 6 Other required operations, supervision, and guidance of the Foundation are determined by Presidential Decree.

Article 12 – (North Korean Human Rights Archives):

§ 1 Investigate and systematically collect, record, and preserve materials related to North Korean human rights violations in the North Korean Human Rights Archives at the Department of Justice.

§ 2 The Minister of Justice can request working relationships with the heads of government agencies and local governments required for the operation of the North Korean Human Rights Archives, and the relevant government agency or local government official that received the request shall respond unless a special reason not to do so exists. (This is the edited version.)

§ 3 Other matters related to the establishment and operations of the North Korean Human Rights Archives as determined by Presidential Decree.

Article 13 – (North Korean Human Rights Survey and Report to the Assembly):

§ 1 The Minister of Unification must submit a report to the National Assembly on the results of a survey of North Korean human rights conducted by the Foundation under Article 10, § 3(1).

§ 2 The survey conducted in accordance with Article 10, §3, paragraph 1 should be performed specifically by content and type of human rights.

Article 14 – (Education and Promotion for Improvement of Human Rights):

§1 The Minister of Unification shall establish and conduct national education and promotion measures regarding the North Korean human rights situation and strategies for improving human rights. (This is the edited version.)

§2 The Minister of Unification must include matters pertaining to North Korean human rights in the Uniform Education Plan according to Article 4 of the Uniform Education Act, and The Minister of Education, Science, and Technology shall strive to reflect that in elementary and secondary curricula in accordance with the Elementary and Secondary Education Act.

Article 15 – (Strengthening Inter-Korean Exchange and Cooperation):

The Nation shall strive to promote the human rights of North Korean citizens through the strengthening of inter-Korean exchange and cooperation by expanding the range of targets like private sector inter-Korean exchange and cooperation.

Article 16 – (Active Support of the Private Sector):

§ 1 The government must actively support private organizations enabling activities related to promoting human rights through the Foundation.

§ 2 The government can aid all or part of the necessary expenses of the private sector discussed in § 1 through the Foundation.

§ 3 Additional requirements and procedures of other private organization activities under § 1 shall be determined by Presidential Decree.

Article 17 – (Cooperative Relationship of Local Governments and Central Government):(edited version)

The Minister of Unification may request cooperation from relevant heads of local governments and central government agencies in situations necessary to North Korean human rights, and the head of the relevant agency or local government who receives the request must respond absent special justification.

Article 18 – (Securing Reliable Funding):

The government must ensure stable financial resources necessary to implement the Nation's responsibilities and projects prescribed by this Act.

Article 19 – (Delegation of Authority and Trust):

§1 The Minister of Unification can entrust part of the authority in this Act and prescribed by Presidential Decree to the heads of organizations or heads of local governments.

§2 The Minister of Unification can entrust part of the authority in this Act and prescribed by Presidential Decree to the heads of central government agencies or related corporations and organizations.

Article 20 – (Officials with Penalties Applicable):

The employees of the following will perform duties in accordance with this act and face related criminal law, other law, and applicable penalties as public officials.

1. Foundation employees in accordance with Article 10
2. Employees of a business or organization entrusted with duties under Article 19, § 2

Article 21 – (Penalties):

Those who receive funding under Article 15 by false or other fraudulent means are punishable by up to 3 years imprisonment and a fine of up to 10 million won.

Addendum

Article 1 – (Effective Date):

This law will become effective six months after being ratified.

Article 2 – (Establishment Preparation):

§ 1   The Minister of Unification will be made to handle the affairs of establishing the Foundation and appointing seven committee members within 30 days from the effective date of this Act.

§ 2   The committee members must write bylaws for the Foundation and obtain approval from the Minister of Unification, and establish registration of the Foundation without delay once approved with joint signature.

§ 3   After establishing registration of the Foundation, the committee members must turn over affairs to the Chairman of the Foundation, and when the Chairman takes over he will be become the head.

§ 4   The cost of establishing the Foundation shall be borne by the government.

Additional Cost Breakdown of the North Korean Human Rights Act

I. Cost Estimate Summary

1. Financial Factors

    Article 5   Allowances for private members of the North Korean Human Rights Advisory Committee

    Article 7   Recruitment of the North Korean Human Rights Policy Ambassador

    Article 10   North Korean Human Rights Foundation

    Article 12   Establishment of the North Korean Human Rights Archives

    Article 14   Education and promotion to further North Korean Human Rights

    Article 16   Active support of the private sector

2. Cost Estimate Assumptions

    • Estimates are based on a period of one year

    • The North Korean Human Rights Survey, education and public relations, and support of private organizations are excluded

3. Cost Estimate Results

    • 11.7 billion won

- A budget will be possible after preparing a detailed plan for promotion of human rights, education, publicity, and support of private organizations

4. Author
Representative 황진하 assisted by 유종구 (02-788-2347)

II. Breakdown of Cost Estimate

A. Allowances for private members of the North Korean Human Rights Advisory Committee (Article 5)
- 250,000 won × 12 times (once per month) × 6 people = 18,000,000 won

B. North Korean Human Rights Policy Ambassador (Article 7)

Article 7 is regulating consultation and cooperation for improvement of North Korean human rights with the international community related to North Korean human rights, and places the Minster of Foreign Affairs and Trade under the North Korean Human Rights Policy Ambassador in order to effectively perform government policy in this regard. The Ministry of Foreign Affairs is now activating the Human Rights Ambassador (Foreign Ambassador) on behalf of the Republic of Korea for domestic and foreign improvement of human rights. (Note 1)

The North Korean Human Rights Advisor will be a "B" class senior official position, considering the positions of the foreign affairs public official identified as the Energy Resources Ambassador in the Ministry of Foreign Affairs and Trade, and the Consular Ambassador for Overseas Koreans. The annual salary of a "B" class senior official is 98,000,000 won, if following "Government Official Employment Compensation Processing Guidelines," and considering that labor costs account for 74.1% of the operational budget for the Ministry of Foreign Affairs and Trade (based on 2007), the additional budget is estimated as follows. (Note 2)

Expenses attributed to the North Korean Human Rights Policy Ambassador (Unit: million won)

	2013	2014	2015	2016	2017	Total
Salary	105	113	121	129	138	606
Operation	78	84	90	96	103	451
Sum	183	197	211	225	241	1057

Notes:

1. "B" class senior official salaries are based on 2009 budget guidelines, NABO financial baseline outlook report, and estimated costs based on 2007 financial statements for the Ministry of Foreign Affairs and Trade
2. Foreign affairs public officials and foreign energy resource ambassador projections

C. Establishment of the North Korean Human Rights Foundation (Article 10): 10 trillion won.
    *   Recurring expenses and major expenses of the Foundation
        – Recurring expenses: 4,043 million won
        – Major expenses: 595,700
    *   Education and promotion to improve North Korean human rights (Article 13)
        Education and promotion to improve North Korean human rights budgeting should be based on a detailed long-term plan, instead of events, and it is possible to distinguish between that targeted for the Nation's citizens from that targeted for North Korean citizens.
    *   North Korean human rights situation survey and report (Article 12)
        Necessary expenses related to the operation of the National Human Rights Commission will be supported from the National Human Rights Commission separate budget
    *   Private sector support (Article 15)
        The current government is providing support for the private sector to many organizations according to group size and the nature of support.
        Further examine extensive screening standards of groups that meet North Korean human rights and humanitarian aid needs in order to improve promotion of the support that the government is currently executing.
D. Establishment of the North Korean Human Rights Archives (Article 12): 630 million won.
    *   The Archives personnel needs are assumed to be five people
        – Salaries: 30 million won × 5 personnel = 150 million won
        – Business Expenses: 400 million won
        – Recruitment: 6 million won × 5 personnel = 30 million won
        – Operational: 50 million won (about 1/3 of the salary cost)
E. Education and Public Relations for the Promotion of North Korean Human Rights (Article 14)
    Education and public relations for the promotion of North Korean human rights can be divided into targets for the Nation's citizens and for North Korean citizens, and long term requirements instead of events should drive the detailed requirements of a provided budget.
F. Active Support of the Private Sector (Article 16)
    Private sector support in the current government depends on the size of the organization and the nature of the support for many organizations.
    Further examine extensive screening standards of groups that meet North Korean human rights and humanitarian aid needs in order to improve promotion of the support that the government is currently executing.

Appendix II Organizations addressing the North Korea crisis

These organizations have all sought to address the existing crises in and around North Korea. I personally have supported a number of them. I have not been employed by any of them nor do I receive anything for listing them here. Royalties from this book will continue to support organizations from this appendix, or ones similar to them. They provide a means to make a difference for the North Korean people—as well as all who may be impacted by North Korea.

Organization	Website	Contact	E-mail	Phone	Location
Amnesty International	www.amnesty.org/en/region/north-korea				International
Baroness Cox's Humanitarian Aid Relief Trust (HART)	www.hart-uk.org		office@hart-uk.org	44-2-208-204-7336	United Kingdom
Caritas Korea	www.caritas.or.kr/english/		caritas@caritas.or.kr	82-2-460-7637	South Korea
Christian Solidarity Worldwide	www.dynamic.csw.org.uk/country.asp?s=gi&turn=North_Korea		Csw-dc@csw.org.uk; admin@csw.org.uk	44-0-845-456-5464	International
Citizens' Alliance for North Korean Human Rights	www.eng.nkhumanrights.or.kr:444/main.htm	Young-ja Kim	bongsa@nkhumanrights.or.kr	82-2-723-1672	South Korea
Community of Sant'Egidio	www.santegidio.org		info@santegidio.org	39-06-899-22-34	Italy
Crossing Borders	www.crossingbordersnk.org/wp/	Mike Kim	contact@crossingbordersnk.org		United States
Database Center for North Korean Human Rights	www.nkdb.org/aboutus111.htm		nkdbi@hanmail.net		South Korea
Emancipate North Koreans (ENoK)	www.enok.org		enok.group@gmail.com	224-500-7893	United States
Fighters for a Free North Korea	www.ffnk.net	Sang Hak Park		02-508-3563	South Korea
Free North Korea Radio	www.fnkradio.com			02-2699-0977	South Korea
Free the North Korean Gulag	www.nkgulag.org	Tae Jin Kim	ktjmn@hanmail.net		South Korea

Organization	Website	Contact	E-mail	Phone	Location
Freedom Now	www.freedom-now.org		info@freedom-now.org	202-223-3733	United States
HanVoice	www.hanvoice.wordpress.com; hanvoice.org	Randall Baran-Chong	randall.baran.chong@hanvoice.ca		Canada
Helping Hands Korea	www.helpinghandskorea.org	Tim Peters	tapkorea@gmail.com		South Korea
Human Rights Education Associates	www.hrea.org				
Human Rights Watch	www.hrw.org/asia/north-korea			1-212-290-4700	International
International Coalition to Stop Crimes Against Humanity in North Korea	www.stopnkcrimes.org/index.php		kekyoung@gmail.com	82-505-471-7470	South Korea
International Justice Mission	www.ijm.org			703-465-5495	
Jubilee Campaign	www.jubileecampaign.org				
Justice 4 North Korea	www.justice4nk.org/en/	Peter Jung	justicenk@gmail.com	703-503-0791	United States
Korean Church Coalition	www.kccnk.org	Sam Kim	nfo@kccnk.org	800-222-7082	United States
Liberty in North Korea	www.libertyinnorthkorea.org	Hannah Song	hannah@linkglobal.org		United States, South Korea
Life Funds for North Korean Refugees	www.northkoreanrefugees.com	Kato Hiroshi	nkkikin@hotmail.com	81-3-3815-8127	Japan
Mercy Corps	www.mercycorps.org.uk			800-292-3355	International

Organization	Website	Contact	E-mail	Phone	Location
Network for North Korean Democracy and Human Rights	www.en.nknet.org	Han Ki Hong	solidarity@nknet.org	82-2-723-6711	South Korea
New York Commission to Help North Korean Refugees	www.chnkrnyc.org/index.htm	Dr. Young Goo Son	info@chnkrnyc.org	516-280-2188	United States
No Fence	www.nofence.netlive.ne.jp/english/	Song Yun Bok	songyb777@yahoo.co.jp		Japan
North Korea Freedom Coalition	www.nkfreedom.org	Suzanne Scholte	nkfcadmin1@gmail.com		
North Korea Intellectuals Solidarity	www.nkis.kr/board.php?board=nkisbmain&command=skin_insert&exe=insert_iboard1_home	Heung Kwang Kim	nkis2009@naver.com	02-718-5560	South Korea
North Korea Now	www.northkoreanow.org	Jack Kwon	jack.kwon@northkoreanow.org		
North Korean Refugees in the U.S.A. (NKUS)	www.nkinusa.org/, info@nkinusa.org, 1-425-329-9393, United States				
OneFreeKorea	www.freekorea.us		onefreekorea@yahoo.com		United States
Open North Korea	www.english.nkradio.org	Kwon Eun Kyoung	kekyoung@gmail.com		South Korea
Prayer Service Action Love Truth for North Korea (PSALT)	www.psaltnk.org	Michelle Kim	michelle@psaltnk.org		United States

Organization	Website	Contact	E-mail	Phone	Location
PSCORE	www.pscore.org/xe/en_home	Young-Il Kim	pscore@pscore.org	82-2-6497-5035-5770	South Korea
Pyongyang University of Science and Technology	www.pust.kr		HR.pust@gmail.com	86-433-291-2616	North Korea
Save North Korea	www.snkr.org	Chun Chong You	content@snkr.org		United States
The Committee for Human Rights in North Korea	www.hrnk.org	Greg Scarlatoiu	committee@hrnk.org	202-499-7970	United States
The World Food Program	www.wfp.org/countries/korea-democratic-peoples-republic-dprk		WFP.PyongYang@wfp.org	850-2-3817219	International
The World Health Organization	www.who.int/countries/prk/en/	Dr Stephan P. Jost	dorjit@searo.who.int	850-2-3817914	International
Voice of the Martyrs	www.persecution.com/	Eric Foley and Hyun Sook Foley	susa@seoulusa.org	(877) 337-0302	United States and international
Worldwide Coalition to Stop Genocide in North Korea	www.stopnkgenocide.com		connect@stopnkgenocide.com		International
YUST PUST Foundation	www.yustpust.org		yustpust@gmail.com	1-312-805-8646	United States

Appendix III

THE NATIONAL LAW JOURNAL

FEBRUARY 17, 2014

An ALM Publication

Opinion

We Can No Longer Ignore Atrocities of Kim Jong-Un's North Korea

By Morse Tan

Although shocking to ordinary sensibilities, Kim Jong-Un's execution of his uncle Jang Song Thaek on Dec. 12 fits squarely within the commonplace brutality and cruelty of North Korea.

Even without the execution carried out by the North Korean leader, the country has already earned the dubious distinction as the worst human rights regime on the planet. Massive and horrific crimes against humanity have become banal in North Korea. Extermination, torture, crimes by association and collective retribution are some of the particularly inhumane reports increasingly coming into broader awareness.

Although the Democratic People's Republic of North Korea has officially signed four international human rights treaties, North Korea has not abided by any of these legal obligations.

Those treaties are the International Covenant on Civil and Political Rights; the International Covenant on Economic, Social and Cultural Rights; the Convention of the Elimination of All Forms of Discrimination Against Women; and the Convention on the Rights of the Child. In addition, North Korea's constitution includes nominal rights protections (although override provisions subsume all rights beneath the will of the party and supreme ruler).

The security concerns in the region are legitimate and substantial, but they should not overshadow the worst human rights crisis in the world today. North Korea must be held accountable under the various human rights treaties it has ratified. Accountability may require external intervention—possibly through the continuing investigation by the International Criminal Court, the formation of a hybrid tribunal or the work of the existing commission of inquiry deputized by the United Nations Human Rights Council.

The North Korean people have no due process of law, no freedom of speech, no religious freedom, and are forced to bow to the iron will of their leader's personality cult, lest they find themselves in a prison or concentration camp. Human rights groups now estimate that as many as 200,000 people are being held in North Korean concentration camps in a Stalin-Hitler-Mao-like attempt to crush all political dissent. Those incarcerated often work 14 to 18 hours each day without adequate food and hygiene on top of unrelenting physical, emotional and mental abuse. The severity of the horrendous living conditions kills many of the inmates long before their sentences are complete.

Suffocating levels of governmental surveillance make it difficult and dangerous to act outside of the state's control. Countless testimonies by defectors confirm that North Korea's system of kangaroo courts and political-prisoner camps are notorious for even the most basic human rights violations. A North Korean can be publicly executed simply for asking "Why is the great leader not giving us rations?"

THOUSANDS FLEE

Due to the unbearable living conditions in North Korea, which itself has become a prison, thousands of its people are attempting to flee the country every year—most crossing the northern border into China. This escape route in particular is fraught with peril as human traffickers exploit the desperate refugees, often forcing them into the sex trade.

When in China, the Chinese authorities consider the North Koreans to be illegal economic migrants (rather than refugees) subject to repatriation if caught, in violation of China's obligations under the 1951 Convention Related to the Status of Refugees and its 1967 Protocol. Defectors forcibly returned to North Korea face the predictable plight of imprisonment, torture and/or execution.

Even those North Koreans who somehow avoid detection in China suffer due to inadequate protection of their rights there. The women are often sold into arranged marriages with Chinese men, which is considered one of the less egregious outcomes. If these women are caught and returned to North Korea, their offspring are genocidally destroyed.

Religious persecution is perhaps the gravest of human rights violations in North Korea. Christians are especially vulnerable and "offenders" have been subjected to fanatical retribution in the name of the supreme leader, who is falsely elevated as a deity along with his deceased father Kim Jong-Il and grandfather Kim Il-Sung. Multitudes of Christians have opted for martyrdom instead of renouncing their faith in Jesus.

The human rights crisis in North Korea has been persistently pervasive. Increasing awareness of the more than 60 years of this tyrannical trampling on human rights must fan the flames of change. We can no longer rightfully claim ignorance. As an international community, a legal community or simply a community of human beings, we must not hide from the horrific injustices befalling the North Korean people.

Impunity and oppression should not be allowed to reign unchecked. The healing of the land of the Morning Calm, the stability of the region and the sizeable ramifications around our deeply interconnected world all hang in the balance. The injustices in North Korea, this nation of "rightlessness," simply demand redress.

To better understand the crises of North Korea, and to keep abreast of efforts to uphold the human rights of the Korean people, go to nkdb.org and thebearandthetiger.com.

THE NATIONAL LAW JOURNAL   FEBRUARY 17, 2014
Reprinted with permission from the February 17, 2014 edition of THE NATIONAL LAW JOURNAL © 2014 ALM Media Properties, LLC. All rights reserved.

Morse Tan is an associate professor at Northern Illinois University College of Law. As the most published law review author on North Korea, he is writing a book with Routledge Press on the dual crises of security and human rights in North Korea. Prof. Tan wishes to acknowledge the efforts of his research assistant Sonya Chung toward producing this article.

Appendix IV

North Korea's Strategic Belligerence

Bhumika Ghimire

North Korea is on its bad behavior once again. Right before the U.S. Fourth of July holiday the reclusive regime was back to threatening its neighbors and the United States, test-firing four short-range missiles. This came at a time when U.S.–North Korea tensions were already at a high point following the capture and imprisonment of two American journalists, Laura Ling and Euna Lee.

U.S. President Barack Obama has said he is ready to welcome North Korea back to the six-party talks, in an effort to calm the waters. But judging by its history, North Korea's cycle of belligerence may just be starting.

Professor Morse Tan of the Florida Coastal School of Law says that these events are typical of how the North Koreans operate. They precipitate a crisis, then use negotiations to extract maximum benefit for the regime. They then break their side of the agreement and repeat the cycle again. He says that grasping the pattern in the context of Pyongyang's objectives gives one a better understanding.

Tan explains that North Korea has three main long-term policy goals toward the South: "1) foment positive political sentiment toward itself in South Korea, which has been succeeding to an extent, especially in some parts of the media, the government and the younger generations; 2) eliminate U.S. military involvement on the peninsula—which is why they have repeatedly asked for a peace treaty with the U.S.; 3) re-unify the two Koreas by military force."North Korea has surely been doing its best to precipitate a crisis in recent weeks, with its nuclear and missile tests, closure of its joint venture factories with South Korea, and the detention of the U.S. journalists and one South Korean citizen.

Now reports suggest that North Korea was behind cyber attacks on U.S. and South Korean business and government websites this week. In the United States, the Pentagon, New York Stock Exchange and White House were targeted. In South Korea, the Defense Ministry, Presidential Blue House, and numerous media websites were hit by suspected North Korean cyber attacks.

This saber-rattling is not likely to result in a North Korea–U.S. peace treaty any time soon. Most observers think the six-party talks are the best hope of bringing some resolution. Professor Tan, however, cautions against expecting early success through the talks.

"The six-party talks will continue only if North Korea thinks they can gain through them," he says. "Five-party talks without North Korea could help coordinate the other five countries in response to North Korea. However, China and Russia have aided North Korea in various ways, notwithstanding their agreement to U.N. Security Council Resolutions 1874 and 1718, due perhaps to international pressure."Lost in North Korea's high-risk game of nuclear brinkmanship is the plight of the country's regular citizen. The regime appears least bothered about its starving and suffering people, and instead continues to spend millions on weapons programs.

A report from the World Food Program says that North Korea is now severely limiting the distribution of food aid in the country. The U.N. children's aid agency, UNICEF, is also restricted in the country; recently it was banned from working in the country's most impoverished region.

Day-to-day life for a normal citizen in North Korea is a steep struggle, Tan says. "Far from any system that rewards merit and work, the North Korean regime divides the populace based on perceived political standing. The three basic categories are: core, wavering and hostile. Within these three categories, there are fifty some sub-categories."

"The core are the elite, while the 'hostile' are sent to concentration camps where they are subjected to severe malnourishment, relentless heavy labor— about 14 to 16 hours every day—cruel torture, and in many instances death through malnourishment, over-work, torture, sickness or outright execution. The middle categories make up the large peasant populace that resort to eating bark, grass and leaves in a despondent attempt to ward off starvation."North Korea's acts against its own citizens are indeed criminal and evil. But there is hope; the international community and even regular citizens can do their bit to help the people and isolate the regime. Professor Tan suggests that U.S. groups could invite North Korean sports teams and cultural groups to help break the ice and initiate people-to-people contact, as the South Koreans have done. The New York Philharmonic's performance in Pyongyang last year stands out in this regard.

The failing health of leader Kim Jong Il has been widely reported, and a change in leadership could bring an opening for change, however small. Kim's successor is reported to be his youngest son, Kim Jong Un, who has studied in Switzerland and is in his mid-twenties. His exposure to Western society could be a positive sign, says Tan.

With North Korea things are never what they seem. But no matter how belligerent the regime, the long-suffering citizens of the country are worth every effort to bring the reclusive regime back into the world community.

Previously published at UPI Asia.

Appendix V Satellite images of North Korea

The satellite images provide an idea of what the camps look like from above, though the atrocities committed there boggle the imagination because of their nightmarish proportions. Many families are forced into these camps because they are "guilty by association", with some seeing three generations of their lineage live and die within the walls, most of them punished for a so-called "crime" committed long ago.

There are upwards of 50,000 men, women and children housed in camp 22, a place where prisoners are forced to stone each other to death, women are frequently raped by prison guards and between 1,500 and 2,000 people—many of them children—die from malnutrition or starvation every year.

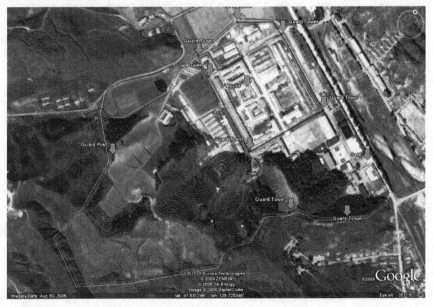

Chongjin-site camp 25: Activists say that as many as 40 per cent of inmates die of malnutrition, while others succumb to disease, sexual violence, torture, abuse by the guards or are worked to death.

Men, women and children are required to work for some 16 hours a day in dangerous conditions, often in mines or logging camps. Very few North Koreans have managed to escape from prison camps and to freedom outside the country's borders, but those who have tell of terrible suffering.

Camp-22-southwest-gate-with-people: Anyone sent to a North Korean labor camp is unlikely to ever leave again, analysts say, while a failed attempt to escape brings execution.

Inmates—who can be imprisoned for life, along with three generations of their families, for anything deemed to be critical of the regime—are forced to survive by eating rats and picking corn kernels out of animal waste.

Taken at night from the International Space Station (ISS), this picture shows North Korea almost completely devoid of lights. In stark contrast, South Korea is shown bathed in light as is China to the north—both clearly visible and powered with ample amounts of electricity. (Copyright is NASA)

Index